Frederick
the Great

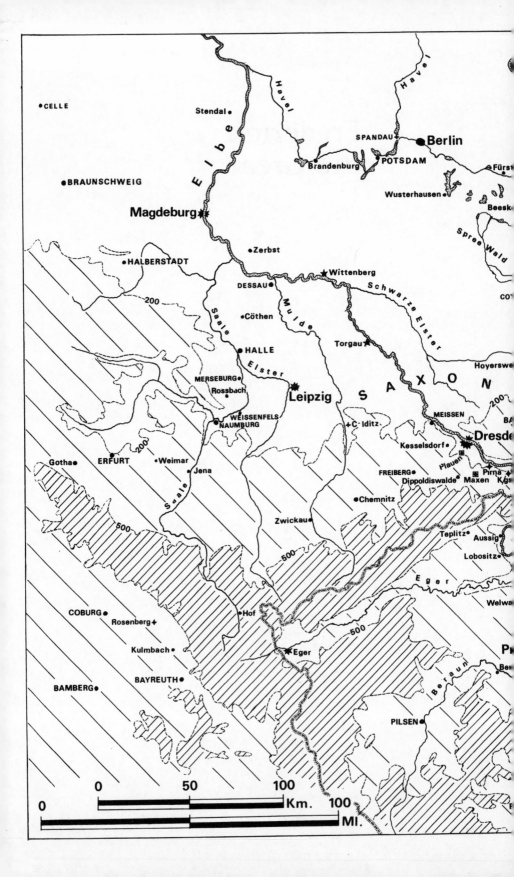

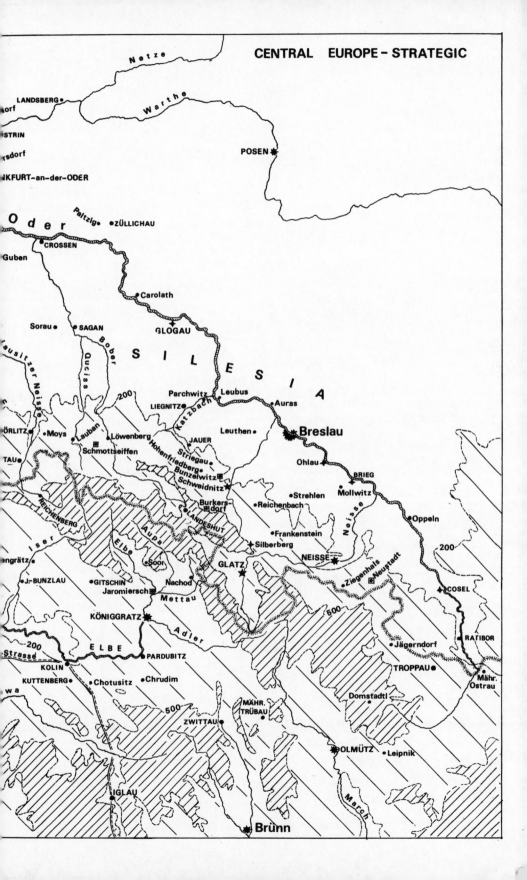

Frederick the Great

A Military Life

Christopher Duffy

London and New York

First published in 1985
Reprinted in paperback 1988, 1990, 1993 by
Routledge
11 New Fetter Lane, London EC4P 4EE
29 West 35th Street, New York, NY 10001

Set in Pilgrim 10 on 12pt
by Inforum Ltd, Portsmouth
and printed in Great Britain
by T.J. Press (Padstow) Ltd,
Padstow, Cornwall

British Library Cataloguing in Publication Data
Duffy, Christopher
Frederick the Great: a military life.
1. Frederick II, King of Prussia   2. Prussia
(Germany)—Kings and rulers—Biography
I. Title
943'.053'0924   DD404

ISBN 0–415–00276–1

Contents

Illustrations

Front endpaper: Central Europe – Strategic
Back endpaper: Central Europe – Political

Preface

This book is a product of the centuries-old British obsession with that most un-British of creatures, Frederick the Great of Prussia. I am confident that my contribution will rank, if not with Carlyle or Mitford, at least with one of our first essays of the sort, which appeared in 1759: *A Succinct Account of the Person, the Way of Living and of the Court of the King of Prussia. Price Six Pence.*

Here I must establish that I do not propose to offer a solution to The Prussian Question, or build psychological edifices on the supposition that Frederick, at some impressionable age, was frightened by a flute. My work is a narrative biography, albeit one with a strong military emphasis. No other literary form is capable of establishing the vital continuities in Frederick's career, or of addressing the notorious contradictions which draw scholars and the public to this fascinating person – a spiritual Frenchman stranded in the remotest corner of Germany, a ruler who was at once a cynical exponent of power-politics, a prince of the Enlightenment, and a lover of the arts who maintained a distance between his inner self and the bloody work in which he was engaged.

Perspectives of this kind will, I hope, attract readers who otherwise harbour an all too well-founded aversion to military history. For their sake I have reduced technical jargon to the essential minimum. Details of uniforms, weapons, equipment, tactics and organisation will be found in the magisterial tomes by Bleckwenn and Jany, and more accessibly in my *Army of Frederick the Great* (1974).

I must, however, urge the timeliness of some kind of military study of Old Fritz. The nature of his administrative achievements has recently undergone the most searching scholarly investigations, but strangely enough, despite a multitude of military historical monographs and narratives, nobody since Theodor von Bernhardi in 1881 has presented a detailed overview of Frederick's life as a soldier. To that extent the re-evaluations of the king have remained incomplete.

Without Hohenfriedeberg, Soor and Leuthen, without the
conquest and retention of Silesia, Frederick would not be
Frederick as we know him, but just one of the more notable
monarchs of his time. What made him 'the first man of his
century'? Not his witty cynicism, not his ambitious corpus of
writings, not his reform of justice – but his bloody battles for the
possession of Silesia. (Augstein, 1968, 265)

In the matter of source material, historians suffered an undeniable loss when the Prussian military archives were destroyed in 1945.
By then, however, the publication of Frederick's *Politische Correspondenz* had been completed, and this material, together with the
king's printed works, makes up no less than seventy substantial
volumes. No other monarch has ever written at such length about his
doings, or (with the possible exception of Louis XIV) has been
observed so closely over such a long period of time. Indeed, it is
remarkable to find how few of the sources cited by historians before
1945 are not available to us today.

Another form of evidence, which has survived mostly intact, is
the physical setting of Frederick's battles and campaigns. With a
certain amount of persistence it is possible to tour the scenes of all of
the more important field headquarters and encampments, and every
battlefield except the two (Mollwitz and Chotusitz) which lie under
aircraft runways. Negatively, this experience helps to preserve the
historian from some of the idiocies he would commit if he stayed at
home and copied what other people have written on the subject.
More positively, it assists him to resolve tactical problems, identify
areas of strategic importance, and to re-create the texture of past
times.

I must acknowledge the benefit I have derived from conversations or correspondence with Hans Bleckwenn, Hubert Johnson,
Jeremy Black and Keith Simpson. In Eastern Europe I received
nothing but the most friendly help in all quarters, official and
private, but I must make particular mention of the assistance rendered by Dr Miroslav Mudra of the National Museum, Prague, and
Lieutenant-Colonel Dr Helmut Schnitter of the Military Historical
Institute, Potsdam.

Abbreviations

Forschungen	*Forschungen zur brandenburgischen und preussischen Geschichte* (1888 etc), Leipzig, Munich and Berlin.
Gr. Gstb. (1890–3)	Grosser Generalstab (1890–3), *Der Erste schlesische Krieg 1740–1742*, 3 vols, Berlin.
Gr. Gstb. (1895)	Grosser Generalstab (1895), *Der Zweite schlesische Krieg 1744–1745*, 3 vols, Berlin.
Gr. Gstb. (1901–14)	Grosser Generalstab (1901–14), *Der siebenjährige Krieg 1756–1763*, 13 vols, Berlin. Publication of this official history was terminated by the Great War, and coverage stopped just short of the battle of Torgau in 1760.
Oeuvres	*Oeuvres de Frédéric le Grand* (1846–57), 30 vols, Berlin.
PC	*Politische Correspondenz Friedrichs des Grossen* (1879–1939), 46 vols, Berlin. According to convention, references are given by document number, not volume or page.
PRO	Public Record Office, London.
Urkundliche Beiträge	Grosser Generalstab (1901, etc.), *Urkundliche Beiträge und Forschungen zur Geschichte des preussischen Heeres*, Berlin.

CHAPTER ONE
Origins

The rise of the future state of Brandenburg-Prussia is perhaps associated in our minds with blurred images of Teutonic Knights, crested helmets, and bloody crusades against the Slavs. By the early modern period those times were long past. The true founders of the eastern marches were in fact those German colonists who pushed slowly across the glaciated lowlands which extended from the Elbe to beyond the Oder. Many of the original inhabitants remained in place. In the north of the region the folk of Polish blood learned to speak the Plattdeutsch of the newcomers, which resembled a primitive English – 'Wat is o Klok?' they said, when they wished to know the time. In the centre and south-east were to be found large unassimilated pockets of the Slavonic Wends, who conversed in a language that was preserved as the *Dienstsprache* of seven of the Berlin regiments in the eighteenth century.

It was through inheritance, rather than conquest, that the prolific German noble line of Hohenzollern acquired the Brandenburg heartland and other territories scattered widely over northern Europe. Already by the beginning of the eighteenth century the Hohenzollerns ruled three groups of holdings, namely:

(a) to the east the Baltic duchy of East Prussia, which was separated from the central core by a corridor of Polish territory;
(b) to the west a number of enclaves in Germany, scattered across the Weser, the Lippe and the Rhine, to wit Minden, Ravensberg, Mark and Cleves;
(c) in the centre the electorate of Brandenburg, and the adjacent territories of eastern Pomerania, Magdeburg and Halberstadt.

In the sixteenth and seventeenth centuries Brandenburg had known the collective ordeals of north-eastern Europe, experiencing the 'second enserfment' of the peasantry, and the devastations of the Thirty Years War. The Saxons and Poles had been hit just as badly,

1

but they became in character identifiably different from the
Brandenburg-Prussians, who by the 1720s were emerging as folk of a
decidedly soldierly aspect. How do we account for the distinction?
The answer probably lies in the fact that the Brandenburgers were to
a remarkable degree moulded by their sovereigns, as Zimmermann
pointed out (1790, III, 219). Frederick put it in a different way in his
Political Testament of 1752: 'the power of Prussia derives not from
intrinsic strength, but from hard work'.

On this reckoning the first 'Prussian' was certainly Frederick
William, 'The Great Elector', who ruled Brandenburg-Prussia from
1640 to 1688. He crushed the local feudal assemblies, and won the
freedom to set up a standing army of 30,000 troops. Independent
military force was now to form the base of Hohenzollern power, and
not the shifts of alliance which had served Brandenburg so badly in
the Thirty Years War.

The new regular army won its spurs in campaigns against the
Swedes, and episodes like the Great Elector's victory at Fehrbellin
(1675) became treasured memories in the developing military con-
sciousness of the Brandenburgers. Dutch models influenced the
formative years of the army, but after 1685 the most modern military
practice of the French was brought to Brandenburg by Huguenot
refugees.

The Great Elector was succeeded by his son Frederick William II
of Brandenburg, a man who, unusually for the new breed of Hohenzollerns, loved pomp and luxury. On 18 January 1701 he assumed for
himself the title of 'King in Prussia', building on the sovereignty he
enjoyed in East Prussia, independently of the German Empire. More
tangibly, this freshly-minted King Frederick I contrived to increase
the military establishment to 40,000 troops, in the face of every
difficulty presented by epidemics and his own extravagance. He hired
out his army in penny packets to the allies in the War of the Spanish
Succession, an experience which proved of decisive importance in the
evolution of the Prussian military tradition. Not only did the Prussian
troops win acclaim on the battlefield, but officers like Prince Leopold
of Anhalt-Dessau ('The Old Dessauer') gained experience of command, and acquired the secrets of the tactics which enabled the Duke
of Marlborough to overcome the armies of Louis XIV in their decline.

Frederick I died in 1713, 'and with him all courtly pomp was
consigned to the grave, to make way for bourgeois simplicity and
military austerity' (Koser, 1921, I, 3). By the age of eight his son,
Crown Prince Frederick William, had owned an impressive array of
military impedimenta, and two years later he wrote a solemn declaration to the effect that he had put aside all childish things. When
he became king as Frederick William I, this formidable individual set

the seal on the character of the Hohenzollern monarchy and its peoples.

In point of size, the Prussian army grew in Frederick William's reign to no less than 83,000 men, which was a remarkably high figure for a population base of about 2,250,000 souls. This achievement was made possible by an increasingly heavy recruitment of foreigners, and by the all-embracing but compact and tightly run administration of the *General-Directorium*, which from 1723 managed both the royal domains and the central and local government.

The material and the symbolic marched side by side in the new Prussia. The Old Dessauer effectively invented the practice of troops marching in step (the 'cadenced step'). It looked good on parade, and on the battlefield it enabled the Prussians to operate in fast-moving and compact formations. The Liège manufacturer François Henoul helped Frederick William to carry out a comprehensive re-arming of the troops, and 1718 saw the introduction of the celebrated Prussian iron ramrod, a device which could be wielded with speed and force, permitting muskets to be loaded much more quickly than with the wooden ramrods of the other services of Europe. In the same year Frederick William accomplished what Hans Bleckwenn has termed the *Stilbruch* in the Prussian officers' uniforms, a deliberate turning-aside from the richly embroidered fashions of western Europe, and the imposition of sober coats of dark indigo blue. Frederick the Great was to retain this weaponry and clothing, and by implication to uphold the values enshrined in them. The new style accorded well with the movement of Pietism which was abroad among the Lutheran people and nobility, and which stressed the virtues of service, honesty and industry.

Brutal, bluff, human and open, Frederick William lent himself easily to caricature. He is known to posterity mainly through the tyrannical treatment of his family, which grew with each re-telling on the part of his daughter Wilhelmine. It is not necessary to repeat what has been written at such length elsewhere concerning the *Tabakskollegium* at Wusterhausen, where the king and his cronies met in an atmosphere reeking of pipe-smoke and cabbage, or to dwell on the giants of the Grenadier-Garde regiment, who lived out their days uselessly in the walled town of Potsdam. Less well known is Frederick William's *Political Testament*, which was opened upon his death, and contained this passage:

> Throughout my life I have been careful not to draw down the envy of the House of Austria on my head. This has forced me to pursue two passions which are really alien to me, namely unbounded avarice, and an exaggerated regard for tall soldiers.

Only under the disguise of these spectacular eccentricities was I
allowed to gather a large treasury and assemble a powerful
army. Now this money and these troops lie at the disposal of my
successor, who requires no such mask. (Bleckwenn, 1978, 65)

It was not a man devoid of perception who bequeathed to
Frederick the finest officer corps in Europe. If a young Prussian
officer's mental equipment was supposed to be constructed around
'the most essential and solid categories of knowledge' (quoted in
Tharau, 1968, 55), those subjects were understood to embrace politics, geography, history and the law.

As for the common soldiery, Frederick William respected the
natural rights of men who had admittedly modest expectations of
what life had to offer (see, for example, Frederick William to Colonel
von Selchow, in Ollech, 1883, 14). Voices from the other ranks are
exceedingly rare in eighteenth-century literature, and it is all the
more interesting to hear the Alsatian-born J.F. Dreyer explain that,
as a foreigner, he was attracted to the Prussian service by the high
standing which its soldiers enjoyed under Frederick William (Dreyer,
1810, 20).

Through the example of the king 'a lazy people . . . a luxury-
loving people' was re-fashioned into a new identity (A. Schlözer,
1777, in Volz, 1926–7, I, 91). Indeed, as early as the 1720s a young
Magdeburg apothecary was refused permission to trade in the pro-
Habsburg port of Lübeck because he looked too *Preussisch*. The
sweetness of life in Talleyrand's pre-Revolutionary Europe never
extended to Hohenzollern Brandenburg-Prussia. *Commodité* and
Plaisir were banished altogether from Frederick William's court, and
they were always difficult to discover in the provinces (Salmon,
1752–3, I, 469).

To the men of the eighteenth century, there appeared to be an all
too direct correspondence between the landscape and the bleak
character of its inhabitants. The Austrian general Lacy, who raided
Brandenburg in 1760, described the villages around Berlin as standing
up in the plain like battalions of infantry. The very name of Prussia,
transmuted into 'spruce', applied both to the conifers massed around
the sandy fields, and to a somewhat artificial neatness of appearance.

Another name, one that was to prove totally inappropriate, was
given to a royal infant who was born on 24 January 1712. This was
'Frederick', a name signifying one who was 'rich in peace'.

Looking back on his childhood, Frederick deplored that so much had
been sacrificed to the demands of his father. He never regretted,
however, that his earliest upbringing had the character of that of the

eldest son of a modest and strict bourgeois household. His language as
a king was shot through with images from the Bible, reflecting one of
the principal sources of his first reading.

It was as a six-year-old that Frederick began to make an impression on observers: 'He is an altogether cheerful and lively prince . . .
Frau von Sacetot, who supervised his education, speaks of him with
unqualified delight. Using an English expression she is fond of exclaiming "He is a little angel!" ' (J.M. von Loen, in Volz, 1926–7, I, 6).

Our little angel had already been introduced to the *Compagnie
Cadets* which was set up for his training, and a lively young officer
called Rentzel introduced him to the rudiments of drill. Frederick
never mastered the technicalities of spelling or mathematics, but his
instincts as lover of the arts and as soldier were guided by a gifted
band of tutors. His French style was formed by his teacher and true
friend, the Huguenot Jacques Duhan de Jandun. His corresponding
military development lay in the hands of two soldiers from East
Prussia: Colonel Christoph Wilhelm von Kalckstein, and the widely
travelled and fine-mannered Lieutenant-General Count Albrecht
Konrad von Finckenstein. These officers were told to imbue Frederick
with the conviction 'that nothing in the world can endow a prince
with more honour and glory than the sword' (Koser, 1921, I, 8).

The celebrated discord between the growing crown prince and
his father is recounted in all the biographies of Frederick. The blame
must be shared liberally among the circumstances of the case and
almost everybody who had dealings with the pair.

In absolutist, hereditary monarchies, where so much of the
welfare of the state hung upon the succession, it was not easy for an
heir-apparent to live up to all the expectations that were invested in
him. The issue was fraught with all the more tension in Brandenburg-Prussia, which was a recent and artificial creation. This having been
said, we must agree with Frederick that the demands of the father
were extreme. This behaviour might have been forgivable in the case
of a grizzled, war-hardened veteran, such as we are tempted to
imagine that Frederick William must have been. In fact he had only
reached his mid-twenties by the time of his son's birth. His tales of the
campaign of Malplaquet might have been, as Frederick complained,
as inexhaustible as the mines of Potosí, but his part in the fighting had
been little more than that of a spectator.

Frederick William's conduct did not even own the virtue of
consistency. What finally broke the son was not an unrelenting
harshness on the part of the king, but his passing moods of blubbering
remorse. At such moments Frederick would respond with the affectionate and trusting nature of his childhood, leaving himself defenceless against the next blow.

The older females of the royal family only served to widen the division between father and son. The blood of Stuarts and Guelphs mingled in the veins of Frederick's mother, Queen Sophia Dorothea. She called forth his love of the arts, but at the same time she drew him into dangerous entanglements with parties at court who favoured a dynastic marriage for him with a Hanoverian princess.

Frederick's elder sister Wilhelmine was closer to him than any other creature. Three years his senior, she had loved him from the cradle, cementing a relationship in which she became at once a step-mother and a partner in a brother-and-sister alliance against the outside world. Many years separated Frederick and Wilhelmine in their turn from their younger brothers and sisters – August Wilhelm, Henry (the favourite of the father), the simple Ferdinand, and the sisters Ulrike and Amalie.

Undoubtedly there were times when Frederick was cast in the role of purest victim. Years later he was plunged into a cold sweat by the memory of the king bursting into his room and sweeping books, papers and flute into the fireplace. At the same time the prince showed a perverse delight in whatever was best calculated to awaken his father's ire. Such were his diamond rings, his embroidered coat, and his 'long, beautiful hair, hanging down on both sides in loose curls' (Hildebrandt, 1829–35, IV, 37).

Frederick's experience of the wider world was greatly broadened when, in January 1728, Frederick William was persuaded against his better judgment to send for the crown prince to join him in Dresden at the court of Augustus II, elector of Saxony and king of Poland. It is scarcely possible to exaggerate the contrast between the two princely residences. Potsdam resembled nothing so much as a Dutch provincial town, with its modest and close-set houses of red brick and its embracing river and canal. In Dresden, on the other hand, the skyline was being transformed by the pinnacles and domes of Italianate churches and palaces. In place of the tobacco-smoked furnishings and dark chambers of the Hohenzollern household, Augustus owned airy apartments, adorned with bejewelled knick-knackery, Chinese vases and porcelain vultures and apes of native Saxon manufacture.

In the matter of morals the court of Augustus was possibly the most corrupt establishment in Europe. An observer might just as well have attempted to define the interrelationships in a warren of rabbits as to give a name to the multifarious couplings of lovers, mistresses, sons and daughters.

The gossips and medical men speculated as to the details of what happened to the sixteen-year-old Frederick during the *chronica scandalosa* of this Dresden visit. It is probable that Augustus furnished the young man with his first mistress. It is possible that on this occasion, or in some later liaison, Frederick contracted an infection which, as Dr Zimmermann claims (1790, I, 79), was cured by an excessively drastic surgical operation. Surmise must be allowed some place in history, and one may conjecture that some intolerable humiliation connected with the Saxon visit (and not necessarily any of the happenings which have passed into recorded history) helps to account for the extraordinary vindictiveness which Frederick as soldier-king displayed towards the electorate. The recording angel who has the story of Frederick's relations with Saxony probably also owns the key to his character and ambitions.

A pale and shaken prince returned to Brandenburg, only to be overthrown shortly afterwards by his continuing passion for Countess Orczelska, who travelled in the suite of Augustus when that monarch came to Berlin in May at the invitation of Frederick William. A third, and for Frederick utterly intolerable, episode in this sequence of disturbing events was occasioned by the Saxon military festivities at Mühlberg in the early summer of 1730. Frederick attended the event with his father. He was now eighteen, and too old for the public humiliations that Frederick William still inflicted on him. He explained much later that 'with regard to making his escape . . . he had long been unhappy and harshly used by his father, but what made him resolve upon it was, that one day his father struck him, and pulled him by the hair, and in this dishevelled condition he was obliged to pass the parade, that from that moment he was resolved, *coûte que coûte*, to venture it' (Mitchell, 1850, I, 358).

The escape in question was a scheme by which Frederick, assisted by two young officers, was to break free from the royal party as it made a progress through western Germany in August of the same year, and claim sanctuary in foreign territory. The plot was easily discovered, and it became only too evident that Frederick William intended something terrible for the prince, whisking him off eastwards in a sealed carriage, and having him tried as a military deserter. The court martial declared itself incompetent to pass judgment on Frederick, who was left in confinement in the castle at Custrin on the Oder. There was, however, to be no mercy for Frederick's fellow-conspirator Lieutenant Hans Hermann von Katte, who was beheaded under the window of the prince's cell on 6 November.

On 19 November Frederick delivered an oath of unconditional loyalty to the king, and two days later Frederick William ordered him to get down to work at Custrin in the *Kriegs- und Domänenkammer*, the local organ of the *General-Directorium*. Frederick was learning to put a distance between his public and private personae, and he now applied himself with unwonted diligence to this bureaucratic drudgery. In time he gained the freedom to ride in the neighbouring countryside of the Neumark, and he sometimes availed himself of the chance to call at Tamsel at the house of Colonel von Wreech, with whose wife he formed a poetically romantic attachment. Tamsel was a little place of one-storey timber-framed houses, straggling between a row of sandy bluffs and the flat wastelands of the Warthe Marshes. It was on land like this that Frederick had the responsibility for establishing lonely outfarms (*Vorwerke*) and clearing or draining the ground for cultivation. This experience brought home to Frederick the extraordinary effort that was demanded to render the lands of Brandenburg-Prussia fertile, and in later years, as director of the state, he was to make it his overriding aim to protect the folk who were engaged in this vital activity.

At the end of November 1731 Frederick was allowed to visit Berlin on the occasion of the marriage of Wilhemine to the Margrave of Bayreuth. The crown prince had been treated as a military deserter ever since his attempt to take flight, but now it was time for him to resume his interrupted military education. Frederick William had told him some years earlier:

> Fritz, pay close attention to what I am going to say to you.
> Always keep up a good and strong army – you won't have a
> better friend and you can't survive without it. Our neighbours
> want nothing more than to bring about our ruin – I am aware of
> their intentions, and you will come to know them as well.
> Believe me, don't let wishful thinking run away with you – stick
> to what is real. Always put your trust in a good army and in
> hard cash – they are the things which keep rulers in peace and
> security. (Koser, 1921, I, 8)

He accompanied these words with a series of taps on the princely cheek, which gradually assumed the force of blows.

It is too much to apply the word 'reconciliation' to the new relations obtaining between the king and Frederick. Rather they recognised that their happiness was best served by living apart. On 27 November 1731 all the generals who were present in Berlin, headed by the Old Dessauer, petitioned Frederick William to re-admit the crown prince to the army. The father not only restored to Frederick the right to wear the officers' coat and sword knot, but granted him the colonel-proprietorship of the recently vacant infantry regiment of Goltz. On 4 April 1732 Frederick set off for Nauen to take up his new command.

Frederick entered on his serious military career at a period when armies knew no formal system of officer training. The Prussian

service, like some others, owned a corps of cadets, but such establishments trained only a small proportion of aspirant officers, and in any
case they were more concerned with inculcating the accomplishments of a gentleman than giving a thorough preparation in military
affairs. Staff colleges, where an officer might have learnt the higher
reaches of his art, were not yet in existence.

What did the eighteenth century offer instead? At the lower
level, the regimental officer simply acquired his trade by living with
it day by day and reading the regulations. At the next stage of their
formation, men of intelligence consulted the histories of the wars and
the standard texts on artillery and fortification. Here was the limit of
what most officers could attain through their own efforts. Successful
generalship was assumed to be part of the personal endowment of
gifted commanders, something which could be transmitted to the
most able members of the next generation only by an almost sacra-
mental process, in which the apostolic laying-on of hands was replaced by direct instruction and the example of the great men.
Frederick went through all of these experiences between 1732 and
1740.

The Prussian service was noted for the absolute priority it gave to
the first degree of the process: the acquisition of the detail of regimental duty. Frederick put it elegantly in his *Art de la Guerre* (1751), in
the first 'song', addressed to ambitious young officers. He reminded
them that they must learn to bear the terrible weight of the musket,
and acquire an instant and silent obedience. He went on to compare
an army to the wonderful hydraulic machinery at Marly, in which
every wheel had an appropriate task, and which could nevertheless
be brought to a halt by the failure of a single part:

> Aimez donc ces détails, ils ne sont pas sans gloire,
> C'est là le premier pas qui mène à la victoire!

In the early 1730s Frederick was still being reminded of his place
of comparative subordination in this hierarchy. He wrote less than
two weeks after assuming command of his regiment: 'Tomorrow I am
off to Potsdam to see the drill and find out whether we are doing
things properly here. I come to the regiment as a new broom, and it is
up to me to master my duties as colonel, and show that I am a
proficient officer who knows everything that is expected of him'
(Becher, 1892, 13). Even in his present rank he had to show due
respect to Lieutenant-Colonel Bredow at Nauen and Captain Hacke
in Potsdam, who were responsible for reporting on his conduct to the
king.

Like the other regiments of foot, the regiment of Prinz von
Preussen was a body of about seventeen hundred souls – officers,

NCOs, men and supporting personnel. The two component battalions were stationed at Neu-Ruppin and Nauen, about forty miles north-west of Berlin. This region was to become known as the military heartland of Brandenburg, from its associations with the sacred field of Fehrbellin, the little estate of the Zieten family at Wustrau, and the activity of Crown Prince Frederick as colonel. Towards the south the country was a generally open land of marshy-banked streams, peat bogs, and vast fields that were relieved here and there by billowing poplars. Along the eastern side it was bordered by the reedy lake of Neu-Ruppin. In the direction of Rheinsberg in the north the soil was a deep and fine sand, densely clad in pines – a very forbidding landscape in winter, but dark green and aromatic in the summertime.

Frederick made his headquarters with his first battalion on the fringes of the wooded zone at Neu-Ruppin, at the northern end of the lake. This was a poor and miserable town, where he dwelt in two mud cottages which had been knocked into a single unit. In an attempt to create a more civilised environment he laid out a garden in a narrow tract of dusty ground, extending between the old brick town wall and an outlying earthern rampart. His newly appointed architect, Georg Wenzeslaus von Knobelsdorff, went on to adorn the scene with an elegant little Temple of Apollo.

Drill and office work filled every morning from daybreak until Frederick stopped for lunch. Afterwards he issued the *Parole* (password) for the next twenty-four hours, an important little ceremony which gave the colonel a regular opportunity to express his opinion on the regiment's performance. Frederick liked to give the impression that he spent every day in unrelenting toil, but in fact he allowed himself ample time for recreation in the afternoons and evenings. We learn of the crown prince playing the flute and reading, of twice-weekly gorgings on hampers of oysters and other delicacies which came from Hamburg, and dark legends of how he and his companions ranged through little villages like Bechlin and Bienenwalde, breaking windows and chasing the girls.

The element of cruelty was openly displayed on one occasion, when Frederick and his young officers revenged themselves on the censorious chaplain of their regiment, 'first smashing the windows of his bedroom, then throwing in a swarm of bees which drove the chaplain and his pregnant wife out of their bed, through the court-yard, and finally into the dunghill. In his old age the king was much given to repeating this tale in a humorous tone of voice, and he was glad when he provoked laughter from his guests, and even among the pages and servants who were standing in attendance' (Büsching, 1788, 20).

We have the most contradictory assessment of the character of the officers at Neu-Ruppin and Nauen. They were witty and urbane, according to some accounts, but inarticulate and limited on the evidence of others. However, the type was clearly established – it was that of the poorish country nobility, which was valued by perceptive military men wherever it was to be found in Europe, but which in the Prussian service was predominant. Its peculiar qualities lent powerful support to the claim that the landed aristocracy was to be considered the natural officer class:

> Discipline in a German army is best upheld when the officer comes from the highest element in society, and the soldier from the lowest. This reflects the habit of command which the nobility exercises on its estates, and the corresponding habit of obedience among the peasantry . . . Danger loses much of its horror for a young lad who gives full credence to all those tales he hears from his relations about their bloody hunting accidents, who sees their scars and crippled limbs (those tokens of courage), and who notes the light-hearted way in which all these inherently frightening things are brought into the conversation. (Garve, 1798, 161)

To modern eyes, the eighteenth-century officer devoted a remarkably high proportion of his time to the business of acquiring recruits. Frederick William expected foreign cannon fodder to make up about half of the manpower of the army, so as to prevent the military establishment from becoming an intolerable drain on the native population. Hundreds of Prussian officers and agents accordingly ranged over Europe in the search for suitable material, and especially for men of five feet nine inches or more, so as to furnish the first rank in the line of battle. The recruiters did not hesitate to employ force or fraud as necessary – a policy which nearly brought about a war with Hanover in 1729.

Frederick sent one of his recruiting officers to Naples, and another, who was too enterprising, was arrested in French Lorraine. In Holland he purchased a man who stood six feet four inches high, 'a phenomenon as rare and as extraordinary as the passage of a comet' (Becher, 1892, 49). A shepherd, reputed to be equally tall, was discovered in Mecklenburg. Frederick reported to his father: 'Persuasion has no effect on him. But a couple of officers and a pair of reliable NCOs can make off with him soon enough, when he is alone in the fields tending his sheep' (ibid., 44). Frederick William gave his blessing to the enterprise, which was by any measure a strange subject for correspondence between a sovereign and his heir.

Not long after Frederick acquired his regiment the king put the native recruiting of the army on a solid basis. This was accomplished by the Cantonal System, which was introduced in 1732 and 1733 and created a pool of conscripted native manpower for each regiment.

The Cantonal System attracted the lively interest of political economists and military observers, who attached to it a host of real or supposed advantages. The recruiting of natives now became a controllable process – a matter of administration rather than of the *razzia*-like forays by which the foreigners were still obtained for the service. The element of servitude was ameliorated by the many exemptions, and by the practice of calling up the cantonists for mustering and drill for only two or three months of the year, at seasons when they could best be spared from the land. The damage to farming was therefore minimised, and the economy actually benefited from the systematic way the regiments were stationed in the provinces. The captains liked this arrangement, because an agreeable custom allowed them to keep the pay of such men of their companies as were on leave. Finally the local associations of the cantonal-based regiment helped to promote comradeship on campaign, and the deep reserves of trained manpower rendered units 'immortal', to use Frederick's word, over the duration of long wars.

Every April the cantonists were recalled to the colours. Frederick subjected his regiment to intensive drilling at Neu-Ruppin, and then, like the other Colonels, he had to take his men to Berlin to put them through their paces under the eyes of the king. The process ended in a 'general review' on the Tempelhofer-Feld, when the regiments marched past Frederick William and carried out a number of gruelling joint evolutions. Sagging with heat and exhaustion, the officers finally learnt of the royal judgment at *Parole* in the afternoon.

We can be sure that merit alone could have earned Frederick the praise which his father measured out to him at these annual ordeals. Frederick was promoted to major-general in 1735, as a direct consequence of his performance in the review of that year, but he always awaited the verdicts with trepidation.

By now Frederick's military imagination had leapt over the confines of the drill square. For years now he had been in the habit of making the short journey south from Neu-Ruppin to the battlefield of Fehrbellin, where he sought to re-create the events of 1675 by walking the ground in the company of old men who had seen the Great Elector's famous victory.

Still more of the tradition of the glorious past was transmitted to Frederick through the medium of Leopold I, Prince of Anhalt-Dessau. The Old Dessauer's active service had begun with the Prussian contingent in the Netherlands in 1695. In the war of the Spanish Succession he became a comrade of Prince Eugene of Savoy on the fields of Blenheim and Cassano, and in 1709 he put Crown Prince

Frederick William in his eternal debt by shepherding him on the campaign in Brabant. Prince Leopold was made field-marshal in 1712, and in the following year, as effective chief of staff to the new king, he began to re-work the Prussian army in his own image. Now the officers discovered that they were expected to make military duties their first concern in life, even in peacetime, which was something of a novelty in contemporary Europe.

Prince Leopold wrote compulsively on military affairs. He tore up his manuscript history of the army in a fit of rage, but his historically based *Stammliste* was accepted for nearly a century to come as the definitive text on the lineage of Prussian regiments. He was probably also responsible for expanding Frederick's grasp of the technicalities of warfare. Until the later 1730s Frederick's military education had been oddly thin. His scratchy sketch maps have a vigour of their own, but he never learnt to draw as well as most of his contemporaries, and he showed a positive disinclination towards the subjects of mathematics and geometry, which were then considered the foundations of military training.

The Old Dessauer was an expert in the formation of crown princes, and for the instruction of Frederick he compiled a *Clear and Detailed Description*, which was based on the orders of the day which were issued in the campaigns against the Swedes between 1715 and 1720. The text was illustrated by a set of sixteen huge plans, and this mass of paper was bestowed on Frederick in January 1738.

The Old Dessauer's communications with Frederick, as crown prince and later king, remained elaborate and deferential. To the other military men Prince Leopold addressed himself with a violence that was accepted as part of his style. This self-consciously tough and *altpreussisch* way of Dessau soldiering was perpetuated by Leopold's sons and nephews, and by protégés and admirers like the colonels Friedrich von Manstein and Hermann von Wartensleben, and the generals Winterfeldt and Fouqué.

Another strand in the Prussian military tradition was embodied by Kurt Christoph von Schwerin (1684–1757), who represented one of the ideals of Frederick's youth, and became his mentor on his first campaign as king.

Schwerin was born in Swedish Pomerania, which brought with it a disposition towards international adventuring, and he served in the Dutch and Swedish employ before he entered the army of Brandenburg-Prussia in 1720, as a battle-scarred and highly revered major-general. Schwerin's way of life was associated with gracious manners, a magnificence of food, wine and furnishings, an openness to the French culture, and a willingness to cultivate the society of agreeable civilians. Towards Frederick, Schwerin adopted the affable tone of a man of the world: 'I am out of wine', he wrote to him on campaign in 1741, 'and have to make do with miserable beer. Your Majesty, be so good as to send me a barrel of Rhenish wine – you have such a lot that you will not miss it. I can then drink your health in the company of our brave officers' (Schwerin, 1928, 105).

Schwerin's school of devotees was still longer-lived than that of the Old Dessauer, and it embraced Frederick's younger brothers as well as celebrated generals like Forcade and Ferdinand of Brunswick. The enemies of the Schwerin manner were inclined to forget that it rested on some firm Prussian virtues. Schwerin prayed alone in his room every morning before he mounted horse. He was at least the equal of the Old Dessauer in fitness, nerve and physical courage, and, as Hans Bleckwenn has discovered, the regiments that were brought up in the Schwerin fashion survived the battering of the Seven Years War much better than did the German princely regiments of the Dessau tradition. Bleckwenn attributes the difference to a more enlightened way of leadership. However, it is worth pointing out that Schwerin was renowned in his own time for the exactitude of the order he maintained among his troops. He meted out death penalties much more readily than did Frederick, and the armies under his command won general admiration for the restraint they exercised in enemy territory, which again offered a contrast to Frederick's way of doing things. Altogether the Schwerin code of discipline appears to have been more effective, more consistent, and less sentimental than the better-known Dessau variety.

In 1734 Frederick made the acquaintance of the greatest of all the commanders of the older generation, and at the same time he had his first direct encounter with active operations. The occasion was the War of the Polish Succession, when a dispute over rival candidatures to the throne of Poland led to a confrontation on the Rhine between the French and a mixed army of the states of the German empire, which stood under the leadership of that celebrated old Austrian war-horse Prince Eugene of Savoy.

As his contribution to the Teutonic host, Frederick William dispatched a corps of 10,000 Prussian auxiliaries, comprising five regiments of infantry and three of dragoons. This force left Berlin in April, and on 30 June Crown Prince Frederick and a small party of officers set off to join the men on the Rhine. The king had furnished him with a long instruction, in which the desire to advance military knowledge was tempered with a concern for the young man's moral welfare.

Frederick reached the army at Wiesental on 7 July. He at once repaired to headquarters, where he exchanged compliments with

Prince Eugene. At noon he dined with General von Groesfeld, and during the meal he heard for the first time cannon being fired with lethal intent. He proposed several healths, and he was delighted when the raising of glasses coincided with the sound of the French artillery.

Frederick had reached the German forces at a not-uninteresting stage of the campaign. The French had clamped a siege on the little Rhine fortress of Philippsburg. They had 95,000 troops in all, but the lie of the ground had forced them to split their men into three parts, leaving only 50,000 men on the 'German' bank of the Rhine. Eugene had arrived on the scene with a respectable army of relief numbering 74,000. He had overcome much greater odds in his famous old campaigns against the Turks, and the expectation was that he would now turn his local superiority to good account.

On 8 July, the day after his arrival, Frederick orientated himself with the progress of operations by repairing to the tower at Wachhäusel, from where he observed the French camp and batteries. He returned to carry out an inspection of the Prussian infantry, and he was halfway through when he encountered Prince Eugene, who invited him to his headquarters for the first of their tête-à-têtes. Frederick now discovered that this ancient, cadaverous warrior was usually plagued with indigestion after dinner, and that it was worth catching him before he sat down to table.

The next day, the 9th, was the most exhilarating of Frederick's expedition. He began by turning back a group of soldiers who were fleeing under fire, and in the course of a mounted reconnaissance he and his party became the target of the French artillery as they rode through a wood. Frederick earned golden opinions for the coolness with which he kept up the conversation, while the trees about him were splintering under the impact of the cannon shot. In the evening Eugene and the Duke of Württemberg came to the tent of our young hero. They talked for a long time, and when the guests were departing Frederick gave the duke a kiss. Eugene turned about and declared: ' "Well now, doesn't Your Highness think my old cheeks are worthy of a kiss?" "Oh, with the best will in the world!" answered the crown prince, and with that he planted several noisy kisses on Prince Eugene. And so they parted' (Anon., 1787–9, XII, 9).

King Frederick William in person arrived at the army on 13 July and betook himself at once to Prince Eugene. After a long conversation the king finally raised the question of whether Frederick would ever make a good soldier. Eugene replied that he could not only reassure him on that point, but declare that his son would be a great general.

To the chagrin of the army, Eugene allowed the French to

prosecute their siege undisturbed, and on 18 July Frederick watched from a house in Wiesental while the garrison of Philippsburg, having surrendered the place to the French, marched out of the fortress with drums beating. Four days later Prince Eugene's army burnt the untransportable equipment and decamped from the scene of its failure. In an atmosphere of confusion the Germans undertook a slow march towards the Neckar, and on 2 August Frederick saw how poor staff work caused the original seven columns to merge into four.

Frederick William left the army on 15 August, now that the campaign was effectively over. People noticed that 'immediately following the departure of his papa, the crown prince of Prussia has fitted himself out with a mass of entirely new and extraordinarily smart gear. Likewise . . . his attendants have been given a fresh and very expensive livery' (Koser, 1891, 226). Significantly, in Frederick's journal of the campaign, the notes and the topographical sketches gave way to ruled staves of music and ideas for compositions.

By now the joint army had spilled in gorgeous profusion into the valley of the Neckar at Heidelberg. The French did not threaten to trouble the proceedings, and the Heidelberg camp became the gathering-place of the gilded youth of Germany. This episode brought home to Frederick how little he shared with his nominal compatriots. He never concealed his contempt for the petty potentates who each strove to build his Versailles, or who, like the Duke of Weimar, maintained an army that was scarcely large enough to put on a stage battle.

Frederick cemented two lifelong friendships during this otherwise frustrating period. Prince Joseph Wenzel von Liechtenstein was sixteen years older than Fritz, but he was by any standards a worthwhile acquaintance. As a discerning patron of the arts he helped Frederick to build up his collection of paintings, and he maintained a friendly correspondence with him even after, as the reformer of the Austrian artillery, he had destroyed the best of the Prussian infantry in the Seven Years War.

The less responsible side of Frederick's character warmed to François Egmont, Comte de Chasot. This was a renegade Frenchman who had killed a man in a duel and fled to the German camp. He lived as dangerously as ever, and he came to Frederick's attention when he wagered the last coin in his pocket in a game of cards and ended up by breaking the bank. Frederick chose this entertaining individual as one of his companions on his return journey to Berlin.

The Prussians had left with Eugene an impression of their remarkable proficiency, and they confirmed him in his fears that an enemy, potentially more dangerous than the Turks or the French, was arising on the northern flank of the Habsburg empire.

Frederick in his turn had been struck by the muddle and indiscipline that had reigned in the joint army, and by the vision of Eugene as an example of the appalling decrepitude which could overtake military men. Frederick's experience of command gradually ameliorated the asperity of these judgments. He commented in 1758: 'if I understand anything of my trade, especially in the more difficult aspects, I owe that advantage to Prince Eugene. From him I learnt to hold grand objectives constantly in view, and direct all my resources to those ends' (Catt, 1884, 42; also 'Refléxions sur les Projets de Campagne', 1775, Oeuvres, XXIX, 80). The term 'grand strategy' had not yet been invented, but it was an awareness of this dimension that was Eugene's legacy to Frederick.

In the high summer of 1735 Frederick's military passions were at a fever pitch, excited by his promotion to major-general and by the prospect of travelling once more to the theatre of operations on the Rhine. His disappointment was all the more acute when, at the beginning of September, Frederick William suddenly withdrew his consent for the journey. Ostensibly the king was of the opinion that it would be undignified for a Prussian prince to be associated with another inactive campaign (it turned out to be the last of the war). In private Frederick William feared that a further spell of service with the Austrians and their allies might give the crown prince an 'Imperial' and un-Prussian perspective on German affairs.

As a partial compensation, Frederick was sent in the autumn to inspect East Prussia. His censorious wit had been sharpened by the experience of the Heidelberg camp, and he conceived a very unfavourable idea of the amenities, climate and character of the people of that isolated land. It was also on the tour of 1735 that Frederick saw the grubby and chaotic court of King Stanislaus Lesczynski, the French candidate for the Polish throne, who had sought refuge in the East Prussian capital of Königsberg. 'The insights, which Frederick gained on this occasion into the intrigues and corruptibility of the Poles, were to colour his opinion of those folk for the rest of his life' (Koser, 1921, I, 99–100).

It is difficult for us to imagine that Frederick was a married man, and that he had lived in that state from the middle of 1732. His unfortunate partner was Princess Elizabeth Christine of Brunswick. She was a good-hearted, ill-educated and passably attractive lady, and never represented for Frederick anything more than one of the keys to his escape from Cüstrin.

In the autumn of 1736 Frederick won a further important degree of independence, when he took up house on the estate of Rheinsberg, which lay close to the Mecklenburg border, at the end of a sandy track leading through a great zone of resin-scented pinewoods. The old castle was transformed by Knobelsdorff, who ran a colonnade between the two round towers on the open side that faced the Grienericksee, thus framing the view across the water to the magnificent woods of oak and beech on the far side.

The Rheinsberg sojourn lasted until 1740, and it is rightly allowed by the biographers to be the most happy interval in Frederick's life. Rheinsberg lay close enough to the garrison at Neu-Ruppin to enable him to fulfil his regimental duties, but otherwise this blessed place permitted him to indulge all the instincts which had for so long been repressed, and to explore some new ones. Now at last Frederick could launch an assault on his private library, which by 1730 had already amounted to 3,775 volumes. He devoured Caesar's *Commentaries*, Rollin's writings on the wars of the Greeks and Romans, and the histories of the campaigns of Charles XII of Sweden. His non-professional reading ranged through the classics (in French translation), his beloved French dramatists of the seventeenth century, and the philosophical works of Locke and Christian Wolff. Begrudging every hour he spent unconscious, he once drank up to forty cups of coffee every day over a period of time in an attempt to discover whether it was possible to do without sleep altogether. It took his innards nearly three years to recover from the ordeal.

Frederick discovered more pleasure than ever in music, a recreation that was to sustain him through the trials of his military life. As a performer, he was acquainted with the harpsichord and violin, but he showed his greatest accomplishment with the flute. The evening concerts at Rheinsberg were semi-private affairs. Frederick and the little band of musicians would run through three or four concerti by his tutor Quantz, after which the prince played a couple of solos from the growing list of his own compositions.

Much of the life at Rheinsberg was invested with an atmosphere of agreeable mumbo-jumbo. Frederick took it into his fancy to call the place 'Remusberg', to accord with the theories of the early seventeenth-century pedant Eilhardus Lubinus who, as he was delighted to discover, had seriously proposed that it owed its origins to Remus, who was supposed to have wandered there after he had been exiled from the first settlement of Rome. In keeping with the spirit of this happy time Frederick enrolled the closest members of his Rheinsberg circle in the mock-chivalric Order of Bayard. The membership embraced not only Frederick's young associates, but respected members of the older generation like *der alte Major* – the cheerful and one-legged Johann Wilhelm von Senning, who had taught him military engineering. The grand mastership was assumed by Henri-Auguste de la Motte-Fouqué, a youthful officer of Huguenot descent who was to become one of the most determined and trusted captains in Frederick's wars.

There is no need to look for any change of character or purpose to explain how the crown prince of the Rheinsberg idyll could turn into the author of the aggressions of 1740. The drilling of the blue-coated musketeers at Neu-Ruppin went ahead without a check, and it was to an unreal Frederick that Voltaire first opened his heart in 1736, greeting him in a letter as the type of the philosopher-prince. Frederick was undoubtedly flattered, since Voltaire was already firm in his European reputation, and with this man as his audience and critic he was encouraged in 1739 to compile his first fully thought-out statement on the responsibilities of monarchy, the *Réfutation du Prince de Machiavel*. Frederick re-worked the first draft with the help of Voltaire, and it emerged as the refined and forceful *Antimachiavel* of 1740.

Frederick's tract took its name from his desire to take Machiavelli to task for maintaining that a prince must adopt different standards for his public and private conduct. On the contrary, asserted Frederick, one was inseparable from the other, since it was to the advantage of princes to attract the love of their subjects. Frederick's 'refutation' of the old Florentine was, however, just a single strand in his arguments, and one which, considered in isolation, has accentuated false contrasts between Frederick the crown prince and Frederick the ruling monarch. In fact the continuity is strong.

There were two kinds of princes in the world, wrote Frederick – those who saw and managed everything in person, and those who let themselves be governed by their ministers. Frederick intended to be counted in the first category. The truly sovereign prince would manage his armies in person, and direct the peaceful increase of the state by encouraging the prosperity of manufactures, agriculture and knowledge. The subjects were to be granted the freedom of their religion, and sectarian fanaticism was to be permitted no place in warfare. The soldiers, indeed, were assumed to be motivated by no altruistic force whatsoever, and Frederick was determined to hold them to their task by iron discipline.

In the interest of his subjects, a prince might be justified in going to war in any one of three main eventualities – to fight off an actual invasion, to maintain his legitimate rights, or (most illuminating of all) to anticipate a threatening danger. In the event, Frederick invoked the second argument when he went to war in December 1740, and the third when he attacked Saxony in 1756.

Voltaire as yet had no direct acquaintance with the crown prince. Many of those who possessed that advantage were left in no doubt that one of Frederick's driving principles was the acquisition of military glory. Dr Zimmermann, who had several long conversations with him in his last illness, draws our attention in particular to the frustrations which Frederick experienced as a young man when he read about the progress that was being made by the Russian field-marshal Münnich in the Turkish war of 1735–9 (Zimmermann, 1788, 198).

Frederick William had already indicated that Prussia's military power might justly be turned against Austria. The Habsburgs had indeed lived in fear of Prussian competition in the German Empire since the early years of the century (Ingrao, 1982, 58), hence Frederick William encountered nothing but obstruction and delay from the Austrians when he pressed the well-founded Prussian claim to the succession to the duchy of Berg in western Germany. Emperor Charles VI accepted Prussian help in the Rhenish campaign with patent reluctance, and in 1735 he suspended hostilities with France without so much as telling the Prussians what was going on. Frederick William pointed to his son as one who would avenge him, all the more so as he knew that Frederick was free of his own crippling reverence for the institutions of the Empire.

The reconciliation of Frederick with his father was completed on 28 May 1740, when Frederick William, already mortally ill, was embraced by his weeping son. The old king, to Frederick's admiration, followed the advance of his illness with the detachment of a doctor, and he died early on the morning of 31 May. 'What a terrible man he was', said Frederick much later. 'But he was just, intelligent, and skilled in the management of affairs . . . it was through his efforts, through his tireless labour . . . that I have been able to accomplish everything that I have done since' (Catt, 1884, 34).

1   Frederick the young king

2 Frederick as crown prince

3   Prince Leopold, 'The Old Dessauer' (by Menzel)

Moritz
Fürst zu Anhalt

4   Prince Moritz of Anhalt-Dessau

5　Hans Joachim von
Zieten

6　Kuttenberg. The church
of St Barbara (top left) and
the great gorge

7 Field-Marshal Otto Ferdinand von Abensperg und Traun

8 Rohnstock Castle. The Bayreuth Dragoons entered by the gate in the centre

9   Hans Carl von Winterfeldt (by Menzel)

10   Königstein fortress

11   Frederick receives the surrender of the Saxons under the Lilienstein

12　Field-Marshal
Kurt Christoph von
Schwerin (by
Menzel)

13　Field-Marshal
Leopold Daun

14 Prince August Wilhelm

15 Friedrich Wilhelm von Seydlitz

16   The Prussian cavalry at Rossbach

17   Frederick at Parchwitz

18   Hochkirch. The battle at the entrance to the Blutgasse

19 Hochkirch. Langen's gate, at the rear side of the churchyard wall. These few square yards witnessed the massacre of the survivors of the regiment of Margrave Carl

20 Prince Henry (by Menzel)

21 Old Fritz (after Chodowiecki)

22   The concert room, Sans Souci

23   The Chinese Tea House, Sans Souci

24 Frederick, the last days

CHAPTER TWO

The Silesian Wars, 1740–5

For two months in the midsummer of 1740 it was possible to believe that Frederick would live up to all the expectations of his subjects and the *philosophes*. The new king abolished the judicial use of torture within three days of his accession. He rebuked the body of his generals for their brutality, and reminded them that humanity and intelligence were as desirable qualities in a soldier as courage and boldness. He issued a prohibition (later rescinded) of physical punishment for the cadets of the Potsdam corps. The Giant Grenadiers, symbol of all that was forced and artificial in the old order, were disbanded except for a battalion of Grenadiergarde, retained in pious memory of Frederick William. Instead, a new unit of household cavalry, the Garde du Corps, was instituted to project an impression of glamour and nobility.

The vision of the philosopher prince, intent on filling his court with savants, poets and ballet dancers, did not survive the autumn. Colonel Louis Charles de Beauval observed: 'The king of Prussia . . . actually regarded all these things as recreations, or consolation in the kind of life he has chosen. His true inclinations drive him on to serious action and to war' (Volz, 1926–7, I, 153).

The celebrated invasion of Silesia was indeed just the second of the blows which brought the idyll to an end. A dispute had arisen with the bishop of Liège concerning the sovereignty of the barony of Herstal. The bishop's title was much weaker than that of the Hohenzollerns, and the local people had put themselves in the wrong by seizing a Prussian recruiting party in 1738, but rather than pursue his claim by peaceful means Frederick sent a most forceful ultimatum to the bishop, demanding to know whether he intended to continue his support for the 'mutineers' of Herstal. The Prussian cabinet minister Podewils, accustomed to normal diplomatic usage, declared, 'That's strong, that's lively – that's the language of Louis XIV!' (Schoenaich, 1908, 239).

When Frederick visited the small castle of Moyland in Cleves on

11 September 1740, it was not just to meet Voltaire for the first time, but to supervise the progress of Major-General von Borcke and his armed 'execution corps'. Borcke seized the Meuse town of Maseyck on 14 September, and the Prussians released the barony to the bishop only after he made over 180,000 thaler in compensation, on top of the 20,000 which the Prussians had already exacted from Herstal as contributions. This was a hard bargain, since Herstal yielded revenues of only 2,000 thaler per annum, and so Frederick received a handsome return for his small investment of force. 'It is impossible to exaggerate the influence which this small episode had on the violent measures which ensued, and how it encouraged the presumption of the king of Prussia' (Valori, 1820, I, 93–4).

Much more was put at stake in October, when Frederick was suddenly presented with the opportunity of pushing through a vast south-eastwards extension of the Prussian territories. The Emperor Charles VI of Austria died on the 20th of that month. Immediately on hearing of the news Frederick bought in stocks of grain for his army, and he summoned Podewils and Field-Marshal Schwerin to an urgent meeting at Rheinsberg. It was evident on 28 October, the first day of the talks, that Frederick had already made up his mind to seize the· Austrian province of Silesia. The debates at Rheinsberg merely concerned the practical details of the forthcoming military operation, and the justifications that were to be made to the world.

Podewils entered a strong protest against the scheme, but on 6 November Frederick told him why he was determined to press ahead. First of all Silesia was 'the part of the Imperial inheritance to which we have the strongest right'. Next the king drew Podewils's attention to the preparedness of the Prussian army, 'which gives us a vast superiority over all the other powers of Europe, in an unexpected eventuality like this'. Lastly the state of international affairs argued for immediate action, to anticipate Frederick's fellow-robbers (though he did not use that term) (PC 140).

How well founded and how complete were these arguments? The statement concerning Prussian rights never carried much weight, since the Hohenzollern claims had extended at most to only about one-fifth of Silesia, and were in any case much less firmly based than those to Berg or Herstal. The advantage of this acquisition was, however, very evident. Directly, the duchy of Silesia offered Frederick the prize of a territory of 14,000 square miles immediately adjacent to the Brandenburg heartland, with busy centres of trade, a well-established linen industry, and a population of 1,500,000, many of them Protestant Germans. Indirectly, the enterprise would lend weight and authority to the Prussian state.

His officers were considered as mere adventurers in the trade of
arms; his soldiers, as vile mercenaries; and the name of
'Prussian' seldom occurred without some contumelious jest, or
some disgraceful epithet. The country itself, notwithstanding
its royal appelation, formed an undescribed species of
hermaphrodite monarchy, which partook rather of the
meanness of an electorate, than of the dignity of a kingdom.
(Gillies, 1789, 66–7)

In 1740 the population of Prussia before the Silesian conquest
reached scarcely two and a quarter million. By normal calculations
the reduction of Silesia might have seemed an impossible undertaking, but Frederick understood that the unique war-readiness of his
army gave him a facility rather like that of a serpent, which may
unhinge its jaws to swallow a disproportionately large prey. He had
at his immediate disposal a contingency reserve of 10,000,000 thaler,
which proved in the event more than enough to defray the costs of the
entire war. The army already stood at the respectable total of 83,000
troops, and Frederick was carrying out an 'augmentation' of 10,000
further men and an increase in the cadres of his field infantry from
sixty-six battalions to eighty-three. The arsenals were gleaming with
weapons enough to equip this force twice over. To Frederick's way of
thinking, the opportunity of making this conquest became its own
justification (PC 125).

As Frederick had foreseen, he faced the problem of shouldering
aside neighbours who were as rapacious as himself, rather than
having to confront any power which might come rushing to the help
of Austria. The Saxons, Spanish and Piedmontese all entered claims
at the expense of the Austrian body politic, and the Wittelsbachs of
Bavaria went on to make a successful bid for the vacant Imperial title
itself. The French and British were already locked in war. The
Russians, though long connected with the Austrians, were put out of
the reckoning by the death of Empress Anna on 9 November. Lastly,
Frederick made what appeared to be an astute evaluation of his
victim. The crisis found the House of Austria leaderless, its finances
exhausted, its army ruined, and many of its provinces ravaged by
plague, war and famine.

Frederick's announcements to the Austrian envoy and the
foreign courts were of the most cynical kind, and they need not detain
us for very long. Acting, he claimed, with the purest motives, he was
doing the Austrians a favour by leading his army into their territories,
and he required the cession of the whole of Silesia as an appropriate
reward for his services.

Military preparations began on 29 October, the day after the first

of the conferences with Schwerin and Podewils. Cereals were purchased in corn-rich Mecklenburg, and transported along the Spree
and the Friedrich-Wilhelms Canal to the main avenue of the Oder
(water transport was of crucial importance at this time of the year,
when the roads were impassable to heavily laden carts). One day
Frederick watched a mass of the gathering troops, and he told the Old
Dessauer of his impressions. He found it remarkable that all those
thousands of men, who were all individually stronger and better
armed than himself, should be trembling in his presence. Such was
the working of the Prussian discipline (Hildebrandt, 1829–35, V, 46).

Frederick left Rheinsberg for Berlin on 2 December. He found a
society alive with speculation, for the masquerades and balls of the
season continued unabated, while the regiments were already on the
march with sealed orders. On Sunday 4 December the congregations
deserted the churches in order to watch the artillery train trundling
along the Unter den Linden. All of this uncertainty proved too much
for one of Frederick's old tutors, Christoph Wilhelm von Kalckstein,
who made so bold as to approach his young master:

Kalckstein: Your Majesty, am I right in thinking there is going to be a
    war?
Frederick: Who can tell!
Kalckstein: The movement seems to be directed on Silesia.
Frederick: Can you keep a secret? (Taking him by the hand.)
Kalckstein: Oh yes, Your Majesty.
Frederick: Well, so can I!

                                        (Anon. 1788–9, III, 60)

Even the Old Dessauer was excluded from Frederick's counsels. He
moped around, spreading despondency and distrust, but Frederick
was determined on the principle that was at stake: 'This is an
enterprise which I must reserve for myself, so that nobody is left with
the impression that the king of Prussia goes to war in the company of a
court tutor' (*PC* 178).

Having seen to the last of the preparations and given a patriotic
address to the officers of the departing Berlin regiments, Frederick
allowed himself the relaxation of attending a masked ball in the
apartments of his queen in the Berlin Schloss. The next morning, 13
December, he awaited the arrival of his travelling coach in the
company of a large crowd and dismissed the pleas of his young
brothers Henry and Ferdinand, who clung to his coat tails and begged
to be allowed to go with him to the war. At nine, Frederick and three
adjutants entered the carriage and set off for the army, which had
been assembling on the border with Silesia.

Frederick hoped that the conquest, or rather the occupation of the Silesian plain, would be complete before the Austrians could feed reinforcements into this most northerly of their possessions. No Habsburg had set foot in Silesia for 130 years past, and Frederick expected to meet resistance only from the isolated garrisons of the fortress towns, of which the most immediately important was Glogau, barring the access up the Oder to Breslau, the main city of Silesia. To this operation Frederick devoted a little over 27,000 troops, comprising about 20,400 infantry, 6,600 cavalry, and a small complement of gunners.

At noon on 14 December Frederick reached Crossen. This was the last town in Brandenburg, and it was set on a height overlooking the Oder, flowing purposefully from Silesia. The superstitious townspeople were in a state of some alarm, for the king's advent coincided with the fall of the bell in the great church, but Frederick assured them that the omen was an auspicious one, signifying the collapse of the House of Habsburg.

On 16 December Frederick and the leading troops marched through a zone of woodland and crossed the Silesian border. One of his lieutenants made for Grünberg, and seized the town key from the thunderstruck burgomaster, sitting with the municipal fathers in the *Rathaus*. The king himself was met just inside Austrian territory by two black-cloaked figures who stood by the roadside like crows. These were Protestant clergymen from Glogau, come to beg Frederick to spare the heretical churches in case of bombardment. The king greeted them as the first of his Silesian subjects.

Frederick spent that night in a baronial house at Schweinitz, and he wrote to Berlin: 'My dear Podewils, I have crossed the Rubicon with flying colours and beating drums. My troops are full of enthusiasm, the officers are fired by ambition, and our generals are avid for glory' (PC 208).

The further advance across the plain took the Prussians to Herrendorf, hard by Glogau. Bad weather set in on 18 December. The baggage and artillery dragged far behind, and the soldiers marched in mud and water up to their knees, ruining their white gaiters. Glogau proved to be rather better fortified than had been expected, and although the Austrian commandant declined to take the initiative in opening hostilities the Prussian invasion threatened to bog down a few miles inside the Silesian border. Frederick was all the more anxious to press on to Breslau because he knew that the city authorities, although riddled with Prussian sympathisers, were engaged in talks to admit an Austrian garrison. Frederick accordingly left Glogau under blockade by an improvised 'II Corps', and on 28 December he set off for Breslau with the advance guard of the main body.

On 31 December Frederick and his grenadiers arrived outside the massive ramparts of Breslau. The main gates were shut against them, but the wickets were open, and a stream of tradesmen's lads made for the lines of brass-capped Prussians, bearing wine, bread, fish and meat, and dragging casks of beer behind them on little sledges.

Through his emissaries Frederick guaranteed the city fathers that he would uphold all the municipal privileges and that he had no intention whatsoever of establishing a garrison there. In return he desired only that Breslau should keep out the Austrians as well. The magistracy agreed to these terms, and the appropriate document was signed on the morning of 3 January. Frederick preceded his assent with the formula 'in the present circumstances and as long as they hold good'. This was dismissed as an unimportant detail at the time.

Meanwhile Frederick and a symbolic suite were allowed to make a ceremonial entry. Just before noon on the same 3 January the royal train entered by way of the Schweidnitzer Tor. Frederick's table silver was first through the gate. It was borne on pack-horses, which were draped with hangings of blue silk, all a-dangle with gold tassels and little bells. Frederick himself was mounted on a mettlesome steed. His blue silken cloak was bedaubed with the falling snowflakes, but he repeatedly uncovered his head to acknowledge the greetings of the crowd. He descended at the house of Count Schlangenberg in the Albrechtstrasse, and twice appeared on the balcony in response to the continuing applause.

In retrospect the beginning of the Prussian presence in Breslau may be seen as inaugurating the first of the sequence of modern wars. It is strange that it was invested with all the ceremonial of the *joyeuse entrée*, which was so much a part of the medieval era that was slipping away.

In military terms, Frederick had won the freedom to cut off the Austrian garrisons, and to sweep the remaining enemy field forces out of Silesia. For this purpose the 'I Corps' was divided into two wings. Frederick and the left continued the march up the Oder, and on the night of 8 January they received the capitulation of the little fortress of Ohlau. Schwerin meanwhile took the right wing on a roughly parallel course out to the west, scouring the fringes of the hills bordering the Austrian provinces of Bohemia and Moravia. Five depleted companies of Austrian grenadiers were slow to make their escape, and they were bottled up by Schwerin at Ottmachau on the left bank of the river Neisse. Frederick arrived at the scene of the miniature siege on 12 January, and found that the Austrians were ensconced in a castle perched at the top of a steep mound. The king was able to persuade them that they must surrender as prisoners of war, and he watched as they marched down with shouldered muskets and sounding music to the town square, where they deposited their arms.

Unaccountably, Colonel Wilhelm von Roth, although one of the few Lutherans in the Austrian employ, refused to surrender the sizeable fortress-town of Neisse nearby. This was an embarrassment, for Neisse stood close to the passes with Moravia, and it might offer the Austrians a strategic bridgehead for an eventual counter-offensive into Silesia. Formal siege was unthinkable at this wintry season, and 'a bombardment is the only thing worth attempting – the place is a nest of Papists, and there are not many troops inside' (Gr. Gstb., 1890–3, I, 268). Cold shot, red-hot shot (heated in the local brickworks) and mortar bombs rained down on the town until 22 January, when the enterprise was abandoned as useless. This was to be far from the last time that an Austrian stronghold put a term to a run of Prussian successes in the open field, and it revealed an important shortcoming in the proficiency of Frederick's army.

It was high time to think of giving the troops some shelter and rest. In his *Principes Généraux de la Guerre* (1748) Frederick condemned winter campaigns 'as being the most pernicious of all operations of war'. They spread sickness among the troops, and they deprived the monarch of the opportunity of recruiting and re-equipping the army for the next campaign. However, Frederick always considered his Silesian operation of 1740–1 as fully justified, for if he had waited for the spring 'it would then have taken me perhaps three or four hard-fought campaigns to acquire what I could now obtain simply by marching into Silesia' ('Principes Généraux', *Oeuvres*, XXVIII, 93).

Frederick left blockading forces around the Austrian garrisons at Glogau, Neisse and the upper Oder fortress of Brieg. He entrusted Schwerin with the command in Silesia, and commissioned him to sweep the tiny remnant of the Austrian field forces out of Troppau and into the Moravian border hills. The rest of the Prussian troops were quartered in the Silesian towns and villages, and Frederick set out for Berlin on 25 January.

There has been an inclination among some historians to ask whether Frederick's theft of Silesia was particularly noteworthy or reprehensible. Gerhard Ritter claims that the moral indignation on this head was 'conditioned by Europe's much later experiences of the military energy of the Prussian state' (Ritter, 1954, I, 31). Likewise Hans Bleckwenn, in correspondence with the present author, has suggested that we should place the episode alongside the colonial aggressions of the British that were going ahead in the same period.

No doubt there is little to choose in the matter of moral probity between Frederick and the other high-minded gentry who were bent on rearranging other people's property in the 1740s. However, what struck observers at the time was the unique style of the Silesian operation, which had been determined in a couple of days and carried to completion in six weeks. The Danish envoy to Berlin, Lieutenant-General Andreas August von Praetorius, expressed his astonishment at the speed, energy and facility of the thing. 'As for the future', he added, 'I am unwilling to be a prophet, but this monarch surely has some great project in mind. He will not be content with conquering a province, but will strive to become the arbiter of the German Empire' (Volz, 1926–7, I, 146–7. See also the nearly identical comments of Colonel de Beauval and Baron von Schwicheldt, *ibid.*, 154, 180–1).

The time had not yet come for Frederick to take any useful decisions concerning politics and strategy for 1741. So far he had no allies in his adventure, and he even found some difficulty in identifying the character of the Austrian leadership. Vienna was certainly proving unexpectedly obstinate in its refusal to renounce Silesia, but Frederick did not yet associate the source of this defiance with the new head of the House of Habsburg, the young and inexperienced Maria Theresa.

Meanwhile the impudent Colonel Roth had got into the habit of kidnapping the pro-Prussian nobility who lived within range of his raids from Neisse, and he spirited his captives away to his friend General Maximilian von Browne, who hovered in the Moravian hills with a screen of Austrian troops. These activities went unchecked by the Prussian hussars, who were still but a pale imitation of the genuine Hungarian originals in the Austrian service. The Prussian inferiority in *der kleine Krieg* of ambush and surprise was brought home directly to Frederick when he was nearly captured by a party of Austrian hussars at Baumgarten on 27 February.

Frederick received a measure of needful cheer on 9 March, when he learnt that the Hereditary Prince Leopold of Anhalt-Dessau (one of the sons of the Old Dessauer) had taken the fortress of Glogau by a surprise night escalade. Almost all of the open country of Silesia had long been in the possession of the Prussians, but Glogau offered them a solid gain, and it opened the navigation of the Oder up to the region of Breslau.

Frederick had still settled on no firm plan to consolidate his hold on Silesia when, at the beginning of April 1741, the initiative was snatched from him by the Austrians. About 16,000 Austrian troops had been assembled in Moravia, and Field-Marshal Neipperg now led them in a boldly conceived march from the border hills, aiming to relieve Neisse and recover the open country of Silesia. This move found the Prussians still scattered in quarters facing the hills along a frontage which reached from Troppau to Schweidnitz, and extended as far back as the Oder between Ratibor and Ohlau. Frederick was in the hills at Jägerndorf when the first tidings of the offensive were brought to him by seven Austrian deserters, and at once an outburst of firing from the pickets served to underline the urgency of their message. In fact his position was even worse than he believed, for the Austrians had already slipped past his right, or western flank, and they were well on their way to Neisse.

Why had Frederick been caught so badly off his guard? In part the answer lies in the lack of responsiveness of the over-drilled Prussian army. More important still, Frederick was inexperienced in war and he distrusted his own correct instincts, which had been to pull back his detachments and magazines from the hills, in accordance with such reports as had reached him concerning the Austrians who were gathering in Moravia. Schwerin, on the other hand, was anxious above all to secure fodder for the cavalry, and he wished to keep the screen well forward so as to conserve the fertile neighbourhood between the Oder and the hills. Frederick had met Schwerin on 29 March to debate the point, but he allowed himself to be overborne by the veteran. The consequences taught him never to defer so lightly to another's strategic judgment again.

The Prussian troops were now summoned from the companionable fug of their billets, and they joined their king as he hastened north across the snowy landscape to regain the time he had lost. The Austrians were well ahead of him. They relieved the fortress-town of Neisse on 5 April, and gained the far bank of the river of the same name. Frederick was for a long time unaware of the location of the enemy, but he knew that a battle could not long be postponed. He wrote to one of his old companions:

> My dear Jordan . . . you know the uncertainties of combat, and how chance has no more respect for the life of kings than it does for that of private individuals. I do not know what will become of me, but if my fate is sealed I wish you to remember me as a friend who loves you still. (*Oeuvres*, XVII, 98)

The ninth of April brought snows so heavy that at times it was impossible to make out objects at twenty paces. From what could be discerned of the Austrians it was evident that they were reaching out to their isolated garrison at Brieg. As long as Neipperg was in communication with the force there, he was firmly emplaced across the routes to Lower Silesia and Breslau (only the battle of Liegnitz in 1760 found the Prussians in equal peril, and there too the enemy were across Frederick's communications).

Frederick, like the rest of the army, resigned the management of the coming battle to the greatly experienced Schwerin:

> By 1741 the Prussians had been twenty-six years absent from
> war. When there was talk at the *Parole* of 'columns', and the
> sequence of the battalions that were supposed to make them up,
> our brave idiots got together and muttered 'What the hell are
> these columns? Well, I know what I shall do. I'll follow the man
> in front, and where he goes I'll go as well!' (Berenhorst, quoted
> in Koser, 1894, 302)

Frederick and Schwerin had about 21,600 troops to pit against the
19,000 Austrians. The Prussians owned the advantage of the solidity
of their 16,800 infantry, so well schooled on the parade square. The
Austrians had just 10,000 foot soldiers, many of them recruits, but in
compensation their 8,000 cavalry gave them a powerful offensive
capacity, and they had a great depth of recent experience among
their officers and generals. These gentry declared: 'We'll throw them
back where they came from . . . we'll have their guts for garters!' (Gr.
Gstb., 1890–3, I, 392).

The sun rose into a clear sky on 10 April 1741, illuminating an
expanse of thick but hard-frozen snow. The troops loaded their
knapsacks onto the company baggage waggons, then formed up in
five marching columns. Frederick probably shared the feelings recorded by one of his drummers: 'Only a fool will claim that he is as
calm in his first battle as in his tenth . . . I know that my heart was
pounding when reveille sounded on the morning of that memorable
day' (Dreyer, 1810, 16).

No further news was yet at hand concerning the whereabouts of
the Austrians, and the army set off at 10 a.m. in the direction of
Ohlau. A little later, news reached Frederick from peasants and
captured hussars that the enemy were disposed among the villages of
Mollwitz, Grüningen and Hünern close under Brieg, and he accordingly swung the columns to the left.

Little could be seen of the Austrians through the gaps in the
woods, but the Prussian army was still 3,500 paces short of Mollwitz
when at noon the order came to enter battle formation. The right
wing was told to align itself on the prominent village of Hermsdorf (or
a small wood to its left), and the left wing was to look for the church
tower of Pampitz. Frederick later reproached himself for not continuing the advance directly on Mollwitz, where he believed he
might have caught the Austrian infantry intact, like the French
troops who were bottled up in Blenheim village in 1704. He was being
too hard on himself, for we now know that the Austrian infantry was
scattered over a wide area around Mollwitz, and could never have
been trapped in this way. However, the move into lines of battle was

undoubtedly premature, and it made its contribution to the one and a half hours of confusion which nearly cost the Prussians their advantage of surprise.

Such a head-on approach to an enemy force was a move which Frederick sought to avoid in his later battles, for it brought a check in the advance so as to allow the columns (which were not considered a tactical formation) to make a right-angled turn and rearrange themselves into the two lines of battle, about 250 paces apart. Only when the lines were formed could the onward march be resumed. Moreover, at Mollwitz the level, snow-covered ground and the low and harsh sunlight seem to have conspired to throw out the Prussians' sense of distance. If they thought they were much nearer Mollwitz village than they really were, then they underestimated the space they needed to win for their lines, and they tried to crowd all of their forces onto a frontage of about 2,600 paces when 800 more would not have been excessive. A number of units therefore found themselves without a home – namely a grenadier battalion of the second column, two regiments and one battalion of the infantry of the fourth column, and the whole of the battalions of the fifth column – and they all had to be fitted in haphazardly along or between the lines of battle. The effective width of front was constricted still further by the Conradswaldauer-Bach and a companion stream on the south of the field, which served to isolate the left wing of the cavalry from the rest of the army.

After the deployment was complete, Frederick gave the order to advance at 1:30 p.m. Now at last the Prussian proficiency in drill showed to full advantage. 'A captured Austrian lieutenant-colonel had to admit . . . that it did not appear to be infantry that was marching towards them, but moving walls' (Captain von Thile, in Geuder, 1902, 115).

The right, or northern, wing was slanting forward towards the enemy, and the Prussian heavy artillery went in front by bounds, unlimbering, firing, then advancing to the next battery position. The Prussian guns were concentrating their fire on a mass of Austrian cavalry that was seen to be forming up to the north-east of Mollwitz. Some of the Prussians saw that the ground turned black when the cannon shot ripped the snow aside. Another witness noted that a strong wind whipped the surface of the snow into a dense, billowing cloud, which enveloped the enemy horse (Geuder, 1902, 94). Out of this haze burst the entire left wing of the Austrian cavalry.

On this side of the field the hostile cavalry comprised 4,500 troopers under the command of General Römer, who was now intent on winning time for the rest of the Austrian army to form up. The 2,000 horsemen of the Prussian right received the Austrian charge at the halt, and they laboured under the further disadvantage of being interleaved with isolated battalions of grenadiers, who got in their way. The Schulenburg Dragoons (D 3; see Map 1, p. 341) had already been shaken by their experiences in the skirmish at Baumgarten, and they now fled without more ado. Frederick was with the Winterfeldt grenadier battalion (5/21) only a short distance along the line, and he set off with the Leib-Carabiniers (C 11) in the hope of staving off the collapse. He was already too late, and he was borne away with the mass of struggling cavalry along the front of the first line of the army.

These events left the Winterfeldt and Bolstern (3/22) grenadiers isolated on the far right of the line, and they blazed away to front and rear on friend and foe alike. A perhaps more valuable service was performed by the Kleist grenadiers (1/25) and a single battalion of Anhalt-Dessau (10), which, although they had been stranded between the two Prussian lines of battle during the muddled deployment, were now well placed to prevent the Austrians from penetrating the interval.

What happened next is difficult to reconstruct with any conviction, but it is evident that Römer's cavalry, although broken into groups, returned to the attack on at least two occasions. The fighting was certainly intense. Römer and the Prussian General of Cavalry Schulenburg were killed at this confused stage of the proceedings. The king's friend, Count Chasot, was intent on throttling an Austrian officer, but before he could finish the work he was wounded in the head by a sword cut, and both he and his intended victim fell to the ground.

Schwerin now advised Frederick that he ought to absent himself from the scene. The field-marshal had noticed that the Prussian line had opened fire without orders, and his experienced tactical judgment told him that things were in danger of getting out of control (Schwerin, 1928, 141). Frederick probably needed little prompting, for he was alarmed by the sequence of sudden reverses. At about 4 p.m. the king therefore took some important papers from his baggage, and he galloped from the field on a fresh and powerful grey horse.

Frederick and his party of companions rode almost without rest through the evening and the early hours of the night to the supposed shelter of Oppeln. They found that the town gates were shut, and when they announced that they were Prussians they came under fire from a force of fifty Austrian hussars which had got there before them. Frederick pulled his horse around and was off before the Austrians could open the gates. The mathematician Maupertuis and other slow-moving members of his suite were overtaken by the

pursuers, but Frederick and an aide-de-camp made good their escape
to the village of Löwen. 'There he strode up and down the room,
giving vent to loud lamentations. "My God", he cried, "this is too
much! Why are You so intent on punishing me?" ' (Valori, 1820,
104–5). An officer now arrived with a message from Schwerin. He told
Frederick not about the final stages of some disaster, but of how his
master had reassembled the shattered cavalry and pushed the Austrians from Mollwitz with the infantry. It is said that the king 'never
forgave Schwerin for having rendered a service too important in
itself, as well as too wounding to the vanity of a sovereign such as
Frederick' (Wraxall, 1806, I, 155).

Frederick was back with his army on 11 April, but he allowed the
Austrians to retire with their forces intact. He was still a novice in
warfare, and he was too glad not to have been beaten to be able to
think of exploiting the victory (Gisors, 1868, 106). With their 4,850
dead, wounded or missing, the Prussians had actually lost 300 more
men than the Austrians. However, the importance of the victory can
be judged only by reference to what would have happened if Neipperg
had won, for then 'not only would all Silesia have been restored to the
Queen of Hungary [Maria Theresa], but the King of Prussia and his
entire army would have been forced into an unconditional surrender'
(Geuder, 1902, 101).

Frederick's tactical summary was forceful and accurate: 'It is to
our incomparable infantry alone that we are indebted for the continuation of my good fortune, the preservation of our valiant army,
and the welfare of the state . . . but the cavalry is damnably awful –
none of the officers can do anything with it' (Gr. Gstb., 1890–3, I,
419).

Regarding the campaign as a whole, Frederick censured his own
conduct with unnecessary harshness, and cited three major mistakes:

(a) He allowed his army to be caught in scattered positions when
    the Austrians opened their advance.
(b) He permitted himself to be cut off from his forces on the left bank
    of the Neisse, and he was ultimately compelled to fight under
    circumstances in which a defeat would have been disastrous.
(c) He lost precious time in forming his army up well short of
    Mollwitz village. (*Oeuvres*, II, 77)

It is agreeable to record that Frederick, so ungrateful to humankind, never forgot his debt to the long-striding animal which had
carried him to safety. The 'Mollwitz Grey' (*Mollwitzer Schimmel*)
was put into retirement and tended for the rest of its long life.
Frederick rode the horse occasionally for exercise, but in fine weather
it was allowed the freedom to gallop and graze in the Lustgarten at
Potsdam:

Sometimes this coincided with the season for the reviews, when the ensigns brought out the colours from the Schloss and the whole corps of drums beat out a march. Then the old horse would rear up and go through its paces of its own accord, until the flags and drummers had passed by. (Nicolai, 1788–92, IV, 51)

Frederick was disinclined to make the further effort that was needed to push the Austrians from Neisse and Upper Silesia. His army required rest and repair, and he did not wish to plunge into a further campaign until the new patterns of European alliances had assumed recognisable shape.

From 20 April to 25 May 1741 Frederick devoted all his efforts to fashioning a battleworthy army in his camp to the north of Mollwitz. Belle-Isle and Törring, the French and Bavarian envoys, could scarcely believe what they saw. Frederick rose at four every morning and made a rapid tour of the camp and the surroundings. He returned to give instructions to the generals, to dictate letters to his two overworked secretaries, and to question spies, deserters and prisoners. The cavalry was the object of Frederick's particular attention, as may well be imagined, but he drove the entire corps of officers so hard that several hundred of them asked to resign. The requests were refused. With all of this going on, Frederick still found the leisure to entertain sittings of forty officers at a time in his tent and to write verse to Charles-Étienne Jordan, his secretary of the Rheinsberg days.

During this period of reconstruction Frederick looked naturally to the assistance of the Anhalt-Dessau tribe. The Old Dessauer himself was drilling 26,000 more troops in a camp at Göttin, and Frederick tapped his experience in the course of a lively correspondence. The eldest of the Anhalt-Dessau sons, the Hereditary Prince Leopold Max, had already proved his coolness and resolution when he stormed Glogau, and Frederick readily entrusted him with independent commands. However, the third in the line, the amiable and respected Dietrich, stood closest to Frederick in terms of friendship. He was made field-marshal in 1747, but three years later Frederick gave in to his repeated demands to be allowed to retire from the military life.

The Old Dessauer's fourth and last son, Prince Moritz, was a bizarre assemblage of practical ability and brutal ignorance. He was said to have been left without any education whatsoever, as an experiment on the part of his father, and he emerged into adulthood as an almost complete *Naturmensch*. It is easy to see why contemporaries believed that he was totally illiterate, whereas he probably just gave the appearance of being so. Frederick, at any rate, found that he could comprehend letters that were written in simple language and short sentences.

Moritz and the others came to Frederick as a legacy from the Old Dessauer. However, in the spring of 1741 we can already discern the rise of the first of a new generation of commanders, singled out by Frederick from among the ranks of their comrades. This was a lieutenant-colonel of hussars, Hans Joachim von Zieten, who on 17 May played the leading part in routing a force of Austrian cavalry at Rothschloss.

Zieten was already in his forty-third year, and his slow promotion owed as much to his poor performance as a peacetime soldier as to the clogging of the senior ranks by venerable warriors. He was born to a family of the poor squirarchy at Wustrau in Brandenburg. Every Sunday from the age of nine he travelled to nearby Ruppin, to have his hair dressed and powdered in the military style by a hired musketeer, and he persevered in his military vocation, despite a series of appalling disqualifications. His stature was slight, his voice on parade was feeble, he maintained bad discipline among his men, he was easily overcome by drink, and his sensitivity and quarrelsome temperament led him into two duels, a period of fortress arrest, and a temporary cashiering.

In 1741, however, the achievement of Zieten and his six squadrons of hussars wrung a compliment from the defeated Austrian commander General Baranyay. In the next year Zieten was to spearhead the advance of the army into southern Moravia, and his men skirmished to within sight of the spires of Vienna. The hussars, under Zieten, were by then an effective force in the field, and their prowess was to be the seed of the regeneration of the whole of the Prussian cavalry.

In the weeks after Mollwitz Frederick came to appreciate that other powers regarded the friendship of Prussia as a desirable commodity. This sensation was all the more agreeable because the Austrians were obstinate in refusing to recognise the Prussian gains in Silesia. On 4 June representatives of Frederick and Louis XV signed a secret fifteen-year alliance. The French gave Frederick a guarantee of his possession of Breslau and Lower Silesia, and in return Frederick promised his vote to the Elector of Bavaria or any other French candidate for the throne of the Emperor of Germany. The main burden of military operations was to be assumed by the French and Bavarians who, Frederick hoped, would push straight down the Danube on Vienna.

Operations in Silesia languished until August 1741, while Frederick and Neipperg built up and trained their rival forces. Desiring to have his hands free for possible joint action with his allies,

Frederick breached the already tenuous treaty of neutrality with the city of Breslau. Early on 10 August 4,500 troops seized the gates, and within a few hours Schwerin exacted the oaths of loyalty which made Breslau a Prussian city.

Just as had happened in the spring, Field-Marshal Neipperg and the Austrians were the first to declare their hand when operations resumed in the high summer of 1741. On 23 August Frederick blocked their first move, which was a strike from Neisse against the Prussian magazine at Schweidnitz. Now that the two armies were mobile again, Frederick hatched a scheme to cut around Neipperg's right flank and reach the prize of Neisse, which would have given the Prussians an important political and military advantage before the coming of winter closed down operations. The Prussian advance guard and the bridging train set out from Frederick's camp at Reichenbach on the evening of 7 September, but in the autumn mists they described a circle and ended up behind the main army, which was not at all what had been intended.

The lost time was never made up. Neipperg was quick on his feet over short distances, and he twice headed off Frederick's attempts to make an undisputed passage of the Neisse river at Woitz, downstream from Neisse town – on 11 September and again on 14 September. Frederick broke forth in foul language, and in his *Principes Généraux* of 1748 he described the frustrations of this episode in a section he entitled 'Des Hasards et des Cas fortuits qui arrivent à la Guerre'.

In the late autumn Frederick discovered that the Austrians, faced with the disintegration of their monarchy, were willing to pay him very handsomely for the freedom to divert their forces against the French and Bavarians on the Danube and in Bohemia. Frederick was a bad partner in any joint enterprise, whether a marriage or an alliance, and now he did not hesitate to throw over his obligations to the French, and come to terms with the enemy at Klein-Schnellendorf on 9 October. Neipperg sent off the first of his troops on the next day, which was an indication of how urgently the Austrians needed these men in the western theatre.

In immediate terms the Klein-Schnellendorf treaty extended and legalised the Silesian conquest of 1740. Lower Silesia was ceded to the Prussians outright. In addition Frederick was allowed to quarter his troops in Upper Silesia, and the fortress-town of Neisse was to be surrendered to him after he had subjected the place to a siege of a certain length. This last curious stipulation was deemed necessary to keep up the appearance of hostilities, and so conceal Frederick's perfidy from the French and Bavarians.

Neisse capitulated on 31 October, which was somewhat earlier than had been arranged. The siege commander, Hereditary Prince

Leopold, had not been privy to the secrets of Klein-Schnellendorf, and he had prosecuted the siege with excessive energy. Leopold then proceeded westwards, and he clamped a blockade on the citadel of the town of Glatz, which was the capital of the border enclave of the same name.

The southern borders of Silesia were now secure. If Neisse gave the Prussians a fortress-depot within easy range of Moravia, then the County of Glatz offered them a fine passage into the corresponding westerly province of Bohemia. However, a much greater prize had been within Frederick's grasp: 'He was never to know again such an opportunity as he let slip in the autumn of 1741, when he suffered Neipperg's troops – the only field army left to Austria – to withdraw perfectly intact, without battle or pursuit. His fate was now sealed' (Koser, 1921, I, 367).

Engagements to an enemy sat still more lightly on Frederick's conscience than did his obligations to his friends. The king had left Berlin on 9 November, and he was looking forward to spending the first weeks of 1742 at his beloved Rheinsberg. Early in January, however, came news of the amazing recuperative power of the Austrians, who were pushing along the Danube against Bavaria, and were threatening to recover their own province of Bohemia, which was swarming with the French, Bavarian and Saxon troops of the anti-Habsburg coalition. Frederick accordingly decided to re-enter the war.

Schwerin had already pushed the zone of the Prussian winter quarters deep into the almost undefended Austrian province of Moravia, and Frederick hoped that by advancing a short way from this base in the direction of Vienna he could make an effective diversion on behalf of his associates, without running the risk of drawing the main Austrian army upon his head. He set out from Berlin on 18 January, and two days later in Dresden the Saxons agreed to place their powerful contingent of well-trained troops under his command. Frederick was thereby able to win a disproportionate amount of control over the allied forces, and the Saxon prime minister, Count Brühl, received from Marshal de Saxe the single-line message: 'Now you have no more army!'

Frederick then travelled east to his forces in central Moravia, passing through Prague and the County of Glatz, and emerging from a range of snowy hills into the plain of Olmütz. The flat and fertile countryside reminded Frederick's party of the familiar landscapes of Magdeburg, and the city of Olmütz proved to be agreeably impressive. The massive stucco walls of the churches and colleges were interspersed with open spaces, which were embellished by fountains. One of the smaller squares was dominated from one end by the

Renaissance façade of the episcopal palace, where Frederick and most
of his suite were accommodated. The bishop, little Count Lichten-
stein, was a cordial host, and 'a large part of the Moravian nobility
had established themselves in that town, where the carnival was in
full train, with all the attendant comedies, masked balls and assemblies' (Stille, 1764, 9).

Frederick remained in Olmütz only a week, from 28 January to 4
February. News came during this period that the Austrians were
continuing their advance up the Danube, and Frederick prepared to
assemble his own force on the northern flank of the enemy communications through Lower Austria. Altogether he had about 34,000
troops at his disposal, comprising 14,900 Prussians, more than 16,000
Saxons, and Lieutenant-General Polastron's contingent of 2,870
French.

Taking care to give a wide berth to the fortress-town of Brünn,
which was held by a frisky Austrian garrison, Frederick made his way
south-west through some of the most picturesque country of Central
Europe. The narrow tracks led at first through foggy woods and
gorges. There was, however, an interval of civilisation at Namiest,
where the royal party crossed the Oslawa by means of a modern
bridge, tastefully adorned with statues of saints. To the right a
gentleman's castle hovered over the valley, reminding one of the
king's friends of the frontispiece to the text of The Tempest (Stille,
1764, 16–7; Stille mistakenly locates this castle at Budischau). Finally
in the second week of February the army assembled between Budischau, Gross-Bitesch and Gross-Meseritsch on an uneven tableland,
set with stands of pines, outcrops of rock, and innumerable lakes and
ponds. From here the force moved south across a continuous pine-
covered ridge, and so to the vast undulating plain which led to the
Danube.

Frederick arranged his troops in quarters along the river Thaya,
whose deep and wide gorge wound below the dirty little town of
Znaym, where the king had his headquarters from 20 February to 8
March. He sent a mixed Prusso-Saxon command ranging the short
distance across Lower Austria to the Danube just above Vienna.
However, all the motions were very feeble, when we consider the size
of Frederick's army, and how close he was to the enemy capital. He
did not know the whereabouts of the Austrian forces, and he was still
unwilling to exert anything but the most indirect pressure on behalf
of the French and Bavarians in Bohemia.

In the course of March Frederick regrouped his forces a little
further to the north, so as to maintain a more effective blockade of
Brünn, and safeguard his communications with Silesia against the
depredations of the Hungarian insurrection. Frederick now installed

his royal person in the large but still incomplete palace of Seelowitz, 'a charming location, worthy of accommodating a great prince' (Stille, 1764, 32). The little river Svratka separated this establishment from a large, arid hill which afforded views over the surrounding plain and in the direction of Brünn, just ten miles to the north. Frederick resided in Seelowitz from 13 March to 4 April. As was to be his habit, when he occupied spacious lodgings during a lull in the campaign, he took the opportunity to compose tactical directions for his army. There were three of these 'Seelowitz Instructions' – one each for heavy cavalry, the hussars and the infantry (see p. 309).

Frederick believed that it was quite possible that he would have to do battle with the Austrians at short notice, and with this in mind he selected a suitable site at Pohrlitz. In fact the encounter still lay two months ahead; meanwhile the Moravian half-campaign did nothing to advance Frederick's reputation as statesman, commander or prince.

Frederick's demands on the Austrians were so extreme that he destroyed all English attempts at mediation. He no longer required Upper Silesia, which he regarded as barren, remote and hostile, but instead he insisted on the cession of the circles of Pardubitz and Königgrätz, which were blessed with the most favourable climate and some of the richest soils in Bohemia. To the rear the region was readily accessible from the County of Glatz, while a couple of marches by the Prussians to their front would sever the Austrian communications with Prague. Put in other terms, once Frederick was legally established in that part of the world, he would have made Bohemia untenable for the Austrians, and completed the virtual encirclement of the electorate of Saxony. Like the Herstal episode of 1740, Frederick's demands in the spring of 1742 have received little attention from the historians, but they tell us a great deal about the ambitions of our hero.

Meanwhile it became increasingly clear that one of the principal objectives of Frederick in holding his forces inactive in Moravia was to turn the province into a strategic desert. Seelowitz itself was plundered, and out in the country the peasants were forced to reveal the location of all their stores of grain, which were then destroyed or carried off. 'Altogether the marquisate of Moravia, which had been reputed the finest and richest in Germany, was reduced to a scene of pitiable desolation' (Mauvillon, 1756, II, 64).

Frederick's harshness extended to his own allies. Saxon officers came to Seelowitz and protested against the king's practice of assigning them to the most arduous duties in the blockade of Brünn and denying them proper supplies and shelter. Frederick's younger brother Henry later took him up on the point: 'You allocated the worst quarters to them. You refused to listen to the representations which their generals made to you, and finally their troops returned to Saxony half-dead' (Herrmann, 1922, 253). We can only assume that Frederick was already engaged in the process of destroying Saxon military power.

Frederick abandoned the desolate surroundings of Seelowitz on 5 April. He had done his work in Moravia, and now at last he made up his mind to move into Bohemia and lend a more direct kind of support to the French who, it was wrongly reported to him, were facing an imminent Austrian counter-attack. Frederick described an anti-clockwise circuit around to the north of Brünn, and marched his leading elements rather quickly across the border highlands into north-eastern Bohemia. On 17 April he planted his headquarters in the little walled town of Chrudim, which was set in a fertile hollow. This move is better described as a new 'dislocation of quarters', in the contemporary parlance, than as proper advance, for the parasitical Prussian army was still scattered over a wide tract of countryside.

It took Frederick a long time to appreciate that he himself was the target of the hostile designs. The Austrians, so often taxed by historians with lack of enterprise, had determined that Frederick was their most dangerous enemy, and by taking considerable risks they were to maintain the strategic initiative until almost the end of the coming campaign. They reduced their troops in Bohemia to a mere 10,000, and commissioned Prince Charles of Lorraine, the brother-in-law of Maria Theresa, to build up a striking force of some 30,000 men in Moravia and come at the Prussians from the rear.

All of this remained unknown to Frederick. His body of hussars was small in number and inexperienced in reconnaissance work, and thus 'throughout the campaign the Prussians were compelled to ask every traveller or peasant for what they knew about the enemy movements' (Schmettau, 1806, II, 283). Such information was not readily forthcoming, and it was of particular relevance for what was to ensue that Bohemia was separated from Moravia by a screen of low, rocky and heavily wooded hills, inhabited by 'a rough intract-able set of men' (Marshall, 1772, III, 313). The Hungarian militia seconded the work of these wild gentry, and the Prussians were able to penetrate this region only in sizeable parties.

At last on 10 May an accumulation of reports convinced Frederick that large Austrian forces were on the move westwards from Moravia, and that an enemy corps from southern Bohemia was coming up to join them. Frederick therefore ordered the army to leave its quarters and assemble at Chrudim. The king staked out the lines of the camp in person, and at eight on the morning of 13 May he set out from Chrudim with the two battalions of the Garde, and reached the summit of a hill which lay to the west.

> It was a spendid day, and you could not imagine a more agreeable view than the one we had from our hill, extending over plains and mountains . . . the columns of our infantry and cavalry could be seen approaching from every direction, like lines being drawn from a circumference towards a common centre. You are aware of the splendour of our troops and military gear, but I assure you that in your wildest imaginings you could not have conceived . . . a more perfect picture.
> (Stille, 1764, 68)

This concentration amounted to thirty-five battalions, two companies of grenadiers and seventy squadrons.

The sunny weather struck no warmth into Frederick's heart. The Marquis de Valori, a French diplomat, joined him at Chrudim and found that he was in a state of near-panic. 'The condition of the king of Prussia was frightful, and it made his expression quite ferocious. All his remarks were cutting, and his smile was forced and sardonic' (Valori, 1820, I, 154).

Even now Frederick did not fully awaken to his danger. The Austrians were already slipping past his southern flank, but he assumed that Prince Charles was merely intent on gaining some marches in the direction of Prague. Frederick put his forces in motion with no great sense of urgency. He set off with the advance guard on 15 May, leaving the Hereditary Prince Leopold Max of Anhalt-Dessau to follow on the next day with the remaining two-thirds of the army.

The tableland to the west of Chrudim terminated in a brow above Podhorschan, where the road described a turn to the left and descended steeply through woodlands to the plain of Tschaslau. Standing on a mighty boulder, later called the *Friedrichstein*, the king had a clear view to the west to the slender spire of Tschaslau, seven miles away. The ground was empty, but in the more broken country further to the south Frederick espied an Austrian camp near Wilimow. He estimated the enemy at between seven and eight thousand, and reached the wrong conclusion that they must represent the corps of Prince Lobkowitz, who was approaching from southern Bohemia. In fact this force was the army of Prince Charles, which owned no less than 28,000 combatants. Frederick marched on to Kuttenberg, and distributed his troops in quarters.

Prince Leopold followed in Frederick's tracks on 16 May. On reaching the Podhorschan viewpoint he was startled by the sight of the Austrian camp, which now extended between Schleb and Ronow. By counting the rows of tents he made an accurate assessment of the size of the force, and he appreciated that the Austrians had their main army close to the routes between the now widely separated elements of the Prussian army. His troops were already exhausted by the hot and dusty march, but Leopold urged them to further efforts, and in the late evening, after eighteen hours on their feet, they reached a hastily chosen camp to the north of Tschaslau. Leopold sent word to Frederick, who replied that he would arrive to support him on the 17th.

The Austrian army marched through the starlit night of 16 May to do battle with Prince Leopold before he could be joined by Frederick. In crude numbers the Austrians were the equal of the total Prussian force, but they were inferior in regular cavalry, and weaker still in artillery and line infantry.

Frederick set out from Kuttenberg at 5 a.m. on the 17th and hastened in the direction of the main army, gathering up the troops of the advance guard as he went. The dragoons hurried ahead of the infantry, but Frederick halted for a moment at the Romanesque church in the village of St Jacob. A stone effigy of Christ gave the near-pagan king a stiff blessing as he passed beneath him through the entrance, but Frederick rushed unheeding inside and mounted the stairs of the narrow tower, from where he saw that the Austrians were already on the near side of Tschaslau and were advancing north-wards. After this rapid orientation Frederick rode on to the main army, and the infantry of the advance guard trailed in behind him. Frederick met Leopold at about 7.30 a.m. and gave him the responsi-bility for the left flank.

In military jargon, this was going to be an 'encounter battle' – an action in which successive forces were incorporated in the line of battle as they happened to arrive on the field. It was impossible to formulate a proper plan, but it seems that Frederick intended to throw his cavalry at the Austrians, and so win the time to form up his infantry. The extensive Cirkwitzer Pond conveniently closed up the right or western flank of the gathering Prussian forces, and close by this body of water Lieutenant-General Buddenbrock assembled the thirty-five squadrons of the cavalry of the Prussian right. To the left of the cavalry Frederick in person gradually assembled a full twenty-three battalions of infantry in a tract of low-lying ground, concealed from view and fire, from which one historian has concluded that this wing was intended to deal the main counter-attack against the Austrians (Herrmann, 1894, 340-6).

The corresponding left or eastern wing of the infantry was commanded by Lieutenant-General Jeetze who, perhaps contrary to Frederick's wishes, pushed his dozen battalions onto an exposed position on the open plateau in front of Chotusitz. This village, which gave its name to the battle, was a straggling affair of lightly built and indefensible houses. The left wing of the cavalry, commanded by Lieutenant-General Waldow, was approximately equal in size to Buddenbrock's force, but it was awkwardly positioned beyond the rather steeply banked little Brslenka-Bach, and consequently experienced some difficulties in crossing this obstacle to reach the Chotusitz plateau.

Both Leopold and Frederick sent orders to Buddenbrock to attack without more ado. From his position in the hollow Frederick probably saw nothing of the ensuing action except the clouds of dust, but he afterwards heard how the Prussian first line of twenty squadrons of cuirassiers hit the left wing of the Austrian cavalry with commendable speed, overthrowing the leading ranks 'like a house of cards' (Stille, 1764, 77).

Buddenbrock then lost the advantage of his impetus by halting to rally his squadrons, as the regulations actually demanded. He enjoyed no support in these critical moments from his ten squadrons of dragoons, which made up his second line, for this force veered too far to the left in all the dust, and it was badly mauled by the left wing of the advancing Austrian infantry. Buddenbrock now found himself assailed by a counter-attack of two regiments of cuirassiers and one of dragoons, and the Prussian troopers finally gave way in confusion when Austrian hussars fell on their fear. By about 9.30 a.m. the cavalry of the Prussian right had ceased to take any further part in the battle.

Meanwhile on the centre and east of the field the Austrians moved steadily over the plateau. In order to stay their progress Waldow most courageously threw the three regiments of the cuirassiers of the first line of the left against the advancing lines of white. Historians argue as to whether the initial clash between the rival forces of cavalry was staged on the east or west side of the Brslenka, but it appears that the three Prussian regiments carved a way clear through the Austrian horse and foot to the open country beyond, and executed a circuit behind the back of the Austrian army as far as the scene of Buddenbrock's dying cavalry action to the west. They discovered that there was little to be done on this part of the field, and the Prinz August Wilhelm Cuirassiers (C 2; see Map 2, p. 342) made back in the direction of Chotusitz, once more braving the fire of the Austrian infantry. One of the squadron commanders, Major Georg Wilhelm von Driesen, was taken prisoner by the enemy cavalry, but in a moment of general confusion he broke free and cut his way to safety.

The battle was now reduced to a struggle around the village of Chotusitz, where Prince Leopold had now assembled a tangled mass of twelve battalions of infantry and fifteen squadrons of dragoons. Here the undoubted hero was Joachim Seegebart, a field preacher of the infantry regiment of Prinz Leopold (27). He first of all rallied his comrades to throw back the Austrian grenadiers and cavalrymen who had penetrated between their ranks: 'While I was thus engaged the bullets flew around my head as thickly as a swarm of stinging gnats. None of them hit me, thanks be to God, and even my coat was untouched. In the mêlée a soldier tried to kill my horse with his bayonet, but one of our men turned it aside' (Berenhorst, 1845–7, I, 99–100). Seegebart then restored a semblance of order to a body of Prussian cavalry, in all likelihood some of the dragoons of the second line. The Austrian assaults were supported by a powerful concentration of artillery, however, and by about 9 a.m. the Prussians were forced to abandon Chotusitz after the enemy troops set fire to the houses about their ears. Leopold re-formed on the north side of the village, but Frederick later criticised him for having attempted to hold the wretched place at all.

The greatest mystery of this confused morning concerns the prolonged inactivity of Frederick and the powerful right wing of the Prussian infantry, who were hiding all the time in the hollow. When Frederick at last got on the move, the effect was decisive. It was at about 10.30 a.m. that the Prussian lines began to press forward. They marched some six hundred paces onto the plateau, then executed a giant wheel to left, and opened a long-range fire of musketry against the left flank of the Austrian forces around Chotusitz. The Austrians immediately sensed the danger to the path of their retreat to Tschaslau, and within minutes their regiments dissolved over the fields.

The battle was over by 11 a.m. The chief Prussian staff officer, Carl C. von Schmettau, urged Frederick to launch an immediate pursuit and received the interesting reply: 'You are quite right, but I don't want to defeat them too badly' (Schmettau, 1806, II, 222). In any case, as Frederick mentioned in a conversation much later, his own cavalry was in disorder, and he could not have advanced his infantry too far without reducing them to the same condition (Gisors, 1868, 106).

The battle had been costly to both sides, depriving Frederick of 4,800 of his troops, and Prince Charles of 6,330. A large proportion of the Austrian losses were made up of prisoners, and the Prussians had actually suffered more than 1,000 more battle casualties than the enemy, which reinforced the general impression that the victory was more one of discipline and morale than of tactics.

Frederick blamed Leopold for the unreadiness of the army when the Austrians struck early on the morning of the 17th. With greater justice he promoted Buddenbrock to full general of cavalry, advanced

Driesen to lieutenant-colonel, and hung the *Pour le Mérite* around the neck of his crony Count Chasot, who had rescued the royal baggage from Austrian hussars. Seegebart's deeds became known even to Voltaire, and Frederick rewarded this heroic clergyman by presenting him with a comfortable living.

Frederick pondered the tactical lessons at his leisure, and did not incorporate them into comprehensive instructions until July 1744. Meanwhile it was evident that the infantry was basically as sound as ever, and that the cavalry, although lacking a sense of ensemble, had acted with much more spirit than at Mollwitz.

Frederick was delighted at the figure he was sure he must be cutting in European opinion. He wrote to Jordan: 'This is the second time in thirteen months that your friend has been victorious in battle. Who would have said a few years ago that your philosophy pupil . . . would now be playing a military role in the world?' (undated, *Oeuvres*, XVII, 213–14). Voltaire in secret deplored the bloodshed, but he complimented Frederick on the simplicity of his official relation of the battle, rebuking him only for not having beaten the Austrians in a location more euphonious than Chotusitz. Frederick replied that Voltaire would discover that the place rhymed well enough with somewhere called Mollwitz.

Displaying all the tenacity of the Austrian military tradition, Prince Charles rallied his troops within a distance of a couple of marches of the Prussians. On 21 May Frederick advanced warily to a camp at Brscheschi, and he remained there until it became clear that the Austrians were moving west against the French. So as to be prepared for any eventuality, Frederick formed the celebrated camp of Kuttenberg on 1 June. This position faced south-east, and extended for rather more than three miles across a low plateau which commanded views over the immense and fertile plain of the upper Elbe. Frederick had his headquarters at Maleschau, near to the right flank at the little settlement of Bykan, where a cluster of redoubts stood above a bare slope which descended to a rivulet. The left flank extended to Neschkareditz, close to the old and substantial mining town of Kuttenberg, with its prominent church of St Barbara, a box-like structure sprouting three slender spires. The rear of the camp was closed up by a steep gorge produced by old silver workings. Frederick was delighted to have the facility of such a barrier against desertion, and he accepted the risk of denying his army any retreat if he once more came under attack from Prince Charles.

At Maleschau Frederick heard that the Austrians had been successful in bringing together their Bohemian and Danubian armies, and that this combined force was threatening to throw the French back to Prague. Frederick told himself that he had now done more than enough for his allies, and, fearing that the French might shortly be driven into signing a separate peace, he decided to anticipate them by making an advantageous accommodation with the Austrians.

The negotiations went ahead at Breslau through the mediation of the British envoy Hyndford. Acting under Frederick's instructions, the foreign minister Podewils reached preliminary terms of peace with the Austrians on 11 June. The definitive treaty was concluded in July, and became known as the Peace of Breslau. It put an end to the Prussian and Austrian conflict which is called the First Silesian War.

The Austrians made over Lower Silesia with Breslau, and all of Upper Silesia except for some of the border townships and passes. Frederick was sorry not to have gained Königgrätz and Pardubitz in Bohemia, but he congratulated Podewils on 'a great and happy event that has terminated this glorious war by putting us in possession of one of the most flourishing provinces of Germany' (PC 888).

Frederick felt under an obligation to justify his conduct to himself and others. In a long letter to Jordan he made the dubious assertion that he had been let down by his allies, and he claimed that having already acquired sufficient conquests, glory and military experience he would have damaged his army and state if he had remained at war any longer; lastly he sought to persuade Jordan that the modern sovereign should be revered as a kind of martyr, for he must be prepared to injure his conscience and his engagements for the good of the people (13 June, Oeuvres, XVII, 226–7).

Frederick later worked up these ideas for the first printed volume of his Histoire de Mon Temps, but a more positive and expansionist driving force is revealed in the preface to the first draft, which was written in 1743: 'Whether the state in question is tiny or huge, we may be sure that aggrandisement is the fundamental law of the government . . . The passions of princes are limited only by the extent of their power. This is the immutable principle of European politics, and every statesman must conform with it' (Koser, 1921, I, 401–2).

Frederick's conduct amounted to a clear contradiction of those few, and probably uncharacteristic, passages of the Antimachiavel in which he had once maintained that public and personal morality were inseparable. Voltaire was too flattered by the attentions of a great man to be able to break off his relationship with the King of Prussia, but his confidence in Frederick, as a unique assemblage of private and civic virtues, was never restored.

Frederick was now recognised as the legal master of the duchy of Silesia and the County of Glatz. These territories represented a huge accession of force to the Prussian monarchy. By 1752 Silesia yielded more than one-quarter of the state revenues, and out of all the

Prussian lands it was to make by far the greatest single contribution (18,000,000 thaler out of 43,000,000) to the cost of the Seven Years War.

The British major-general Joseph Yorke travelled through the region in 1758, and he commented:

> The mountains are well-cultivated and peopled, and great manufactures [exist] in all parts of them; indeed, the whole duchy of Silesia is as fine a country as one can see and well worth fighting for, and the inhabitants of it [are] beautiful; out of England I never saw so handsome a race of people as the Silesians, very different from their neighbours in Brandenburg and Bohemia, who are very plain. (Yorke, 1913, III, 210)

The linen industry was well established, 'the soul of Silesia', in Frederick's words (Voltz, 1926–7, II, 260), but the mineral wealth of Upper Silesia and the Waldenburg Hills was at first little appreciated, and so it played no part in the calculation of the statesmen in the great wars. After 1777, however, a new minister of mines, Friedrich Anton von Heinitz, exploited the reserves of coal on a large scale, and within six years the air was fouled with the exhalations of more than 5,000 coal-fired furnaces.

Frederick always regarded the administration of Silesia as something to be held under his personal control. The otherwise all-embracing General-Directorium was allowed no share in the running of this region, and Frederick instead appointed Count Ludwig Wilhelm von Münchow as the first of a series of Silesian ministers, directly answerable to himself – an arrangement which greatly facilitated the operations of the army in Silesia. Münchow reached a number of sensible compromises with the local interests, and Frederick's nominee as the Catholic bishop of Breslau, the dissipated Count Philipp Gotthard von Schaffgotsch, sought (with no great success) to establish good relations between the Prussian authorities and the native Catholics of Upper Silesia.

The policy of leniency did not apply to the border enclave of the County of Glatz, where the royal favourite Henri-Auguste de la Motte-Fouqué exercised virtual vice-regal powers from 1742 until 1760. As an embittered Huguenot, Fouqué treated the Catholics harshly, and he finally succeeded in producing a genuine religious martyr in the person of the priest Andreas Faulhaber, who went to the gallows on 30 December 1757 rather than break the seal of the confessional (Bach, 1885, passim).

The conquest of Silesia accentuated a Prusso-Austrian antagonism that was to endure for almost one and a half centuries. A commentator wrote in 1756:

Everybody knows that Silesia and the country of Glatz are of a quite different order of importance to the Queen of Hungary [i.e. Maria Theresa] than the Netherlands or Lombardy. The two former territories are some of the richest in Germany, and they are the keys to Bohemia, Moravia and Hungary. Their possession lends to the king of Prussia a credit and influence in the Empire that was denied to his predecessors. (Mauvillon, 1756, III, 142)

These wars brought an awareness of the things that set the two monarchies apart. As early as 1741 Frederick sought to inculcate a hatred of the Austrians among the Prussian troops. At the level of personal encounter in peacetime, the Austrian traveller in Prussian territories was distinguished by his religion, his accent, and his ample and rich clothing. Like Count Ernst Friedrich Giannini, he might detect a tincture of hostility mingled with the otherwise courteous treatment that was extended to him as a foreigner (Thadden, 1967, 194).

Language and style were indeed matters of some moment. The *Political Correspondence* is enlivened in one of its volumes by an attempt on the part of Frederick and his ministers in 1758 to forge a convincing 'Letter from a Secretary of Count Kaunitz to Count Cobenzl. It was not difficult to obtain bad paper and a battered old typeface, to convey the impression that the document was printed somewhere in Germany outside Prussia, but what defeated them for some time was Frederick's requirement to render the text 'in Austrian German', by which he understood not the tongue of the peasants, but something 'after the Viennese way of writing, in the usual high-flown, bombastic and complicated Austrian style, which loads down the name of the Empress and Kaunitz, every time they occur, with all the customary Viennese epithets' (*PC* 10363). Frederick's cabinet secretary Eichel gave up after three or four attempts, but somebody in the foreign office at last produced a credible version.

The Prussian officers despised the lack of comradely cohesion among their Austrian counterparts, as well as the stifling regard for rank and etiquette which prevailed among them in their off-duty hours. Frederick's officers, on the other hand, had the key to all society. A Prussian lieutenant once asked an Austrian how he, as a military man, would be received in Vienna. 'You will be greeted courteously enough', he was told, 'but you will have as little chance as an Austrian officer of being invited to the table of the great men' (Friedel, 1782, 42). The emphasis on these distinctions derived from the non-homogeneous nature of the Austrian corps, which embraced everyone from the sons of small tradesmen to the grandees of the houses of Liechtenstein and Esterhazy. Frederick described the army shut up in Prague in 1757 as 'that Austrian race of princes and rabble' (*PC* 8983).

Conversely the Austrians derided the apparently mindless obedience of the Prussian officers, and their conscientious wearing of the regulation uniforms, which smacked to them of servants' livery (Mansel, 1982, 110). Chancellor Kaunitz deplored the inhumanity of the Prussian system of forcible recruiting, and the theme was taken up by a publicist who claimed:

> The Prussian soldier is in every regard a wretched creature . . .
> The officer exercises an unlimited despotic power over him . . .
> In Berlin you have a certain General Lettow. I remember him as
> a colonel in Frankenstein when I saw him smash in six of the
> teeth of an old grenadier with his stick, simply because the man
> could not hold his head as straight as *Herr Obrist* demanded.
> (Anon. *Zehn Briefe*, 1784c, 60–2)

The quarrel was given coherence and personification by the natures of the rival sovereigns. By 1742 Frederick had come to appreciate that he was no longer struggling with the corpse of Emperor Charles VI but with the new leader of the House of Habsburg, the queen and archduchess Maria Theresa. She was of the same generation and spirit as Frederick, but she resembled him in no other particular. While Fritz conserved and expanded his domains as a base of power, Maria Theresa regarded her inheritance as a sacred and inalienable family trust. Where Frederick gave the appearance of being trenchant and cool, Maria Theresa was intuitive, almost 'biological', and concerned to soften the asperities of Enlightenment reform by ordinary human considerations. For the image of Frederick, the self-proclaimed 'first master of the state', Maria Theresa substituted a concept of herself as the head of an extended family, the 'mother of her dominions'.

Frederick knew that Prussia could not stay out of the war for very long. His ambitions were unfulfilled, his suspicions as lively as ever. Meanwhile the Austrian counter-offensive against his former allies was gathering further force. It cleared Bohemia, eliminated Bavaria from the strategic map, and ultimately threatened the borders of France.

Meanwhile the interlude of peace gave Frederick time to put his army in order. At Mollwitz and Chotusitz the infantry had rescued him from his own miscalculations, and more than compensated for the failings of the other arms. No great change was required here. The *Infantry Regulations* of 1 June 1743 therefore amounted to little more than a simplification of Frederick William's rules of 1726. With partial revisions in 1750 and 1757, the regulations of 1743 determined the routine of the infantry for the rest of the reign. For tactical guidance, Frederick directed the officers to the *ad hoc* emendations which he introduced, as the inspiration took him, over the following years.

The lessons of the recent campaigns were perhaps more directly reflected in the instructions which Frederick composed specifically for the cavalry. The cavalry commanders were encouraged to attack without waiting for orders, if they believed that they could do so with advantage, and indeed they were threatened with cashiering if they allowed the enemy to attack them first.

The early morning of Chotusitz had found the Prussians divided and unprepared, and under the necessity of fighting on ground of which they knew little. Frederick now told the hussars to venture out in large detachments of two and four thousand at a time, and act 'like a spider in a web, which is alive to every disturbance' (Hussar *Reglement*, 1 December 1743). The commanders' responsibilities did not end when they had seen the army properly settled into a new position: 'Afterwards the generals . . . must reconnoitre the terrain around the camp, and take due note of every small feature of the ground' (*Ordres für die sämmtlichen Generale*, 23 July 1744, *Oeuvres*, XXX, 121).

The lessons were brought home to the army during the spring reviews and autumn manoeuvres of 1743. In addition, officers were summoned from the provinces in order to attend the larger and more instructive of these assemblies, or to learn from the example of crack regiments like the Gens d'armes, the Zieten Hussars, or the super-large regiment of the Bayreuth Dragoons.

The manoeuvres of September 1743 were of especial importance in the learning process, for on two occasions Frederick staged minia-ture operations with combined forces of infantry and cavalry. Here was the foundation of the great autumn manoeuvres of the mass conscript armies of Continental powers in the nineteenth and early twentieth centuries.

No manoeuvres were staged in 1744, because the Prussians were again at war. In one perspective Frederick was acting in the spirit of the passage in the *Antimachiavel* in which he had written that a prince was justified in opening hostilities in order to forestall a threatened attack. The war between Maria Theresa and her enemies was certainly turning to the Habsburg's advantage, as we have seen, and she now enjoyed the support of a 'Pragmatic Army' of British, Dutch and German auxiliaries. As a needful measure of security Frederick concluded an alliance with the French on 5 June 1744.

Frederick reserved the right to go to war only when he saw fit, but he was very soon overtaken by events: at the end of June Prince Charles and the Austrian army crossed the Rhine above Germersheim, and threatened to invade Alsace. On 12 July Frederick sent Louis XV a firm promise to begin operations, and a month later the leading Prussian columns crossed the Saxon border on their way to Bohemia.

Frederick did not move only in the interests of maintaining the European equilibrium or his own safety. For Prussia this was also a period of real and potential expansion. In May 1744 the principality of Ostfriesland came to the House of Hohenzollern by way of legitimate inheritance, after the death of the last native ruler. Ostfriesland was isolated on the North Sea coast, and was of no strategic consequence whatsoever. The same could not be said of the districts of northern Bohemia which had slipped from Frederick's grasp in 1742. Four months before the new war broke out, Frederick was already marking on the map of Bohemia the territories which he desired for himself. These embraced the circle of Königgrätz, the trans-Elbe bridgeheads of Pardubitz and Kolin, and all the ground on the near side of the river as far as Saxony (PC 1390) – a rich and (as Frederick thought) eminently defensible little empire. (See Map 3, p. 342.)

Frederick's intention for the coming campaign was to make directly for the Bohemian capital, Prague, seize it, and then establish himself in western Bohemia before Prince Charles and the Austrian army could return from the Rhine. Bohemia was still almost completely undefended, and Frederick assembled provisions to sustain the army for only a matter of weeks, being sure that the campaign would have been convincingly won before that time was out.

Frederick assembled the forces for the Bohemian invasion in three main groups. The 40,000 troops of the royal army were to march from Berlin, barge through neutral Saxony, and strike up the left bank of the Elbe against Prague. Inside Bohemia Frederick was to join the Hereditary Prince Leopold of Anhalt-Dessau, who was coming with 15,000 men from the north-eastern provinces by way of Zittau and the Iser valley. Field-Marshal Schwerin brought 16,000 further troops from Silesia by way of Glatz.

The mobilisation was accomplished smoothly and secretly, and between 12 and 23 August 1744 Frederick and the leading elements of his army made the passage of unoffending Saxony. Zieten and his 1,300 hussars spearheaded the advance into Bohemia from the border hills, and then the slower-moving infantry of the three great Prussian columns assembled around Prague in the first week of September.

Prague was a large city, but weakly fortified, and more than three-quarters of the total garrison of 18,000 men were made up of unreliable militia and civic guards. The Prussian gunners proceeded to knock a wide breach in the ramparts of the Neustadt. The Austrian commandant surrendered unconditionally on 16 September.

Weighing up his conduct afterwards, Frederick was certain that he should now have consolidated himself at Prague by establishing a sizeable garrison there, and allowing time for his supplies of flour to be unloaded at the head of the Elbe navigation at Leitmeritz and transported overland to the army. Frederick believed that once he was firmly based he should have struck south-west to eliminate the sole remaining Austrian forces in Bohemia, namely the 18,000 men of Carl Batthyány, and prevent Prince Charles from re-entering Bohemia from western Germany.

None of these things was done. The French and Bavarians instead pressed Frederick to make for the wilds of far southern Bohemia and capture the castles and little walled towns which had figured so prominently in the campaigning of the French in 1742. This, they hoped, would open a way to the Danube valley from the north and threaten Prince Charles's communications with Austria. Frederick gave way, later admitting: 'It was quite wrong of me to have pushed my condescension so far' (*Oeuvres*, III, 76).

The Prussian army assembled just south-west of Prague. On 19 September Lieutenant-General Nassau marched off with a powerful advance guard, and proceeded to reduce Tabor (23 September), Budweis (30 September) and the castle of Frauenberg (1 October). Frederick and the main army left Prague on 21 September, and they climbed gradually into an almost Scandinavian landscape of steep hills and tall black pines. At last on the 27th they were rewarded with the sight of the walls of the old Hussite town of Tabor, crowning a rocky ridge above a fertile plain. In heavy rains the army skirted the Tabor Pond and the town, and encamped a short distance to the south-east. The advance was resumed on 1 October, and took the Prussians south-west to Moldautheyn, where they crossed the upper Moldau on a bridge of boats.

Frederick had a total of 62,000 troops under his command, and it was disconcerting for him to be so ill-informed as to where the enemy were. On 25 September he learnt that the Saxon army had thrown off its neutrality and was about to move in support of the Austrians, and on 2 October came reports that Prince Charles and the main Austrian army were already well into Bohemia. They were thought to be advancing on Budweis, but nothing was known for certain.

In his inexperience, Frederick assumed that, once an active campaign had begun, a battle would very shortly follow. On 4 October and again the next day he rode out to the little settlement of Zaborsch, passing through a silent countryside of broad meres, massive stands of conifers and vast empty fields. The hills of the Böhmer-Wald stood out ever more clearly along the horizon, confirming the isolation of this remote corner of Bohemia, but of the enemy main force there was nothing to be seen. In fact Prince Charles was twenty-five miles distant at Mirotitz. He had already united with Batthyány, which gave him a force of 50,000 troops, but he (or rather his adviser, old Field-Marshal Traun) wisely withheld the Austrians from more positive action until they had been joined by the Saxons.

Frederick had passed the culminating point of this year's campaigning. His line of communication was tenuous in the extreme, and on 9 October he began a slow retreat in the direction of Tabor and Prague, hoping all the time to seize the opportunity of bringing the Austrians to battle. The enemy did not allow themselves to be drawn, but gave notice, by gathering in fodder and planting a depot at Beneschau, that they might be interested in establishing themselves athwart Frederick's communications with Prague. On 17 October Nassau and Schwerin averted the immediate danger by pouncing on the Beneschau magazine. Frederick arrived on the scene the next day, and arrayed the army behind a chain of lakes between Konopischt and Bistritz. The weather was by now bitterly cold, and the soldiers gave themselves what shelter they could by building crude huts, or covering their tents with straw.

On the 22nd the balance of numbers turned to the advantage of the enemy, when Prince Charles was joined by the Saxon contingent, giving him a superiority of 10,000 troops over the Prussians. Charles and Traun saw that the time had come for a show of force, and on the night of 23 October they advanced to a position within six miles of Frederick's camp. On the 24th Frederick's army executed a short but tedious march as far as the heights between Sajetschi and Lang-Lhota, close enough to the enemy for their camp fires to be clearly made out on the cold and moonlit night that followed. Frederick was warming himself by a fire when his quartermaster, Carl C. von Schmettau, returned from a patrol to announce that the allied position was impregnable. Frederick rarely gave credit to unwelcome news, and on the 25th he rode out on reconnaissance with a party of grenadiers and hussars, while the whole army marched slowly up behind.

The allied position became known as the Camp of Marschowitz, and it was set in a central Bohemian scenery of round bosky hills and broad undulating fields, interspersed with rivulets, rows of ponds and little woods. The enemy camp formed a pronounced salient to the north, where the lines sloped back on both sides at steep angles, which rendered it impossible for Frederick to grasp the extent of the position from a single standpoint.

The long flank to the south-east came first within Frederick's view, and he could see that the enemy were lining the crest of an extensive ridge, from where the ground fell in an open and even slope to a damp hollow, presenting a natural killing-ground. Frederick knew from his principles of fortification that the salient of a defensive position normally offered the most vulnerable point to an attack, but at Point 525 at Marschowitz the Saxons had made an abatis (obstacle of felled trees), and the approaches were impeded by two outlying hills that were obviously inaccessible to the Prussian troops and guns.

The Prussian army trailed over to its right past the salient, and from the direction of Neweklau Frederick caught his first view of the allied left, extending away to the south-west. Here the access was obstructed by three large lakes. Frederick now had a comprehensive picture of the Marschowitz camp, and he was not tempted to make the assault. Food and fodder were already running short, and later on the 25th the Prussians began to fall back in the direction of Prague.

At the end of the nineteenth century the historians of the German General Staff roundly declared: 'The Frederick who struck at Prague, Leuthen and Torgau would not have shrunk from the assault' (Gr. Gstb., 1895, III, 254). To this it is legitimate to rejoin that if he had launched such an attack, he could well have encountered the same reception as at Kolin or Kunersdorf. Frederick's caution was amply justified when we consider the natural and artificial strength of the position, the numbers of the enemy, and the state of his own troops, who were cold, tired and hungry. The Marschowitz confrontation of 25 October was in fact an episode of some importance in the history of Frederick the commander, for it presented him for the first time with a tactical dilemma of the kind that was to dominate his conduct of operations in the final campaigns of the Seven Years War.

More immediately, in Bohemia in the late autumn of 1744, Frederick had by now everywhere surrendered the initiative to the enemy. His conduct of strategic affairs was decidedly 'sticky', compared with the uncompromising nature of his resolutions in the Seven Years War, and it had occurred to him too late that he ought to do something about evacuating the garrisons which he had left in southern Bohemia. By nightfall on 23 October the strongpoints of Budweis, Frauenberg and Tabor had all fallen to the Austrians, with a loss of nearly 3,000 men.

Frederick was extravagant in his criticism of his own misjudgments, when he wrote up his history of the campaign. He was, however, probably correct when he concluded that what finished the Prussians in Bohemia was the Fabian strategy of Prince Charles and Field-Marshal Traun, and the utter hostility of the environment. It was quite impossible for the Prussians to get their hands on the fodder and grain which ought to have been at their disposal in the better-cultivated stretches of the countryside. Frederick asked his readers to bear in mind that 'in Bohemia the great nobles, the clergy and the stewards are all devoted to the house of Austria, and that the common people, who are stupid and superstitious, were much embittered against us on account of the difference of religion' (*Oeuvres*, III, 60). The Austrian hussars and Croats skirmished right up to the perimeters of the Prussian camps, and the foragers could venture forth only in heavily escorted masses of several thousand troops at a time.

Saxony was now to be considered hostile territory, and Frederick could no longer return along the path by which he had entered Bohemia. If he moved quickly, however, he would still have open to him a good communication with Prussian territory by way of the low passes from north-east Bohemia to Glatz and Silesia. Frederick accordingly swung his army half-right towards the upper Elbe, and sent Lieutenant-General Nassau with the advance guard to occupy Neu-Kolin and Pardubitz. Marching through storms of rain the Prussians suffered heavy attrition all the way through desertion, typhus and dysentery. The seventh of November nearly brought a battle near Kuttenberg, but the allies shrank from the encounter, and Frederick was now intent only on gaining the far bank of the upper Elbe and affording his troops some rest. Finally the Prussians made their passage at Neu-Kolin on the 8th and 9th.

It was no coincidence that the line of the upper Elbe corresponded with the southern border of the part of Bohemia that Frederick intended to keep for Prussia at the peace. He assumed that all major operations were at an end, and he scattered his troops in quarters with the intention of staying in Bohemia through the winter. In all of this he reposed altogether too much trust in the passive barrier of the Elbe, which along this stretch presented a slow-moving body of shallowish water just ninety paces broad.

Early on 19 November the Austrians and Saxons crossed the Elbe in the neighbourhood of Teltschitz and nearly annihilated the grenadier battalion of Wedel, which was the only Prussian unit that was close enough to offer any opposition. Frederick at once recognised that his refuge north of the Elbe was untenable. On the 20th he sent the sick and the spare baggage ahead towards the border, and a number of *Feldjäger* made off at speed to Lieutenant-General Einsiedel at Prague, bearing separate but identical orders to evacuate the six battalions that were in garrison there.

Frederick called in his detachments, and, after giving his united army a short rest at Königgrätz, he made for the passes with Silesia and Glatz. The snow was being driven by a strong wind, burying the narrow roads that were already obstructed by broken-down waggons and the bodies of cart horses. On 27 November the Croats and hussars caught up with the struggling Prussians. The rearguard came under heavy attack at Pless, while the rearward elements of the main army were overtaken on the way to Trautenau, and about two hundred men were lost.

For the royal army the campaign came to an end on 8 December, when the border abatis at Braunau was completed, and the last of the troops withdrew into Silesia. The ordeal of the garrison of Prague was continuing. Einsiedel and his men had withdrawn from the city on 26 November, and they were now retreating on Upper Lusatia by way of the difficult paths through Gabel and Friedland.

The total Prussian losses in 1744 can be guessed only from a few details. The Austrians reckoned that nearly 17,000 men had come over to them as deserters. Other sources estimate that 36,000 troops returned to Silesia, and that about half of these died from dysentery (Mamlock, 1907, 12). When we make every allowance for exaggerations, the damage to the Prussian army was still very great. The survivors roamed about Silesia in disorder, the officers were demoralised, and the generals' trust in Frederick's leadership was temporarily broken. As for the king, 'he had lost something of his over-confidence. He was willing to listen, and his replies were gentler and less biting. These changes were obvious to everyone. He had just experienced his first misfortunes' (Valori, 1820, I, 204).

There is something impressive about the frankness with which Frederick owned that the campaign had been as much won by the Austrians as lost by his own mistakes. He paid handsome tribute to Traun in his *Histoire de mon Temps*, and many years later, when he met Austrian officers on social terms at Neisse and again at Mährisch-Neustadt, he eagerly sought out veterans who had served with that elderly gentleman in 1744. 'Did you know who taught me the little I know?' he asked the Prince de Ligne. 'It was your old marshal Traun. Now there's a man for you!' (Ligne, 1923, 158).

Frederick pondered deeply about the chastening but instructive experiences of 1744. In future he took full account of the peculiarly frustrating conditions of warfare in Bohemia. He had also learnt something about the concentration of forces, and discovered that it was more advisable to defend river lines from the front than from behind. He knew that the Prussian army must never again be exposed to conditions which eroded its formal discipline – once this constraining force was relaxed, there were scarcely any limits to the disintegration.

Frederick's search for the tactical decision proceeded unabated, despite the failure at Marschowitz, for his military reputation still hung upon the battleworthiness of his army, and more specifically the infantry. In the strategic dimension, his record was still one of almost unrelieved failure. His rapid progresses in December 1740, February 1742 and September 1744 looked impressive enough on the map, but they amounted to little more than promenades into an empty countryside. Once the main Austrian army arrived on the theatre of operations, Frederick was forced on every occasion to conform with the strategic initiatives of the enemy.

The destructive effects of the campaign of 1744 were felt through the winter and well into the following spring, and the task of restoring the shattered army was aggravated by a series of skirmishes along the borders of Glatz and Upper Silesia.

Frederick took energetic measures to draw recruits from the cantons and abroad, but the approach of the campaigning season of 1745 found him still short of 8,000 infantry and 700 cavalry. Money too was a matter of concern. This was a fallow period in the Prussian finances, since the resources inherited from Frederick William were at last exhausted, and Frederick still had to build up the reserves and the structures that were to support him so effectively through the Seven Years War. He was unable to raise a loan on the Dutch money market, and the *Stände* (the provincial assemblies of the nobility) were able to contribute little more than one-fifth of his needs.

Frederick employed promotions, cash grants, and judicious rebukes in an attempt to restore enthusiasm and a sense of purpose in the army. 'Is this the right moment to ask to resign?' he challenged Lieutenant-General Kalckstein. 'I had always assumed that you were devoted to the state, and it never crossed my mind that you could wish to remove yourself when things are going so badly with us' (Gr. Gstb., 1895, II, 124). All the time it was evident that confidence could be restored only through some success in the open field.

Frederick decided to stage this encounter inside Prussian territory since, for the first time in his career, he renounced the ambition of carrying the war to the enemy – he knew that his troops and his finances were not up to the ordeal. He therefore told the French that they must assume the active role in 1745, by establishing an army of 60,000 men in western Germany, and sending another 60,000 troops down the Danube against Vienna (*PC* 1738). On his own theatre, 'if the Austrians come at me, I shall let them cross the hills in peace, after which I shall march directly against them . . . Prince Charles will have no adviser [i.e. no Traun] at his side during this campaign, and there is a good chance that he will make some stupid mistakes' (*PC* 1781, 1796).

The clouded face of diplomatic affairs also indicated caution.

Frederick's allies appeared to be failing or falling away, and he still hoped that the British negotiators would be able to secure an acceptable peace on his behalf. Only by the early summer of 1745 did an accumulation of evidence make it clear that Austria and Prussia were not fighting for third parties, or for compensations or equivalents, but for the possession of Silesia and the very existence of the Prussian state. The nature of this new contest did not differ in kind from the Seven Years War.

First of all Maria Theresa had raised the stakes in a speech of 1 December 1744, absolving the Silesians from their allegiance to the House of Brandenburg. Then the Emperor Charles VII died on 20 January and his native Bavaria was shortly afterwards overrun by the Austrians. This put an end to the useful device by which Frederick had been able to hold himself at a certain distance from the war, by representing the Prussians not as full belligerents, but as auxiliaries intervening on behalf of the Emperor. Now he was a principal in the conflict.

Then in the second week of March 1745 came news of a hostile Quadruple Alliance of Britain, Holland, Saxony and Austria. For the last two powers 'it was no longer just a question of humiliating him by depriving him of Silesia. What they wanted was to reduce him to a nullity . . . This means nothing but his destruction, and [they] would sacrifice the liberties of mankind to compass it' (Valori, 1820, I, 211; Thomas Villiers, 3 September, PRO SP 88/66).

On 14 March Frederick had laid the foundation stone of the 'summerhouse at the top of the vineyard near Potsdam' – the future Sans Souci. He left for Silesia the next day, and after stopping for a time in Breslau and Neisse he established his headquarters on 29 April in the Cistercian monastery at Camenz, standing in the plain of the upper Neisse below Glatz. Frederick was tormented with impatience, waiting for the enemy to declare themselves, but the month of May was warm and sunny and Abbot Tobias Stusche provided agreeable *Tafelmusik* when the king sat down every day to dine under the great trees in the garden.

At Camenz Frederick received the first agreeable news for a very long time indeed. This concerned an action at Bratsch in Upper Silesia on 22 May, when Margrave Carl and 6,000 men beat off an attack by superior Austrian forces against a convoy. Frederick heaped praise upon the Württemberg Dragoons, and he later dated the revival of the whole of the Prussian cavalry from this episode. It taught him how men could surpass themselves when they were subjected to a judicious process of correction and encouragement, and when a few heroes gave them an example to follow.

During this period the allies were drawing their forces together inside Bohemia – namely a contingent of 19,000 Saxons, and Prince Charles with his 40,000 Austrians. On 26 May Frederick received from Colonel Winterfeldt the news that the enemy were at last on the march to invade Silesia. In his new camp at Frankenstein the king accordingly assembled 42,000 infantry, 14,500 cuirassiers and dragoons, 2,300 hussars and a train of fifty-four heavy pieces, making up a force of about 59,000 men. He had summoned up all the troops from the side theatres, for the campaign of 1744 had taught him 'that the man who tries to hang onto everything ends up by holding nothing. Your essential objective must be the hostile army' ('Principes Généraux', 1748, *Oeuvres*, XXVIII, 37–8).

Frederick's immediate concern was to tempt the allies down from the hills. He had a double spy, an Italian, in Charles's headquarters, who told the Austrians that Frederick was intent on falling back under the guns of Breslau. The mobile detachments of Winterfeldt and Du Moulin were ordered to spread the same report, and they lent colour to this story by retreating in the sight of the Austrians to Schweidnitz.

On 1 June Frederick arranged his army between Schweidnitz and Alt-Jauernick. On this day and the two following mornings he rode to the low swells of the Ritter-Berge, near Striegau, from where he had a view across an expanse of flat ground to the wooded folds of the Riesen-Gebirge foothills at Freyburg, Hohenfriedeberg and Kauder.

The first of the Austrian troops put in an appearance on 2 June, and in the evening Prince Charles and the Saxon commander, the Duke of Weissenfels, made their way to the gallows hill to the west of Hohenfriedeberg. They could see little of interest, since Frederick had hidden most of his troops behind the Nonnen-Busch or in hollows in the ground. The allies were therefore encouraged to venture into the plain the next day.

Early on 3 June Frederick made his usual ride to the Ritter-Berge, and he noticed that the enemy soldiers had already lit their cooking fires, from which he concluded that the allied army would soon be on the move. Frederick returned briefly to the Prussian camp, and he was back at his viewpoint in the afternoon. Towards 4 p.m. he

saw a cloud of dust which arose in the hills, and then advanced and descended towards the plain, snaking forward from Kauder to Fehebeutel and Rohnstock. The dust disappeared, and we now had a clear view of the Austrian army which was debouching from the hills in eight great columns . . . to the sound of drums, trumpets and all those military instruments which appeal so much to the Germans. This pleasing harmony,

together with the neighing of horses, made a concert of sound
that was calculated to inspire anybody to combat. Further
embellishment was provided by the glittering of the weapons,
the spectacle of the countless colours and standards floating in
the air, and the contrast between the grave, disciplined march
of the main forces, and the speed of the light troops as they
hastened in front. All of this was lit by a radiant sun, presenting
a sight at once enchanting and terrible. (*Oeuvres*, III, 111;
Mauvillon, 1756, 261)

In the evening the allies shook themselves into a loose line which
stretched for just over four miles between Kauder and Hohenfriedeberg. They were negligent and overconfident, and they made no
attempt to occupy any features of tactical importance.

Frederick departed at a gallop, and at about 6 p.m. he reached his
headquarters at Alt-Jauernick and made a few necessary arrangements. As a soldier-king he was under no obligation to summon a
council of war, and he could now enjoy a little rest in the darkness of
his tent. His friend Chasot entered at 8 p.m., and Frederick told him:
'Now at last I have got what I wanted. I have just seen the enemy
army leave the hills and spread out in the plain. Tomorrow will be an
important day for me' (Kröger, 1893, 34–5).

Frederick's intentions for the coming 'Battle of Hohenfriedeberg'
were to execute an overnight march to the north-west, make an
undisturbed crossing of the obstacle of the Striegauer-Wasser, and
finally roll up the enemy flank from the east.

The Prussian army set off at 9 p.m. on 3 June. The roads were
reserved for the artillery, and 'the soldiers had to march on either
side, up to their knees in water for most of the time. But nobody left
his rank' (Valori, 1820, I, 228). The men knew what was at stake, and
they religiously observed the orders which forbade smoking and all
unnecessary noise. The army stopped short of the Striegauer-Wasser
in the early morning, and the troops rested under arms for a couple of
hours. Frederick was among them, wrapped in his cloak against the
chill of fresh and starlit night.

At 2.30 a.m. on 4 June Frederick assembled the generals and
issued his verbal orders. The columns were to pass the Striegauer-
Wasser in the region of Striegau, Gräben and Teichau and make
northwards in the general direction of Pilgramshain until they had
covered enough ground to be able to form a line of battle. The
Prussians were then to advance to the west, with the right leading in a
staggered echelon of brigades.

Hohenfriedeberg was to be the most episodic and compartmen-
talised of all Frederick's battles, and within the limits of the present

study it is scarcely possible to do more than describe the character of the succeeding events.

The first confusions derived from the fact that the allies had extended themselves much further to the east on the far side of the Striegauer-Wasser than Frederick had suspected. Only the main body of the Austrians had lit camp fires during the night, and, unknown to Frederick, the Saxons and bodies of Austrian cavalry and grenadiers were roaming around in the darkness directly to his front. The leading Prussian elements, instead of enjoying a clear run towards Pilgram-shain, therefore found themselves engaged in a private battle which ultimately absorbed all of the cavalry of Frederick's right wing.

Lieutenant-General Du Moulin led the way across the Striegauer-Wasser with an advance guard of six battalions of grena-diers and twenty-eight squadrons of hussars. Du Moulin set out well ahead of the main body, and he was under orders to seize the isolated hills beyond Striegau. These features were already occupied by a mixed detachment of four companies of Saxon and Austrian grena-diers. Just after 2 a.m. 'a Prussian hussar came up to this force and enquired: "Are you Austrians or Prussians?" On hearing that they were Austrians he removed his cap, and duly announced "and I am a Prussian hussar!" and he rode down from the hill' (Carl Egidius Grosse, in Hoffmann, 1903, 32–3).

Du Moulin's report of the enemy presence reached Frederick at about 4 a.m., when the columns of the main army had been on the march for half an hour and the sun was about to break over the horizon. Frederick sent a battery of six 24-pounders in support of the advance guard, and he hastened the march of his leading cavalry and infantry across the Striegauer-Wasser. There was no question of forming in a proper order of battle, and the second line actually found itself taking the lead.

Between four and five the Duke of Weissenfels succeeded in deploying the Saxon horse and the cavalry of the Austrian left wing to the south-east of Pilgramshain, and the battle proper opened against Du Moulin's hussars and the cavalry of the Prussian right. In his address to the generals Frederick had mentioned that the cavalry was to give no quarter in the heat of the action, and a murderous excitement spread among the troopers.

The Prussian cavalry enjoyed the advantage of numbers, the slope of the ground, and the support of the two batteries of artillery, but Count von Rothenburg, who commanded the twenty-six cuiras-sier squadrons making up the first line, was soon in need of support from the dragoons and hussars to his rear. The Prussians broke ranks in their eagerness to get at the enemy, and within a few minutes dragoons, hussars, cuirassiers and enemy mounted grenadiers were engaged in a disorderly hand-to-hand combat, swirling about like a swarm of bees. Two battalions of Saxon foot grenadiers were caught up in the battle, and more than one of the Prussian officers was appalled to see how these fine-looking men were being cut down without mercy. The Saxon general Schlichting was very lucky indeed to fall unscathed into the hands of the Prussians.

While the cavalry battle roared off to the north, the Prussian infantry had begun to cross the Striegauer-Wasser by the bridges at and near Gräben. The Hereditary Prince Leopold of Anhalt-Dessau arrayed the first nine battalions at his disposal in an improvised line of battle, and he advanced against the gathering Saxon infantry without more ado. Further battalions hastened up to prolong the line to right and left, and ultimately a force of twenty-one battalions moved with shouldered muskets, flying colours and beating drums against the enemy, who were standing firm in a broken country of ditches, bogs and bushes. The Prussians braved the Saxon canister fire which opened up at four hundred paces, and pushed well into the zone of effective musketry before delivering their own fire in the faces of the enemy: 'This began a slaughter which within a few hours covered the field with blood and corpses' (quoted in Hoffmann, 1912, 28).

The eviction of the Saxons was complete by about 7 a.m. Frederick had been directing the arrival of his army on the battlefield, and upon hearing the news of the triumph over the Saxons he cried out: 'The battle is won!' It was true that the course of events by no means corresponded with his original plan, but the Austrians were only now setting themselves in motion – far too late to be able to help the Saxons – and Frederick was well on his way to defeating the allies in detail.

Now that the Saxons were out of the reckoning, Frederick's concern was to build up sufficient forces to face the Austrians. He halted the march of reinforcements to the north, and wheeled all the available battalions to the left. Owing to a muddle in orders, young Prince Ferdinand of Brunswick and the five regiments of his brigade were left unsupported in open ground one thousand paces to the east of Günthersdorf village. Prince Charles did not respond to this opportunity of turning the flank of the as yet unformed Prussian left: 'Indeed the fate of states and the reputation of generals sometimes rest on the most trifling incidents. A few seconds are enough to determine their fortune' (Oeuvres, III, 117). Frederick was ultimately able to confront the Austrians with a force of about 10,400 infantry, comprising thirteen battalions of musketeers, and Infantry-General Polentz's command of five battalions of grenadiers.

The corresponding left wing of Prussian cavalry was, however, still dangerously placed, for its inferiority in numbers to the Austrian horse (6,000 against 7,000) was compounded by the difficulties which the Prussians experienced in crossing the Striegauer-Wasser. Major-General Kyau with ten squadrons of cuirassiers crossed by the bridge at Teichau, and they advanced over-confidently across the plain between Thomaswaldau and Halbendorf, unaware that the rickety structure had collapsed behind them and that they were stranded. The Austrian cavalry bore down, and the isolated Prussian squadrons would probably have succumbed if Major-General Zieten had not discovered a ford between Teichau and Gräben and got across the stream with the Zieten Hussars (H 2; see Map 4, p. 343) and the Alt-Württemberg Dragoons (D 12). Zieten promptly fell on the Austrian second line before it could intervene against Kyau.

Lieutenant-General Nassau fed twenty-five further squadrons into the battle across Zieten's ford, and the left wing of the Austrian cavalry came under effective musketry fire from the village of Thomaswaldau, which had meanwhile been seized by Poleutz's grenadiers. At about eight o'clock the Austrians gave way in disorder. Many of the troopers became stuck in the marshy ground, and Prince Charles himself was nearly taken prisoner.

Now that the Saxons and the Austrian cavalry had been eliminated, the battle was prolonged only by the 19,500 men of the Austrian infantry, falling back east over the open fields on either side of Günthersdorf. In places they contested the ground bitterly, 'giving rise to a terrible fire. It did not last nearly as long as at Mollwitz, but it was much noisier. The two sides often exchanged fire simultaneously (though our men got off more rounds than the enemy, thanks to their speed in loading), and all the time the rival artillery maintained its bombardment, making a frightful, almost indescribable din' (officer of the regiment of Margrave Carl, quoted in Hoffmann, 1903, 21–2).

Frederick's whereabouts at this time are difficult to trace with certainty, though Saxon prisoners caught sight of him behind the lines of battle, dressed in an old overcoat and hat, issuing orders from time to time, and making constant use of his telescope.

Neither the king nor any other of the senior officers noticed that the ten-squadron-strong elite regiment of the Bayreuth Dragoons (D 5) had so far been without useful employment. First light had found the regiment on guard near the Nonnen-Busch, lest the enemy light troops should emerge from the trees and harass the Prussian flank. From there the dragoons marched in the tracks of the infantry, crossed the Striegauer-Wasser at Teichau, and finally arrived south of Günthersdorf with the infantry of the second line. First Lieutenant Chasot (Frederick's old companion) commanded the three right-hand squadrons, and he halted the march of the regiment immediately behind a dangerous-looking gap which yawned in the first line of infantry, between the regiment of Bevern (7) and the brigade of Prince Ferdinand of Brunswick. Prince Ferdinand made Chasot very welcome, and drew his attention to a line of Austrian grenadiers who were drawn up three or four hundred paces to the front, screening the main force of the enemy infantry.

Victory is a child of many fathers, as von Moltke has remarked, and the initiative behind the ensuing charge of the Bayreuth Dragoons, the most celebrated episode of the Silesian Wars, has been variously attributed to Chasot himself, to Lieutenant-General Gessler, and to the immediate regimental commander, who was the hard-drinking and amiable Colonel Otto Martin von Schwerin.

All we know for certain is that the dragoons filtered through the gaps and intervals in the Prussian infantry, and that some time about 8.15 a.m. they opened their attack along a frontage of some six hundred paces. Chasot records:

> I immediately set the squadrons of the right wing in motion, and at first we progressed at a walk. We crossed several ditches one rank at a time, and on each occasion I made the leading rank halt on the far side so as to give the rearward two ranks time to catch up. Then we broke into a trot and finally into a full gallop, putting our heads down and running into the Austrian grenadiers. They at first stood bravely and delivered a volley at twenty paces, after which they were overthrown and mostly cut down. (Kröger, 1893, 38)

Behind the grenadiers the Bayreuth Dragoons collided with the main force of the Austrian infantry, and when the smoke lifted the troopers were seen to be hewing into a mass of fleeing Austrians. In twenty minutes the regiment took five cannon, sixty-seven colours and 2,500 prisoners, losing just ninety-four men in the process.

Only three regiments of Austrian infantry remained intact to cover the retreat:

> The Prussians continued to advance, but as slowly and in such good order as if they had been at a review. They halted about two thousand paces behind the battlefield, and not a single man bent down to plunder the dead and wounded on the way. This was quite admirable, but it was no more than was expected of Prussian troops. (Valori, 1820, I, 234)

The battle finished at 9. a.m. precisely.

In his joy Frederick wrote to the Old Dessauer: 'This is the best thing i have ever seen. The army has surpassed itself' (PC 1869). If the military education of the king and his troops was still incomplete, they had shown for the first time an impressive proficiency in nearly all of the branches of the art of war. The preliminaries of the battle had been a personal triumph for Frederick, since the concentration of force, the successfully sprung trap, and the overnight march amounted to the first strategic advantage he had ever gained over the cunning Austrians. Frederick maintained the momentum of the advance beyond the Striegauer-Wasser, even after the locations of the enemy turned out to be much more widely spread than he had expected. He was therefore able to attack the allies 'in such a position that they could only fight battalion by battalion, being never able to engage at the same time with their whole army' (Villiers, 7 June, PRO SP 88/65). In the further battle, all of the arms of the service lived up to the ideal of *immer vorwärts* – the two batteries of artillery which gave support to Du Moulin's advance guard, the infantry brigade commanders who responded to the challenge of the fluid combat, and the cavalry which twice got the better of the Austrian horse in open battle.

Concerning the hammer-blow which finished the action, Frederick exclaimed: 'These men of the Bayreuth regiment are veritable Caesars. You can imagine what monuments would have been raised to their honour in Ancient Rome!' (Koser, 1921, I, 500). Interestingly enough, their intervention in no way corresponded to the role assigned to the dragoons in the cavalry *Disposition* of July 1744, which was to form the second line of the cavalry and fall on the flanks of the enemy infantry only after it had been beaten. The very size of the Bayreuth regiment (the equivalent of a small brigade) made it something of an oddity among the regular horse. At Hohenfriedeberg it escaped being incorporated in the cavalry order of battle, and so it remained uncommitted until it launched its independent attack head-on against the shaken but still intact regiments of Austrian infantry. This mode of action corresponded much more closely to that of the Napoleonic cavalry reserve than to anything known in the middle of the eighteenth century, and it is disappointing to find that Frederick was not inspired to look any further into the matter, except perhaps in one of the battle schemes in the *Principes Généraux* of 1748 (*Oeuvres*, XXVIII, 79).

After the battle Frederick established his headquarters in the tall and rather grim palace of Rohnstock, which was to become a favourite resort whenever he was campaigning in this part of the world. On the morning of 5 June the kettle-drummers of the Bayreuth Dragoons came hammering into the interior, followed by two bodies of troopers who bore fifty captured colours and standards, which were dipped by the successive ranks as they passed under the archway.

Frederick then had the trophies set up in his room while all the kettle-drummers continued to thunder away.

The Prussians gained some idea of the magnitude of their victory after all the prizes and wounded had been gathered up, the dead buried, and the armies of prisoners counted. In most of Frederick's battles the Prussians usually lost more men than the enemy, regardless of which side had won, but at Hohenfriedeberg the terrible lists represented a balance in their favour of nearly three to one. The total allied losses amounted to about 13,800 men, of whom 3,120 had been killed, and the Prussians had bought their victory with 4,751 casualties, including 905 dead (Keibel, 1899, 438).

We do not know whether all of this won any merit in the next world; Hohenfriedeberg certainly earned the Prussians few friends in the present one. The Austrians were determined to renew the fight at a favourable opportunity, for 'it is characteristic of the court of Vienna that it is puffed up by the slightest success, yet never deflated by misfortunes' (Valori, 1820, I, 211). The Saxons bore their grudge into the next war, when their cry *'Dies ist für Striegau!'* recalled not only the massacre at Hohenfriedeberg, but the ordeal of their survivors in the following weeks, when they were starved and beaten until they donned the uniforms of the Prussians. Trooper Nicolaus Stephan of the regiment of Maffei was one of those who managed to escape. A Saxon clerk duly entered the report: 'The said carabinier is willing to do further duty. He declares he would more willingly serve the King of Poland for twenty years than the King of Prussia for one' (Hoffmann, 1903, 45).

Shortly after the battle the Austrians and Saxons fell back into Bohemia unmolested. No single convincing reason has ever been put forward to explain why Frederick did not launch an effective pursuit. At various times he spoke or wrote about his inexperience in managing that kind of operation, or the difficulty of replenishing the army in bread and ammunition with a transport train that had still not recovered from the ravages of 1744. 'The battle of Hohenfriedeberg had saved Silesia. The enemy were beaten, but not destroyed. It was not within the power of this victory to flatten the Bohemian hills, over which we had to carry the provisions for the army' (*Oeuvres*, III, 120). More relevant, perhaps, is the possibility that Frederick failed to appreciate the resilience of the Austrians, and the changes which had taken place in the character of warfare since 1742, when the single battle of Chotusitz had been enough to bring the enemy to terms.

In the weeks after Hohenfriedeberg Frederick confined himself very narrowly to one military objective: 'My intention in this campaign was to live at the expense of the enemy, eating up and exhausting completely all the supplies and fodder in the area of Bohemia adjacent to our borders. We would then retire towards the frontier, consuming as we went, and proceeding by short marches as a measure of precaution' (PC 2004). The region in question was the part of north-east Bohemia extending from the passes with Silesia and Glatz down to the neighbourhood of Königgrätz. The mere consumption of fodder and grain might appear to be a strange concern, but a countryside that was eaten out in this way would embarrass the enemy for the movement of his transport and cavalry, and constitute a direct equivalent to a successful strike against the fuel supplies of a modern army.

In accordance with this overall scheme of operations, the Prussian army executed a very slow clockwise movement inside Bohemia for the three months between the middle of July and the middle of September 1745.

The first unresisted advance brought Frederick through the rolling and lightly wooded country east of the upper Elbe to within sight of the Austrian and Saxon positions, which extended behind the Adler to the sizeable but unfortified town of Königgrätz.

Once the Prussian horses had munched their way through all the grass and grain north of the Adler, Frederick moved his army to the west, and on 20 July he crossed the upper Elbe on four bridges. On the far bank he first of all ensconced himself on the low plateau of Chlum (the scene of the Austrian defeat in 1866), then on 24 August he retreated a short distance upstream to an extensive camp bordering the river from Semonitz to Jaromiersch. All the time Prince Charles kept ponderous pace with the Prussians. Frederick tells us: 'I had my tent on a hill, and every day I could see the enemy generals coming to reconnoitre my position. They observed the Prussians through enormous telescopes, and then deliberated together – you might have taken them for astronomers' (Oeuvres, III, 131).

The Prussians' position was gradually becoming untenable, however. The communications with Silesia could be safeguarded only by strong detachments, and the enemy Croats and hussars put the Prussian camp under virtual siege. One night a group of sixty such 'partisans' penetrated a suburb of Jaromiersch and raided the house of the Marquis de Valori, the French envoy. They mistook his secretary for the great man himself, and Valori remained in his room undetected:

> Frederick laughed at this little adventure, but it was really disgraceful to have allowed an enemy detachment to reach the centre of his army. Generalising about the Prussian service, we can say that no other army is quite as badly guarded. They are

so afraid of their men deserting that they dare not place their
pickets any distance into the country. There is not a post which
is more than one hundred paces out from the army, and they
make no attempt to send out patrols between one outpost and
the next. (Valori, 1820, I, 244–5)

At five o'clock on the foggy morning of 18 September the army
re-crossed to the left bank of the Elbe at Jaromiersch and resumed its
northward march. Two days later the Prussians climbed a tree-
covered slope, and emerged onto an undulating plateau. The
Königreich-Wald had fallen away to their left, and its birches and
mighty conifers presented an agreeable border to the open fields of red
earth. In front, the ground rose slightly before it dipped away to the
wide valley of Trautenau, and ahead of that again rose the blue wall
of the border hills. Here was a good site for the last of Frederick's
foraging camps, before the Prussians made the final bound to Silesia.

The foragers and convoy escorts from this 'Camp of Staudenz'
faced their endless battle with the Croats and hussars, but Frederick
began for the first time to look forward to his return to Potsdam,
where the garden-palace of Sans Souci was a-building. He wrote on 24
September to his valet Michael Gabriel Fredersdorf:

I want the fire screen to be sent to Potsdam, together with the
table, the two statues, and the four portraits by Watteau which
Count Rothenburg has sent from Paris. These are to be stored in
my chambers until I arrive. I labour under many burdens and
sorrows at the moment, but I shall be glad to see Knobelsdorff
again. (Frederick, 1926, 51; Knobelsdorff was the architect of
Sans Souci)

The Austrians had other plans for Frederick. On the same day
Prince Charles examined the Prussian camp from a hilltop, and he
saw the potential for a surprise attack. Not only did the Königreich-
Wald provide an impenetrable cover for a left-flanking approach
march around to the west of the camp, but a short push from the trees
would be enough to carry the allies to the summit of the Graner-
Koppe, a broad, smooth mound which dominated the open country to
the east and south. Through a terrible oversight on Frederick's part,
the right flank of the camp of Staudenz terminated in a damp hollow
one thousand paces short of the hill.

In the course of 29 September and the early hours of the ensuing
night the Austrians and Saxons made the difficult passage of the
Königreich-Wald, and began to emerge on the open ground along a
wide front. The main allied forces were arrayed south of the Graner-
Koppe, but the mound itself was jammed with a concentration of ten

battalions of musketeers, fifteen companies of grenadiers, thirty squadrons of cuirassiers and dragoons, fifteen companies of elite carabiniers and mounted grenadiers, and sixteen heavy guns pointing east towards the Prussian camp. Only a dense mist, and some rearrangements along the six thousand paces of the line of battle, prevented the allies from attacking at daybreak on 30 September.

Meanwhile the Prussians were enveloped in the mental fog generated by their indifference to their surroundings, and by Frederick's failure to grasp the Austrians' determination. His thoughts at this time extended no further than arranging a leisurely start to the march to Trautenau for ten in the morning. The many detachments had reduced his army to 22,000 men, which was scarcely half the number of the enemy, and in the *General-Principia* of 1753 he would warn his senior officers against making the same kind of mistake.

At 5 a.m. on 30 September 1745 Frederick was talking with his generals in his tent when the first report reached him that enemy forces had been seen to his right. The single drummer of the headquarters guard beat out the *Generalmarsch* in a thin rattle, and Frederick and Hereditary Prince Leopold of Anhalt-Dessau galloped to the outposts to confirm the danger for themselves. Meanwhile the Marquis de Valori admired the facility with which the Prussian battalions and squadrons were ranging themselves in order without any kind of higher direction.

The hastily formed Prussian units marched out of the camp by their right. Since the position formed a rough east-west perpendicular to the enemy, Frederick made the columns execute right turns south-east of the village of Burkersdorf, then pushed them north until the heads arrived at the foot of the Graner-Koppe, permitting him to form a line of battle parallel to the allies. Frederick's intention was to hold back the centre and left as a reserve, and concentrate on his right or northern flank in the region of the Graner-Koppe (Stille, 1764, 181). He hoped thereby to eliminate the very great danger to his communications, which ran through Trautenau to Silesia. This preliminary manoeuvre was almost accomplished when the mist dissolved at about 8 a.m., giving way to a warm and sunny autumn day.

The battle of Soor opened with an Austrian cannonade against the horse of the Prussian right, moving beneath the Graner-Koppe:

Our cavalry withstood this ordeal with a composure that was all the more admirable when you consider that the enemy bombs frequently landed in the middle of the squadrons, carrying away eight or ten horses at once. After every explosion the troopers collected themselves, filled the gaps, and continued the march with sword in hand. (Henckel von Donnersmarck, 1858, I, part 1, 127–8)

Frederick directed the cavalry around to the north side of the mound, where they were to clear away the enemy squadrons and thereby open the way for the direct infantry assault. The Gens d'armes (C 10; see Map 5, p. 344) and the Buddenbrock Cuirassiers (C 1) formed the first line of attack, and three further regiments and the squadron of Garde du Corps moved up in support.

The wheel around to the right of the Graner-Koppe took the Prussian cavalry out of the arc of fire of the allied guns, but it swept the squadrons into a steep little valley which, almost certainly unknown to Frederick, guarded the access to the mound from the north. Only a tight discipline could have prevented the Prussians from piling together in disorder at the bottom, and only powerful and well-fed mounts could have carried them up the further slope. Horsemen ever since have wondered how the thing was done.

The forty-five squadrons of the allied left failed to seize their opportunity, and they met the Prussians at a stand with carbine and pistol fire. In the confused fighting which followed, the twenty-six Prussian squadrons maintained enough momentum to push most of the enemy horse back into the woods, but the Austrian infantry, now that their front was unmasked, were at last able to open fire, and the attack broke up into a multitude of smaller combats.

By this time the Graner-Koppe was coming under frontal assault from the right wing of the Prussian infantry. The first line was made up of some of the best troops the army had to offer, comprising three battalions of grenadiers, and three more of the large regiment of Anhalt (3) – a body which had been formed under the eye of the Old Dessauer. These troops were set the task of marching across six hundred paces of open ground to the muzzles of the Austrian guns – 'never have we undergone a more terrible cannonade' (PC 2002). The casualties among all ranks were dreadful. The young Prince Albrecht of Brunswick, brother of the queen, was struck dead in front of the grenadiers, and the battalion of Wedel (15/18), already badly hit in 1744, now lost three-quarters of its effectives. The advance was finally turned back 150 paces short of its objective by five companies of Austrian grenadiers, who surged from the Graner-Koppe crying 'Es lebe Maria Theresa!'

Frederick now committed the five battalions of his second line, and the issue of the day hung upon the Geist Grenadiers (13/37) and two regiments of musketeers – the Blanckensee regiment (23) from Berlin, and the Pomeranians of La Motte (17). These last people came from around Cöslin, and Frederick regarded them as Low Germans of the crudest sort. 'You are pigs', he used to say, 'and when I come into your camp it stinks to high heaven. You must spend your whole time eating and shitting' (Anon., 1788–9, II, 23–4).

The wreckage of the first line filtered through the intervals of the second and began to rally in the rear, which once more gave Frederick a force of eleven battalions. The fire of the Austrian guns was now masked by their own grenadiers, and this time the Prussian attack was carried all the way up the Graner-Koppe. The mass of intermingled bluecoats and Austrian grenadiers swept over the summit, leaving the deadly battery in Prussian hands.

While the issue was still in doubt on the Graner-Koppe, the Prussian centre and left, which were supposed to stay back in reserve, instead pressed forward on a broad front. Possibly they mistook the lead given by the second battalion of the Kalckstein regiment (25), which had been sent to clear the village of Burkersdorff. This spontaneous attack was in danger of sticking fast in front of a powerful Austrian battery, south-south-west of the village, until Prince Ferdinand of Brunswick sprang from his horse and led the second battalion of the Garde (15) in a bayonet attack which broke open the centre. The cavalry of the Austrian right made no attempt to intervene, which permitted the Bornstedt and Rochow Cuirassiers (C 9, C 8) to snatch up 850 of the Austrian infantry as prisoners.

Soon after midday the enemy disappeared into the woody depths from which they had emerged, and Frederick strove to organise a pursuit:

> My cavalry came to a halt not far short of the enemy rearguard. I hastened up and shouted: 'Marsch, vorwärts, drauf!' I was greeted with 'Vivat Victoria!' and a prolonged chorus of cries. Again I called out 'Marsch!' – and again nobody wanted to move. I lost my temper, I struck out with my stick and fist, and I swore (and I think I know how to swear when I am angry), but I could do nothing to bring my cavalrymen one step forward. They were drunk with joy and did not hear me. (Gr. Gstb., 1895, III, 84)

If the battle of Soor is so much shorter in the telling than Hohenfriedeberg, it is because the action was so much simpler – essentially one fulminating counter-attack – and not because it was any less hard fought, or because less had been at stake. Altogether 7,444 of the allies had been killed, wounded or taken prisoner. The Prussian losses reached 3,911, of whom 856 had been killed, which fell short of the butcher's bill at Hohenfriedeberg in absolute terms, but was much higher in proportion to the numbers engaged.

Frederick was certain that 'out of the four battles in which I have been engaged, this was the most bitterly contested' (*PC* 2002). In the *Principes Généraux* of 1748 he classed Soor as one of the actions which arrived unbidden, for it had compelled him to do battle to protect his communications with Trautenau. 'I have never been in such a fix as at Soor', he wrote to Fredersdorf, 'I was in the soup up to my ears' (Frederick, 1926, 58); or, as he put it more elegantly to Valori, at Hohenfriedeberg he had been fighting for Silesia, and at Soor for his life.

Frederick admired the strategic surprise which had been accomplished by the Austrians, and he believed that he owed his victory not to any superior combinations of his generalship, but to 'the most brave, the most valiant army that has ever existed' (*PC* 2206). Frederick's confidence in his troops was never to stand higher. He maintained that they were fully capable of storming batteries from the front, if it could be managed in the same way as the second assault on the Graner-Koppe ('Principes Généraux', 1748, *Oeuvres*, XXVIII, 75), and in general terms he used the experience of the battle of Soor to justify his claim that offensive action suited the genius of the Prussians, and that they owned an inherent advantage even when they faced superior numbers of the enemy (*PC* 2068, 8770).

Frederick's personal affairs had been thrown into disorder by a minor episode of the battle, when General Nádisti and a corps of Austrian hussars had discovered the convoy containing the royal baggage. The Austrians made off with his tents, horses, money chests, table silver, clothes and flutes, leaving him with just the shirt on his back, and without so much as a spoon he could call his own. He asked Fredersdorf to send him a service of light silver, and 'Quantz is to make me some new flutes of a highly extraordinary kind – one with a powerful sound, and the other which must be easy to blow and have soft high notes. He is to keep them for me until I return' (Frederick, 1926, 56). He feared, however, that nothing would be able to take the place of his beloved whippet Biche, who was thought to have been hacked to pieces by the hussars.

The army remained for five days in a camp to the south-west of the battlefield, 'for the sake of honour', and resumed its leisurely retreat on 6 October. The Prussians crossed the Silesian border on the 19th, and at the end of the month Frederick departed for Berlin. He believed that the war was effectively over.

Frederick enjoyed his peace for little over a week before he learnt from a Swedish diplomat that the Austrians and Saxons were making ready to surprise him in a winter campaign. Unlike the invasion of June, which had debouched into Silesia, Prince Charles's army of 20,000 Austrians and Saxons was going to advance from the Saxon territory of Upper Lusatia, which was more than fifty miles further to the west and offered a more direct route to the Brandenburg heartland.

Frederick decided to make a two-pronged counter-attack. The western jaws of the pincers were constituted by an *Elbe-Armee* of 25,000 men, which the Old Dessauer had been gathering over a period of two months, and which was poised to invade northern and central Saxony from Halle. Frederick set off for Silesia on 16 November to reassemble the victorious troops of Soor for the other offensive, which was to cut into Lusatia from the east, before the enemy could assemble to give battle.

Frederick held the royal army short of the Silesian-Saxon border for a few days, until it was clear that the Saxons had admitted Austrian troops to their territory, and thereby become full belligerents. On 23 November the four columns of the army crossed the Queiss into Lusatia by the bridges and fords at Naumburg, and in the fine afternoon of the same day Zieten's hussars caught a force of Saxons in their quarters at Katholisch-Hennersdorf. Frederick sent a body of cavalry in support, and by the evening the Prussians had more than nine hundred prisoners in their hands. The fast-moving detachments seized the important allied magazine at Görlitz on 25 November, almost under the eyes of Prince Charles, and two days later, when the Austrians were turning back towards Bohemia, their rearguard was pushed in disorder through Zittau.

This five-day pre-emptive campaign in Lusatia had, at negligible cost, eliminated an immediate threat to Brandenburg, and deprived the enemy of 5,000 men and precious provisions and transport. The Marquis de Valori suspected that Frederick's achievement was still greater than at Hohenfriedeberg or Soor:

> It is true that the enemy forced him into moving, but what he did was no less admirable. He acted with a boldness that surpasses belief, making use of an army that was exhausted and reduced by a good one-third of its effectives. And all of this in a season of harsh weather. (Valori, 1820, I, 260)

Frederick remained for a few days in Görlitz, hoping in vain that the Saxons would come to terms. At the same time he detached Lieutenant-General Lehwaldt with 8,500 troops in order to threaten Dresden from the east and establish communications with the Old Dessauer.

There seemed to be no end to Frederick's capacity for being surprised by the resilience of the Austrians. On 5 December he learnt that Prince Charles had ducked behind the hills, and was moving down the Bohemian Elbe in support of the Saxons. A detachment of

6,000 Austrians under Grünne had in fact already accomplished a union near Dresden. It would be some time yet before Frederick's army could arrive on the scene, and meanwhile the Old Dessauer and his *Elbe-Armee* seemed to be moving with intolerable slowness from northern Saxony.

At last, on 13 December, Frederick learnt that the Old Dessauer had just reached Meissen, and had drawn Lehwaldt to him on the west bank of the Elbe. From there the combined force marched south to do battle with the Saxons and Grünne near Dresden.

On the 15th the royal army made the passage at Meissen. Early in the afternoon it was reported to Frederick that 'the whole sky seemed to be in flames in the direction of Dresden' (Berenhorst, 1845–7, I, 128). At five in the evening an officer brought news of the great victory of Kesselsdorf, in which the Old Dessauer had overcome the 25,000 Saxons and the 6,000 Austrians in a bloody frontal assault.

On the morning of 17 December the king met the Old Dessauer at the Lerchenbusch outside Dresden. Frederick dismounted, took off his hat, and embraced the veteran as a sign of reconciliation.

The Saxons and Austrians were at last willing to accept the verdict of battle, and in the agreeable days before the arrival of the Austrian plenipotentiary Frederick bought cartloads of porcelain for the palace of Charlottenburg, and attended the opera *Arminio* by Hasse, who was one of his favourite composers. On Christmas Day the Peace of Dresden put an end to the war. Maria Theresa recognised Frederick in his sovereignty over Silesia and Glatz, and gained in return only Frederick's agreement to the election of her consort Francis Stephen as Emperor of Germany.

Frederick truly believed that the peace would be a durable one, but he reflected with satisfaction on what his army had achieved during the campaigns of 1745. The cavalry had made a powerful contribution to the recent victory at Kesselsdorf, as well as at Hohenfriedeberg and Soor, and the historians of the German General Staff concluded at the end of the nineteenth century: 'King Frederick never commanded a better infantry than in the Second Silesian War. These troops were equalled only by the men of the first campaigns [1756–7] of the Seven Years War' (Gr. Gstb., 1895, III, 253).

Frederick returned to Berlin looking rather older than his thirty-three years. There was no sign of the plumpish prince of 1740, with the luxuriant hair of chestnut brown. Now the king's complexion was weatherbeaten, the cheeks had fallen in, and deep lines ran past the corners of the mouth. This was nevertheless the highpoint of Frederick's life (Koser, 1921, I, 538). Valori noticed: 'This last campaign had given him the opportunity of deploying all the talents of a great general. He now believed that he had all those qualities at his command, in the same way as those of monarch and writer . . . He ran after a universal reputation' (Valori, 1820, I, 226).

A final cause for celebration remained. The whippet Biche was discovered to have survived the battle of Soor as a prisoner of the Austrians. She was in the keeping of Nádasti's wife, who was unwilling to let her go, but 'her restitution became almost an article of the treaty of peace' (Valori, 1820, I, 248).

Biche was received by Frederick's friend Lieutenant-General Rothenburg. He 'slipped her quietly through the door, without the king noticing, and in an instant she was standing on the table in front of him, with her front paws about his neck. Tears of joy sprang into Frederick's eyes' (Anon., 1787–9, I, 21).

CHAPTER THREE
The Armed Camp, 1745–56

'It is splendid to have acquired some glory, but we should be much at fault if we slipped into a sense of false security. We must prepare our resources well in advance, in the knowledge that the time or occasion might arrive when we will have to employ them' ('Principes Généraux', 1748, *Oeuvres*, XXVIII, 4). This was the rule which Frederick laid down for his army after the war.

The physical means of war-making accumulated impressively during the years of peace. Frederick made good the losses in manpower by the brutal expedient of retaining the Austrian and Saxon soldiers who had been made prisoner in the last war. He transformed the strategic geography of Silesia by extending the fortifications at Neisse, the portal towards Moravia, and by planting a new fortress at Schweidnitz, close to the border passes with Bohemia. New muskets, artillery and stocks of ammunition were set out in the arsenals, and the regiments piled up stocks of clothing in churches and other suitable large buildings.

Likewise Frederick rapidly overcame the financial embarrassments of 1745. 'Ants are careful to use the summer months to accumulate the provisions they will eat during the winter. In the same way the prince in peacetime must save the money he will have to expend when he is at war' (*Oeuvres*, IV, 7). By the time of the mobilisation of 1756 Frederick had 13,500,000 thaler at his disposal – enough, he thought, to see him comfortably through three campaigns.

If the army of 1745 had been a not unimpressive force, 'the Prussian army that went to war in 1756 was the ultimate creation of the era of enlisted armies. With every justification it bore on its glorious colours the inscription: *Pro Gloria et Patria!*' (Osten-Sacken, 1911, I, 205).

In part his masterpiece was the production of the care which Frederick devoted to the theoretical formation of his officers. On 2 April 1748 he completed the last of those five notebooks with gilded edges that made up the manuscript of *Les Principes Généraux de la Guerre appliqués à la Tactique et à la Discipline des Troupes Prussiennes*. He revealed the work first of all to Prince August Wilhelm, the eldest of his younger brothers, and then after a long interval he supervised a German translation and printing as *Die General-Principia vom Kriege*, which was issued to the generals in 1753.

The *Principes Généraux* represent Frederick's most complete and coherent statement on the management of war. It is therefore of some interest that he first turned his attention not to tactics or strategy, but to the specific problems of maintaining the Prussian army in good order. He stressed the unique nature of the Prussian forces – the only army in modern times to adhere to a truly Roman discipline, but also one which was peculiarly susceptible to breakdown, thanks to the very high proportion of foreign mercenaries in its ranks. Hence 'the constitution of our troops is such that those who command them must be tireless in their attention' (*Oeuvres*, XXVIII, 4). Frederick listed no less than fourteen safeguards against desertion, in the first article of the work, 'Des Troupes prussiennes de leurs Défauts et de leurs Avantages'. All of this was designed to avert a disintegration of the kind which had overtaken the army in 1744.

Articles II to X were of a useful but routine character, concerning the evolution of plans of campaign (omitted from the *General-Principia*) and the subsistence and encamping of the army. Article XI, unpromisingly entitled 'Quand et pour quoi il faut faire des Détachements', contained an important statement on the principle of the concentration of force: 'Small minds want to cling on to everything, but sensible men keep their attention on the principal object . . . The man who tries to hang onto everything ends up by holding nothing' (*Oeuvres*, XXVIII, 37; see also p. 59 above).

Article XII, 'Des Talents qu'il faut à un Général', was one of the sections which did not appear in the German edition, for it revealed too much about Frederick's arts of man-management.

The next fourteen articles were devoted to the science of reading the intentions of the enemy, and to the conduct of active military operations. After ruminating on the infinite variety of marches, the precautions to be taken against the Austrian light troops, and the ways of crossing or defending rivers, Frederick turned to the heart of the matter, namely the general battle. The army was not to shrink from an encounter with a superior enemy, for 'these are the occasions on which my oblique order of battle can be employed to great effect. You refuse one wing to the enemy, but you reinforce the attacking wing, with which you deliver the assault against a single wing of the enemy forces, taking them in flank. An army of 100,000 men, outflanked in this way, may be beaten by 30,000, because the issue is decided so quickly' (*Oeuvres*, XXVIII, 74).

As the leader of an army with an unbroken run of five victories to its credit, Frederick could proclaim with some enthusiasm: 'Battles determine the destiny of states. When you go to war you must seek to bring on a rapid decision – whether to extricate yourself from an embarrassment, to put the enemy at a disadvantage of the same kind, or in order to finish a quarrel that might otherwise drag on indefinitely' (*Oeuvres*, XXVIII, 83). Transferring these principles to the strategic plane, Frederick added: 'our wars must be short and lively. It is not at all in our interests to engage in protracted campaigning. A war of any length would bring about a slow destruction of our admirable discipline; it would depopulate our country, and sap our resources' (*ibid.*, 84).

In the final articles Frederick dealt interestingly with the element of chance in warfare, the evils of councils of war, and the cost of winter campaigns, returning in Article XXIX to his new battle tactics, a system 'founded on the speed of every movement and the necessity of being on the attack' (*Oeuvres*, XXVIII, 88).

From January 1753 the *General-Principia* was entrusted to the keeping of the generals as a most holy document. Frederick attached personal letters to the recipients, warning them not to leave the book lying about, 'or even to read it in the presence of servants – your own or anybody else's. When you want to read it, make sure you are alone. As soon as you are finished, you must seal it up again and lock it away somewhere safe' (to Major-General Schmettau, 2 December 1754, quoted in Preuss, 1832–4, I, 238).

The great secret was preserved until 20 February 1760, when a copy was captured in the possession of Major-General Czettritz at Cossdorf. By the end of 1762 a variety of editions had been published in Leipzig, Frankfurt and London, and as far afield as Spain and Portugal. The loss of security was regrettable, but the world admired the design and purpose which, as they could now see, informed Frederick's conduct of war. In the Austrian camp, Field-Marshal Daun found himself in hearty agreement with almost everything that Frederick had written, though Article XXIII confirmed his belief that 'he has often done battle without good reason. To my way of thinking, you should give battle only when the advantages of a victory are greater in proportion than the harm that will be the consequences of a retreat, or of the loss of the battle' (Kriegsarchiv, Vienna, *Kriegswissenschaftliche Mémoires*, 1760, II, 27). The Prince de Ligne simply called the work the best book on warfare that he knew.

Since 1748 the Prussian generals had already been in possession of two more narrowly focused directives – the *Instruction für die Major-*

Generals von der Infanterie, and the corresponding Instruction für die Major-Generals von der Cavallerie. Frederick's secretary Eichel tidied up the final drafts for printing (a very needful process, because Frederick's spelling was so bad), and the two books were distributed among the generals under the usual conditions for safekeeping. In the preliminary remarks, Frederick reproached himself for having left the major-generals for so long without a guide to their responsibilities as managers of their brigades. As we might have expected, he went on to give a prime place to a list of precautions to be taken against desertion. In battle, the two arms were to seize and maintain the initiative in their different ways – the infantry by advancing with shouldered muskets, and the cavalry by attacking without hesitation. These two sets of instructions were revealed to the Austrians when Fouqué's corps was overthrown on 23 June 1760.

The same confidence in the effectiveness of offensive action was just as marked in Frederick's Art de la Guerre of 1751:

> Attaquez donc toujours! Bellone vous annonce
> Des destins fortunés, des exploits éclatants,
> Tandis que vos guerriers seront les assaillants!

Inspired by the Rêveries of Marshal de Saxe, this lengthy poem was intended for publication from the start, and indeed Frederick sent a draft to the garrulous Voltaire. L'Art de la Guerre comprised six 'songs', relating to the essential foundation of training and discipline, the positioning and moving of the army, the desirable qualities in a commander, the science of fortress warfare, the business of quarters and supply, and the weighty and fearsome experience of battle. This work was to hold a strong appeal to the warriors of the time, for it seemed to them to convey the truths of their profession in a poetic and compelling way.

In 1752 Frederick committed the most weighty matters of state to his first Testament Politique, a paper so sacrosanct that for more than a century after Frederick's death it was safeguarded as one of the innermost secrets of the monarchy. We shall refer on many occasions to this work, and to the companion Testament of 1768.

In outline, the Testament of 1752 laid bare the foundations of the Prussian state – its financial system, the nature of the component peoples, the social structure, and the directions of desirable territorial expansion. Frederick treated the administration of the army in great detail, with particular reference to the cantonal system of recruiting, and he returned yet again to the prime importance of good order: 'A well-disciplined regiment will be as well behaved as a community of monks' (Frederick, 1920, 87).

The last in this most revealing series of works was represented by the *Pensées et Règles Générales pour la Guerre* of 1755. This was a discursive and private paper which he addressed to his confidant Winterfeldt. We find here a good deal of repetition of the *Principes Généraux*, but in much the most interesting section, entitled 'Des grandes Parties de la Guerre', Frederick neatly reconciled his horror of the costs of war with his desire for aggrandisement:

> I believe that no intelligent man, when he considers matters calmly, will begin a war in which he knows that he will be forced onto the defensive from the outset. Putting all high-flown sentiments aside, I maintain that any war which fails to lead to conquests is a war which weakens even the victor in the conflict, and which undermines the strength of the state. Therefore, you should never embark on hostilities unless you have an excellent prospect of making conquests. This will determine the way you go to war, and give that war an offensive character.

Frederick was aware that once a war was under way, Europe inevitably divided into two rival systems of alliance, which tended to impose 'a certain balance' among the powers. For decisive and positive results, therefore, the effort must be concentrated on a single enemy, and every possible advantage must be taken of the initial offensive which could 'decide the whole war, if you have the ability to exploit all the advantages which might be offered by the state of your forces, the timing of the attack, or the facility of anticipating the enemy on some important position' (*Oeuvres*, XXVIII, 124-25).

With all the reading in the world, the Prussian army would not have been fashioned into the physically and mentally active force of 1756 without the experience of the strenuous peacetime reviews and manoeuvres.

The season of the springtime and early summer reviews served the same purpose as in the time of Frederick William, namely to give the men and the junior officers practice in the skills of the parade ground, to enable the king to see the regiments in detail, and to enable to regiments to see him.

The autumn manoeuvres were an invention of Frederick's, and they were a development of the first gathering of the kind at Spandau in 1743. Day after day Frederick put large forces of mixed arms through simulations of real actions, reproducing attacks, retreats, foraging expeditions, the defence of positions, and the like. The 'enemy' positions were at first represented only by flags or strips of cloth, signifying the brigade boundaries, but in later years the forces were sometimes divided in two and carried out genuinely contested manoeuvres. The outcome helped Frederick to determine the practicability of various formations, and how long the forces took to cover the ground, and these experiences could make or break the careers of some of the generals. At the manoeuvres of the Magdeburg and Altmark regiments in 1748 Frederick watched from a hill while a brigade struggled towards him across a zone of swampy meadows. The confusion was

> made still worse by Lieutenant-General Count von Haake, . . . who burst into smoke and flames, and tried to put things right by resorting to shouts, rebukes and blows. The king came shooting down from his hilltop like a bolt of lightning. He told the yelling Haake to betake himself to the rear, and within a few minutes Frederick had restored order among the infantry. The rest of the manoeuvre was accomplished with the greatest precision. (Haller, 1796, 13–4)

The largest and most important of these gatherings was held between Spandau and Gatow from 2 to 13 September 1753, and it concerned no less than forty-nine battalions and sixty-one squadrons, making a force of 44,000 men. Frederick commissioned Lieutenant-Colonel Balbi to draw up an entirely misleading account of what was taking place, and he allowed the hussars to plunder any unauthorised spectators.

On occasion, the inherent unreality of the autumn manoeuvres left Frederick with a totally false impression of the worth of some of his commanders. He later admitted that he had badly misjudged the abilities of Zieten, whose talents were not of a kind to shine in peacetime.

Field-Marshal Schwerin was more adept at this kind of exercise. On the second day of the celebrated Spandau manoeuvres, as commander of an enemy force he contrived to lure Frederick out of a strong position, then launched the left wing of his horse into an attack which caught the king's cavalry at a disadvantage. 'At once the troops were brought to a halt. The events of the manoeuvre were subjected to examination, and His Majesty embraced his former enemy' (Ernst Friedrich Giannini, quoted in Thadden, 1967, 198).

Schwerin had become the doyen of the Prussian army after the Old Dessauer died in 1747. However, in spite of the show of warmth at Spandau, Frederick had long ceased to live on cordial terms with his old mentor. It seems that the falling-out went back to 4 November 1744, when Schwerin had left the stricken army in Bohemia, pleading ill-health.

Field-Marshal James Keith was a newcomer to Frederick's small circle of fellow-spirits. A Scotsman by blood, and a veteran of the Russian service, Keith was prized by Frederick for his experience, his courage, and his resource in action. As a friend, Keith further appealed to the king as a man of fine manners and cosmopolitan culture. The troops liked and respected him, though the Prussian officers harboured a lingering resentment of Keith as an outsider, and they were amused by his subservience to his mistress Eva Merthens, who was a large lady from Finland.

Not even Keith could aspire to the place which Frederick reserved in his trust for that corpulent yet shadowy figure Hans Carl von Winterfeldt. 'There can rarely be another man of such repute who, like Winterfeldt, has ever occasioned such divisions or even total contradictions of opinion' (Kaltenborn, 1790–1, II, 36). Winterfeldt's enemies were willing to admit that there was much about the man that was impressive and appealing. He had a bluff, engaging manner, he issued his orders with clarity and confidence, and he was able to carry a multitude of matters in his head. We are told at the same time that Winterfeldt was vindictive, a sower of discord, and the prey of dark ambitions and resentments. His upbringing had been in the rural simplicities of Pomerania, and he could not forget his failure to launch himself into the frenchified culture of Berlin after the Second Silesian War: 'At that time the society of Berlin was most brilliant. The ladies were amiable to an extraordinary degree, and they said that military reputations meant nothing to them, unless the officers in question were agreeable company as well' (Kalkreuth, 1840, II, 12).

This was the man whom Frederick chose as his confidant in the secrets of statecraft, his spymaster, his effective chief of staff, and whom he assigned as his nark, or personal deputy, with commanders like Schwerin, Keith, Prince August Wilhelm and the Duke of Bevern.

The contemporaries of Winterfeldt linked his name with the processes which brought Prussia into the Seven Years War – that experience which carried the state to within days of its disintegration. It does not take long to outline the essential events.

By the early 1750s the Austrians, still intent on recovering Silesia, had cast over the old connection with Britain, and begun to establish a liaison with the French, their former enemies. The French were for the moment unwilling to commit themselves to an actual alliance, or to go to war.

The Austrian links with Russia were of much longer standing. Here the problems for the Austrian chancellor Kaunitz were of a different nature, for in 1753 the Empress Elizabeth and her counsellors had made the decision in principle to go to war with Prussia, and the Austrians feared that the Russians might drag them into hostilities before the French were willing to join in. 'It must indeed be counted as one of the proudest memories of Prussian history, that the resources of thirty-six million people were considered inadequate to overcome a mere four million' (Lehmann, 1894, 29; actually about 4,500,000).

Frederick unwittingly gave the Austrians a helping hand. He feared that the Anglo-French colonial war would spread to Europe, and with every reason he suspected the hostile designs of the Russians. He dreaded the prospect of ending up entirely friendless, and he therefore turned to the British, with whom he concluded the defensive Treaty of Westminster of 27 January 1756, 'the worst mistake of his career' (Augstein, 1968, 175). He reckoned without the response of the French, who, despite Frederick's betrayals of 1742 and 1745, had still considered themselves Prussia's ally. Outraged by Frederick's action, the French moved closer to the Austrians, and in the First Treaty of Versailles of 1 May 1756 they cancelled their guarantee of the Prussian possession of Silesia. Frederick began military preparations in June, and on 29 August he launched a pre-emptive invasion of the electorate of Saxony.

Now that hostilities had begun, the Austrians completed their circle of alliances. On 2 February 1757 Austria and Russia determined on a plan of military co-operation, and on 1 May the French signed a Second Treaty of Versailles which made them active members of the alliance, which was widened to embrace the Swedes and Saxons. Finally the call of Maria Theresa's consort Francis Stephen, as Emperor of Germany, drew many of the states of southern and western Germany into the war on behalf of the league. By the summer of 1757, therefore, Prussia was at war with the greater part of Europe. The French stood to gain nothing directly from the alliance, but Austria, Russia, Saxony and Sweden made territorial claims which would have reduced Prussia to the status of a minor principality of north Germany, and extinguished for ever the pretensions of the House of Brandenburg.

The allocation of 'war guilt' is a question which has divided historians for generations. In 1894 the controversy assumed new life when Max Lehmann argued that Frederick too had aggressive designs in the middle 1750s: 'There were accordingly two offensives which clashed in 1756: that of Maria Theresa, aiming at the recovery of Silesia, and that of Frederick, who intended to conquer West Prussia and Saxony' (1894, 85). The complexity of the ensuing debate threatens to surpass human understanding, for it embraces a range of conflicts which were fought on theatres extending from the leafy

Ohio valley to the cold shores of the Baltic. Herbert Butterfield (1955), Winfried Baumgart (1972) and Theodor Schieder (1983) made heroic attempts to summarise the state of the argument, but we still lack the key to understanding that can be furnished only by a knowledge of Frederick's intentions. These ambitions remain a matter of surmise.

It has been claimed that Frederick was presented with a danger of encirclement that was more real than he knew, and that 'The revelation of the Russian war aims has given a depth of meaning to Frederick the Great's maxim "Better to anticipate than to be anticipated" such as the king of Prussia himself would not have thought possible in his lifetime' (Baumgart, 1972, 158). This perhaps leaves out of account the gap between intentions and practicabilities. In fact the preparations of the Russian army lagged well behind the warlike policy of the ministers in St Petersburg, and the Russians were in a condition to make offensive war only in August 1757, and even then on a limited scale. Without the spur of hostilities, the Russians would probably have taken the field much later still (Duffy, 1981, 73–5).

Likewise the first, tardy Austrian orders to mobilise the regiments were issued on 16 July 1756, in response to the Prussian preparations, and 29 August found the Austrian forces in Bohemia and Moravia still without a single piece of mobile artillery. It by no means suited Frederick's politics to find the Austrians so completely unready. He had recalled Lieutenant-General Schmettau, Field-Marshal Keith and the commander of the first battalion of the Garde from the 'cure' at Karlsbad in Bohemia at the end of July, and when they returned he was infuriated to find that they had seen no trace of any Austrian military activity (Schmettau, 1806, I, 306).

The evidence for active Saxon complicity also lacks weight. Hertzberg, one of Frederick's ministers, had been given the job of making propaganda out of the diplomatic documents which were captured in Dresden, and he admitted long afterwards that his own arguments were unconvincing. Hertzberg had known for three years of the existence of an Austro-Russo-Saxon agreement of 1746, providing for a partition of Prussia in the event of war, but he was also aware that the project was to be put into effect only after Frederick had taken the initiative in opening hostilities. It remained an open question whether it would really have been more dangerous for Frederick to bide his time rather than precipitate matters.

Interestingly enough, Frederick's protagonists are willing to use arguments about indefinitely postponable ambitions in defence of the king when it comes to interpreting some of the more aggressively worded passages of the *Testament* of 1752. There Frederick had written:

> Our state is still lacking in intrinsic strength. All our provinces together contain only five million souls [actually less]. Our military establishment is respectable enough, but it lacks the number of troops required to resist the enemies who surround us . . . Of all the territories of Europe, the ones which are most suitable for our state to acquire are Saxony, Polish Prussia and Swedish Pomerania, for all three would serve to round off our borders.

Frederick wrote that the conquest of Saxony might be facilitated if Saxony happened to stand in alliance with Maria Theresa at a time when she or her successors threatened to break with Prussia, for this would give the Prussians every excuse for marching into the electorate. Frederick was inclined to leave this commission to his heirs, if only because, in his hypochondriac state, he believed that he did not have long to live.

Did Frederick really intend to annex Saxony in the Seven Years War? Was this why the captured Saxon troops at Pirna in 1756 were sworn into the Prussian army as complete regiments, and not incorporated piecemeal into Prussian units as in the Second Silesian War? Does this explain why Frederick ordered Saxon city fathers to swear an oath of allegiance to him (*PC* 9789)? Was it significant that the Prussian administration of Saxony so closely resembled the style of rule established in Silesia? There is no conclusive evidence on these points. However, in defence of Frederick as upholder of the territorial *status quo* it is worthwhile pointing out that it did not necessarily serve his interests to incorporate Saxony into the Prussian monarchy, despite the statement of the *Testament* of 1752.

In 1756 Frederick was only too glad to find Saxony at once defenceless and potentially hostile, for then he was at liberty to ransack the electorate for cash, fodder and manpower; Saxony as a Prussian province would have had to be treated much more leniently. Long after the Seven Years War Frederick continued to build his finances on the assumption that in the event of hostilities Saxony would be conquered and lie at his disposal. It was therefore something of an embarrassment when good relations were established with Saxony in 1778, and Frederick was forced to consider how to put the finances on a new foundation (*Réflexions sur l'Administration des Finances pour le Gouvernement prussien*, 20 October 1784). Possibly Frederick also regretted that he was now denied any further opportunity of wreaking his vengeance on things Saxon. He had written to his brother August Wilhelm before the Seven Years War about 'the pleasure of humiliating, or rather annihilating Saxony' (19 February 1756, *PC* 12125) – a sentiment very inadequately translated by one of Frederick's admirers as 'reducing Saxony to a political nullity' (Herrmann, 1895, 245).

The hostile testimony of Frederick's officers is cumulatively impressive, even when we have made every allowance for their jealousy of Winterfeldt, and the fact that they were excluded from the innermost processes of the king's thought. The courtier Lehndorff, little Count Podewils the minister of foreign affairs, the veterans Gaudi, Kalkreuth, Retzow and Warnery, and the royal brother Henry all believed that the war was an unnecessary one, and most of them ascribed it to the sinister power of Winterfeldt (Warnery, 1788, 214; Retzow, 1802, I, 53–4; Kalkreuth, 1840, II, 120; Naude, 1888, 235; Jany, 1901, I, *Heft* 3, 21; Lehndorff, 1907, 336; Lehndorff, 1910–13, I, 249). Indeed, Winterfeldt's ambitions extended well beyond the confines of Saxony to the creation of a new Protestant German Empire, a dream which came to an end in June 1757. 'I am convinced', wrote Warnery, 'that if the King of Prussia had won the battle of Kolin, he would have sought to bring the Hereditary Lands of Maria Theresa under his dominion' (Warnery, 1785–91, II, 310; see also Warnery, 1788, 12; Bleckwenn, 1978, 190).

Ultimately the 'guilt' for the Seven Years War is one of those intractable questions which depend on how widely we draw the boundaries of our inquiry. Most immediately, Frederick was justified in acting on the reports which reached him from The Hague, to the effect that the Austrians, Russians and French planned to attack him in the following spring. A wide perspective brings to light a little more of the ambitions and hatreds of Frederick and his confidant Winterfeldt, and reveals that by seizing the military initiative Frederick created the conditions which made it possible for Austria to complete the alliance.

Allied statesmen, like the Russian chancellor Bestuzhev, rightly suspected that Frederick believed that the period of Prussian expansion was not yet over. When we look at Frederick's career as a whole, we will recall not only the events of 1756, but the invasions of Herstal and Silesia in 1740, and the claims which he lodged to north-east Bohemia in 1742 and 1744. In other words our hero emerges as the prime begetter of violence in Central Europe in the middle of the eighteenth century.

In military terms, the arguments for undertaking a pre-emptive attack on Saxony were irrefutable. The Saxon change of sides in 1744 had shown Frederick how dangerous it was to leave a hostile or even a neutral power astride the central Elbe. 'I was also determined to gain as much ground as I could in this first campaign, and provide better cover for my states by holding the theatre of operations as distant as possible by carrying the war into Bohemia, if this proved at all practicable' (Oeuvres, IV, 39).

As a prize in its own right Saxony was rich in agriculture, trade and men of military age, and the Saxons had 'a story . . . that His Prussian Majesty has often said, that the thing in the world he most repented was that, when he was master of this country, he did not carry off all the troops' (Lord Stormont, Dresden, 11 August 1756, PRO SP 88/78).

For a number of years now Winterfeldt had pondered the details of the invasion. On two occasions he had found it agreeable and instructive to make the journey by way of Saxony to take the cure at Karlsbad. He prospected the Bohemian passes (deciding that the Aussig route was the most suitable), and he made a leisurely inspection of the whole of the celebrated position of Pirna and Königstein. He concluded that the camp was tactically strong, but that if the Saxon army took refuge there it would soon run out of fodder for its horses.

It was therefore on the basis of well-established contingency plans that Frederick and Winterfeldt made arrangements to assemble 62,000 troops for the invasion and break across the Saxon border in three main groups. They hoped, if possible, to catch the Saxon forces before they could concentrate, and establish the Prussians in winter quarters in northern Bohemia up to the line of the river Eger. Meanwhile Schwerin and 23,800 men were to stand by in Silesia.

Frederick's intentions for the continuance of the war are remarkably vague. At heart he shared the confidence of some of the junior officers like Ewald von Kleist, who believed that the Prussian army was capable of confronting any eventuality (Kleist to Gleim, 20 July 1756, in Volz, 1926–7, II, 3). In fact the king had no inkling of the weight of the counter-offensive that was going to break upon his head after 1756. Blinded by their presuppositions, Frederick and Winterfeldt chose to ignore the intelligence which indicated that the Austrians and Russians had been making considerable progress in the arts of war, and especially gunnery. Frederick dismissed the Russians as a horde of ignorant barbarians, over the protests of Keith (Retzow, 1802, I, 182–3). He derided what he was told of the important peacetime manoeuvres of the Austrians in the camp of Kolin in 1754 (Gisors, 1868, 103), and he roundly declared 'the Empress has no money' (to Schwerin, 12 March 1757, PC 14367), not appreciating that the French would lend financial help to their Austrian allies, as well as siege technicians who could crack open the lightly built new Prussian fortifications in Silesia.

Winterfeldt managed the mobilisation with undoubted technical skill. The necessary reserves of clothing, ammunition, flour and grain had been at hand since 1752, and in the second half of June 1756 the orders went out to buy horses for the transport train, and recall the first troops from leave to their colours. Frederick, Winterfeldt and the supply superintendant Wolf Friedrich von Retzow were probably the only people who were aware of the objective of all these preparations.

Frederick probably took the political decision to open hostilities on 20 or 21 July, after weighing up the reports he had received from von der Hellen, his envoy at The Hague, concerning the allies' hostile plans for 1757.

In August, Frederick dispatched two ultimata to Austria, and received unsatisfactory replies. On the 26th he sent a third message to Vienna, declaring that he must take the necessary measures for his security, but that he was still prepared to call back his troops if Maria Theresa promised not to attack him in this year or the next. On the morning of the 28th Frederick raised himself into the saddle before the Schloss at Potsdam, put the troops of the garrison through a few drill movements, then led them across the bridge over the Havel on the way to Saxony.

CHAPTER FOUR
The Theatre of War

Locked in the heart of Central Europe, the scene of Frederick's wars warmed but slowly in the springtime sun. The snow continued to accumulate in the highlands until it reached its greatest thickness in February. It lingered for about two hundred days on ground above 4,200 feet (1,200 metres), and in some summers it was never entirely banished from the highest crevices of the Riesen-Gebirge. Again and again, promising thaws were interrupted by 'returns of winter', which made it difficult for commanders to think of opening the campaigning season before the last days of April.

The grass began to grow in the first half of May, which was a consideration of vital importance for the maintenance of the horses. Then, in most years, a sequence of sunny spells and cold rains finally gave way to a high summer of clear skies and hot temperatures, which extended into the autumn. The troops suffered severely, for this was the season of the forced marches and the great battles (one young officer gave all the money he had for a hatful of water after the battle of Zorndorf). Finally the cold, the rains and the snows descended on the theatre of war with unpredictable abruptness. In 1761 they arrived in Silesia at the beginning of October, and in north-east Bohemia in 1778 as early as August.

Physically, the setting of the campaigns extended over three regions:

(a) *The northern plains of Brandenburg, Saxony and Silesia*
    Two major rivers (the Elbe to the west and the Oder to the east) transversed these lowlands from south-east to north-west. They offered good navigation, as well as open and fertile land on one or both of their banks, and they consequently became important avenues of operations. A huge tract of heath and forest stretched from the Brandenburg-Saxon borderlands into the Neumark and north-western Silesia, however, rendering subsistence difficult in the middle of this theatre.

(b) *The border hills*
These were a more or less continuous chain of heights which
stretched all the way from southern Germany to Hungary and
constituted the highest ground between the northern plains and
Vienna. 'The people who come from this low-lying and flat
country are given to uttering a great shriek, when they catch
sight of the first hill worthy of the name. They believe they have
glimpsed the very pillars of Heaven' (Riesebeck, 1784, II, 4). It is
true that the hills were not particularly high, by Pyrenean let
alone Alpine standards, but in operational terms they constituted significant obstacles. The passes became impenetrable in
wintertime, so a commander had to establish himself solidly
and deeply on the enemy side of the heights if he was not to be
forced to retreat before the end of the campaigning season.
Moreover at every time of the year the hill country favoured the
work of the Austrian hussars and Croats who preyed on the
Prussian convoys.

(c) *The Austrian provinces of Bohemia and Moravia*
These two territories lay south of the hills, and exhibited a great
variety of terrain which will be investigated shortly.

To make some sense of what happened in the wars it is necessary
to rearrange our basic physical geography into strategic zones, reflecting the influence of forces like politics, strategies, agriculture,
and the legacy of the past in the shape of bridges and fortresses. Three
such geopolitical systems appear in the middle of the eighteenth
century:

Berlin and the eastern approaches

Frederick's way of war was greatly influenced by the vulnerability of
the Brandenburg heartland. Berlin was an open city which could
scarcely be defended by less than 20,000 men, for the feeble excise
wall did not come into the reckoning. The royal residence of Potsdam
was quite untenable. Spandau, the weapons smithy of the Prussian
state, also stood open to the invader. It was true that Spandau citadel
was tactically strong, and covered by the marshes of the Spree and
Havel, but it was too small to be of any strategic account.

In the Seven Years War the Russians found it convenient to avail
themselves of the navigation of the Netze and the Warthe, and to
establish their main depot at Posen in western Poland. Thereafter
they could turn south into Silesia, or push on due west through the
Neumark of Brandenburg against Berlin. In the latter case the only

natural obstacle to their progress was the line of the Oder, which they reached at the little fortress of Cüstrin or at the university town of Frankfurt, according to whether they chose the routes to the north or the south of the Warthe Marshes. Once they were across the Oder, the Russians were separated from Berlin by fifty miles of level heathland and fields, where could be seen 'scattered spires of wheat, rye, barley and oats, shooting from the sands, like the hairs upon a head almost bald' (Adams, 1804, 3).

Magdeburg, Dresden, Prague and the system of the Elbe

The Brandenburg heartland lacked any position whatsoever which could be held against an enemy approaching from the south. A raiding force could have reached Berlin in less than ten hours from the nearest Saxon frontier post at Mittelwalde. A more respectable army, basing itself on the Elbe at Wittenberg, could cover the eighty-five miles to the capital in six marches, which was still dangerously close in strategic terms. Frederick concluded: 'The best defence we can make is to march into Saxony, as we did in the winter of 1745. If we retired behind the Spree or the Havel we would lose the whole country' ('Principes Généraux', 1748, Oeuvres, XXVIII, 16).

Now it became evident that the strategic centre of the monarchy lay not in Berlin, but in the fortress-depot of Magdeburg. This was a large and rather ugly town, encased in fortifications built by Frederick William I. It was rarely visited by foreign tourists, and it never figured in the histories of the campaigns. However, Magdeburg stood at one of the most important road junctions and river crossings of the region of the lower Elbe, and it commanded the province of Magdeburg-Halberstadt, the richest in the Prussian state, which extended as a fertile and open plain from the Harz Mountains in the west to the Brandenburg heathlands in the east.

In times of hostilities Magdeburg served as 'the repository of whatever he [Frederick] finds necessary to place out of reach of sudden insult' (Moore, 1779, II, 111). Thus in the Seven Years War it received the royal treasury and the court of the queen. For offensive action, the Elbe was capable of bearing provisions, ammunition and heavy artillery from Magdeburg all the way through Saxony and into northern Bohemia (PC 9007).

Saxony and Bohemia as far as Prague may therefore be considered an extension of the 'system' of the Brandenburg heartland. The direct route from Berlin to Dresden ran through barren territory, and Frederick preferred to come at Saxony from the north-west, basing himself on Magdeburg, and assembling his troops in the area of Halle.

A march of two days carried the Prussians from Halle to Leipzig (with a population of 130,000), which was the trading centre of the electorate. Thereafter the army pushed up the open plains along the west (left) bank of the Elbe to the weakly fortified Wittenberg: 'That makes you master of the course of the Elbe, which will furnish you with your supplies' ('Principes Généraux', 1748, *Oeuvres*, XXVIII, 9; also *PC* 10725). The next town of strategic consequence was Torgau, which owned a permanent crossing of the Elbe and became of great importance for the Prussian transverse communications on the northern plain. Frederick fortified the old town in the Seven Years War with earthworks and palisades, and there was a good position on the open ridge to the north-west.

When Frederick or his corps commanders wished to threaten Dresden without committing themselves too deeply in Saxony, they arranged their troops for seven or eight miles along the heights which extended from the Katzenhäuser, Krögis and Schletta to the spur which terminated at the site of the castle overlooking the Elbe at Meissen. The forward edge of the position was defined by the Triebisch stream: 'This rivulet is in itself most contemptible, but its banks on both sides are very high and impracticable in most places. The country behind for two German [ten English] miles is extremely uneven, cut with deep hollow ways, ravines, and by small brooks formed from the neighbouring mountains' (Mitchell, 24 May 1760, PRO SP 90/76).

Such was the celebrated 'Camp of Meissen', which aroused the admiration of commentators like the Piedmontese staff officer de Silva. He observed in 1760 that the shape of a campaign or an entire war could be determined by the proper choice of a defensive position: 'That is the case with the one at Meissen, which yields him an abundance of resources. He seized it at the beginning of the struggle, and I doubt whether anybody will be able to get him out again! This camp gives him the possession of Saxony, and Saxony in turn furnishes him with everything he needs to continue the war' (Silva, 1778, 254).

The route from Meissen to Dresden ran for fifteen miles alongside the Elbe, as the river described a series of gentle curves through a beautiful landscape of woods, vineyards, meadows and sandstone bluffs. It was in the region of Dresden that the Austrians, once they had arrived in Saxony in the Seven Years War, found the means to wage a protracted positional warfare. The city of Dresden itself was of the greatest political and strategic consequence, for it was at the same time the capital of the electorate and a powerful regular fortress sprawling over both sides of the Elbe. There was a beguiling view from the long stone bridge of nineteen arches: 'The river, which is confined within narrow bounds until a short distance from Dresden, now becomes a mighty stream, corresponding to the splendour of the city and the landscape. The hills in the direction of Lusatia offer a quite magnificent sight' (Riesebeck, 1784, II, 5).

Dresden, as a fortress, was large enough to accept a powerful garrison. Moreover in the Seven Years War the Austrians cunningly integrated its defence with that of the adjacent Plauensche-Grund, a broad valley which was dominated by a succession of wall-like heights along the eastern side. Frederick found that this emplacement was too strong to be taken by direct assault (Ligne, 1923, 170), and in addition the extensive Tharandter-Wald interfered with the Prussian movements around the flank.

Behind Dresden again the ground rose gradually to the hilly region of the 'Saxon Switzerland'. The landscape was bizarre in the extreme. Isolated sandstone mesas, which would not have appeared out of place in the Wild West, here sat incongruously among verdant fields and beechwoods. The river Elbe was reduced to a simulacrum of the Colorado, a narrow brown ribbon describing loops around the foot of the massy heights.

The Austrians discovered that the access to this region, and thus to the Bohemian border, could be barred by holding the heights above the Müglitz, a stream which ran through a very steep and densely wooded valley until a short distance above Dohna, and thence across the narrow riverine plain to the Elbe. On the far, or eastern, side of the Elbe, the Austrian field-marshal Daun enjoyed another good site for his encampments among the basalt crags of Stolpen.

To the rear of the Müglitz line, the last coherent defensible position inside Saxony was offered by the famous 'Camp of Pirna', where we shall find ourselves shortly. It was, however, too much of a self-confining prison to be able to commend itself to the Prussians or the Austrians, and it became of strategic importance only in the peculiar circumstances of the autumn of 1756. For Frederick's purpose the one useful position in the neighbourhood was the height of Cotta, on the upper Gottleuba, where he could place a corps close to the Bohemian border.

Frederick did not need to progress as far as Pirna, the Müglitz or even the Plauensche-Grund in order to take advantage of the transverse routes inside Saxony. As Tempelhoff pointed out, the commercial life and therefore the communications inside north-west Bohemia were poorly developed. In Saxony, on the other hand, towns like Chemnitz, Freiberg and Bautzen were important trading centres, and 'the interconnecting roads are as good as they reasonably can be, in a hilly region. Hence it is easy for an army to move inside the Saxon frontier, and support whatever detachments are positioned there to defend it' (Tempelhoff, 1783–1801, I, 132).

A Turkish envoy once described Bohemia as 'the real pride and core of the Austrian power' (Achmet Effendi, 1762, in Volz, 1908, II, 207). Bohemia had been renowned since the Middle Ages for the wealth of its mines of iron, tin and silver, and in the eighteenth century the prosperous woollen industry of the north-eastern hills and the Bohemian-Moravian borders made the kingdom a still greater prize. The menfolk were the foundation of he Habsburgs' artillery and the backbone of their infantry: 'Beyond comparison they are the best soldiers of all the Imperial subjects. They are the ones most able to endure all the hardships of military life without going under' (Riesebeck, 1784, II, 412). The conquest of Bohemia remained the ultimate objective of all Frederick's plans for offensive war against the Austrians. What avenues lay open to him for a direct invasion from Saxony?

Frederick never led the main army across the frontier to the east of the Elbe. The country closest to the river was tangled and nearly trackless, and suitable only for attempts at strategic surprise, such as those launched by Field-Marshal Browne in 1756 or Prince Henry in 1778. Scarcely more attractive was the long and vulnerable road stretching from Zittau in Upper Lusatia, or the one from the neighbouring corner of Silesia that led between the Iser-Gebirge and the Riesen-Gebirge to the valley of the Iser. The base areas for such an offensive stood equally remote from the supply lines of the Elbe and the Oder, and the prospects in Bohemia depended on how completely the Austrians allowed themselves to be taken by surprise.

Frederick much preferred to invade Bohemia by way of the western side of the Elbe. It was necessary to escort the train of boats through the sandstone gorge of the Saxon-Bohemian border, but the main Prussian army always moved quickly enough to be able to cut across country over the low Elbsandstein-Gebirge, descend to the valley of the Biela, and then make the passage of the isolated Bohemian Mittel-Gebirge before the Austrians had time to make an effective response (in 1744, 1756 and 1757).

Except for the border hills, the Austrians had no tenable positions except the narrow river Eger and the low ridge of Budin on the southern side. Here they could be turned by a Prussian corps advancing down the Eger from the west (Moritz in 1757). The whole country therefore lay open to the Prussians. 'Behind Lobositz we enter open landscapes, fine plains and rich agriculture. This is the Circle of Leitmeritz, the region the local people call "the Garden of Bohemia" ' (Guibert, 1803, I, 251). Leitmeritz town offered the Prussians a convenient crossing of the Elbe (comparable with Torgau for the Saxon Elbe), and it was the best landing place for the heavy artillery and stores, though the actual head of navigation for the larger boats lay twenty miles upstream at Melnik.

From Leitmeritz the Prussians could reach the capital city of Prague in three marches. As a fortress, the capital of Bohemia was extensive but not particularly strong, and scarcely tenable by anything short of a large army. Even when Frederick took the place, in 1744, it was something of an embarrassment for him. Conversely, all the other Bohemian towns were too small to serve as depots for the invading army, and in any case it was found to be difficult to gather provisions and intelligence in central Bohemia, where the communications were rudimentary and the population implacably hostile. After the experiences of 1744 Frederick renounced the ambition of plunging any further south, and his thoughts turned more and more to the attractions of the wide, fertile and warm valley of the upper Elbe as it stretched east past Kolin towards Pardubitz and Königgrätz.

The Silesian Oder, and the avenues to Moravia and north-east Bohemia

It is time to turn back north of the hills and pass to the regime of the Oder and the Silesian strategic system. This was country that was dominated by the Prussians. The short and easy avenue from Brandenburg to Silesia lay by way of Crossen, 'a very pretty, neat town, handsome square; a wooden bridge over the Oder; the road pleasant, through meadows and oak woods along the banks of the Oder' (Mitchell, 1850, II, 40). Next upstream came Glogau in Silesia, another agreeable town, where Frederick established an important artillery depot and extensive magazines of cereals (the counterpart of Magdeburg on the Elbe). Convoys of boats, bearing military requisites of all kinds, made their slow way upstream to the armies and garrisons in Silesia. Frederick commented in 1758 that the clothing for the recruits had failed to arrive in proper time. 'It has a lot to do with the water level this spring, which has been so low that the boats can only accept half loads, and they take six weeks over a journey that usually lasts five' (Orlich, 1842, 123). When Frederick marched to do battle with the Russians in August 1759 it was actually possible for his cavalry to wade the river below Frankfurt (see p. 183).

A good fast road followed the west (left) bank of the Oder to Breslau, the fortress capital of Silesia. Here Frederick bought the former Spätgen Palace before the Seven Years War, and he began to enlarge it in a style befitting a royal residence. This establishment was to prove most convenient for him, since Breslau was the strategic heart of Silesia.

Wheat, rye and barley were heavily cultivated in the immediate neighbourhood of the capital, and Lower Silesia as a whole was fertile and greatly admired by the contemporary standards of beauty. Except for the level and open ground in locations like Hohenfriedeberg, Leuthen and Reichenbach, the province presented the aspect of an undulating and verdant countryside, agreeably interspersed with lush mixed woodlands of spruce, beech, ash, birch and the omnipresent oak. This fat land was recognisably part of northern Europe, and it contrasted most strikingly with the ambience of Bohemia and Moravia, where the bare landscapes, the harsh light, and the air of poverty and servitude already hinted at the Orient.

The western flank of the Silesian system was traversed by a number of little rivers which flowed north from the Sudeten hills. These streams could normally be crossed with little ceremony, but they offered obstructions of some moment when they were swollen by heavy rains or melting snows, or when the enemy were waiting on the far side to contest the passage. The Bober ran from the Riesen-Gebirge above Hirschberg by way of Sagan to the Oder at Crossen. The companion stream, the Katzbach, flowed a dozen miles further to the east, and was of such strategic weight that Frederick composed a memorandum in its honour after the Seven Years War: 'In the last war it was evident that the stratagem in which the Austrians had the most confidence was to establish themselves behind the Katzbach. They hoped they could cut off the Prussians from the Silesian fortresses, and besiege these places at their leisure.' He explained that Daun had sought to make use of the Katzbach in this way against Bevern in 1757, and against the royal army in the campaign of Liegnitz in 1760 (Taysen, 1882, 129).

The corresponding eastern flank of the Silesian system was formed by the borders of Upper Silesia with Hungary and Moravia. The Hungarian frontier was always something of a nuisance for the Prussians, for they could never seal it effectively against light forces irrupting through the Jablunka Pass. However, the avenue to Moravia exercised a strong fascination for Frederick throughout his military career.

Using the fortress town of Neisse as his base, Frederick could seize Troppau without difficulty to serve as an advance depot, and then strike across a low plateau into the heart of Moravia, which lay much closer to Vienna than did Bohemia:

I know that kingdom [Bohemia] too well not to be aware of the difficulties we have in establishing ourselves there. The way to take it is by diversion, and Moravia alone offers a suitable theatre. The great families have their estates in Moravia, and

operating from there we can make the Austrians fear for the
safety of Vienna, which is of a different order of importance for
the House of Austria than Prague. (To Henry, 2 June 1778, *PC*
26422)

Inside Moravia the only obstacles to Prussian progress were artificial
ones, namely the old fortress town of Brünn, and Olmütz with the
new works which were built before the Seven Years War.

In this way the Silesian strategic system reached well into
Moravia. It also marched with north-eastern Bohemia. Along this
sector the County of Glatz formed a strategic appendix or sub-system.
Its southern and eastern rims were high and mostly inaccessible. The
corresponding northern side was screened from Lower Silesia by the
Eulen-Gebirge, which was of no great height, but very precipitous
and thickly wooded. The Eulen-Gebirge was to prove an embarrassment to Frederick in his later campaigns, for if he was off his guard the
Austrians could gain the passages of Wartha and Silberberg in a
couple of marches from the Silesian border, and so effect an entry to
the Silesian plain. This was why Frederick built a fortress at Silberberg after the Seven Years War.

Offensively, the County of Glatz offered Frederick a choice of
routes either due west up the steepish path over the border and then
down to Nachod, or more conveniently by the broad valley to
Braunau.

At Nachod and Braunau we meet what was by far the most
important of the corridors between the Prussian and Habsburg states.
At the northern end it brought the Austrians into the heart of Silesia
close to Breslau, and 'Lower Silesia is the vital part of the duchy. We
must hang on to it' (Frederick to Schwerin, 2 August 1956, *PC* 7796).
At the southern end the avenue extended into north-eastern Bohemia
by way of Königgrätz and Pardubitz.

In Lower Silesia Frederick owned two strategic bulwarks towards
the border hills. Schweidnitz (fortified from 1747) stood in a fertile
region an easy twenty-five-mile march from the Oder. 'It has the
highest steeple in all Silesia, and from which there is an extensive and
beautiful prospect over the wide plains which surround the town to
the distant mountains, which look like a wall round the horizon'
(Adams, 1804, 185).

In 1745, and in almost every campaigning season of the Seven
Years War, the armies contested for the piedmont region above
Schweidnitz and Hohenfriedeberg, where the rounded bosky foothills
of the Riesen-Gebirge swept down to the plain and interlocked with
the green fingers of the valleys reaching into the higher ground.
It was hard to evict the Austrians when they emplaced themselves

immediately above Schweidnitz in the region of Waldenburg, as they did in 1760 and 1762. As some compensation the Prussians usually had the facility of a second strongpoint: the important road junction of Landeshut, standing about fifteen miles west-south-west of Schweidnitz. Landeshut was sited in a hollow, but in 1758 Fouqué built ten forts on the surrounding hills, which made the place into the strategic equivalent of a fortress. Ahead of Landeshut again the Prussians had an important defensive camp between Liebau and Schömberg, just short of the enemy frontier.

More than twenty miles of the Silesian-Bohemian border were absolutely barred to strategic movement by the curtain of the Riesen-Gebirge. This was the highest ground in Central Europe, and patrols faced a climb of nearly 5,000 feet to the top of the ridge. They passed through rocky forests of tall spruce, then a zone of waist-high pine (Pinus mughus), and emerged at last on a clattering scree of dark grey stones. They were rewarded by a view which stretched deep into Saxony, Silesia and Bohemia, taking in the scene of two-thirds of Frederick's campaigning.

The invasion route closest under the eastern flank of the Riesen-Gebirge ran by way of the Liebau position to Schatzlar and Trautenau in Bohemia. It was winding and steep, and decanted the Prussians into the depths of the Königreich-Wald. They usually found it more convenient to use the avenue to Braunau and Nachod which, as we have seen, presented no natural difficulties, 'besides the Braunau route is to be preferred because, whenever we are campaigning in Silesia, we must regard the Oder as our nursing mother' ('Principes Généraux', 1748, Oeuvres, XXVIII, 10). Here Frederick was thinking about the facility of communications from the river at Breslau.

The effective strategic border of north-east Bohemia ran about fifteen miles inside the political one. It was easy enough for the rival armies to pass through Nachod and Braunau, but they came into prolonged confrontation in the area of Jaromiersch and Königgrätz. This was where the dark masses of the Königreich-Wald and the Königgrätzer-Wald came together, and where the Aupa, the Mettau and the Adler converged on the upper Elbe – an accumulation of natural obstacles which formed the most important choke point in the theatre of Frederick's wars. The king came this way in 1744, 1745, 1758, and again as an old man twenty years later. It was no coincidence that the last battle between Prussia and Austria was to be fought on the same ground in 1866.

Minor features of the terrain

As we shall have occasion to notice, the routes of Central Europe answered passably well to the needs of contemporary armies. What they lacked in hardness and consistency of surface they made good by their magnificent profusion, and their very lack of definition made it possible for troops and vehicles to by-pass the worst of the ruts and muddy patches.

The cereals were the ancient tall-stalked strains of the kind which may be seen in Silesia today, reaching six feet or more high. This mass of vegetation offered fair concealment to infantrymen, and after midsummer showers it exuded dense banks of vapour in the warmth of the sunshine.

The most common material used in the construction of villages was wattle and daub – whether supported by well-built half-timbering, as in the Neumark settlements, or heaped up in something cruder, as in Bohemia and Moravia. Brick-built houses and barns were, however, to be found in the neighbourhood of Breslau, and on both the Silesian and Bohemian sides of the Riesen-Gebirge the cabins were made of horizontally laid squared-off logs. Thatch was the usual roof covering in Austrian territory, while red tiles were almost universal in Silesia.

Throughout the theatre of war the general aspect of the villages was one of astonishing uniformity. The dwellings were oblong, single-storey affairs, about forty-five feet in length, and arranged parallel or perpendicular to the dusty road in front. Barns and connecting walls of clay might lend a deceptive air of continuity and solidity to the centres of some villages; more frequently, however, the houses stood apart in little plots of ground, marked off by low picket fences, which had the effect of stringing the villages at some length along the main street, or even for miles up some of the higher Silesian valleys. Altogether the light construction, the open plan, and the lack of depth of the villages of Central Europe rendered most of them completely unsuitable for defence. Usually the only feature of tactical significance was the village church, standing in a prominent position behind a thick cemetery wall.

Conversely, the ponds were numerous and extensive, for they served for the rearing of waterfowl and carp, which were important sources of protein. Frequently they were artificial constructions, running in chains down the course of a little stream. Even after the earthen retaining dams were opened in springtime, to allow grass to grow in the beds, the pond sites presented muddy and deep obstacles. Field-Marshal Schwerin experienced this outside Prague in 1757. The

larger standing ponds, like the Dorf-See at Kunersdorf, were capable
of diverting the path of an entire army.

CHAPTER FIVE

The Seven Years War, 1756–63

The Prussian army crossed the Saxon border on a wide frontage on 29 August 1756. On the right flank the regiments of Prince Ferdinand of Brunswick poured through Leipzig under the eyes of the astonished citizenry. The main force made direct for Dresden, but the Prussians were not quick enough to catch the Saxon army of 19,000 troops, who at once recoiled out of Frederick's reach to the Camp of Pirna.

Frederick entered the undefended city of Dresden on 9 September, and the next day he rode south-east in search of the Saxons. He found them entrenched on the left bank of the Elbe in one of the most tactically strong positions in Central Europe. The western salient of the Camp of Pirna rested on the old walls and modern casemated bastions of the castle of Sonnenstein, overlooking the main square of the little town of Pirna. The corresponding eastern bulwark was formed by the great fortress of Königstein, which had been hewn out of the living rock by generations of Saxons to serve as the ultimate refuge of the electorate. The winding gorge of the Elbe rendered the long side of the encampment absolutely inaccessible. On the southern, or landward, side, the Saxons had cut abatis through the tangled country from Königstein to the neighbourhood of Neuendorf. The continuation to Sonnenstein bordered the near side of the wide Gottleuba valley, and it was along this more open sector that the Saxons concentrated their forces and their earthworks.

Frederick lodged himself in the baroque mansion of Gross-Sedlitz, from which he had a clear view of the southern front of the Saxon position beyond the Gottleuba. The sheer-sided plateau of Königstein was visible to the right, and beside it rose the bulky lump of Lilienstein, which was actually on the far side of the Elbe. Frederick carried out further reconnaissances on 11 and 16 September, but he found ample time to tour the lines of the Prussian camp: 'He is as relaxed and happy as if he was living in a time of profound peace. He is never morose, in spite of his great and manifold occupations. He has a word for everybody he encounters . . . and he mixes with his

101

soldiers as amicably as among children' (Ewald von Kleist to Gleim, in Volz, 1926–7, II, 4).

Both the armies were anxious not to take the initiative in opening hostilities, and indeed the first Prussian soldier was not killed until 12 September – the victim of a minor skirmish. Historians have wondered ever since why Frederick, having gone to so much trouble to secure a strategic surprise, now seemed oblivious of the passage of time. Perhaps he hoped from one day to the next that starvation was about to force the Saxons to surrender, and so yield him a rich prize of hungry but intact troops.

Frederick pushed the first troops across the border into nearby Bohemia on 13 September. He wished to open fresh foraging country to his cavalry, and he was anxious to know of the exact whereabouts of the Austrian field-marshal Browne, who was assembling the enemy troops somewhere in north Bohemia. Frederick became dissatisfied with the quality of the reports he was receiving from Keith, who was in charge of the growing Prussian force in Bohemia, and so on the 28th he betook himself to the camp of Johnsdorf and assumed personal command.

On 30 September Frederick directed the 28,500 men of the army on a forced march up the stony roads of the Bohemian Mittel-Gebirge and over the pass of Paschkopole to Wellemin, just short of the Bohemian plain. The departure had been delayed by one of the heavy autumn fogs that are so common in those parts, and in order to make up the time the troops had to hurry through the afternoon and well into the night, which fell at seven in the evening.

Frederick was taken by the resemblance between the name of Wellemin and that of his favourite sister Wilhelmine, and he was in a good humour as he settled for the night in the relative comfort of his travelling coach. His generals and staff officers lay around him under the open sky: 'They served, as it were, as a protection for the greatest treasure which Providence has bestowed upon mankind in this present age' (Pauli, 1758–64, V, 55).

At 5.30 on the misty morning of 1 October Frederick and his generals set out to join the six battalions of the advance guard at the southern exit of the last valley of the Mittel-Gebirge. On the way he was met by an officer who reported that, as far as could be distinguished in the fog, the Austrian army appeared to be deploying on the plain below. Frederick rode on a little further, then abruptly turned his horse around and hastened back to rejoin his main force. At six he advanced the infantry down the valley in two columns, while the cavalry moved up close behind in three lines, taking up almost the entire width of the valley floor.

In its small compass the field of Lobositz owned almost every conceivable variety of landscape. Out to the north-east it was bounded by a bend of the river Elbe. To the south there rose the little town of Lobositz, and in front of that stretched the channels, ponds and swamps of the Morellen-Bach. Further west, the direction from which the Prussians were advancing, the plain of Lobositz narrowed into a valley as it entered the curious landscape of a denuded range of extinct volcanoes. To the left, as the Prussians saw it, the eerie cone of the Lobosch Hill rose to a height of 420 metres above the valley floor. The summit was a basalt plug, and on the steep slopes the fertile soil had been terraced into vineyards, divided from one another by dry-stone walls of grey volcanic rock.

On the right or southern side of the valley exit the ground rose to the lower but still respectable height of the Homolka-Berg. This was a smooth-topped, commanding height, a kind of elder brother to the Graner-Koppe at Soor, and, since it was unoccupied by the Austrians, Lieutenant-Colonel Moller planted one of the heavy batteries there. This seems to have comprised four 24-pounders, five 12-pounders, and one or more howitzers.

Frederick followed the right wing of the infantry as it advanced up the Homolka-Berg. The summit was bathed in sunlight, but in the plain to the east the town of Lobositz could be discerned only 'as if through a veil' (PC 8378). In fact he notes that 'the fog was so thick that all that you could make out was a sort of enemy rearguard. It appeared that one attack would be enough to make this force recoil to the rear. I am short-sighted, and I asked some officers with better eyes than mine to tell me what was going on, but they could see no more than I did' (PC 8144).

This 'rearguard' consisted of the main Austrian army of 34,000 men, which Field-Marshal Browne had artfully disposed in concealed positions over the landscape. His Croatian light infantry on the Lobosch was supported by the regulars of the corps of Lacy, standing in readiness behind the hill. The bulk of the Austrian horse and foot was held to the south, behind the Morellen-Bach, and between this force and Lacy a line of grenadiers and Croats was hidden in a sunken road. Many of the Austrian infantry were lying flat on the ground, and at least one of Browne's batteries of heavy guns was concealed behind a screen of cavalry. His plan was to stage a limited holding action around Lobositz, and later slip across to the right bank of the Elbe and lead a flying corps to the relief of the Saxons.

The Austrians opened the battle with a cannonade from their powerful battery in front of Lobositz. The regiment of Hülsen (21; see Map 6, p. 345) was standing at the foot of the Lobosch Hill, an easy target for the Austrian guns, and musketeer Franz Reiss recalled:

When the cannon at first spoke out, one of the shot carried
away half the head of my comrade Krumholtz. He had been
standing right next to me, and my face was spattered with
earth, and brains and fragments of skull. My musket was
plucked from my shoulder and shattered in a thousand pieces,
but in spite of everything I remained unscathed, thanks be to
God. (*Urkundliche Beiträge*, I, *Heft* 2, 30)

The bombardment continued with a violence that was beyond the
Prussians' experience, and whole files of their soldiers were being
carried away at a time.

Frederick and his companions on the Homolka-Berg were in the
path of the shot which flew over the regiment of Alt-Anhalt (3),
standing directly to their front. Early in the cannonade Major-
General Quadt was hit by a splinter from a shattered stone, and he
tumbled, mortally wounded, over the back of his horse. Frederick was
urged to take cover from the raging missiles, but he replied, 'I did not
come here to avoid them' (Brunswick, 1902, I, *Heft* 4, 36).

The Prussian battery on the Homolka exacted a revenge from the
bodies of Austrian cavalry which were dimly seen to be manoeuvring
in chequer-board formation on the plain. The Austrians lost
Lieutenant-General Radicati, one of their most popular leaders (his
red marble monument is to be seen in the cathedral at Leitmeritz),
but their squadrons calmly continued their evolutions, so as to throw
the Prussian gunners off their aim. The Prussians deployed two
further batteries in the course of the action – one on the valley floor,
and another a short way up the Lobosch – but Frederick's army
enjoyed no respite from the Austrian cannonade.

Before 7 a.m. Frederick ordered the solid and genial Duke of
Bevern to clear the Lobosch with the left wing of the infantry. Bevern
advanced three regiments up the slopes, and he sent word before long
that he was heavily engaged with the enemy.

At about the same time Frederick allowed himself to be persuaded by his brother August Wilhelm to dispatch a reconnaissance
in force to clarify the situation in the plain. Eight squadrons of
cavalry were chosen for this task, and while they were filtering
through and around the battalions of infantry to the foot of the
Homolka, their commander, Lieutenant-General Kyau, told
Frederick that he believed he could detect a force of Austrian grenadiers in a dangerous flanking position in a little village (Sullowitz),
and that there were two lines of enemy cavalry behind. 'At this the
king became impatient, and told him to attack regardless' (Brunswick, 1902, I, *Heft* 4, 35).

The glittering troopers of the Garde du Corps (C 13), the Gens d'armes (C 10) and two squadrons of Prinz von Preussen (C 2) soon discovered the presence of the Austrians for themselves. During the advance the Garde du Corps veered sharply to its left, in order to avoid the musketry fire from Sullowitz, and by this movement they exposed the right flank of the Prussian force to a counter-attack by the Austrian Erherzog Joseph Dragoons (D 1). Frederick had raised himself in the saddle, and when the first clash came he sat back and exclaimed, 'Now they are off!' (Westphalen, 1859–72, I, 157). The Prussian Bayreuth Dragoons (D 5) intervened to rescue the cuirassiers, whereupon the Austrian horse withdrew swiftly and expertly behind their batteries, exposing the Prussians to a devastating fire of roundshot and canister.

The broken Prussian squadrons streamed back towards the Homolka in disarray, but Frederick saw that one of the Garde du Corps, bleeding and hatless, had forced his horse about and was making back towards the Austrian positions. ' "Wait a moment!" said the king. He drew his handkerchief from his pocket, and an adjutant took it to the cavalryman to enable him to bandage his head. "My thanks", replied the Garde du Corps. "You won't see it again, but I'll get my own back on the enemy and make them pay for it!" ' (Anon., 1787–9, XI, 19). With this he spurred away.

Frederick had rather less sympathy for the rest of Kyau's force, and he told the Alt-Anhalt musketeers, 'Pay attention to what the officers order you to do. Don't let the cavalry through. Shoot them down if you have to' (Urkundliche Beiträge, 1901, I, Heft 2, 3). In the event the survivors re-formed on the remainder of the Prussian cavalry (forty-three squadrons), which had meanwhile filtered through the intervals of the infantry and formed two disorderly lines. These 10,000 troopers became restless under the Austrian cannonade, and without waiting for any command they surged towards the Austrian positions. Frederick exclaimed, 'My God, what is my cavalry doing! They're attacking a second time, and nobody gave the order!' (Brunswick, 1902, I, Heft 4, 37).

The attack divided into two main masses. The Austrian grenadiers and Croats made rapidly to either side as the left-hand group broke across the sunken road, and the Prussians were badly shot up by artillery and musketry, and hit by a counter-attack of three regiments of Austrian cuirassiers.

To the right, a number of regiments spilled into the Morellen-Bach. Kalkreuth writes that 'many horses were too weak to struggle up the high bank from the swampy hollow. I remember seeing a Schönaich Hussar lying dead in the lines of the Austrian infantry. A lot of the cavalry stuck fast in the mud on the far side, and they lost a great number of dead and wounded' (1840, II, 129). Colonel Seydlitz of the Rochow Cuirassiers (C 8) was one of those that had to be rescued from the mud.

The disorganised cavalry was now good for nothing except to help to fill out the single line of infantry which stretched across the valley floor. All the rest of the battalions were being fed into the battle on the Lobosch – the Jung-Billerbeck Grenadiers (5/20), the second battalion of Itzenplitz (13), the Kleist Grenadiers (3/6), and finally the first battalion of Munchow (36) and the second battalion of Hülsen (21). Frederick told Ferdinand of Brunswick to arrange to have thirty cartridges taken from each man of the unengaged battalions on the right and sent to the battling troops on the Lobosch.

The resistance of the Croats on the hill was now stiffened by three battalions and three grenadier companies of Austrian regulars, which were dispatched by Colonel Lacy from behind the hill. Meanwhile in the plain the mournful thudding of the Austrian drums carried across to the Prussians, and a force of Austrian infantry (cavalry, according to some accounts) appeared to be making ready to launch a counter-attack from Sullowitz. They were driven back by artillery fire from the Homolka, and some well-lobbed howitzer shells set fire to the houses of Sullowitz, which made the village untenable for the Austrians.

By 1 p.m., some of Frederick's generals on the Homolka were in the grip of panic. The heavy batteries were almost out of ammunition, as was the infantry. The cavalry horses could hardly drag themselves along, for their strength was sapped not only by the two exhausting attacks, but by the previous days of hard marching and inadequate fodder. Everywhere the initiative seemed to be passing to the Austrians, in spite of the check at Sullowitz, and the fog had long since lifted from the plain, revealing the unengaged main force of the Austrian army drawn up in two lines behind the Morellen-Bach.

Frederick took his leave of the battle, after sending word to Bevern to make one last attack on the Lobosch. The king was still riding away from the field when Bevern's troops made a push with the bayonet and dislodged the Austrians from their walls and ditches. Ferdinand asked Keith if the infantry of the right wing should advance in support, and he was told, 'Yes, go ahead' (Brunswick, 1902, I, *Heft* 4, 41).

The battle roared up again outside Lobositz town, where the Austrians rallied and opened fire from windows and holes in the roofs. Ferdinand brought up some howitzers, which usefully set fire to a number of houses, and the Jung-Billerbeck and Kleist Grenadiers and some of the musketeers of Arnim led a successful assault on the little town, where the flames were claiming the Austrian dead and wounded. The action came to an end between 3 and 4 p.m., when the fresh and intact Austrian force made a simultaneous right turn and was pushed by Browne north to the Elbe behind Lobositz, forming an impenetrable barrier to the pursuit.

Major Oelsnitz found the king at the village of Bilinka, and persuaded him only with some difficulty that the Austrians had been dislodged. Frederick ordered the generals to meet him in Wchinitz, hard under the Homolka mound. Here they held a kind of council of war, in which Ferdinand of Brunswick was able to carry the argument against the generals who spoke in favour of retreating. The nerves of the Prussians were still on edge, however, and a single round from an Austrian heavy cannon was enough to awaken fears of an enemy counter-attack. This was in fact Browne's signal for the Austrian army to withdraw from its blocking position behind Lobositz, leaving the ground to the Prussians.

In the late afternoon the Prussians pitched their tents among the dead and wounded, and, as happened so often after battles, the heavens responded with peals of thunder and showered the field with rain. The Prussians had suffered about 2,900 casualties, which slightly exceeded the enemy losses. The gallant Garde du Corps to whom Frederick had given his handkerchief was nowhere to be found in the ranks. 'After an intensive search he was discovered dead on the field. He had received many cuts and bullet wounds, and his empty pistol was in his right hand. The king's handkerchief was still wound about his head' (Anon., 1787–9, X, 19–20).

The immediate tactical victory undoubtedly lay with the Prussians. As Frederick wrote to Moritz of Dessau on 2 October: 'You might think you know our army, but I assure you that after yesterday's test you would believe that nothing is beyond its powers' (PC 8146). Admittedly the cavalry had shown that aggressive instincts alone were of no account unless subject to discipline and control, but once more the incomparable infantry had carried the day.

As for the management of the affair, Frederick conceded that he had misread the field in the early morning mists, and run into an Austrian army when he thought he was chasing a rearguard. After the repulse of the second cavalry attack he had posted the horse in the centre of the line of battle, and 'by means of this novel and slightly unorthodox manoeuvre I was able to outflank the enemy right with my weak force of infantry, and ultimately take the town of Lobositz, evicting the enemy and compelling them to retreat' (PC 8146). He did not mention that the last sentences covered a period when he was already absent from the field, and incapable of exerting any influence on the decisive phase of the combat.

It is not at all easy to identify the moral victory. This was the most disconcerting action in which Frederick had yet been engaged.

It was also the longest drawn out, and it finished with the Prussians at the end of their resources and the Austrians with the bulk of their troops intact. The enemy had appeared to absorb themselves into the texture of the landscape. Their infantry had stood with a firmness which it had never displayed before, and their artillery now seemed capable of dominating a battlefield. Frederick at once grasped the implications. He told Schwerin: 'We will have to be very careful not to attack them like a pack of hussars. Nowadays they are up to all sorts of ruses, and, believe me, unless we can bring a lot of cannon against them, we will lose a vast number of men before we can gain the upper hand' (PC 8144).

In the *Principes Généraux* Frederick had written sternly about the necessity of concentrating all available forces for combat, yet at Lobositz he went into action at the head of less than half of the troops he had brought into Saxony. Most of the rest were still blocking the Pirna camp. The Austrians were not displeased to find that Frederick was committed so deeply inside Bohemia on the western side of the Elbe. This gave Field-Marshal Browne the chance he had been seeking to assemble a flying corps of 8,800 men on the east bank, and march through the hills and attempt to break through to relieve the Saxons.

On 13 October the king left Lobositz for Saxony, and told Keith to make arrangements to evacuate the army from Bohemia, since it was impossible for the cavalry to subsist any longer in this exhausted countryside. Frederick was hastening north because he had learnt of the unexpected appearance of the Austrian corps of relief on the right bank of the Elbe nearly opposite the Pirna camp. He reached Struppen early on the afternoon of 14 October, and was told that the starving Saxons had crossed to the right bank the day before. These wretched folk had been unable to establish contact with Browne, and were now piled in demoralised confusion at the foot of the Lilienstein rock.

The Saxon commander Rutowski opened negotiations later on the afternoon of the 14th, and harsh terms of capitulation were soon agreed. The Saxon officers were allowed their freedom, but the men were yielded 'at discretion' – in other words, left to the mercy of the Prussians. One of the Gardes du Corps caught sight of Frederick dining with the Saxon generals after the document had been signed: 'Opposite the king sat the deserving Field-Marshal Rutowski, who had commanded the Saxons. His situation was at once sad and humiliating, but Frederick was speaking to him about "Joseph", the king of Poland's court dwarf, and he went on to express his delight at the skill of the clown Petrini in these comic arts' (Kalkreuth, 1840, II, 131).

On 17 October the Saxons filed back across the Elbe by a bridge of boats which had been built by the Prussians. Frederick had long harboured the ambition of incorporating the Saxons in his army, and the hideous process of enrolling the troops extended into the 19th:

> Frederick was present in person while they forced the soldiers to swear allegiance to him. The auditors murmured the words of this so-called oath of loyalty in front of the men, and those who refused to repeat it were punished by the Prussian soldiers . . . The king so far forgot himself as to use his own stick on a young nobleman, an ensign in the regiment of Crousatz, and he told him: 'You must be totally devoid of ambition and honour, not to wish to enter the Prussian service!' (Lieutenant-General Vitzthum, in Vitzthum, 1866, 251–2)

The Prussian army was used to dealing with involuntary recruits, but Frederick unwisely rejected the usual expedient of dividing the captives among existing Prussian units, and instead he formed the 18,500 surviving Saxons into ten complete regiments, commanded by second-rate Prussian officers. The result was that by the spring of 1757 the Saxons were deserting in whole battalions and regiments. Many of them were re-formed into auxiliary units in the Austrian army, which gave them the opportunity to continue their long-enduring blood feud against the Prussians.

In November 1756 the army was distributed in quarters in Saxony, and soldiers and officers settled into the overheated tobacco-laden fug that was the environment of the Prussian army in wintertime. Frederick fixed himself for the season in the Dresden palace of Count Brühl, the Saxon prime minister, and discovered that this gentleman had left behind 304 pairs of breeches in his wardrobe. The king played the flute in evening concerts, and he passed many agreeable hours at the oratorios of Herr Hasse, or in listening to the elaborate masses in the Catholic church. He frequently betook himself to the celebrated royal picture gallery and sat for minutes at a time in front of Correggio's *Notte*.

Meanwhile Saxony lay at the Prussians' disposal. The British envoy to Dresden had already reported on 12 September:

> I think it is every day more evident that His Prussian Majesty's design is to keep this country as a deposit during the war, and to take upon himself the whole management of the affairs of Saxony. All the royal chests, and, in short, the whole revenue, is already seized, and all the officers in the several branches of it, removed. (Lord Stormont, PRO SP 88/79)

This unholy business was to be managed by a special department of the military commissariat, acting under the immediate orders of Frederick. Between the autumn of 1756 and February 1763 the Saxon resources in recruits, fodder and cereals made an important and direct contribution towards maintaining the Prussian army in the war, while the exactions in cash amounted to the huge sum of 48,000,000 thaler, which greatly exceeded the 27,500,000 thaler of Frederick's subsidy from the British, and amounted to more than one-third of the total cost of the war (Hubatsch, 1973, 120; Johnson, 1975, 170).

Frederick did not hesitate to take hostages and threaten military executions against property, so as to extort the necessary sums from Leipzig and other trading centres (PC 9789, 10352, 10546, 10555, 10572, 10617). Even the British envoy Mitchell, who was a friend of the king, was taken aback when on 5 January 1761 the Prussians arrested between fifty and sixty merchants in Leipzig and incarcerated them in the town hall.

All of this could be justified in terms of military necessity. There remained, however, an element of vandalism for which it is difficult to find any explanation save personal vengeance on Frederick's part. Many of the Prussian officers were disturbed by what they saw, and two episodes in particular aroused much comment and debate. In October 1757 Frederick was said to have allowed the Garde to plunder the castle of Grochwitz, which belonged to Count Brühl, one of the alleged authors of the enemy alliance. Still better authenticated was the treatment meted out in 1761 to the hunting lodge of Hubertus-burg, which Frederick knew to be dear to the heart of the king and elector Augustus. The upright Saldern flatly refused Frederick's order to ransack the castle (see p. 334), and 'the free battalion of Quintus Icilius was given the commission instead. This business was completed within a few hours, and carried through with such zeal that nothing was left but the naked walls' (Archenholtz, 1840, II, 99).

In the autumn campaign of 1756 Frederick had removed the Saxon army as a formed body from the potential enemy order of battle, and won a most important strategic and material base for continuing the war. Nevertheless, the veterans and commentators often asked themselves whether gains even of this magnitude were worth the expenditure of considerable advantages which by the nature of things Frederick could not recover, namely the unique peacetime war-readiness of the Prussian army and the initiative in opening hostilities.

The cavalryman Kalkreuth was among the first troops to enter Bohemia, and he claims that the 'most expert of the Prussian officers were of the opinion that we could have left the Saxons under some kind of blockade, and marched directly on Prague and Vienna. The Austrians were moving up so slowly that Frederick might have been able to settle the issue of the war in the course of this campaign'

(Kalkreuth, 1840, II, 126). The historian Delbrück suggests that if
Frederick had not delayed he could have brought between seventy
and eighty thousand men into Bohemia by the middle of August,
followed by thirty or forty thousand more after Pirna had fallen
(Delbrück, 1890, 32–6; Delbrück, 1892, 10–11; Lehmann, 1894, 80–2).

Now the Austrians were in the war with their forces intact, and
they were able to exploit the Prussian breach of the peace by conclud-
ing their offensive alliances with the Russians and the French.
Frederick described the campaign of 1756 as 'setting out the pieces in a
game of chess' (PC 8255). It was more like the opening of a cage of
lions.

'To read the newspapers you might think that a pack of kings and
princes was bent on hunting me down like a stag, and that they were
inviting their friends to the chase.' So Frederick described the state of
affairs to Wilhelmine on 7 February 1757, by which time the allies
were concerting their plans for military operations against Prussia.
The king nevertheless added: 'As for myself I am absolutely determined not to oblige them in this respect. In fact, I am confident that I
am the one who will be doing the hunting' (PC 8580).

The design of Frederick's spoiling attack in Bohemia in the spring
of 1757 was to exert a particular fascination for German historians at
the end of the nineteenth century. Some of them perceived the spirit
of Napoleon and von Moltke the Elder in the way Frederick brought together converging forces to effect a powerful concentration of troops
deep in enemy land, and then engaged the foe in a decisive battle (e.g.
Caemmerer, 1883, 4–6; Malachowski, 1892, 348–9; Gr. Gstb., 1901–14,
II, 150–4; Koser, 1904a, 248; Koser, 1904b, 71–4). The heroic simplicities of this concept were, however, brought into some doubt by Hans
Delbrück and his school, who drew attention to Frederick's frequent
changes of mind, and the extent to which his strategy fell short of the
ideal of 'overthrow' (Delbrück, 1892, 9–41; Delbrück, 1904a, 69).

It was probably not until the second half of March that Frederick
could be reasonably confident that the French were as yet unready to
take an immediate part in operations, and that he therefore had
several weeks at his command in which he could devote his almost
undivided attention to the Austrians. In the meantime he kept open a
number of options, ranging from proposals for a vigorous attack into
Bohemia, to various schemes for waiting for the enemy on the near
side of the border hills.

Frederick debated the practicability of the possible strategies
with Lieutenant-General Winterfeldt and the seventy-two-year-old
Field-Marshal Schwerin. On 19 March Winterfeldt focused
Frederick's attention on the central issue, which was the danger of

allowing the Austrians the leisure to build up their forces in Bohemia
until the French arrived on the scene. He therefore proposed a blow
against the important magazines at Königgrätz and Pardubitz (*PC*
8757). The principle of pre-emptive action was reaffirmed on 30
March, when Schwerin, Winterfeldt and Frederick's representative,
Major-General von der Goltz, met in conference at Frankenstein in
Silesia.

The report of the Frankenstein meeting reached Frederick in his
new headquarters, at Lockwitz near Dresden, on 3 April. Frederick
now brought together the proposals of Winterfeldt and Schwerin with
the results of his own cogitations, and he rapidly outlined the features
of something far more ambitious than the original design to strike at
the magazines on the upper Elbe. The 116,000 men of the available
field army (including gunners) were to advance from Saxony and
Silesia across the Bohemian border on an initial frontage of about 130
miles. The break-in was to be accomplished by four widely separated
columns, which would combine two-by-two into two armies, one on
each side of the Elbe. From west to east the disposition ran as follows:

(A) West bank of the Elbe
1   Prince Moritz of Dessau (19,300) advancing from western Saxony
     and down the valley of the Eger.
2   The royal army (39,600) moving up the left bank of the Elbe.
(B) East bank of the Elbe
1   The Duke of Bevern (20,300) crossing from Lusatia and descending
     the Iser in the direction of the large magazine at Jung-Bunzlau.
2   Schwerin with the Silesian army (34,000) entering Bohemia near
     Trautenau, and moving smartly west to join Bevern.

According to the original scheme the two armies were to unite inside
Bohemia in the region of Leitmeritz, 'as the navigation of the Elbe is
most essential, and must be preserved' (Mitchell, 19 April, in Mitchell, 1850, I, 239). The transport trains carrying the dry fodder would
see the Prussians through the first days of their advance, after which
they looked to the supplies in the captured Austrian magazines.

By timing his invasion before the grass was growing, Frederick
might hope to catch the enemy at an important disadvantage. The
Austrian commander, Field-Marshal Browne, was now the prey of
tuberculosis, and in his feverish over-optimism he could contemplate
nothing but his schemes for the eventual Austrian offensive. Meanwhile the Austrians remained in quarters in four scattered groups,
namely (again from west to east) Arenberg with 24,000 troops around
Plan, Browne's own 30,000 between Prague and the Eger, Königsegg
with 28,000 at Reichenberg near the border with Lusatia, and the

sluggish Serbelloni with 27,000 well to the east around Königgrätz.

Nobody has established with conviction whether or not Frederick hoped from the outset to bring the whole war to an end by some Armageddon in northern Bohemia, or whether he merely intended to snatch a rapid advantage at the expense of the Austrians and then turn back and confront the French. No less an authority than the retired *Generaloberst* Count Schlieffen pronounced on the subject shortly before the Great War. He concluded that for really decisive results against the Austrians, Frederick should have employed no less than 150,000 men, which he could have assembled by stripping East Prussia, Pomerania and the Prussian Rhineland. Schlieffen conjectured that Frederick shrank from committing himself too fully in Bohemia because he desired to conserve his resources for the battle against the French, whose military qualities he overestimated (Boehm-Tettelbach, 1934, 23–4, 27).

While his troops were in the process of gathering, Frederick maintained a security as strict as that before the invasion of Saxony in 1756, and initiated only ten other people into the great secret (*PC* 8834). He ordered Bevern and Moritz to carry out limited raids along the borders, so as to confuse the Austrians and throw them onto the local defensive, and on 18 April 1757 and the following days the Prussians descended from the hills in full force. Surprise was complete, and the enemy were thrown into consternation. (See Map 7, p. 347.)

The royal army passed the Mittel-Gebirge without opposition, and on 25 April it reached the plain of Lobositz, which was still reeking from the dead of the action of the year before. On this day Frederick completed the union with the corps of Prince Moritz, giving him a combined army of nearly 60,000 men. Well beyond the Elbe, Bevern evicted the Austrian corps at Reichenberg from its positions on 21 April, and four days later he was in contact with Schwerin's army on the Iser.

Casting aside the original scheme of waiting for all the Prussian forces to unite around Leitmeritz, Frederick pressed south against the river line of the Eger, where Browne and the hastily reassembling Austrian army were expected to make a stand. The Prussians marched all through the night of 26 April, and between four and eight the next morning they passed the little river Eger by two bridges of boats at Koschtitz. They encountered no opposition, for Moritz had chosen a site well upstream of the Austrian camp at Budin.

The army hastened across the meadows on the far side of the Eger, and climbed the long, tree-covered Budin ridge which should have offered the Austrians an excellent blocking position. The ground descended beyond the ridge then rose again to the bare plateau of Charwatetz, opening up a view over an immense horizon to the east and south. Clouds of dust were rising from the plain, and Frederick feared at first that the Austrians might be moving to attack the Koschtitz crossing, but at noon the enemy were distinctly seen to be retreating south-east towards Welwarn.

Frederick moved his headquarters to Charwatetz on the 28th, and learnt on this day that Bevern and Schwerin had joined on the Iser. His own army had found enough supplies in Budin to carry it all the way to Prague, and on 30 April the force set out in battle order. The British envoy Mitchell wrote:

> The country is an open and fertile plain cut sometimes with ravines but has very few trees. Along the road was spilt a great quantity of oats occasioned by the precipitate march of the Austrians from Budin to Welwarn, and in the market place of Welwarn I saw about eighty large barrels of flour which they had not the time to destroy, having only knocked out the tops and bottoms of the barrels. (PRO SP 90/69)

On 1 May Frederick's army pushed to within a single march of Prague. Frederick was with the advance guard, which followed close on the heels of the Austrians, and he established his headquarters for the night in the Jesuit house at Tuchomirschitz, standing on a bluff with a view along a pretty wooded valley which led down to Prague, just six miles away. He was told that Browne and the newly arrived Prince Charles of Lorraine had only just vacated their lodgings in the same building, and that they had argued so violently that they had nearly come to blows.

Frederick had hoped to bring the enemy to battle on the west, or near, side of the Moldau, but at this time the Austrians were actually in the process of withdrawing to the far bank of the river at Prague. They were now stationed in the strategic triangle formed by the confluence of the Moldau and the Elbe, and they might, with more energetic leadership, have exploited their central position in order to fall on Frederick or Schwerin while the two Prussian armies were still separated. Schwerin, indeed, was out of touch with Frederick for a number of perilous days, and he crossed the Elbe at Brandeis into our triangle only on 4 May, which was about four days later than Frederick had supposed.

Frederick presented himself before Prague with a powerful advance guard on 2 May and discovered that the Austrians had eluded him. The rest of the army arrived in the evening, soaked by rain and in some disorder, and on 3 May the king allowed the troops some much-needed rest. This day was one of heavy showers, bursts of sunshine and rainbows, and in the clear air the Prussians could see the Croats as they stalked the ramparts of Prague in their red cloaks. More significantly, Frederick's telescope revealed the lines of the Austrian army, which had taken up position on the far side of the Moldau on the plateau immediately to the east of the city. Prince Charles's generals had rejected all talk of retreating any further into the centre of Bohemia (something which Schwerin at that time was in no position to prevent) and they had determined to make a stand outside Prague. Frederick was going to have his battle after all.

Mitchell dined with Frederick on 4 May. 'He was very hearty and cheerful, and told me in a day or two the battle of Pharsalia between the Houses of Austria and Brandenburg would be fought' (Mitchell, 1850, I, 325; on Frederick's ambitions see also Henckel von Donnersmarck, 1858, I, part 2, 192).

Frederick's plan was to bring his army into the Moldau-Elbe triangle, unite there with Schwerin under the noses of the Austrians, and attack without delay. Thirty-two thousand troops were to be left under Field-Marshal Keith on the left bank of the Moldau opposite Prague (apparently to prevent the Austrians from escaping to the west), but Frederick and Schwerin combined would still have 64,000 men at their disposal, which exceeded the Austrian army by about 4,000.

On 5 May the royal army crossed to the right bank of the Moldau by a bridge of boats which had been cast across the river at Seltz, four miles below Prague. No word arrived from Schwerin, but Frederick sent an adjutant to tell him to bring his army early next morning to the plateau of Prosek, about three miles north of the Austrian camp.

Frederick's army was on the march again at five on the morning of 6 May, and just over an hour later Schwerin's columns swung into alignment, forming the left or eastern wing of the united force. Frederick was glad to see Schwerin and Winterfeldt again:

> With his usual cheerfulness he called out, 'Good morning, gentlemen!' Then he rode with them and a few adjutants to the heights of Broditz, and saw the whole enemy camp stretching before him. 'Good morning to you too!' he shouted in a jocular way to the Austrians, when the appearance of the royal suite induced them to fire a few cannon in the direction of the hill. One of the shot buried itself in the earth close to the king.
> (Hildebrandt, 1829–35, III, 175–6)

Winterfeldt timed the reunion of the commanders at 6.30 a.m., and noted: 'The king was determined to attack the enemy without more ado – a sentiment shared by Field-Marshal Schwerin as well as my humble self. Now we had to find a suitable gap' (Volz, 1926–7, II, 18).

For some minutes Frederick and his party remained on the highest point of the Prosek ridge, examining the Austrian positions. Many men in the Prussian army could see that their fate was being decided, and their speculations afterwards engendered a host of detailed but contradictory accounts as to what was debated on the hilltop.

Frederick eventually concluded that a frontal attack held little prospect of success, for the Austrian camp stretched along a broken plateau which overlooked the difficult valley of the lower Rocketnitzer-Bach. He accordingly sent Schwerin and Winterfeldt galloping off to the east to determine whether there was any prospect of reaching around and behind the Austrian right. He did not go with them in person for his stomach was violently upset. The two officers made a rapid reconnaissance, and saw that the eastern side of the plateau fell gently into a zone of green meadows which might indeed offer the Prussians an easy avenue to the rear of the enemy position.

The army moved off to the left in three columns at about seven o'clock on this fine morning, and it seemed that the whole landscape on both sides of the valley was covered by the troops of the rival forces. (See Map 8, p. 348.) The leading regiments veered to the right in the neighbourhood of the village of Hlaupetin, and hastened south so as to win an adequate frontage for their attack.

For a time the Austrians lost sight of the dark columns as they passed to the west of Chwala, but by about ten in the morning the direction of the movement had declared itself and the Austrian commanders began to rush detachments from their main body to-wards the open eastern flank. Forty companies of grenadiers were among the infantry whom Field-Marshal Browne collected for this purpose, and a mass of Austrian cavalry (twelve regiments of cuirassiers and dragoons, and five weak regiments of hussars) arrived at a blocking position between the village of Sterbohol and a large pond to the south.

The character of the opening phase of the battle was shaped by Schwerin, who was determined to throw in whatever troops first came to hand, in order to gain the eastern slopes of the plateau before the Austrians. Thus Lieutenant-General Schönaich and the twenty leading squadrons of the Prussian horse were pushed willy-nilly into combat with the multiple lines of the Austrian cavalry near Sterbohol. This gave rise to a long and indecisive battle while the cuirassiers and dragoons surged backwards and forwards, and the rival hussars sought to win the southern flanks of the enemy.

The first guns of the heavy artillery followed the cavalry for some time, but at Unter-Poczernitz the pieces stuck fast in the narrow streets. This blockage deprived the Prussians of the artillery support they so badly needed on this part of the field, and forced the regiments of the first line of the left wing of the infantry to spill over the meadows. Only now did the Prussians discover that some of the rich green levels on either side of the upper Rocketnitzer-Bach were in fact the drained beds of fishponds, and that the shoots of oats (upon which the carp would feed when the ponds were re-filled) sprouted from a soft black silt. In the worst patches the men were sinking up to their waists.

The Austrians were already forming a coherent line of infantry on the eastern slopes of the plateau, and Winterfeldt and Schwerin ordered their first fourteen battalions to press home the attack across the meadows. Frederick arrived near Sterbohol and questioned Schwerin as to the wisdom of this unsupported advance. The old field-marshal replied, 'We must strike while the iron is hot!' (Gr. Gstb., 1901–14, II, 131), and hastened ahead to assume personal control.

In accordance with the Prussian tactical doctrine obtaining at the start of the Seven Years War, the infantry were expected to frighten the enemy out of their positions just by advancing towards them with shouldered muskets. In the event the Austrians opened a long-range fire from a heavy battery on the low Homole-Berg (a Czech pillbox of the 1930s stands on the same spot), then employed the canister of their battalion guns, and finally engaged with their musketry. Whole files of the Prussians were being brought to the ground, and in the face of this ordeal the regiment of Kurssell (37; see Map 9, p. 351) fled under the scandalised eyes of the king, and the regiment of Fouqué (33) made off in total disorder and cast aside its muskets. Some of the men, Catholics from Silesia, stayed behind and loaded their muskets for the Austrians.

At this critical juncture the Prussians lost two of their leaders in rapid succession. Some time before 11 a.m. Winterfeldt was riding in front of the regiment of Schwerin (24) when a ball wounded him in the neck, and he fell unconscious from the saddle. Field-Marshal Schwerin now came hastening up on a little brown Polish horse and had the bleeding form of Winterfeldt hoisted onto a spare mount. Schwerin was disturbed to see that the men of his regiment were inclined to run away, and he snatched a colour of the second battalion in order to set an example to the troops. He had ridden forward no more than a few paces before a blast of canister removed half his head and lodged balls in his heart and stomach. As he fell to the ground the green flag collapsed at his side. It was, in the words of a royal archivist, 'the finest death in combat that has ever been related in the annals of Prussian military history' (Augstein, 1968, 279).

The news was brought to Frederick. 'Our great hero was shattered. A tear sprang from his eye, but few people noticed. He did his best to conceal his emotion and shouted out "There is nothing we can do about that. Let's be as determined as he was. March on!" ' (Dreyer, 1810, 35).

At about 11 a.m. the victorious Austrian infantry descended the slope from the plateau and began to push back the twelve battalions of Schwerin's second line. Things would have gone badly for Frederick if the infantry of his centre had not begun to exploit an opportunity which was opening up further to the north along the axis of the Kaiser-Strasse. This was a gap which yawned at the angle of the Austrian forces – between the positions of the main army, which was still facing north, and the detached regiments, which had hastened south-east and were now pushing back Schwerin's wing.

Altogether twenty-two Prussian battalions advanced through this region of lakes and headlands. Lieutenant-General Hautcharmoy led the march with the regiments of Hautcharmoy (28), Tresckow (32) and Meyerinck (26), and the Duke of Bevern exercised nominal control of the remainder of the force. In fact many of the regimental commanders groped their way forward on their own initiative, and Colonel Hertzberg found himself heading a small group of battalions in what turned out to be a decisive attack against the uncovered north flank of the detached Austrian wing. He had pushed his immediate command, the first battalion of Darmstadt (12), between the two ponds of Kej and up to the plateau, 'and such a silence had fallen on the battle that they could not hear a single shot during the whole of their march through the abandoned camp of the Austrian cavalry'. From here Hertzberg discovered the exposed wing of the Austrian infantry to the south, and he wheeled his men to the left. The following regiments of Prinz von Preussen (18) and Kannacher (30) conformed with this change of direction, and the scratch force of Prussians began to roll up the enemy units in succession, beginning with the regiments of Wied (28) and the Mainz auxiliaries. 'Nowadays the printed accounts ascribe this movement to the king. In fact it was quite impossible for him to have issued the appropriate orders, for he was far distant on the left wing' (Berenhorst, 1845–7, I, 102).

At about the same time Lieutenant-General Zieten at last turned the cavalry battle near Sterbohol to the advantage of the Prussians, by carrying twenty-five fresh squadrons around to the south of the pond and joining the Puttkamer and Werner Hussars (H 4, H 6) for an attack against the right wing of the Austrian cavalry. Zieten simply pronounced, 'Overthrow any enemy who appear!' and the word was taken up among the squadrons.

The Austrian right wing was therefore taken between two threats to its flanks and rear – from Hertzberg's force from the north, and the forty-five or so squadrons of Prussian cavalry to the south.

The counter-attack against Schwerin's infantry promptly collapsed, and ultimately many of the Austrian troops on this wing were cut off altogether from their main army and had to escape in the direction of Beneschau.

At about noon the Prussian breakthrough to the north began to roll up the principal Austrian position from its right flank. 'Now our fine and agreeable day was plunged into gloom. The whole air was darkened by the powder smoke, and by the dust thrown up by the thousands of men and horses. It was like the last day of the world' (letter of an Anhalt musketeer, *Urkundliche Beiträge*, 1901, I, *Heft* 2, 51). On his own initiative Major-General Manstein intervened from the north with four grenadier battalions of the right wing of the Prussian infantry, dislodging the Austrians from their earthworks on the ridge between the Kej and Hlaupetin ponds, and in the early hours of the afternoon the Austrians were gradually unseated from their further positions along the northern edge of the plateau.

General Kheul rallied the main force of the Austrians from a stand behind a steep little valley which ran north from Maleschitz to the bend of the Rocketnitzer-Bach at Hrdlorzez. This new battle occasioned the heaviest fighting of the day, and the regiment of Winterfeldt (1) was massacred when it tried to climb the slope from the bottom of the ravine.

Once again the Austrians were to be evicted only by a double threat to their flanks. First of all their right or southern wing had to be pulled back when the advance of Zieten and Frederick from Sterbohol carried on in the direction of Neu-Straznitz. However, the Austrian troops to the north remained in ignorance of what was happening, and they held their positions until they were taken in their left flank by the regiment of Itzenplitz, which Prince Henry in person led across the Rocketnitzer-Bach. The soldiers had at first shrunk from wading the stream, and their fears were almost confirmed when the diminutive form of Prince Henry strode into the water and nearly disappeared from sight.

By 3 p.m. the main force of Austrian infantry was withdrawing on Prague, protected by the almost suicidal counter-attacks of the Austrian cavalry. Frederick himself was nearly captured when the Stechow Dragoons (D 11) were caught by three regiments of Austrian cuirassiers.

News of the king's whereabouts on this terrible day is in fact remarkably scanty. Two further sightings were made when the battle was finally over. The hussar officer Warnery tells us that Frederick joined him close under the citadel of Wischehrad, at the southern end of the Prague fortifications, and that he remained under artillery fire for half an hour. 'He had his telescope to his eye, and he laughed at our anxiety . . . the cannon shot were ploughing the earth around him, which kept his horse in restless motion, but he seemed to find the experience amusing' (Warnery, 1788, 118–9). The following scene is added by the Garde du Corps Kalkreuth:

> I do not know where the king was during the battle but between four and five he came straight to Prince Henry. The king was in a pitiable state. He dismounted and sat on one of those turf banks which enclose the fields. He then opened himself to the prince in agonised lamentations: 'Our losses are frightful. Field-Marshal Schwerin is dead!' He went on to enumerate the other casualties, and he was so distressed that he could scarcely speak. (Kalkreuth, 1840, II, 155)

Frederick told his reader Catt that 'the battle at Prague must be the greatest and bloodiest in history' (Catt, 1884, 236). He had overcome by far the most powerful concentration of force which the Austrians had yet put in his way, and to all appearances he had left them with no means of recovery. The enemy losses approached 14,000, of whom about 5,000 were prisoners, and Field-Marshal Browne had been mortally wounded in the counter-attack at Sterbohol.

With hindsight the Prussians appreciated that they ought to have done better still. It was now seen that Schwerin's infantry had been set an impossible task – to march with shouldered muskets against heavy guns and grenadiers – and Frederick noted that the flanking march ought to have been prolonged by at least another 2,000 paces (Warnery, 1788, 121). Zieten had certainly done magnificent work with the cavalry of the left wing, but during the battle the cavalry on the far right had been stranded uselessly facing the north side of the Austrian camp, from which it was separated by the valley of the Rockenitzer-Bach.

Some commentators apply the criticism of unused resources still more strongly to the 32,000-man-strong corps of Field-Marshal Keith, which had been left on the west bank of the Moldau. In response to an order from Frederick, Keith had dispatched Prince Moritz on the morning of the battle with four battalions and thirty squadrons to pass the Moldau above Prague. If these forces had arrived on the scene, they might well have prevented any of the Austrians from escaping to Beneschau. In the event the bridging train stuck for a time in a sunken road, and when the carts reached the river in the early afternoon Moritz discovered that there were not enough pontoons to reach the far bank. Nobody was inclined to follow the example of Colonel Seydlitz, who tried to ford the river and became stuck in quicksand. His horse sank up to the pistol holsters, and Seydlitz had to be hauled out with a rope.

What influence had Frederick exercised over the events of 6 May? He said to Catt: 'I felt ill throughout the battle. I voided everything I had eaten the day before, but we can't allow ourselves to take notice of such things – we had to act, and we acted well' (Catt, 1884, 236). He had left the vital reconnaissance to Schwerin and Winterfeldt, and he appears to have deferred again to Schwerin when the field-marshal urged the vital necessity of attacking at Sterbohol without delay. It is true that von Hoen, the author of the most detailed and authoritative account of the battle, ascribes the decisive exploitation along the Kaiser-Strasse directly to Frederick's orders (Hoen, 1909, 391). However, some at least of the commanders on the spot remained ignorant of any such directions (see p. 118), and the few recorded glimpses of the king indicate that he spent most, if not all, of the action on the southern part of the field.

Frederick rode over the ground on the day after the battle, accompanied by Zieten and Prince Henry. A few of the dead had been interred by their friends, who had inscribed their names on boards or crude crosses, but all the rest awaited the burial parties.

Frederick mourned the deaths of Major-generals Schöning and Blanckensee, his friend Lieutenant-General Hautcharmoy, and above all the heroic Schwerin, 'one of the greatest generals of this century' (to George II, PC 8908). More disturbing still was the loss of so many of the veterans whom Frederick called 'the pillars of the Prussian infantry', and the implications of the flight of Schwerin's troops at Sterbohol, which was the first time that this arm had failed him in battle. The total Prussian losses amounted to 14,287 officers and men (Hoen, 1909, 413), which in absolute terms was slightly higher than the enemy losses, and comprised a much higher propor-tion of dead and wounded.

Henckel von Donnersmarck noted in his diary: 'Hardly any battle up to the present time has been more murderous. We are condemned to the lamentable fate of having to earn our laurels with the blood of multitudes of brave men, with tears and endless afflic-tion' (1858, I, Part 2, 201).

For a number of days after the victory of Prague Frederick was gripped by the sensation that it was in his power to bring the war with the Austrians to an end, and so gain the freedom to march west and settle accounts with the French. Mitchell observed:

> His affairs do not admit of long wars, and it is in his interest to think of a peace in the midst of victory. His enemies are

numerous and powerful, have great resources, whilst the king of Prussia's superiority depends entirely on himself . . . as he has an excellent understanding, he certainly sees that at last he must succumb before the united powers of Austria, France and Russia. (17 May, PRO SP 90/69)

Frederick was elated to discover that the greater part of the defeated army had not escaped into the country, but was piled up in Prague. He did not have the means of prosecuting a formal siege, but he was confident that the mass of humanity in Prague, which according to his estimates comprised 70,000 citizens and 50,000 (actually 46,000) soldiers, would soon run through the provisions. He hoped that a bombardment might hasten the process by setting fire to some of the Austrian supply magazines.

The necessary siege train was shipped up the Elbe from Magdeburg to Leitmeritz, and transported from there overland to the batteries around Prague. Finally at midnight on 29 May a rocket snaked into the sky from the Zisaka-Berg, and the Prussians opened fire simultaneously from nearly sixty mortars and heavy cannon. On 31 May and 1 June very thick clouds of black smoke were seen rising from the city, encouraging Frederick to believe that a couple of stores had actually caught fire.

By 4 June, however, Frederick had begun to fear that his bombardment was doing little effective damage, and that the city was much better stocked with provisions than he had expected. He was now also aware that the Austrians, as resilient as always, were building up a big army of relief in eastern Bohemia. They had entrusted the command to Field-Marshal Daun, of whom Frederick knew little, though Austrian deserters told him that he was not a man who was likely to risk battle for the sake of rescuing Prague. Frederick had given Lieutenant-General the Duke of Bevern the responsibility of holding these people at a distance from the city. Bevern was gradually reinforced to a strength of 24,600 troops, and in accordance with Frederick's instructions he took the offensive against Daun and pushed him some way from the Kaiser-Strasse.

As a precautionary measure Frederick set out on 13 June to join Bevern with a reinforcement of four battalions, sixteen squadrons of cavalry and fifteen heavy guns. He had scarcely settled himself for the night at the *Zum letzten Pfennig* inn when an officer arrived from Bevern at eleven bearing the totally unexpected news that the whole of the Austrian army was on the advance.

On the 14th Frederick's little corps marched on through Schwarz-Kosteletz and over a plateau to a wooded brow above the village of Zdanitz. He took in the wide but as yet empty view over the plain of

Kolin, then descended in the path of his hussars. He had to scamper back at some speed when powerful forces of Austrian cavalry were detected beyond Zdanitz, but Frederick resumed the march later in the day, and at Malotitz he was joined by Bevern's army and four detached battalions under the command of Lieutenant-General Tresckow. In order to complete his concentration Frederick sent word to Prince Moritz to bring up all the disposable troops from the neighbourhood of Prague.

The reassembled Prussian army rested at Malotitz on 15 June, and Frederick still could not bring himself to believe that Daun's main force was in the immediate vicinity. The country round about was a small-scale landscape of hillocks and steep-sided bushy hollows, and the *Capitaine des Guides* Gaudi accordingly climbed the church tower of Ober-Krut, from where, in the afternoon sun, he had a clear view of the white tents of part of the left wing of the Austrian army just three miles away. Frederick at first gave no credence to this report.

In an atmosphere of rising tension the army waited in the Malotitz camp throughout the 16th. There was now little doubt that Daun's army was in the offing, and that the Prussians were facing the prospect of a new battle less than five weeks after the carnage of 6 May. Frederick's reader Catt learnt afterwards from 'personnes sûres' that Bevern advised the king against launching a new assault on the Austrians. While he was speaking, the reinforcements from Prague arrived at the camp, and Frederick drew Moritz into the conversation. That intelligent ignoramus cried out: 'Your Majesty, your presence alone is worth 50,000 men! You must attack!' (Catt, 1884, 237). In gross physical terms Frederick probably had little more than 35,000 troops under his command, and he was going to commit them in battle against about 53,000 Austrian effectives (Hoen, 1911, 28). The Austrian infantry alone was probably equal in number to the entire Prussian army.

A convoy of carts from Nimburg arrived on the morning of 17 June carrying bread for six days, and in the afternoon the army moved to the left in two columns in the direction of the Kaiser-Strasse. This was the finest road in Cental Europe, and it might offer possibilities of turning the Austrian army from the north. During the march, however, Frederick looked east across the pond of Swojschitz and caught sight of the Austrians drawn up on the rounded hills on the far side. In other words Daun had sensed his intention, and had shuffled the enemy army north during the night. The Prussians encamped near Kaurschim, and at 8 p.m. the outposts espied great clouds of dust from the Austrian camp. Daun was on the move again. He had abandoned most of his original westward-facing position, and he was now constructing a new angle looking north over the Kaiser-Strasse.

To Frederick, the strength of any position held by the enemy was probably no longer of overwhelming consequence:

> The cause of our misfortune is chiefly owing to the great success the king of Prussia's arms have had in eight successive battles against the Austrians; and, particularly to the victory obtained near Prague, on the 6th of May, which made His Prussian Majesty imagine, that he could force them from the most advantageous posts. (Mitchell, 29 June, PRO SP 90/69)

The Prussian army set out from the Kaurschim camp at 6 a.m. on 18 June. A thick mist still hung in the hollows, but the sunlight threatened a day of crushing heat. The initial direction of the march was north to the neighbourhood of Planian, where the army made a right turn and continued east along the Kaiser-Strasse. Frederick climbed the main tower of the sombre church at Planian, but he found that the site was so low-lying that he still had no view of the new Austrian positions. He rejoined the army, whose advance guard was now pushing some way along the Kaiser-Strasse.

The short ascent from the Planian hollow carried Frederick into a landscape far grander than the close-set country of the last few days. The plain of the Elbe stretched limitlessly to the left, and a couple of thousand paces to the right the open ground rose smoothly but impressively to a long rounded ridge. A line of Austrian troops stretched across the summits of the nearest hills.

Frederick halted his army, which was already exhausted by the forced march of ten miles in the increasing heat. Croats were swarming in the fields of cereals to the south of the Kaiser-Strasse, which prevented a closer investigation of the ridge, and Frederick therefore ascended to the upper storey of the tall inn of the *Zlaté Slunce* ('Golden Sun'). He made a very close examination of the ground with his telescope and remarked that the Austrians had skilfully posted their cavalry wherever the terrain best suited its action, and not in text-book style on either flank. Nothing that Bevern or Zieten could say, however, would persuade Frederick that he was facing overwhelming odds. The engineer captain Friedrich Giese is said to have assured the king that the attack was practicable, while Prince Moritz, who would act as second in command in any battle, kissed the royal coat and declared: 'Things are certain to go well, wherever Your Majesty happens to be!' (Henckel von Donnersmarck, 1858, I, Part 2, 230).

Where should the attack be directed? The two component hills of the ridge, the Przerovsky Hill to Frederick's front and the Krzeczhorz Hill to the east, did not present themselves very clearly to an observer at the *Zlaté Slunce*. From here the ridge appeared not so much to run parallel to the Kaiser-Strasse as to descend slant-wise to meet it a couple of miles to the east. This was the deceptive effect of the low spurs which projected to the north around Krzeczhorz. Nothing could have seemed more natural than to continue the march down the excellent Kaiser-Strasse across the front of the Austrian position, and then ascend the heights and gain the enemy right or eastern flank.

The stalwart Major-General Hülsen was to lead the way with the infantry of the advance guard and the Stechow Dragoons (D 11; see Map 10, p. 352), leaving the road just after passing on a level with Krzeczhorz, and then working around and behind this village to form a line facing west on the ridge. Lieutenant-General Zieten was to cover his left flank with fifty squadrons of light horse, and one hundred further squadrons of cavalry were to be close at hand alongside the leading divisions of infantry, following in Hülsen's tracks. The rearward or right-hand divisions of the army were to be 'refused', in the classic style of the oblique order of battle. The cavalry at the tail was made of the merest handful of regiments, in contrast with the large force which had waited uselessly at Prague.

Frederick gave his generals a verbal briefing on the upper floor of the *Zlaté Slunce*, indicating features of the ground through the windows. He then entered a nearby room and repeated the details to the generals' adjutants. He explained that for the first time in his battles he would hold the cavalry in reserve, so that it would remain fresh enough to exploit the success of the infantry. He left the inn early in the afternoon, mounted his horse and drew his sword, 'something which he had never done before' (Warnery, 1788, 151).

The extraordinary complexities of the battle of Kolin were never convincingly unravelled until Hoen wrote on the subject in 1911. In outline, however, we shall describe two phases of combat, namely:

(a) when the intended flanking attack of the Prussians was converted, by Frederick's last-minute changes of mind, into a frontal one, and
(b) when the Prussians repeatedly opened potential breaches in the enemy line, only to fail in face of the tenacity and superior numbers of the Austrians.

The Prussians moved off to the left in lines at about 1 p.m. Zieten's hussars and Hülsen's battalions were passing on a level with Krzeczhorz when they came under fire from the miniature artillery of a force of Croats – an incident which told Frederick that, contrary to expectations, this village was occupied by the enemy. Frederick decided to await news of Hülsen's further progress, and he ordered the army to halt on the Kaiser-Strasse: 'You could not have imagined a

finer day, or a more splendid sight' (Ligne, 1795–1811, XIV, 19).
Already Frederick's scheme had undergone its first disruption.

Towards 2 p.m. Hülsen's force climbed towards Krzeczhorz with
sounding music. The Prussians evicted the Banal Croats from the
walled churchyard and an ancient earthwork extending to the west,
and within half an hour they had cleared the village and reached the
celebrated Oak Wood behind. After this first success, instead of
finding himself master of an empty ridge, Hülsen discovered that he
was face-to-face with the Austrian division of Wied, which Daun had
moved laterally from his reserve. Hülsen was glad to receive a
reinforcement of three battalions of grenadiers from the main army,
and he used the newcomers to prolong his front to the right.

Zieten meanwhile had moved on a wide arc to the east, keeping
approximate pace with Hülsen's left. In the process he swept back
Nádasti's force of 4,000 Croats and 6,700 Austrian and Saxon light
cavalry. Zieten then halted in line, to the east of the Oak Wood, in
full accord with the spirit of Frederick's instructions.

Down on the Kaiser-Strasse the army had been waiting in pla-
toon columns, ready to move in support of the advance guard.
Frederick gave the expected command shortly before 3 p.m., and
when the infantry shouldered their muskets a blaze of reflected light
flashed along the columns. Frederick seems to have been encouraged
by the lack of substantial opposition to Hülsen (for the movement of
Wied's division was probably hidden from him by the crest of the
ridge), and rather than follow all the way in Hülsen's tracks, as had
been originally intended, he now sought to save time by ordering the
army to make straight for the Oak Wood.

The columns had scarcely begun to climb the slopes from the
Kaiser-Strasse when Frederick issued the astonishing order for the
division of the left wing to wheel their component platoons into line,
then advance against the ridge on a broad battle frontage. Prince
Moritz was determined to adhere to the original scheme of marching
all the way to the ridge in columns, and over Frederick's shouted
protests he ordered the troops to continue on their way:

> For the third time Frederick called out: 'Prince Moritz, form
> into line!' The prince repeated: 'Forwards, forwards!' At this the
> king galloped up and halted with the muzzle of his horse against
> the prince's saddle. 'For God's sake', he shouted, 'form front
> when I tell you to do so!' The Prince at last gave the appropriate
> order in a sorrowful tone of voice, and he commented . . . 'Now
> the battle is lost!' (quoted in Duncker, 1876, 76).

Why had Frederick changed his mind yet again, abandoning the last elements of his flank march in favour of a frontal attack? Hoen concludes (1911, 380–6) that the king had become belatedly aware of the clouds of dust which betokened the shift of Austrian reserves to the east. He therefore decided not to move up behind the advance guard, but to bring the leading battalions of the main army up to Hülsen's right and sweep the Krzeczhorz Hill by a concerted push.

Nine battalions stood under the immediate command of Prince Moritz, but the Austrians had sixteen heavy cannon waiting for him and soon the Prussians were climbing over heaps of their own dead and wounded. Moritz had a horse shot under him, 'whereupon the soldiers, who were infuriated against him, yelled that it was a pity that the animal on top had not been killed rather than the animal beneath' (Lehndorff, 1910–13, I, 115).

The frontal attack received a significant extension to the west when the five battalions of the division of Major-General Manstein advanced direct from the Kaiser-Strasse against the commanding Przerovsky Hill. The first move had come from one of Manstein's battalions, which moved into the tall grain to clear the Croats who had been sniping at the motionless troops on the highway. It then appears that Captain the Marquis de Varenne arrived with an order from the king to commit the whole force to the attack, whereupon Manstein swept Colonel Kleefeld's Croats from the village of Choczenitz and pushed on against the Przerovsky Hill behind. Frederick betook himself to the scene in person, which is an indication of the importance he attached to the enterprise, and between 3.30 and 4.30 p.m. the energetic Manstein organised three assaults against the Austrian positions.

Manstein failed to dislodge the enemy, but his persistence had the effect of fixing the Austrian division of Andlau on the Przerovsky Hill. This left the Austrians dangerously weak in the direction of Krzeczhorz, where the Prussian division of Lieutenant-General Tresckow had come up alongside Moritz, and where Hülsen had finally accomplished the capture of the Oak Wood. By the middle of the afternoon, therefore, the battle had become general, and the greater part of the Prussian army was engaged in a frontal assault on the ridge.

South of Krzeczhorz the combat became increasingly fluid, for the Austrian divisions of Starhemberg and Sincère had arrived in support of Wied, and Lieutenant-General Starhemberg had enough force in hand to deliver a counter-attack. The Austrians recovered the Oak Wood, but when they continued on towards Krzeczhorz they were hit in their right or eastern flank by an astonishingly vigorous charge of the Prussian cavalry brigade of Krosigk. The powerfully built Major-General Christian Siegfried von Krosigk led the attack in person, at the head of the Normann Dragoons (D 1; see Map 10, p. 352):

> His courage and zeal for the service were undiminished by two bad sword cuts which he had received to the head. But a lethal canister shot, which took him in the stomach below the breastplate, at last threw him to the ground . . . A dragoon saw him fall. He testifies that he was still able to call out: 'Lads, I can do no more. The rest is up to you!' (Pauli, 1758–64, II, 125)

The commission was taken up by Friedrich Wilhelm von Seydlitz, the thirty-six-year-old colonel of the Rochow Cuirassiers (C 8). Together with the supporting cuirassiers of Prinz von Preussen (C 2), which made up the third regiment of the brigade, the Prussian troopers worked their devastating way west, overthrowing the Austrian Würt-temberg Dragoons and the Saxon Carabiniers, riding down the Hungarian infantry regiment of Haller, and pushing back the 'German' infantry regiments of Baden and Deutschmeister. Only the regiment of Botta held firm at the far left of the division of Sincère.

Over the next two hours Frederick rallied force after force in an attempt to exploit the opportunity which had been opened by Kro-sigk's initiative. The action became nearly continuous along the length of the line, and it absorbed the commands of Hülsen, Tre-sckow, and Manstein, as well as the exhausted survivors of Krosigk's brigade. Most of the anecdotes about Frederick's activity at Kolin derive from this period. The famous and kindly sentiment 'Rogues, do you wish to live for ever!' was advanced (if it was ever uttered at all) to Manstein's troops at about 6.30 p.m. At this time the Prussians were shrinking in the face of four heavy guns and four companies of grenadiers which were emplaced on the Przerovsky Hill, and Frederick set an example to the first battalion of Anhalt (3) by drawing his sword and advancing with the colours. The men con-tinued to fall back in disorder behind him.

These efforts drew in almost all the reserves of the army. Towards 6 p.m. a heavy mass of Prussian cavalry approached the crest of the sector of the ridge to the south-west of Krzeczhorz. This was an altogether slower-moving affair than the brilliant offensive of Kro-sigk. The nominal commander was Lieutenant-General Penavaire, who was in his eighties. He had at his immediate disposal twenty cuirassier squadrons of his first line, and he was supposed to be strengthened by the second line of Zieten's command and possibly also by some of the cavalry of the right. The attack ('charge' is altogether too dramatic a term) was slowed by the slope and the dense growth of rye, and scarcely ten squadrons appear to have reached the crest of the ridge. The Austrian cavalry division of

Serbelloni withdrew to the side, but the infantry of Starhemberg were standing firm behind and threw the Prussians back.

For some time now the Duke of Bevern had been moving eight battalions diagonally across the rear of the army from the Kaiser-Strasse towards the left centre of the line of battle. This body constituted the last uncommitted force of Prussian infantry, and it suffered heavy losses from canister fire before it so much as reached its assigned place in the front. The First Battalion of the Garde (15), which made up the rear of the column, was savaged by the Darmstadt Dragoons (D 19) and lost its battalion guns.

Bevern's command was drawn into one final concerted push over the crest of the Krzeczhorz Hill – an attack in which the king also engaged the remaining battalions of Tresckow's division, a couple of battalions of Hülsen's, and all the available squadrons of Penavaire and the cavalry reserve. At about 7 p.m. the Prussians burst over the ridge, which opened a clear breach in the enemy line, and put the issue of the day in the balance. (See Map 11, p. 354.)

Colonel Prince Kinsky won a few precious minutes for Daun by forming the regiment of Botta (12), the one surviving unit of the division of Sincère, into a coherent flank on the western side of the breakthrough. Reinforcements from the division of Andlau prolonged the line to either side, and soon the bulk of the Prussian infantry swung to its right and engaged in a fire-fight athwart the ridge. At this juncture a mass of Austrian cavalry irrupted against their rear from the direction of the Oak Wood.

The initiative in this devastating attack was taken by the young Netherlandish troopers of the de Ligne Dragoons (D 31), who, according to legend, had been put on their mettle by a disparaging remark from Daun. Altogether more than eighty Austrian and Saxon squadrons were directed against the exhausted Prussian troops. The Saxons in particular had many old scores to settle, and their cry of 'Dies ist für Striegau!' (i.e. Hohenfriedeberg) rang in the dying ears of defenceless creatures like the boy ensigns of the Prussian infantry.

The battle was lost beyond recall, and between about 8 and 9 p.m. the Prussians made back towards the Kaiser-Strasse in groups of thirty or forty at a time. Hülsen staged a stand at Krzeczhorz, which helped to deter the Austrians from pursuit, but the last men to leave the field were the hussars of Zieten's first line, who were cursing most mightily in their frustration.

Frederick had long since departed with an escort of thirty hussars and a squadron of the Garde du Corps. He dismounted at Nimburg and sat down on a wooden water pipe, 'gazing fixedly at the ground, and describing circles with his stick in the dust' (Archenholtz, 1840, I, 67–8). He left Prince Moritz in command of the army, and early in the afternoon of 19 June he reached his old headquarters at Klein-Michele outside Prague. He was visited by his brother Henry and a small party of officers, who found him prostrate on a bale of straw. He left it to Henry to draw up the necessary orders for the retreat of the army, 'telling him that he was incapable of doing anything, and that he needed to rest' (Henckel von Donnersmarck, 1858, I, Part 2, 236).

The physical damage to the Prussian army has been assessed at about 13,000 men, nearly all of whom were lost by the infantry, who were reduced by some 65 per cent of their effectives. The shock and demoralisation were of a nature that could be experienced only by an army which had previously been victorious eight times over, 'and indeed, one must be more than human, to be absolutely free from presumption after such a series of successes' (Mitchell, 29 June, PRO SP 90/69). For the king, the experience was all the more painful when he called to mind what might have been achieved through a victory: 'If I had succeeded as I ought to have done, I would have knocked the Austrians out of the reckoning, and proceeded with my plan of marching on the Rhine, attacking the French and pushing into France. But fate was against me and decreed otherwise' (Catt, 1884, 237).

No single episode of Frederick's military career has occasioned more surmise and debate. Kolin was, for the Prussian army, what the charge of the Light Brigade at Balaclava represented for the British in the nineteenth century. For the first time it was possible to entertain serious doubts about Frederick's generalship, and about the wisdom of the war and the nature of its outcome.

Veterans, commentators and historians have ventured a number of explanations of what had gone wrong:

(a) Immediately after the battle of Prague the king had neglected the opportunity of dispersing the Austrian fugitives and driving Daun into Moravia (Mitchell, 1850, I, 353–4; Henckel von Donnersmarck, 1858, I, Part 2, 216).

(b) Frederick should have given battle, if at all, much closer to Prague, where he could have drawn on the siege corps, as Napoleon and Clausewitz have suggested.

(c) Frederick was arrogant and impatient, and underestimated the numbers and quality of the Austrians.

(d) The intended flank attack was converted into an extremely costly frontal assault, in which the Austrian superiority in numbers and position told to the fullest effect. In his letters and histories Frederick put the blame on the over-enthusiasm of the troops, and the mistakes of some of the generals, especially

Manstein. The historian von Hoen attributes the change of plan directly to the king himself.

(e) The cavalry, apart from the brigade of Krosigk, was sluggish and unresponsive. 'When we ordered our cavalry to do anything, we might as well have been speaking to a wall' (Warnery, 1788, 170).

(f) The Austrian position was very well chosen – a natural killing ground. Daun was an expert manager of a defensive battle of this kind, and his gunners, his grenadiers and most of his regiments of musketeers and cavalry fought with skill and tenacity.

In all of this it is necessary to preserve a certain sense of perspective. If Frederick was being judged so harshly, it was because his name had always been associated with victory. There had been many occasions on 18 June when it appeared that Kolin too was going to be counted among his triumphs.

On 20 June the siege of Prague was abandoned with great celerity and no little confusion. The next day Frederick rejoined the army which had been beaten at Kolin, and he began to gather his wits. For the immediate future he was content to adopt a waiting strategy. By holding on to most of the ground he had gained in north Bohemia he would at once keep the Austrians south of the border hills, consume the fodder which the enemy might otherwise use to sustain a counter-offensive, and win the time to orientate himself in the rapidly changing political and strategic situation in Europe.

Frederick still credited the Austrians with little capacity for seizing the initiative, even after the campaign of Kolin, and for logistical reasons he took the very considerable risk of dividing his forces into two approximately equal parts. On the left, or western, bank of the Elbe the king assumed personal command of 34,000 men, who fed off the magazine at Leitmeritz. To the east of the Elbe his eldest brother, August Wilhelm, was entrusted with the direction of 33,800 troops, who were maintained by a long line of communication which stretched back through wild country to the magazine at Zittau in Upper Lusatia.

Frederick reached Leitmeritz on 27 June. He lodged himself in the spacious episcopal palace, which was set between the town and the river. The cool, arched corridors gave onto suites of rooms which offered ample accommodation to Frederick and his staff, and the main hall was a magnificent affair, with a ceiling fresco of Moses striking water from the rock, and alcoved windows which gave views over the Elbe.

In these idyllic surroundings Frederick spent some of the most unhappy days of his life. With the experiences of Kolin all too fresh in his mind, he dictated to the engineer lieutenant Johann Anton Freund some speculations as to how he might order things differently in his battles. Perhaps he might commit his worst troops to the costly initial attacks, instead of sacrificing his best. Perhaps also he might be able to winkle the enemy out of their positions by employing the high-trajectory shell fire of howitzers (*Instruction, so des Königs Majestät Friedrich II., uns allen, die wir Quartiermeister-Dienste gethan haben, selbsten gegeben haben*, summed up as *Aphorismen des Königs über die Befestigungs-, Lager- und Gefechtkunst, Oeuvres, XXX*).

Now that the first blow against Austria had failed, it was evident that 'all Europe was on the march against him' (Henckel von Donnersmarck, 1858, I, Part 2, 238). The French had two armies ready to advance across Germany. Twenty thousand Swedes were at hand on the Baltic coast on the borders of Prussian Pomerania, and the Russian army was poised to invade isolated East Prussia. This crisis evoked in Frederick that extraordinary response of self-pity, iron resolution and philosophical detachment that we shall encounter so often in him during the Seven Years War.

Frederick complained to his sister Wilhelmine that he could see no reason why states like France, Russia or Sweden should have been so wicked as to pick a quarrel with him (*PC* 9198). However, where lesser souls might have sought refuge in a timorous defensive, 'my inclination is to seek somehow or other to bring on a decision by battle. If we fail to come to grips before the end of the campaign, we are lost' (to August Wilhelm, 13 July, *PC* 9197).

Equally characteristic of Frederick was the resort to the pen, which he probably never employed with such intensity as in the summer and autumn of 1757, explaining that misfortune had revived his taste for poetry.

No philosophy could armour Frederick against a further blow which struck him, as secretary Eichel wrote, 'absolutely point blank' (*PC* 9151). Eichel had learnt from the foreign minister that Frederick's mother, Queen Sophia Dorothea, had died on 28 June. Eichel wished to break the news gently and in person, but in spite of everything a message slipped through directly to Frederick. The king's grief was terrible. He wrote to Wilhelmine:

Our mother is no more. This loss is the culmination of my sorrows, and yet I am forced to act, and I do not have time to give full course to my tears . . . All the other losses in this world may be redressed, but those occasioned by death are beyond remedy. (*PC* 9163)

These sentiments reach out to us over the gap of more than two centuries, yet, through his gratuitous cruelty, our suffering hero was shortly to be responsible for the ruin of a member of his fast-diminishing family circle. We left Prince August Wilhelm in command of the Prussian forces on the eastern side of the Elbe. The Austrians, contrary to what Frederick had expected, made their main effort in that direction, and threw the Prussians into confusion. Winterfeldt was at loggerheads with the other generals in the force, and August Wilhelm looked in vain for some guidance from the king. The fast-moving Austrians seized the important road junction at Gabel on 15 July, and on the 23rd they burst into Zittau and deprived the Prussians of the carefully garnered provisions which could have sustained 40,000 men for three weeks.

The loss of Gabel convinced Frederick that his presence was needed in Saxony. He left Keith to evacuate the royal army from Bohemia, and departed from Leitmeritz on 21 July. Frederick met the army of August Wilhelm at Bautzen on the 29th, and the next day he interviewed its exhausted and wilting commander in person. The prince rode away from the meeting in tears, and Frederick pursued him with a letter which heightened his humiliation. Never again, he wrote, would he give him another army to ruin: 'to my way of thinking your splendid expedition was nothing more than the impulse of some superannuated spoiled child, from whom we take a knife lest he should cut himself and injure others' (26 August, *PC* 9291).

The broken August Wilhelm retired from the army. He wrote to his sister-in-law, the wife of Prince Henry:

> Our great man is in the grip of inordinate conceit. He asks nobody for advice, his thoughtlessness is beyond belief, and he is so moody that he refuses to credit the most solid intelligence. When misfortune overtakes him he distances himself from what has happened, and puts the blame on somebody who is innocent. (Volz, 1926–7, II, 33)

August Wilhelm died of a cerebral haemorrhage in June the next year. The generals had liked him for his accessibility, and 'his loss was regretted in the army. After a couple of days he was forgotten, just like Schwerin after his death' (Warnery, 1788, 200).

Meanwhile in the high summer of 1757 Frederick was determined to confront the Austrians who had so impudently emerged into Lusatia. His reassembled force comprised 50,600 men and seventy-two heavy pieces. The hussar Warnery claims that the troops were restored to life by the galvanising presence of their master (Warnery, 1788, 185), but the British envoy Mitchell describes an army that was still demoralised by the defeat at Kolin and still suffering from the privations of the campaign (11 August, PRO SP 90/69).

On 16 August Frederick was in the immediate proximity of the army of 100,000 Austrians in their position on the Eckartsberg plateau north of Zittau. 'We could see him from our camp', wrote one of the Austrians. 'He was riding through his position on a great grey horse, giving orders left, right and centre' (Ligne, 1795–1811, XIV, 36).

Frederick was set on attacking the right flank of the Austrian position. Prince Henry was equally sure that such an enterprise would be suicidal, and in the evening he betook himself to the royal headquarters at Tittelsdorf:

> The king was already at supper under a tree. Several officers
> stood about him. They awaited his orders, and they were
> entranced to be in his proximity and hear his voice. The king
> spoke in a monologue, developing all sorts of splendid plans, and
> proclaiming how he would beat those buggers the next day, and
> so on. (Henckel von Donnersmarck, 1858, I, Part 2, 275)

The royal brothers entered the rough cabin behind, and a crowd of officers gathered outside under a fine and warm rain.

> We could see them both. The prince was speaking with evident
> animation, but we could not catch what they were saying. This
> scene continued for one and a half hours. Finally the prince
> came out to announce the orders, namely 'Tomorrow is a rest
> day!' Everybody was overjoyed. (Kalkreuth, 1840, III, 165)

Henry thereby entered a claim to the enduring gratitude of the army, and established himself in the eyes of many of the officers as a restraining force on what seemed to them to be the bloodthirsty irresponsibility of his brother.

On 20 August the Prussians retreated closer to their magazine at Bautzen. 'They executed this movement with such order and composure . . . as to lend an air of superiority to what was in fact a pretty humiliating episode' (Ligne, 1795–1811, XIV, 58).

The Prague-Kolin phase of operations was now definitely at an end, and Frederick was forced to establish new priorities in his grand strategic calculations now that he had to face the possibility of a converging allied attack. (See Map 12, p. 356.)

On the far eastern flank the field-marshal Hans von Lehwaldt had been commissioned to hold East Prussia against the Russians. He was known as a brave officer, but one who was unused to independent command.

More immediately Frederick had to reckon with a threat to his

homeland from the west. His sole friends in Europe, a force of
Hanoverian and other Protestant German auxiliaries, were defeated
by a French army in north-west Germany at Hastenbeck on 26 July,
and driven against the lower Elbe. Frederick himself was the target of
a second French army which Marshal Soubise was leading from
Strasbourg. In central Germany Soubise was going to act in co-
operation with a third hostile force, the *Reichsexecutionsarmee*,
which had been raised from a large number of the states of Germany
to visit the 'execution' of the Empire on the Prussians.

Since the Austrians had declined to allow themselves to be
brought to battle on favourable terms in Upper Lusatia, Frederick
made the dangerous decision to divide his forces for the second time in
two months. He left the Duke of Bevern on the spot with 41,000 men
to cover Silesia and Brandenburg against the Austrians. The king
himself resumed command of the troops from Leitmeritz, who had
been waiting south of Dresden, and he set off against the French and
the forces of the Empire in person.

With the advantage of hindsight we can see that Frederick was
paying the French and the Germans too handsome a compliment.
The French forces, so effective in the Netherlands campaigns of
1745–8, had become undisciplined and comfort-loving. The 30,500
troops of the *Reichsarmee* had been assembled in virtue of ancient
constitutions of the loose German Empire, and they comprised con-
tingents from no less than 231 of its component bodies politic. The
nominal commander, the able Austrian field-marshal Prince Joseph
Friedrich von Sachsen-Hildburghausen, discovered that his authority
was compromised by an assortment of senior generals who had been
appointed by individual princes of the Empire, and who were given to
turning up at headquarters unannounced. The men as a whole were
decent, sleepy and peaceable. It was unfortunate that some of the
best-trained troops, like those from Württemberg, were Protestants
whose inclinations turned them towards Frederick rather than Maria
Theresa. 'Seydlitz, who was subsequently engaged in many operations against this army . . . said that it was inadvisable to force those
troops to fight, because they would certainly do so. However, since
their hearts were not fully engaged in the outcome of the war, it was
better to make such manoeuvres as would force them to retreat
without compromising their honour' (Warnery, 1788, 332).

This Seydlitz had taken over the direction of Krosigk's charge
at Kolin, and Frederick now selected him for the principal command of the cavalry in the coming campaign in the west. Friedrich
Wilhelm von Seydlitz was born in the duchy of Cleves in 1721. At the
age of fourteen he was appointed page in the suite of the 'Mad' Margrave Friedrich of Brandenburg-Schwedt, under whose influence he

conceived his passion for tobacco, women, and feats of daredevil horsemanship like riding through the sails of a windmill. He learnt his military trade as a hussar in the Silesian Wars, and in the early 1750s he passed into the dragoons and finally into the cuirassiers, which gave him a grounding in all the branches of the cavalry. For his conduct at Kolin he received the Pour le Mérite and was promoted to major-general, and before the year was out he was a lieutenant-general wearing the orange sash of the Black Eagle. Such a rise was without precedent in the Prussian service, but Frederick was never in any doubt that he had done right to advance him over the heads of his seniors.

Seydlitz's notorious promiscuity, a legacy of his Brandenburg-Schwedt days, undermined his health so seriously that any slight wound threatened to incapacitate him for months at a time through shock and infection. This failing apart, Seydlitz was admired for his private as well as for his military virtues. He accepted his rise to high command with a modesty that disarmed any resentment. He was neither an intellectual nor a zealot, yet he held learning and religion in the highest regard. He was an enemy of corporal punishment, but he subjected his soldiers to a hard schooling and he was a stickler for the externals of military discipline. 'His appearance was one of warlike beauty. He was thinly built and very tall. He was a lover of military splendour, and seemed to have been poured into his uniform – a circumstance which added mightily to the impact he made as a soldier, and to the effect he had on his fellows' (Blankenburg, in Volz, 1926–7, II, 275).

In action Seydlitz possessed to a supreme degree the quality which the eighteenth century called *coup d'oeil*. Frederick explained that 'out of all the commanders I have seen, he is the only one who can exploit the full potential of his cavalry' (Catt, 1884, 83). The relationship with the king is in fact of some interest, for Seydlitz was the sole Prussian general who was capable of striking awe into Old Fritz himself. He used to look on with an amused and detached air when Frederick launched himself into his more extravagant flights of rhetoric, and he did not hesitate to challenge the royal opinions on tactics, horsemanship, and the qualities of foreign soldiers, whom the king usually held in contempt.

Seydlitz commanded the Garde du Corps at the head of Frederick's party when it set out from Zittau on 25 August. The weather in the first days of the progress was fine, and 'the king rode all the time at our head, sometimes alone, sometimes with one or other companion, but invariably behaving with the utmost gracious-ness to all who approached him. If it was Seydlitz, Frederick used to beg him to keep his pipe in his mouth, for he knew he was a passionate smoker' (Kalkreuth, 1840, III, 177). At Dresden on 30 August Frederick met the army which had retreated from Bohemia west of the Elbe, which gave him a force of 25,000 troops with which to seek out the French and the *Reichsarmee*.

The further march west across Saxony was by no means so agreeable. 'The soldiers are greatly fatigued, as it has rained constantly since we left Dresden, and the roads are extremely bad; many of the Saxons incorporated into the Prussian troops have deserted, but this is no real loss' (Mitchell, 6 September, PRO SP 90/70). As always Frederick was close up with Seydlitz and the powerful advance guard, and they repeatedly pushed the Austrian hussar brigade of Szecheny out of their path. Seydlitz burst through the little town of Pegau on 7 September, and on the 13th he and Frederick bluffed their way into Erfurt, where the people crowded around the king to kiss his hands, his coat-tails and even his horse. A new spell of fine weather had begun on the 6th. The desertion among the troops considerably abated, and 'as they flatter themselves with the hope of going into Alsace to beat the French, they bear the fatigues of the continual marches with great alacrity and cheerfulness' (Mitchell, 17 September, PRO SP 90/70).

On 15 September Seydlitz swept away the enemy outposts from Gotha, and Frederick entered the town at the head of the Meinecke Dragoons. His admirers among the people found that all of the celebrated traits of his character were gratifyingly reflected in his startling eyes, his straight nose, and the lines etched on his face. 'His complexion and the state of his clothing and shirt serve to confirm what is generally said of him, that in the field he makes himself no more comfortable than the least of his officers' (quoted in Wiltsch, 1858, 15).

Frederick left Gotha on 16 September, and the next day the allied commanders Soubise and Hildburghausen arrived there on a reconnaissance in force with nine or ten thousand men. Seydlitz arranged his 1,500 troopers outside in a thin but impressive-looking line, and sent a 'deserter' and some peasants into the town to announce that Frederick was on his way with the main army. The allies evacuated Gotha in some alarm. Eighty soldiers were captured by the Prussian hussars, together with a huge booty of clerks, lackeys, cooks, ladies, perfumes, dressing gowns and parrots.

Frederick's outward cheerfulness, and the army's enjoyment of the comedy at Gotha, gave no hint of the disintegration in Prussia's wider strategic affairs. First of all on 10 September the king learnt that Lehwaldt had been defeated by the Russians at Gross-Jägersdorf. Then on the 14th we discover Frederick addressing a letter to his confidant Winterfeldt, whom he had left with Bevern's army facing the Austrians: 'Everything is going splendidly here, but I am very worried by a rumour which has come to me from Lusatia. I don't know what to make of it. They write to me from Dresden that you have been killed, and from Berlin that you received a cut in the shoulder' (*PC* 9336). Within a matter of hours came news that Winterfeldt and many of his men had been lying dead for a week, after a detachment under his command had been overwhelmed by the Austrians at Moys.

Frederick took the loss of Winterfeldt much more to heart than that of Schwerin. Towards the end of his life he was talking with a young officer when the conversation turned to the action at Moys. Frederick burst out: ' "That was where Winterfeldt was killed! He was a good man – a man of soul – he was my friend!" His great eyes brimmed with tears as he looked towards the window. He opened the casement, and stood there some time before he turned back to Rüchel and sent him on his way with a perceptible softening in his voice: "Good night, I am obliged to you" ' (Varnhagen von Ense, 1836, 233).

On 17 September, the day of Seydlitz's brilliant coup at Gotha, Frederick was informed that the sorry chapter of the Hanoverian campaign had ended in a capitulation to the French at Kloster-Zeven. The army of the Duc de Richelieu was now free to help Soubise and Hildburghausen in central Germany. As a precaution against Richelieu, Frederick had already sent Prince Ferdinand of Brunswick on the 14th with six battalions and eleven squadrons to protect Halle. Prince Moritz of Anhalt-Dessau was simultaneously dispatched with ten battalions and ten squadrons to the Elbe to cover Brandenburg and the important bridge at Torgau against the Austrians.

Annoyingly enough the French and the troops of the *Reichsarmee* in Thuringia persisted in hanging just out of Frederick's reach. He fell back on 27 September from Erfurt to Buttelstädt, but failed to tempt the allies any further west than Gotha. On 11 October the Prussian army executed a further retreat to the little town of Eckartsberga. The rain turned the road into red clay mud, and Frederick's temper was not improved by reports that the Austrians were sending a raiding corps against Berlin. Frederick ordered the detachments of Ferdinand and Moritz to do what they could to head off the enemy, and on the 12th he dispatched Seydlitz and the Szekely Hussars to help them. All of Frederick's composure had disappeared. In the evening he took up the text of Racine's tragedy *Mithridate*, and through the windows of his lodging he could be seen declaiming the lines with dramatic passion.

Frederick left Field-Marshal Keith with a small corps to hold the line of the Saale against the allies, and he hastened with the advance guard north-east by way of Leipzig and Torgau to save the capital. On the 19th he learnt that the Austrians had occupied Berlin on the 16th, only to abandon it by the next day upon the news of Moritz's approach. The Austrian raiding force was identified as a small one (3,400 troops under Lieutenant-General Haddik), and by the 20th it was evident that the enemy had slipped away, which rendered it pointless for Frederick to continue his march into Silesia to cut off the path of retreat.

On 24 October Frederick was back at Torgau, and he received the immensely heartening news that the enemy in the west had crossed the Saale and were likely to present him with the opportunity for the battle he so much desired. Frederick called his outlying detachments to rally to him at Leipzig, and by the 28th he achieved a concentration of thirty-one battalions and forty-five squadrons. The corps of Moritz had come from Berlin in five and a half days, and that of Ferdinand from Magdeburg in three, 'but what is the most surprising and pleasing at the same time is the spirit the soldiers showed on this occasion; they had marched upwards of twenty-five English miles a day for three or five days successively, and at the moment they arrived they desired to be led again against the enemy' (Mitchell, 27 October, PRO SP 90/70).

Lacking support from Soubise, the *Reichsarmee* fell back across the Saale again on 30 October. However, the allies lingered irresolutely on the western side, which suited Frederick's purpose well enough, and he made up his mind to cross the river and attack them.

Frederick decided to make the passage of the Saale at two points – upstream with the main army at Weissenfels, and downstream with Keith's detachment at Merseburg (see Map 14, p. 359). True to his brisk style in this campaign, Frederick arrived outside Weissenfels with his advance guard at daybreak on 31 October, and at once sent the grenadiers and the Mayr free battalion ahead to burst in the gates. Three hundred German troops were cut off and captured in the town, and when his main army came up Frederick rushed the heavy guns to the bluff beside the massive ducal palace and cannonaded the French grenadiers re-crossing the river.

Frederick in person was at the river bank, watching with some frustration as the French burned the covered wooden bridge behind them. The vines and poplars of this beautiful stretch of riverside were bare, but the willows and aspen still retained a full autumn foliage, and two enemy officers were watching the royal party from a concealed position on an island which lay within close musket shot. One of the Frenchman hastened back to the Duc de Crillon to report that it would be possible for a marksman to shoot down a Prussian senior officer, and that this dignitary was probably the king, from the respect that was being shown to him. 'Crillon handed his loyal Brunet a glass of wine, and sent him back to his post, remarking that he and his comrades had been put there to observe whether the bridge was burning properly, and not to kill a general who was making a reconnaissance, let alone the sacred person of a king, which must always be held in reverence' (Crillon, 1791, 166).

Frederick was spared to range up and down the right bank of the Saale, and he found a suitable crossing point for a bridge of boats downstream from Weissenfels. The infantry made an unopposed passage there on the morning of 3 November, while the cavalry waded across nearby. In the afternoon Frederick and the advance guard reached Braunsdorf and learnt that the allies had established a camp near Mücheln. He could make out little of their position in the falling darkness, though it was evident that the allies were facing north in the expectation that the Prussians would be advancing from Halle. An attack against the allied right wing might therefore offer Frederick a good chance of success. Moritz and Keith had meanwhile crossed the Saale with the rest of the army at Merseburg, and after some blundering through the murk the Prussian forces were reunited at 7 p.m.

Early on the moonlit morning of 4 November Frederick rode forward with the combined cavalry of his army to the north-east slopes of the Schortau heights. He left the main force of the troopers under cover, and proceeded with a party of hussars to the summit, from where he could see that overnight the enemy had responded to the Prussian passage of the river by wheeling their camp about to face east. The allies were well positioned, and reports put their strength at 60,000 men, which was three times the size of his own force. Frederick called off the advance of his main army, and positioned it behind the Leiha-Bach, with the right or northern flank extending to Bedra, and the left to his headquarters at Rossbach. He had postponed, rather than abandoned, his battle, for he knew that the *Reichsarmee* in particular was low on provisions, and that the allies would either have to come out and attack him, or execute a dangerous retreat towards the river Unstrut. The French and Germans had been seven days now without shelter or regular rations, but they were overjoyed by the apparent failure of nerve on Frederick's part. 'All their complements of musicians, trumpeters, drummers and fifers now gave sound, as if they had won some great victory' (*Oeuvres*, IV, 151).

The first impression of the allied strength had been exaggerated, but the combined army amounted to a still impressive 41,000 troops, of whom the Germans of the Empire made up about 10,900 men, and the French, recently reinforced from Richelieu's army, constituted 30,200. Frederick had just 21,000 troops under his command, which put him at a numerical inferiority still more acute than at Soor in 1745.

Soon after daybreak on 5 November the Mayr free battalion found that the allied camp was covered by the corps of Saint-Germain (eight battalions and thirteen squadrons) garnishing the Schortau heights. Behind this screen the allied army spent several hours sorting itself into three columns, which were supposed to execute a grand tactical plan of turning Frederick's left flank. This force lurched into motion towards noon and made initially for Zeuchfeld, as if to escape south out of Frederick's way. Early in the afternoon the allies carried out their wheel to the left, and, despite delays and confusions which gave birth to an unintended fourth column, they began to march over a wide and open ridge which led past the Prussian left flank.

This interesting development found the Prussians still at ease over their lunch. Frederick had his headquarters in the *Herrenhaus* at the southern extremity of Rossbach village, which stood like an island in the open plain of arable land. At the time of the allied march the king was dining unconcernedly with some of his officers in an upper room, but the young *Capitaine des Guides* Friedrich Wilhelm Gaudi had stationed himself in the garret above, where a number of bricks had been removed from the western wall, giving him a clear view to the ridge. Over there he could see that a number of enemy generals were prospecting the Prussian position, and that the allies had changed the direction of their march. Gaudi went downstairs to report to the table what he had seen. At first Frederick angrily dismissed him as an alarmist, but additional confirmation arrived soon enough.

Once aroused, Frederick acted with all possible vigour to head off the advance of the allies and attack them on the march. He immediately seized on the potential of the long, low ridge of the Janus Hill for screening a clockwise movement of the army out to the north-east, and on by a broad sweep south and west to embrace the allied columns. The cavalry had the furthest to go, and Frederick gave the newly promoted Major-General Seydlitz full authority over the disposable thirty-eight squadrons. Seydlitz duly rode up to the cavalry generals and announced: 'Gentlemen, I obey the king, and you will obey me!' (Gr. Gstb., 1901–14, V, 211).

The Prussian cavalry moved off to the left, and five squadrons of the Szekely Hussars (H 1; see Map 15, p. 360) kept pace along the Janus Hill to the south so as to conceal the movement from the enemy. The slower-moving Prussian infantry began to march up the western slopes of the ridge, and when the heads of columns came within a few hundred paces of the crest Frederick dispatched Colonel Moller to the summit with a battery of eighteen heavy guns.

The allies noticed the departure of the king's army shortly before 2.15 p.m.: 'In less than two minutes all the tents lay on the ground, as if they had collapsed like theatrical scenery, and his army was in full march' (Gr. Gstb., 1901–14, VII, 212). It was assumed that Frederick was making his escape, and so the allies plunged recklessly on, with the Austrian cavalry of the advance guard pushing 2,000 paces ahead of the main infantry.

Moller's guns spoke at 3.15 p.m., and the ground miles away shook with the concussion. At the sound of the cannon Seydlitz wheeled his squadrons into line, and he continued the march in this formation until the cavalry reached a suitable attacking position behind the eastward extension of the Janus Hill ridge. At 3.30 p.m. the leading allied squadrons approached to within about 1,000 paces of the crest, whereupon Seydlitz ordered the trumpets to sound the command '*Marsch! Marsch!*' On the far side he was soon engaged in a stern tussle with the two Austrian cuirassier regiments of Bretlach and Trautmannsdorff, which were able to deploy themselves into a passable fighting formation before the impact. The Austrian Szecheny Hussars and three regiments of Imperial German horse were in support, and for some minutes the allies withstood the onset of Seydlitz's first line.

Seydlitz now committed the eighteen squadrons of the second line in a double flanking attack which embraced not only the Austrian and German cavalry but the twenty-four squadrons of French which now arrived on the scene. The Low German cry of '*Gah to!*' burst from the Brandenburgers and Pomeranians of the cuirassiers, giving one of the French officers occasion to wonder what kind of men were these who went into battle crying 'Cake!'

The confused mass of allied cavalry was bundled back as far as the deep sunken road which ran between Reichardtswerben and Tagewerben, and this obstacle completed their rout. Seydlitz was one of the rare cavalry commanders in history who have possessed the discipline over themselves and their men to deal two great blows on one day of battle. He appreciated that he still had a great deal to do, and rather than pursue the already soundly beaten allied cavalry beyond Reichardtswerben, he rallied his squadrons to the north-east of that village and led them to a new position in the hollow of Tagewerben, from where they would be well placed to intervene against the southern flank of the allied infantry.

Meanwhile the Prussian infantry was hastening into view over the ridge. It reached forward by the left in echelon of battalions, with fifty-pace intervals, which usefully gained ground to the south, and the troops wheeled into line short of Tagewerben. The front was prolonged to the south by battalions which were drawn from the second line, until almost the entire Prussian infantry formed a dog-leg facing approximately south-west, while the columns of allied infantry approached the re-entrant angle. There to meet the enemy were not only the Prussian foot soldiers, but the heavy battery of Colonel Moller, which had been brought down from the Janus Hill.

Few details have been transmitted of the ensuing infantry battle, which lasted a matter of minutes and involved only seven of the Prussian battalions. The leading French infantry regiments of Piémont and Mailly braved the fire of the artillery and approached to within forty paces of the Prussian line before being shredded by the salvoes of Kleist (9) and Alt-Braunschweig (5). It was then or shortly afterwards that Frederick strayed in front of the muskets, and the Magdeburgers of Alt-Braunschweig called out: 'Father, please get out of the way, we want to shoot!'

Seydlitz brought his troopers out of the Tagewerben hollow in two lines, fell on the French cavalry which was still streaming past his front, and carried on against the infantry behind. A Frenchman reported: 'Everybody sank into a mob, and it was impossible to restore or stay the flight, whatever the efforts of the entire corps of generals and officers. The Prussian infantry followed on the heels of ours, and fired without checking its advance or having a man drop out of rank or file. The artillery shot us up without respite' (Koser, 1921, II, 542).

The battle ended in scrappy fighting west of Pettstädt, when the light detachments of Saint-Germain and Loudon came south to cover the retreat. A French soldier approached the plainly dressed Frederick and declared: ' "Corporal, I want permission to go back to Auvergne. That's where I come from" . . . While we were chatting he espied one of our NCOs gathering all the prisoners and arranging them in three ranks. "Hey, corporal, look at that bugger over there. He wants to line us up like Prussians, and we've only been here a couple of minutes!" ' (Frederick, quoted in Catt, 1884, 90–1).

By 5 p.m. the field was shrouded in darkness. Frederick had intended to lodge for the night in the castle of Burgwerben, but he found all the rooms full of wounded French officers. Rather than disturb these gentlemen, he established himself in a servant's room in a nearby house.

Frederick wrote to Wilhelmine on the evening after the battle: 'I can now die in peace, because the reputation and honour of my nation have been saved. We may still be overtaken by misfortune, but we will never be disgraced' (PC 9489).

The huge disparity in losses between the Prussians and their enemies was all the more astonishing when we consider that Frederick was fighting at a disadvantage of almost two to one. The allies were diminished by more than 10,000 men, most of whom were probably taken prisoner, whereas the Prussian losses amounted to less than 550. Seydlitz sustained a light wound in the arm, which nevertheless kept him from duty for four months. He was consoled by the attentions of a kindly lady at Leipzig, and by his promotion to lieutenant-general.

How did contemporaries rate this victory? It was evident that, after his first surprise, Frederick had seized and maintained initiative and control until the end of the action. Gaudi harboured no grudge for the harsh words in the Rossbach *Herrenhaus*, and he explained that

> if the king was able to turn the tables so masterfully in his favour, if he managed to counter the deadly designs of the enemy with such skill and speed, he owed it entirely to his own considerable talents. On the day of this battle he showed himself in his true greatness, as will be testified by all informed observers who were present at the event. (Jany, 1901, 10)

The French foreign minister, Cardinal Bernis, appreciated that Rossbach was also a victory for the Hohenzollern style of leadership: 'We must not forget that we are dealing with a prince who is at once his own commander in the field, chief minister, logistical organiser and, when necessary, provost-marshal. These . . . advantages outweigh all our badly executed and badly combined expedients' (to Choiseul-Stainville, in Volz, 1926–7, II, 196).

Frederick was too much the cosmopolitan to rejoice in one aspect of his triumph. Like Prince Henry, he was genuinely distressed at the misery he had inflicted on his spiritual brothers in the French officer corps: 'I can never get used to looking on the French as my enemies' (Archenholtz, 1840, I, 116). These sentiments were not shared by the native Prussian private soldier:

> Another circumstance which was of great advantage to us on this day was the natural hate which the ordinary Germans, but especially the men from Magdeburg, Brandenburg and Pomerania, harbour for everything that is French . . . they fought with real bitterness, as we could see most clearly in the behaviour of our cavalry when they were hacking into the enemy infantry. It was only with great difficulty that the officers were able to prevail on the common soldiers to give quarter. (Gaudi, in Wiltsch, 1858, 256)

The victory at Rossbach was of decisive importance in securing Frederick's western strategic flank. King George II of Britain was thereby encouraged to disavow the shameful treaty of Kloster-Zeven, and on 16 November a new chapter opened in the Seven Years War when Prince Ferdinand of Brunswick set out to assume command of the Hanoverian army. Over the following years his combined force of Hanoverians, British, German auxiliaries and Prussian cavalry was to draw on itself the entire French effort in Germany.

Meanwhile Frederick could think of nothing but the account he still had to settle with the Austrians in the east – 'strictly speaking, the battle of Rossbach merely afforded me the freedom to go in search of new dangers in Silesia' (*Oeuvres*, IV, 156). The royal army therefore followed in the tracks of the French and the *Reichsarmee* for only two days. Frederick then devoted his entire attention to arranging the march back to Lusatia and on to Silesia, where the Austrians appeared to be carrying all before them. Frederick planned to allow only one day of rest in every four, and he ordered his troops to live off their hosts whenever they halted in towns and villages, so as to relieve some of the problems of supply. This was a late time of year to embark on a fresh campaign, but Frederick was assisted by the remarkably mild weather which prevailed from the middle of October until the beginning of December (Mitchell, 1850, II, 305).

On 13 November Frederick began the eastward march from Leipzig with eighteen battalions and twenty-three squadrons. A force of equivalent size was entrusted to Field-Marshal Keith, who made a diversionary invasion of north Bohemia. This might have seemed an expensive detachment, but it attained the desired effect of drawing the Austrian corps of Marschall from Lusatia. On 21 November Frederick learnt that the route to Silesia by way of Görlitz was now free.

Every report from Silesia made Frederick's arrival more urgent. He already knew that the key fortress of Schweidnitz had fallen. On the 24th he reached Naumburg, at the gates of the province. Two days earlier the ominous sounds of heavy gunfire had carried across the plain from the east, and he was now told that the main Austrian army had stormed the Duke of Bevern's entrenched camp outside Breslau, the fortress-capital of Silesia, and that the Prussians had retreated across the Oder. Frederick was determined to retrieve this army, and he sent Lieutenant-General Kyau (later replaced by Zieten) to bring the troops back across the river and rejoin him at the Katzbach crossing at Parchwitz. Frederick resumed his march on the 26th, and the next day he learnt at Lobedau that the isolated garrison of Breslau had capitulated to the Austrians. He was left with no accessible base in Silesia.

Frederick reached Parchwitz on 28 November. He stayed there until 4 December, gathering in the scattered Prussian forces and making the physical and psychological preparations for the great blow that was intended to deliver Silesia. He arranged to have the

Political Testament of 1752 delivered into the shaky hands of August Wilhelm, if that proved necessary, and he composed a morbid *Disposition de ce que doit se faire après la bataille, en cas que je sois tué* (PC 9559).

On 2 December Zieten reached Parchwitz with the demoralised survivors of Bevern's army. Bevern himself had fallen into the hands of the Austrians, and Frederick suspected that he had allowed himself to be captured deliberately. The officers of the defeated army had dreaded their encounter with the king, 'like the criminal who shrinks from the gaze of his executioner' (Lojewsky, 1843, II, 123), but Frederick was bent only on making them useful for the next battle, and he regaled them with wine and reminded them of their past victories. The soldiers were revived by a free distribution of extra rations, and, more important still, by the men who came from the royal camp with tales of Rossbach.

Frederick was never more close to his army than at Parchwitz:

> During these winter days the king camped in the open air like
> one of his private soldiers. He used to warm himself at their
> fires, and then make room for others to take his place. He talked
> with the soldiers as if they were of his own kind. He
> sympathised with the travails which they had undergone, and,
> in the most friendly possible way, he encouraged them to
> behave like heroes just once more. (Professor Johann Georg
> Sulzer, in Volz, 1926–7, II, 120)

Never again was his army more truly national in character, for the Saxons and many of the foreign troops had been shed in the battles and forced marches of the last three months, leaving Frederick with a small but excellent force of 35,000 men, mostly native Brandenburgers, Pomeranians and Magdeburgers. There were ample reserves of musket ammunition (which in battle were to be brought up behind the battalions in carts), and the disproportionately large heavy artillery train of seventy-eight pieces included ten of the thundering *Brummers* – thick-barrelled 12-pounder fortress cannon which Zieten had transported from Glogau.

On 3 December Frederick made preparations to attack the Austrians, whom he expected to find entrenched to the teeth in the Duke of Bevern's old camp between Breslau and the Lohe. He brought together large quantities of bridging materials, and he assembled eight hundred volunteers in two battalions in order to spearhead an attack on the Austrian left. He wished to convey to the army the importance of what was at stake, and he ordered the generals and the regimental and battalion commanders to attend him at his headquarters at Parchwitz in the morning. This was melodrama indeed, by the austere standards of the Prussian service, and there was something about Frederick's weariness, his weak voice, and his shabby uniform which commanded all the more attention.

The 'Parchwitz Address' was delivered in German (unusually for Frederick, who mostly spoke in French), and the most authentic account renders it as follows:

> The enemy hold the same entrenched camp of Breslau which my troops defended so honourably. I am marching to attack this position. I have no need to explain my conduct or why I am determined on this measure. I fully recognise the dangers attached to this enterprise, but in my present situation I must conquer or die. If we go under, all is lost. Bear in mind, gentlemen, that we shall be fighting for our glory, the preservation of our homes, and for our wives and children. Those who think as I do can rest assured that, if they are killed, I will look after their families. If anybody prefers to take his leave, he can have it now, but he will cease to have any claim on my benevolence. (As recorded by Prince Ferdinand, Herrmann, 1918, 101–2)

There ensued a holy silence, which was broken when Major Billerbeck burst out: 'Yes, imagine any pig wanting to do that! What a time!' (Gr. Gstb., 1901–14, VI, 10).

Early on 4 December the army set off eastwards from Parchwitz in four columns and an advance guard. Frederick was riding well ahead with the Puttkamer and Zieten Hussars, and just short of the little town of Neumarkt the peasants in their Sunday clothes told him the almost unbelievable news that the place still held the enemy field bakery and their stocks of bread and flour. Frederick concluded that considerable Austrian forces were nearby, and he saw that he must seize this unexpected prize and anticipate the enemy on the low Pfaffendorfer-Berg beyond. He ordered his hussars to storm the town without more ado, since the grenadiers of the advance guard were still lagging far behind. Some of the squadrons rode around Neumarkt. The rest dismounted, broke in the gates with axes they had seized in nearby farmhouses, and cleared the houses with their carbines. Two regiments of Austrian hussars made good their escape, but the Prussians killed one hundred Croats and captured five hundred more. This was a highly unorthodox way of taking a defended post, but Frederick had already used dismounted hussars for this purpose at Pegau on the way to Rossbach. No Austrian army could yet be discovered, but on the deserted Pfaffendorfer-Berg the king came across some stakes which had been planted there by enemy engineers when they were laying out the site for a camp, which lent credence to some encouraging reports that the Austrians might be abandoning their entrenched position at Breslau.

In the evening Frederick retired to his quarters in a corner house in the square at Neumarkt. Here he learnt that the Austrians had indeed crossed the Lohe and the Schweidnitzer-Wasser, and that they were bivouacking in open ground on the near side. According to one account the report came from a Lieutenant Hohenstock, who had been posted within sight of the Schweidnitzer-Wasser, and who was able to count the standards of the cavalry of the Austrian right as they were carried across the stream (Kalkreuth, 1840, IV, 118–19).

If Frederick attacked early the next day, he could catch the Austrians at a time when they were labouring under all the disadvantages of the defensive without the usual compensations of a prepared position and fresh troops. In one respect, however, the risks were greater than Frederick knew, for Prince Charles of Lorraine had no less than 65,000 men under his command, whereas the king had put the numbers of the Austrians at 39,000, after the rigours of their Silesian campaign (PC 9553).

The fifth of December was to be the most celebrated day in Frederick's military career. Before daybreak he rode from the right wing of the cavalry to the Garde du Corps:

> The weather was fine but very cold. The troopers were standing by their horses and clapping their hands to keep warm. 'Good morning, Gardes du Corps!' 'The same to you, Your Majesty!' replied an old cavalryman. 'How goes it?' enquired the king. 'Well enough, but it's bloody cold!' 'Have a little patience, lads, today is going to be a little too hot!' (Hildebrandt, 1829–35, II, 39)

The army rose in silence at 4 a.m., and by five or six it was on the march by columns in two great wings of infantry, with a wing of cavalry on either side. A powerful advance guard strode in front, and ahead of that again Frederick scouted the way with three free battalions, the foot jaegers, and all the hussars of the army. The sun now climbed through a mist into a cloudless sky and revealed a wide and open landscape. The ground was mantled in a light covering of snow, but Frederick and many of his generals were familiar with every tiny rise and hollow of this plain, for this was where they held their grand autumn manoeuvres in peacetime.

Just short of the low scattered houses of the village of Borne the king advanced his hussars against a line of cavalry that could be distinguished through the mist. This was a force of Austrian hussars and Saxon *chevaulegers*, who were promptly put to rout. Six hundred prisoners were taken, and Frederick had the captives led past his marching columns so as to raise the morale of his troops.

Frederick left the three battalions and the jaegers to hold Borne, and rode out with Prince Moritz and a detachment of hussars to the minuscule Schön-Berg, from where he could see that he had emerged opposite the right-centre of vast lines of Austrians as they extended on a rough north-south axis for about four miles across his front. The details could now be distinguished with great clarity, even though he was facing into the sun, and it was perhaps now that he learnt from reconnaissance parties that the Austrian right, or northern, flank was anchored on the dense oak thickets of the Zettel-Busch (the only extensive area of wooded country on the field), while the left wing fell short of the support of the Schweidnitzer-Wasser. More important, looking to his right Frederick saw that the conformation of the Schleier-Berg and the Sophien-Berg offered him the means of executing a concealed march southwards for a couple of miles, after which a wheel to the east might bring the army into an attacking position perpendicular to the exposed Austrian left at Sagschütz. Almost certainly Frederick could give a name to all the villages he saw, which would have lent force and clarity to his instructions.

Meanwhile it would be useful to persuade the enemy that the Prussians intended to continue the original eastward advance beyond Borne. Frederick arrayed the cavalry of the advance guard for a time one thousand paces east of Borne in full view of the Austrians, and towards 11 a.m. some of the troops of the main army were temporarily deployed as if they intended to march in line directly against the Austrian positions. Prince Charles of Lorraine was watching these proceedings with close attention, and he was fully convinced that the Prussians were going to hit his right flank between Frobelwitz and Nippern. He accordingly moved nine battalions from the reserve and positioned them around Nippern, which was well over an hour's hard marching from the actual point of impact south of Sagschütz.

Late in the morning the Prussian columns wheeled to the south, passing through and around Borne, and by means of a complicated series of breakings-off and re-joinings the wings were converted into lines. For reasons which have never been properly explained, Prince Carl of Bevern and six of the nine battalions of the advance guard remained with Zieten and the right wing of the cavalry – a mixture of horse and foot which harked back to Mollwitz.

The ground in the centre and the south of the field of Leuthen was some of the most open and flat in Silesia, and yet, after the march had proceeded no more than a few hundred paces, the Prussian columns disappeared from the view of the Austrian high command, standing just north of Leuthen village. This conjuring trick was made possible by Frederick's intimate knowledge of the terrain. The king wished to make certain that the movement carried well clear of the enemy flank, so avoiding the confusions which had occurred at Prague and Kolin, and he told the puzzled army to continue marching towards the distant grey pyramids of the Zobten-Berg.

Soon after mid-day the heads of the Prussian columns arrived west of Lobetinz, where Frederick indicated a change of direction half-left to the east-south-east, and so past the Austrian flank. The limit of the march was established when Zieten and the battalions of Carl of Bevern wheeled into line of battle beyond Schriegwitz.

While the centre and left were still marching up to their assigned stations for the attack, Frederick rode out to a perilous viewpoint in a small pinewood near Radaxdorf. This copse was directly in line between some Austrian guns and a number of pieces of Prussian battalion artillery which chose this moment to open a duel. The cannon shot ripped through the trees from either side, and after a few moments Frederick's adjutant Captain Dyhern galloped from the trees waving his hat, and told Prince Ferdinand (commander of the central division) to cease firing on his royal brother (Herrmann, 1918, 103; the Staff history, Gr. Gstb., 1901–14, VI, 34, postpones this incident until the attack on Leuthen village).

The initial breakthrough was to be accomplished by Major-General Wedel with the three remaining battalions of the advance guard, namely the regiment of Meyerinck (26, see Map 16, p. 362) and the second battalion of Itzenplitz (13). To their right rear was a column of four battalions, mostly grenadiers, and a battery of 12-pounders which was moving up to a site on the low Glanz-Berg. The main body of the infantry was arrayed in a staggered line of battalions extending back to the left at fifty-pace intervals. The whole formed a textbook example of the Oblique Order (see p. 310).

Frederick aligned the attack with some deliberation. He gave careful briefings to all the commanders concerned, and he halted to speak to the *Frey-Corporals* Barsewisch and Unruh, who were bearing the colours of the colonel's company of Meyerinck:

> 'Ensigns of the Life Company, take heed! You must march against the abatis, but don't advance so quickly that the army can't keep up with you.' Whereupon His Majesty indicated the position of the enemy line to our battalions, and told the men: 'Lads, do you see the whitecoats over there? You've got to throw them out of their earthwork. You just have to go straight at them and turn them out with the bayonet. I will come up with five [*sic*] grenadier battalions and the whole army to support you. It's a case of do or die! You've got the enemy in front, and

all our army behind. There's no space to retreat, and the only
way to go forward is to beat the enemy.' (Barsewisch, 1863, 32;
the enemy on this sector were actually wearing blue coats)

Prince Moritz came up to Frederick watch in hand to remind him
that the short winter day was already well advanced, and the
Prussian lines finally moved forward into the attack shortly after
1 p.m. Even now Frederick sent adjutant after adjutant to tell the
leading battalions to moderate their speed.

The first enemy forces to feel the impact were regiments of
German auxiliaries, many of them Protestant Württembergers, who
for some minutes put up a surprisingly strong resistance from behind a
line of willows marking a small field ditch (Frederick's 'earthwork').
The Germans suddenly took to their heels when the Meyerinck
regiment came on regardless, and the further Württemberg battalions
to the east collapsed without ever having come under attack. The
Prussian infantry drove northwards in the direction of Leuthen village, powerfully assisted by the extraordinarily mobile batteries of
heavy guns. The pieces of the right and centre opened fire first from
the Juden-Berg north-west of Sagschütz, then joined the guns from
the advance guard on the broad Kirch-Berg.

Meanwhile, on the far Prussian right, Zieten was being forced to
commit all his fifty-three squadrons against his old enemy Nádasti,
who brought the cavalry of the Austrian left down to meet him. This
hard-fought contest ended with the Austrians defeated and in flight.
In the process the Prussian cavalry brigade of Lentulus captured
fifteen guns, and almost annihilated the Jung-Modena Dragoons.

At first Prince Charles of Lorraine sought to restore the battle
south of Leuthen by stripping individual battalions from his second
line, but soon the whole Austrian army had to be wheeled until it
formed along a new south-facing front which stretched through
Leuthen and for several hundred paces on either side. In some
locations the Austrians were piled thirty deep, presenting an excellent target in enfilade for the Prussian guns which had been brought
up to the low swell of the Butter-Berg.

The second phase of the battle opened at about 3.30 p.m. when
the Prussians opened an assault on the new Austrian line, and
especially on the core of resistance in Leuthen village. The attacks of
the Garde Regiment were repeatedly repulsed from the perimeter of
low, brick-built cottages and barns, until finally the way into the
interior was opened by the Third Battalion under the leadership of
Captain Möllendorff, who forced an entry from the south through a
suite of stables (Hoffmann, 1912, 87). Even now the German auxiliary battalion of Roth-Würzburg offered a spirited resistance from the

central churchyard, where the thick surrounding wall had four round corner towers. One of the battalions of Pannwitz (10) was beaten back in an initial assault, and ultimately the Prussians were forced to make a breach in the wall with their artillery.

Leuthen was carried after some thirty minutes of fighting. Behind the village, however, the Austrians stood their ground once more, and the cavalry generals Lucchese and Serbelloni swept down from their right with a force of about seventy squadrons. If the mass of Austrian cavalry had reached the open left flank of the Prussian infantry, it might yet have turned the balance of the day against Frederick.

This dangerous move was noticed by Lieutenant-General Georg Wilhelm von Driesen, whom we last encountered in the thick of the fighting at Chotusitz. Now at Leuthen he held under his command the forty uncommitted squadrons of the Prussian left, standing in dead ground near Radaxdorf, and on his own initiative he decided to intervene against the right flank of the Austrian cavalry as it flowed past him. The celebrated Bayreuth Dragoons (D 5) opened the attack, watched by the cuirassiers of Bevern's old army, who were still under something of a cloud. They were not altogether sorry to see the magnificent dragoons being mauled in the first clash with the Austrians. 'It is true that the cuirassiers in the second line could have given immediate support, but their best officers said: "Let the king's favourite dragoons stew a little first!" Finally, when the danger for the dragoons became too great, the cuirassiers arrived and saved them' (Kalkreuth, 1840, IV, 128).

The Puttkamer Hussars (H 4) came up in the rear and collided with the enemy Kollowrath Dragoons while the Austrians were still in the process of deploying, and overthrew them completely. The thousands of struggling cavalrymen bore down on the Austrian infantry north of Leuthen, and whole battalions of the enemy threw down their muskets and fled. Such troops as sought to make a stand were swept away in the stream of fugitives.

In these confused minutes Frederick was intent only on gathering, in the fast-descending darkness, a force with which he might gain the bridge five miles behind the field at Lissa, and so prevent the enemy from establishing themselves for a new battle behind the line of the Schweidnitzer-Wasser (Weistritz). The Seydlitz Cuirassiers and three battalions of grenadiers responded to the royal summons and set off with Frederick into the night of gently falling snow. On the Breslau highway Frederick was joined by Zieten and a dozen hussars, and at the isolated settlement of Saara he picked up a garrulous innkeeper who strode along by his stirrups with a lantern. The hussars closed in on the king to overhear the conversation, and three hundred paces short of Lissa the party drew a discharge of fifty or sixty musket shots at short range. The Prussians scampered to right and left through the willows that bordered the raised road. Frederick was the first to recover his voice: 'For God's sake, Zieten, this would not have happened if the hussars had obeyed orders! I told them to keep a strict thirty paces ahead of us!' (Nicolai, 1788–92, III, 236).

Frederick waited thirty minutes until his grenadiers arrived in support, and then the little expedition entered the town. There was an exchange of fire with the enemy on the far bank of the Schweidnitzer-Wasser, and with further Austrians who were concealed in houses around the town square. This was no business for a king, and Frederick accordingly turned into the castle of Lissa, which was a cheerful rococo house perched atop a fortified basement. Baron Mudrach, the owner, saw the royal party approaching the gate, and he made Frederick heartily welcome.

Frederick did not share the last spiritual experience of his army in this extraordinary week of December. Not until later did he hear how the entire army, still marching through the night, had raised its voice in the chorale 'Nun danket alle Gott!' The sound breathed fresh life into men who were almost paralysed with cold and exhaustion, and some of the veterans were to remember it as their most vivid experience of the war.

On the day after the battle the dead and wounded formed countless little snowhills. The Prussian casualties amounted to 6,382 officers and men, of whom the majority were probably lightly wounded. The Austrians lost 22,000 all told, 12,000 of them prisoners, together amounting to one-third of the effectives of their very considerable army.

It has never been seriously disputed that Leuthen was the greatest victory of the generation, and perhaps of the century, and that this day alone would have established Frederick's claim to a place among the most celebrated commanders. Almost every commentator has drawn attention to the high morale of the Prussian troops, Frederick's knowledge and exploitation of the terrain, the unhurried speed of the attack, the mobility and destructive fire of the artillery, the responsiveness of the infantry, the devastating intervention by the cavalry of the left wing, and the initiative shown at every level from Lieutenant-General Driesen to Captain Möllendorff. The achievement was of a different order from that of Rossbach, for at Leuthen the Prussians had overcome a hard-fighting and recently victorious enemy.

After the battle the British envoy Mitchell found the king 'pleased and happy, but not elated, with the great and almost incredible success of his arms. He talks of the action of the 5th

December . . . with the modesty becoming a hero, whose magnanim-
ity is not affected with the smiles, nor with the frowns of fortune' (11
January 1758, PRO SP 90/71).

On 6 December the Prussians crossed the Schweidnitzer-Wasser in
four columns, and rounded up four hundred baggage carts and considerable quantities of prisoners. The pursuit proper began only on
the 7th (unaccountably late, according to some of Frederick's critics,
Gr. Gstb., 1901–14, VI, 67–8), when the king dispatched Zieten with
a corps of sixty-three squadrons and eleven and a half battalions. By
that time the main body of the Austrians was making south-east
towards Schweidnitz and the Bohemian border, and thousands more
had surged through the gates of Breslau:

> Just imagine a cloudburst descending from the hills with
> thunder and lightning, and flooding the valley at the foot . . . in
> the same way we saw those countless troops flowing under our
> eyes . . . Every street became a river of men, and every lane a
> torrent. (Belach, 1758, 127)

On 8 December Zieten was checked at the Kleine-Lohe by a strong
Austrian rearguard, and Frederick wrote urgently to him the next
day: 'My dear Zieten, in these circumstances one day of exhaustion
will be repaid by one hundred of repose later on' (PC 9573).
Lieutenant-General Fouqué was sent to replace Zieten as commander
of the pursuing force, and on the 22nd and the 23rd he pushed the last
of the Austrian main army across the Bohemian border.

The Austrians still had many troops stranded inside Silesia at
Schweidnitz and Breslau. The siege of Schweidnitz was a formidable
undertaking which Frederick postponed until the next year, but the
Prussians subjected Breslau to an intensive bombardment and the
demoralised garrison surrendered as prisoners of war on 20 December.
Frederick exclaimed: 'God be thanked! I have drawn this terrible
thorn from my foot' (PC 9612).

On the 21st the Austrians began to march out of the Schweidnitzer Tor in a seemingly endless column. There were in excess of 17,000
troops in all, which was considerably more than some of the Prussians
had expected. Frederick was looking on, escorted only by a small
party of officers, and it seemed extraordinary that none of the
Austrians seized the opportunity to shoot him down (Hildebrandt,
1829–35, V, 127).

The Prussians finally entered winter quarters across central
Silesia and southern Saxony, and in their cramped accommodation a
terrible epidemic carried off far more men than had succumbed to the
bullets of French and Austrians.

The events of 1757 were remembered as 'that extraordinary campaign, the most fertile in battles, reverses and great events, of any
presented in modern history' (Wraxall, 1806, I, 161). Frederick called
it 'a campaign that was like three in one' (PC 9636).

The campaign fell into two clearly distinguishable parts: (a) the
working-out of the last chapter of the Frederician-Winterfeldt plan of
aggression which terminated at Kolin, when the king expended the
final advantages he enjoyed from having seized the initiative in
opening hostilities in 1756; and (b) the opening of the long-drawn-out
struggle for survival on the northern plain, and the unexpected
reprieves which Frederick won for himself at Rossbach and Leuthen.
The French never appeared at his back door again, and the Austrians
were thrown back into Bohemia with scarcely one-quarter of the
90,000 men who had crossed the border in the summer.

Frederick was to experience crises more acute than those he
underwent in 1757, but never was he to know campaigning of such
intensity. F.A. von Retzow explains that the armies of 1757 had been
expertly schooled through the long years of peace, and that their
commanders were burning with ambition: 'Towering above the rest
was the heroic figure of Frederick, at the head of a force of robust
warriors, whose courage was as yet untouched by misfortune. So it
was that one battle was fought after another, and human blood was
poured mercilessly away' (Retzow, 1802, I, 443–4).

On 21 December Frederick established himself for the winter in
Breslau, and he remained there, apart from short excursions, for
nearly three months. He compared himself to a sailor home from the
high seas who was in need of a rest ashore, and he spent many days
alone in the silence of his room.

At the beginning of January 1758 Frederick was confident that
the Austrians, after their catastrophe in Silesia, would be inclined to
peace, but all too soon it became evident that both they and the
French were determined to continue the war. The Austrians and the
Reichsarmee by themselves owned 150,000 effectives, and the Russians and Swedes had 98,000 more. Frederick himself was able to
gather scarcely 135,000 troops, and many of these were enemy prisoners who had been forcibly recruited into the army.

Faced with odds of this magnitude, the king evolved a routine of
operations that he maintained for the next four years. On the far
western flank he learnt to rely on Prince Ferdinand of Brunswick,
who was already displaying that near-genius for independent command that was to keep the French penned up in western Germany for

the rest of the war. With his Hanoverians and his other Protestant German troops, Ferdinand launched a lively offensive in February and early March 1758, and succeeded in turning the French out of Hanover and Brunswick and forcing them to retire across the Weser. Ferdinand ultimately took 100,000 British and Germans under his command, and in spite of every vicissitude of fortune he maintained a successful defence of Hanover and kept the French at a good arm's length from the vital fortress of Magdeburg, which supported the Prussian effort in Saxony.

Prince August Wilhelm was near death, and had been rejected by Frederick for high command. As some compensation, the next in line of the royal brothers, the thirty-two-year-old Henry, began to impress himself on Frederick as a clear-headed and expert, if also notably cautious, officer, very well suited for detached commands on the main theatre of war. We will often see Henry posted in Saxony or on the Oder, holding the enemy clear of Frederick's flanks and rear, while our hero dashes hither and thither intent on carrying out some great stroke with the royal army.

Frederick was certain that the main business of 1758 must be to throw back the Russians, who overran East Prussia in January, and who were sure to advance against the Oder. In order to have his hands free to deal with the Muscovites, Frederick intended to take the field very early and paralyse the Austrians by a grand strategic diversion. This was to take the form of an offensive from Upper Silesia into Moravia, where a siege of Olmütz would open many interesting possibilities. Olmütz lay on the direct path to Vienna, and the Austrians were certain to respond in a dramatic fashion. Perhaps they might offer battle under circumstances favourable to Frederick. At the very least they would pour forces into a theatre of war where they could be of no conceivable use to the Russians.

On 17 March 1758 Frederick planted his headquarters in the monastery of Grüssau, which lay in a small plain in Silesia, beset with pine-covered hills on all sides. From here he could follow the progress of the siege of nearby Schweidnitz, and supervise the gradual assembly of his troops and transport train at Neisse. Frederick encouraged the belief that the thousands of waggons were being gathered in order to convey the magazine at Neisse westwards to Glatz, and thus open the way for an offensive into Bohemia.

The Prussians normally did not excel in the siege of fortresses, but on 18 April Frederick abridged the operation against Schweidnitz by launching a dangerous but successful storming of the Galgen-Fort. The commandant of the whole fortress-complex at once surrendered. This agreeable postscript to the campaign of 1757 delivered nearly 5,000 men into Frederick's power and gave him great quantities of muskets and weapons and other equipment to distribute in the army. More important, Frederick had gained ten clear days for the coming campaign, 'and time is something which is very precious to me just now' (PC 9939).

The concentration at Neisse could now go ahead:

Here I am at the outset of my campaign. God knows how it will go, or what will become of me! I am cursed with having to make war without respite, and yet some people are stupid enough to think that I am fortunate . . . Look what a fine time I have! Every morning I have to read through forty letters – half say nothing at all; one quarter are very routine or very difficult to read; the rest are full of ghastly news. (Catt, 1884, 25)

Frederick's thoughts turned to Sans Souci, and to his long-dead father, who appeared to him in a nightmare and ordered him to be bound and taken under arrest to Magdeburg. He awoke in a sweat.

On 24 April Frederick made an ostentatious reconnaissance of the roads and country around Glatz, then made back at speed to Neisse on the 25th. On that day the army came together 'in such small divisions, and by so many different routes, that it was impossible for anybody who was not previously informed of it, to imagine that so great a force could be collected in and about this town . . . the cavalry are encamped here and there in the bottoms so as not to be seen from the mountains on the other side of the river, and the infantry is all crammed into the town' (Major-General Joseph Yorke, 26 April, PRO SP 90/71). In fact the king was going to take little more than 55,000 troops with him into Moravia. All the rest of the disposable force was with Henry in Saxony, with Lieutenant-General Zieten at Landeshut covering the Lower Silesian border, or facing the Russians beyond the Oder.

On 29 April the royal army crossed the Austrian frontier, and Frederick made an unopposed entry into Troppau – a sizeable but indefensible town stranded on the Silesian side of the border hills. The first of May brought a most tiring march across the steep valley of the rushing Mohra stream, and up through darkly wooded hills to the gloomy village of Alt-Zeschdorf. The snow fell all day long, and the slippery roads accentuated Frederick's obvious exhaustion. The next day the army pushed rapidly across an open, undulating table land (very much like Salisbury Plain, except for the spruce trees), and finally on the 3rd the Prussians reached the edge of the plateau in an area of dense woodland which descended steeply to the plain of Olmütz. (See Map 17, p. 363.)

The Austrian field army was still nowhere to be seen, and Frederick calculated that he had gained six marches on Daun, who must still be located in Bohemia as much as one hundred miles to the west, watching the invasion routes from Glatz. On 4 May the army made the difficult passage of the marshes and multiple channels of the river Morava, or March, and Frederick established himself on the far side near Littau. This was an important strategic gain, for he had interposed himself between Olmütz and the path of relief from Bohemia, and the barrier of the Morava now turned to his own advantage.

On the 5th Frederick had the leisure to reconnoitre the neighbourhood. In appearance it was a Central European Lombardy, complete with dykes, ditches and rows of poplars, and with the spires of Olmütz offering a passable resemblance to Milan or a Parma. Frederick had passed this way in 1742, but Olmütz was no longer the friendly place he had known then. A girdle of permanent fortifications had been cast around the city, and the sun, which was now breaking through the murk, was reflected from extensive inundations which extended to the north and south. The garrison was made up of 8,500 well-found troops, who were commanded by the active old general Ernst Dietrich von Marschall.

Frederick arranged his army in a number of camps around Olmütz, of which the most important were that of Field-Marshal Keith (covering the siege from the north-west), and the one which Frederick in person established further to the south at Schmirschitz, where there was a low ridge that offered wide views over the plain to the east and south. Here also he could stand guard over the fringe of the great tract of low, wooded and rocky hills which extended westwards into Bohemia.

By 20 May the king's old companion Lieutenant-General Fouqué had arrived in the neighbourhood of Olmütz with all the divisions of the convoy of siege artillery. It was a remarkable technical achievement, and one which perhaps misled Frederick into believing that it would be a matter of no great difficulty to maintain his communications with Upper Silesia. Now the siege could begin in earnest. The first parallel was dug against the fortress on the night of 27 May, and on the 31st the Prussians opened fire with forty-three pieces.

Gradually Frederick was overcome by a sensation that things were slipping beyond his control. Daun had indeed gathered his army in the forests to the west, but instead of advancing boldly into the plain and allowing himself to be beaten, he harassed the environs of the Prussian camps with his hussars and Croats, and infiltrated messengers and parties of recruits into Olmütz through the feeble cordon of the Prussians. 'The troops of the blockading force were so weak, and the investment was so loose, that many officers of the siege corps were in the habit of ordering their lunch from the town' (Kalkreuth, 1840, IV, 132).

The siege itself was going badly. The direction of the approaches had been well chosen, namely from the south-west over the high and firm ground of the Tafel-Berg. However, Frederick was at loggerheads with his chief engineer, Colonel Balbi, over the siting of the trenches and batteries. These had been begun at an excessive distance from the fortress, and they were now coming under enfilade fire from one of the Austrian works. Finally at the end of June two blows made it impossible for the Prussians to linger any more around Olmütz.

Frederick had been aware that the continuance of the siege hung upon the safe arrival of a huge convoy of well over 3,000 carts, bearing artillery ammunition, flour, one million thaler in cash, items of equipment, and sutlers' provisions. Large numbers of recruits marched with the column, as much to serve as reinforcements for the army as to act as escort.

On 28 June the convoy survived a first Austrian attack at Unter-Gundersdorf. Later in the day Zieten arrived on the scene from Silesia with two battalions of grenadiers, two regiments of cuirassiers and 600 hussars, and on the 29th he leaguered up the carts into a defensive *Wagenburg* south-west of Altliebe (he was criticised after the event for not having pushed straight on towards Olmütz).

At eight on the rainy morning of 30 June the reinforced convoy set out along the road to Domstadtl. This was a landscape of little rounded hills and valleys, and isolated blocks of conifers. It was not particularly wild, but it was very well suited for ambush. Little or nothing was seen of the Austrians until the advance guard had passed through Domstadtl, but then almost the whole stretch of the road back to Altliebe came under attack from the south-east by the detachment of Major-General Siskovics. Zieten pushed the infantry into two counter-attacks, one each from his right and left wings, but the troops were thrown into disorder when they marched through the woods, and the Austrians were able to drive them back to the road. Late in the morning a further enemy force under Major-General Loudon closed in from the west, and finally Siskovics combined with the newcomers in an attack on the Altliebe *Wagenburg*, which still held two-thirds of the carts.

By the late afternoon the Prussians had been split in two. Zieten and 4,200 men made back towards Troppau, while Major-General Krockow struggled on to the army with eight battered battalions, half a dozen squadrons of cuirassiers, 550 hussars and a sorry train of about one hundred waggons. Around Altliebe and Domstadtl the Prussians left 2,386 casualties and prisoners, twelve cannon and over 3,000 vehicles. Mitchell observed:

The king of Prussia either was not informed of, or he did not believe, the intelligence he had of the strength of the Austrian detachments sent against the convoy. Perhaps it was, unhappily, that the first convoy passed unmolested, though the escort was much inferior to that which accompanied the last, which may have occasioned this fatal security. (8 July, PRO SP 90/72)

Daun's main army had meanwhile cut its way through the woods and emerged in open country at Dobramillitz, twenty miles south of the Schmirschitz camp. On 27 June the Austrians moved north-east to Klenowitz, as if to challenge the Prussians to battle, and Frederick made his preparations accordingly. On the night of 30 June, however, Daun neatly side-stepped Frederick by executing a passage of the Morava in three columns, almost under the noses of the Prussians, and the next day he pushed rapidly up the east bank and established direct contact with Olmütz. Frederick had assumed that if the Austrians crossed the Morava anywhere, it would be further downstream towards Kremsier, where the river formed a single main channel.

The news of the Domstadtl ambush reached Frederick on the morning of 1 July, and even before he heard of the relief of Olmütz he decided to raise the siege 'without losing one moment, or seeming in the least disconcerted' (Mitchell, 8 July, PRO SP 90/72). The contrast with the clogging half-measures of 1744, when the garrisons were left in Tabor, Budweis and Frauenberg, is a measure of Frederick's progress as a commander. He remarked to Keith: 'It is better to make a disagreeable decision than to decide nothing at all, or wait until things become quite impossible' (PC 10104).

Frederick seems to have been put on his mettle by his strategic defeat at the hands of the Austrians. His activity and his inventiveness returned, and over the following five weeks he executed a retreat which must be counted among the most interesting of his achievements. The Prussians were encumbered by 5,000 carts, not to mention the siege train, and the king feared that if he retreated northwards along the familiar Troppau route he might be exposed to a kind of Domstadtl writ large. He accordingly decided to cut loose from his line of communication and make north-west across the hills to Bohemia, where he might seize the Austrian magazine at Königgrätz, and open the avenues to Glatz and Lower Silesia.

The Prussians set off on 2 July. Frederick took the lead with a first column, and Keith came up with the second. The king moved rapidly through Mährisch-Trubau and Zwittau, and, after a two-night halt at the vast Renaissance castle at Leitomischl, he pressed on through Hohenmauth to reach Königgrätz on 13 July. The Prince de Ligne observed that under normal circumstances the Austrians could have expected to pick up many deserters: 'But they say that he so skilfully interspersed the suspect regiments with units of Pomeranians and Brandenburgers that hardly anyone could escape from him' (Ligne, 1795–1811, XIV, 212).

Frederick discovered that the enemy had already destroyed most of their magazine at Königgrätz. However, Keith joined him there on the 14th, and the Prussians could congratulate themselves that they had accomplished the first and most dangerous stage of their retreat. The heavy artillery and the sick were sent ahead on the 17th, and they were soon well on their way to Glatz.

Daun had been slow to come up in support of his light corps under Loudon, but on the 22nd, having crossed the Elbe downstream, he took up an extensive camp to the west of Königgrätz between Urbanitz, Stösser and Stresetitz. Frederick sought in vain for a weak point that might even now offer him the chance for a battle. By this time the Russians were making dangerous progress towards the Oder, and on 26 July Frederick began a stately retreat in the direction of the border passes. He denied the Austrians any opportunity of falling on his columns in the way they had done on the same ground in November 1744.

On 4 August Frederick's army reached Nachod, and shortly afterwards the Prussians fell back across the border into the County of Glatz. 'He retired; but it was the retreat of a lion, who turns upon his pursuers. Frustrated, not vanquished; formidable even in retreat; carrying with him all his artillery and baggage, he left to Daun little more than a negative triumph' (Wraxall, 1806, I, 180).

Frederick had terminated the Olmütz campaign stylishly enough, but he was now forced to choose from a narrow range of unattractive strategic options. He remarked to Catt:

> I do not know, my friend, whether you have a clear idea of my circumstances, and how often I am forced to act contrary to rules that I know to be good. It all comes down to my unfortunate state of affairs. Sometimes it is a question of extricating myself from a dangerous position. At other times I have to ward off one immediate enemy, so that I can rush off to deal with somebody else who is threatening me elsewhere.
> (Catt, 1884, 148)

With the prospect of Daun's army irrupting at any moment into the northern plain, and Prince Henry holding Saxony with just 20,000 men, Frederick reckoned that he had a space of only three weeks in which to deal some decisive blow against the Russians. It is not easy to determine just how serious Frederick expected this clash would be.

He spoke dismissively to Field-Marshal Keith, a veteran of the Russian service, about the military qualities of the Muscovites, but he made the same kind of personal arrangements as he did before the battle of Leuthen: 'It is my intention that, after I am dead, my body shall be disposed of with no ceremony. I am not to be opened by the surgeons, but taken quietly to Sans Souci and buried in my garden' (*Ordre*, 22 August, *PC* 10230).

On 11 August Frederick left Margrave Carl of Brandenburg-Schwedt in charge of the forces in Silesia, and set off in person for the Oder with a corps of just fourteen battalions and thirty-eight squadrons, or about 11,000 men in all. He could not take a greater force with him without revealing his design to Daun. On the eastern theatre he intended to join the 26,000 troops of Lieutenant-General Dohna, who had taken over the command from Lehwaldt in March. He faced an army of some 45,000 Russians, who were making their way westwards to the Oder under the command of General Fermor.

On 15 August the main Russian force opened a bombardment of the small fortress of Cüstrin. Once in their hands, this place would offer them a secure passage of the Oder just fifty miles from Berlin. There could be no question of stopping the Russians somewhere beyond the Oder, as Frederick had originally hoped. His plan was now to join Dohna, relieve Cüstrin, and bring the Russians to battle in the neighbourhood.

Frederick drove his corps relentlessly north-west to Crossen and then down the left bank of the Oder to the pretty university town of Frankfurt, where he arrived on 20 August. He lodged at the house of a clergyman's widow, and as he stood at the door the sound of the Russian bombardment of Cüstrin was carried distinctly from the north. 'I noticed', wrote one of his officers, 'how at every shot the king took a pinch of snuff. It was possible to detect, under that amazing steadfastness which distinguishes the character of that remarkable man, the working of his sympathy for the fate of that unlucky town, and how desperately impatient he was to come to its help' (Anon., 1787–9, II, 13).

The king rode off with a small party at two the next morning, and he reached Dohna's corps at Gorgast, just outside Cüstrin. The troops were in fine external order, with powdered hair and a good carriage, but Frederick did not bother to conceal his dissatisfaction with their commander. Frederick's own corps was resting exhausted at Frankfurt, after its forced marches over sandy tracks under a burning sun.

The Russians promptly abandoned their siege of Cüstrin, and formed themselves up nearby on the east bank of the Oder. Frederick associated Cüstrin with some of the most vivid episodes of his impressionable youth, and now when he entered the town its hideous

aspect made all the greater impression. 'Here and there stood part of a
wall, or some remnants of rooms or stables, but everything was
charred and devastated, and the interiors of the roofless buildings
were filled with wreckage, still glowing within' (Ortmann, 1759,
417).

The two forces, Frederick's and Dohna's, united at Manschnow
on 22 August, making an army of about 37,000 troops. 'Nobody could
have been more avid for battle than were the Prussians at this
juncture. The demon of war seemed to have taken possession of the
entire army, and every man longed for action' (Hülsen, 1890, 86).

Frederick maintained a cannonade on the far side of the Oder
near Cüstrin, but meanwhile he made preparations to cross the river
nearly twenty miles downstream at Alt-Güstebiese. Lieutenant-
General Kanitz went ahead with the pontoon train and two regiments of infantry, and on the night of 22 August he built a bridge
undetected by the Russians. Frederick simultaneously fed some of the
infantry and hussars of the advance guard across the river by boats,
and they established a bridgehead on the far bank. The army hurried
up from Cüstrin on the 23rd. The regiments began to cross the bridge
at noon, and they hastened ahead to a camp between Zellin and
Clossow. The season was as hot as ever, and the strain of covering an
average of fifteen miles on every day's march was now telling heavily
on the troops. 'The men were hungry, but they had to eat their bread
on the march, and satisfy their thirst from whatever puddle they
found by the road. It is safe to say that a good third of the army was
stricken and collapsed' (Prittwitz, 1935, 213). This last push beyond
the Oder was particularly valuable for Frederick, for it enabled him to
cut between Fermor's main army, to the south, and the nearly
12,000-strong corps of General Rumyantsev, which was stranded
downstream at Schwedt.

The 24th was another day of terrible heat, and Frederick allowed
the troops to take a little rest before they set off in four columns in
search of the enemy at two in the afternoon. From a church tower a
lad watched the army advance over the fields, 'or rather we deduced
as much from the way the muskets gleamed in the sun. But soon the
dust arose and hid the sight from our view. People also said that on the
way Frederick repeated an order to the infantry to reverse their
muskets and carry them with the butts uppermost, so as to conceal
the march from enemy reconnaissance parties' (Jakob Wilhelm Bertuch, in Kalisch, 1828, 48).

Late in the afternoon Frederick detected the presence of the
Russian army south of the little river Mietzel. The stream itself was
unguarded, and Frederick pushed the advance guard over the intact
bridge at the Neudammer Mühle and arranged the troops in a bridge-

head position. The main army rested on the north bank, and an additional bridge was built to assure the communications between the two elements of the army. It was an important gain to Frederick to establish himself so easily on the far side of the Mietzel, which was fringed with marshy banks and a rank growth of soggy woods.

The extensive woodlands prevented Frederick from discovering much of the Russian positions, and consequently at the evening *Parole* he could convey little more than the outline of the battle which he intended to give on the next day. It was unlikely that he actually commanded that the Russians were to be cut down without mercy, as has sometimes been alleged, but the army went into battle believing that such was the royal intention. The same had happened at Hohenfriedeberg. Frederick retreated for a couple of hours to a tiny room in the Neudammer Mühle. Catt went there at midnight and found that the king was already taking coffee. 'I addressed myself to the attendant who was on duty, and asked him whether His Majesty had managed to get any rest. "Rest, my dear sir? He slept so well it was difficult to wake him up!" ' (Catt, 1884, 158).

Two forestry officials presented themselves at the mill at the king's command. One of them was dispatched to show the cavalry the way across the Mietzel upstream at Kerstenbrück. The other, who was called Zöllner, was told to guide Frederick in person as he led the army through the woods of the Zicherer-Heide on a wide arc around the eastern flank of the Russian position. After receiving a final report from a scout Frederick delayed no longer; 'The king donned his hat, attached his sword, and left the building to meet the generals and adjutants who were waiting outside. "Good morning, gentlemen!" he called out. "My congratulations – we have won the battle!" He mounted horse, and Zöllner guided him along the path which had been chosen' (Kalisch, 1828, 50–1). Frederick was with the advance guard, and the columns of the main army came up behind. It was 3 a.m. on 25 August.

Daylight found the columns emerging into the open cultivated country around Batzlow. Nothing was to be seen of the Russian army, though the smoke rising from the neighbouring villages told of the Cossacks' handiwork. Suddenly Frederick caught a view to the left of the huge supply train of the Russians, standing out against the skyline at the edge of the sandy bluffs which overlooked the Warthe Marshes near Klein-Cammin. Retzow was one of the first of the many commentators who have posed the question whether the king should now have abandoned his intended attack on the Russian army, and instead snatched a near-bloodless victory by seizing this lightly defended *Wagenburg*, which would have made Fermor's position untenable. Frederick tried to deal such a blow after the battle (*PC* 10254), when he was better acquainted with the prowess of the Russians, but on the morning of the 25th he was already so well on his way against the Russian rear that he was disinclined to call off his grand enterprise.

The Prussian columns executed a sharp right turn south of Batzlow, and they made a shallow inclination as they passed through and around Wilkersdorf. Frederick could as yet distinguish only part of the Russian position, and he let the march continue due west until he halted the columns south of the village of Zorndorf and wheeled them into line. Fermor was now in the process of completing a drastic about-turn of his army, in response to the appearance of the Prussians in his rear, and his powerful flanks and the multiple lines of his reserves gave his position the aspect of a gigantic square.

Frederick had already made up his mind to advance his left wing in an attack in the 'Oblique Order' (see p. 310). To the untutored eye the field appeared 'a large open plain, edged with woods' (Mitchell, 1850, I, 428). In fact the ground was segmented by a number of interesting features, and Frederick chose as his target the unsupported Russian right or western wing, which had been incautiously located in front of the rest of the Russian army, and was standing between the ponds and damp meadows of the deep Zabern-Grund to the west, and the long and shallow indentation of the Galgen-Grund, which was one of the curious little valleys which striped the centre of the field from south-east to north-west.

The Zabern-Grund was to serve as a useful left-hand cover for the northwards advance of the two infantry divisions which constituted the striking force. Lieutenant-General Manteuffel took the lead with the eight battalions of the advance guard, and he was to be closely supported by the left wing of the main army under Lieutenant-General Kanitz, who had nine battalions in his first line, and six more on his flank and rear. Lieutenant-General Marschall von Biberstein came up in reserve with twenty squadrons, and the thirty-six squadrons of Lieutenant-General Seydlitz were ordered to move down the western side of the Zabern-Grund and keep pace with the main attack. The rest of the infantry fell under the command of Dohna, and constituted the 'refused' wing standing on the right.

Colonel Moller was instructed to soften up the Russian right by a lengthy bombardment. For this purpose he positioned one battery of twenty pieces to the north-west of Zorndorf, and another of forty directly to the north of the village.

The cannonade began at 9 a.m., but the gunners ceased fire when they found that the shot was falling short. They advanced the batteries a further six hundred paces and made a heavy and sustained fire. The Russian gunners sought to reply, but they were facing slightly uphill and into the sun, and they were blinded by the dust and smoke which were blowing into their faces. To civilians standing miles away it appeared that 'the ground was shaking in response to a continuous peal of thunder. The windows in the houses were rattling, and the sky was darkened by the dense cloud of smoke which arose from the battlefield and the burning villages' (Bertuch, in Kalisch, 1828, 51–2). The missiles ploughed through the deep files of the Russian infantry, and some of the shot rolled as far as the train of light baggage, causing panic among the drivers and horses. 'What added to the horror of this spectacle was that the Cossacks and Calmucks had set fire to the villages all round, and a great number of Russian powder waggons blew up in the woods which surrounded the field of battle' (Mitchell, 1850, I, 429).

The Prussian army began to march:

> A peculiarly plangent melody was being sounded by the woodwind of one of the regiments, and Frederick asked one of his generals whether he could identify it for him. He replied 'It's the tune of the hymn *"Ich bin ja, Heer, in deiner Macht!"* ("Now Lord, I am in Thy Keeping").' Frederick repeated these words with some emotion, and he listened with acute attention as the music receded gradually in the distance. (Hildebrandt, 1829–35, II, 15)

Ensign Prittwitz of Alt-Bevern (7; see Map 18, p. 364) noted that the players made themselves scarce as soon as the advance of the left wing took it through and around the burning village of Zorndorf.

Beyond Zorndorf the dust hung so thickly that the advance guard came within forty paces of the Russian lines before the rival infantry exploded in a fire-fight. It was about 11.15 a.m. Manteuffel had some of the best units of the army under his command, namely six battalions of grenadiers and the highly regarded East Prussian regiment of Kanitz (2). However, the troops suffered heavily from the blasts of musketry and canister that were delivered in their faces. Worse still, their left wing lost contact with the protection of the Zabern-Grund, a mistake which gave the Russian cavalry the space to throw fourteen squadrons against its flank. The Kanitz regiment lost more than 60 per cent of its effectives, and the survivors and the rest of the advance guard fled in panic.

The left wing of the main army was itself going badly astray. Frederick had failed to convey to Lieutenant-General Kanitz the essence of his task, which was to act in close support of the advance guard. Kanitz instead conceived that he must maintain contact with Dohna on the right wing, and instead of following on the heels of

Manteuffel he swung his division half-right out of the intended axis of advance. His regiments were somewhat disordered by the passage of the birches and spruce of the Stein-Busch, and on the far side they collided with the deep lines of the enemy centre, which had largely escaped the attentions of the Prussian artillery. The Russians enveloped the right wing of the division, and broke through the centre at the vulnerable point between the battalions of grenadiers and the East Prussian regiment of Below (11).

Frederick had meanwhile ridden to join Prince Moritz, who had commandeered Biberstein's cavalry (D 6, D 7, D 8) and recovered a heavy battery which had fallen into the hands of the Russians. The British envoy Mitchell encountered the king at this moment. 'I thought this a sufficient authority for me to wish him joy of the victory, which I did. He received my compliments civilly, and, as I rode along with him, whispered to me with great coolness: *Mon ami, les affaires vont bien mal à ma gauche, je vais y mettre ordre mais ne me suivez point!*' (Mitchell, 1850, II, 60). Frederick dismounted, and seized a colour of the Below regiment in an attempt to rally the fugitives. This gesture was as futile as most of its kind. He could scarcely be seen through the dust, and his voice was lost in all the din. The day had the makings of another Kolin, for the intended rapier-like thrust had degenerated into a wide frontal assault which had cost Frederick nearly two-thirds of his infantry.

If the happenings on the centre and left were now converted into something like a victory, it was entirely the doing of the hitherto unengaged thirty-six squadrons of Seydlitz. For a time Seydlitz held his cavalry on the far side of the Zabern-Grund, aloof from the infantry battle to the east. According to one story, first related by Blanckenburg in 1797, Seydlitz resisted the threatening and repeated orders from Frederick to intervene without more ado. He sent an adjutant with the reply: 'Tell the king that after the battle my head is at his disposal, but meantime I hope he will permit me to exercise it in his service!'

After the defeat of Manteuffel and Kanitz it was impossible for Seydlitz to hold back any longer. He fed his squadrons over the Zabern-Grund by three crossing points, then pushed them diagonally up the steep slopes on the far side against the flank of the victorious infantry and cavalry of the Russian right. The physical obstacles to this complicated movement were still greater than the ones which had faced the Prussian cavalry at Soor. It seems that Seydlitz kept three of the regiments (C 8, H 2, H 3) under his personal command, and formed them into regimental columns on three-squadron frontages, which crashed into the Russian infantry simultaneously and to devastating effect (Immich, 1893a, 147–8). 'This whole wing [that is the right of the enemy] was so ill-treated that it broke and fled into the wood of Quartschen and towards the Mietzel, but unhappily the peasants had burnt the bridges, otherwise it is probable the battle had there ended. But the Russians finding no retreat remained in the wood firing' (Mitchell, 'Notes on the campaign 1758', British Library, Add. Mss. 6867).

This extraordinary battle took on new life at about 1.30 p.m., after Frederick had betaken himself to the right wing, where Dohna held the remaining fifteen battalions of the Prussian army. The king was weighed down by a moral inertia, after the various disasters on the left, and he halted in front of the regiment of Prinz von Preussen (18) and gave vent to the encouraging cry 'May God have mercy on us!'

> Prince Moritz was aware of the unfortunate turn of events, and of how badly things could turn out. He was, it seems, none too pleased with the king's exclamation. He took off his hat, cast it into the sky, and with a resolute air and a deep voice he bellowed: 'Long live the king, we've won the battle!' The line of troops responded with a 'Long live the king!' of their own, which appeared to evoke a fleeting smile from His Majesty. Prince Moritz and General Below told the troops: 'Lads, you see those men falling back over there? They are Russian prisoners under escort. Forward! Long live the king! March on!' (Catt, 1884, 159–60)

The advance had scarcely got under way before the enterprising Russian major-general Démicoud thundered down on Dohna's infantry with the thirty-six squadrons of the Russian left. Within minutes the second battalion of Alt-Kreytzen (40) was taken prisoner, and the Russians captured the heavy battery which it had been guarding. Some of the Prussian regiments came near to breaking in panic when they espied a cloud of dust emerging from around the south side of the trees of the Stein-Busch, but the newcomers proved to be the Plettenberg and Alt-Platen Dragoons (D 7, D 8) which had been summoned by Frederick (or sent by Seydlitz) from the left. The hopes of the men of Alt-Kreytzen now revived. One of their number describes how the Prussian dragoons

> charged with loose reins so frightfully that the earth shook beneath us. They surrounded both us and the enemy cavalry, and threw up such a thick cloud of dust that they mistook us for Russians, and we too began to feel their terrible blows. We infantrymen then grabbed our guns again, fired bravely, and shouted: 'Victory! Long live the King of Prussia!' At this point

the king himself came riding up and said: 'Lads, don't shout victory yet – I'll tell you when the right time comes.' The Russian cavalry was completely cut down, and the blood was running in streams. The king had brought two infantry regiments with him to our aid, but there was nothing left for them to do. (Musketeer Hoppe, 1983, 9)

Further regiments of Prussian cavalry were fed into the battle, and between 6 and 7 p.m. Dohna's wing began a final push which ended in obstinate and confused fighting along the Galgen-Grund:

The troops were striking or stabbing with musket butts, bayonets and swords. The ferocity on both sides was unspeakable. There were badly wounded Prussians who were oblivious of their own preservation, and were bent only on murdering their enemies. The Russians were just the same. A mortally wounded Russian was found lying on an expiring Prussian, and he was tearing away at him with his teeth. (Archenholtz, 1840, I, 169)

Discipline was collapsing on both sides. The Black Hussars (H 5) got behind the Russian lines to the dank hollow of Quartschen, and gave themselves up to plundering the money chests. Some troops of the Observation Corps on the Russian left broke open the kegs of spirits they found in their officers' baggage, and drew fresh heat from the fiery liquid. Amid this madness an officer of Dohna's wing caught sight of Frederick, 'who was riding with perfect composure between the two lines, and peering calmly through his telescope heedless of the shot and shell which flew about him' (Prittwitz, 1935, 227).

The firing ceased at about 8.30 p.m., and the Prussians and Russians drew apart, leaving the battlefield to the dead, the wounded and the abandoned guns. The sheer concentration of Russian numbers on their western flank, together with the final advance of Dohna, had the curious effect of imparting an anti-clockwise wheel to the two armies, so that they ended the day occupying much of the same positions which their enemies had held in the morning. The Prussians were now established in the region of Quartschen and the Langer-Grund, while the Russians were heaped up to the south in the direction of Zorndorf. Frederick's small tent was pitched among the troops, and before he retired for the night the king wolfed a plate of bread and butter and talked with Catt about the terrible things they had just witnessed.

On the following days, when passions had cooled, the most shocking sights of the Seven Years War gave some indication of the nature of the violence of the 25th. A young officer saw places where the cavalry had been slaughtering each other, and men and horses were piled up in heaps. What struck me most was the ferocity that was still written on the countenances of the dead men . . . I could scarcely pick my way with my horse through the bodies and weapons which strewed this awful field in such profusion. Muskets, pistols, swords, cartridge pouches and especially those little Russian copper powder ladles were littered about so densely that it would have been a considerable undertaking to cart them all away. (Prittwitz, 1935, 235–6)

Those nine hours of combat had cost the Russians 18,000 men, and the Prussians 12,800, or one-third of Frederick's force.

Numbers of this magnitude ceased to convey anything to the imagination. What brought the carnage of the day home to Frederick was the loss of his favourite *Flügeladjutant*, Captain von Oppen of the Garde du Corps, whom he was accustomed to keep in readiness a few paces to his left and rear. At Zorndorf he had been sent with a message to Seydlitz, but he had failed to return. A search was made for him after the battle, and he was found dead of forty-seven wounds. Oppen was carried to the royal tent in a blanket, and Frederick had to turn about to hide his grief. He wrote to Wilhelmine, who was lying gravely ill at Bayreuth, that he was unable to stop weeping:

It is to you that I confide all my distress, all my hidden agonies. Just think what would become of me, if I had the irreparable misfortune to lose you! My dear, divine sister! Summon up all your strength, and more, to bring yourself back to health! My life, my happiness, my very existence lie in your hands! (*PC* 10257)

Not the least of the horrors of Zorndorf was the immediate prospect of a further battle. On the morning of the 26th Frederick rode out on reconnaissance in the direction of Zorndorf village. The Russian hussars and Cossacks gave way, but closer to Zorndorf he came under artillery fire and a discharge of canister flogged the ground around him. The Russians kept up their bombardment for the rest of the day, and cost Frederick about one hundred more casualties.

Frederick withdrew his cavalry to the north side of the Langer-Grund, to spare them the useless ordeal of skirmishing with the Cossacks, and he thereby unwittingly left open to Fermor the means of re-establishing contact with the Russian supply train in the Klein-Cammin *Wagenburg*. The Prussians detected that the enemy were on the move only at 5 a.m. on 27 August, by which time the Russians had slipped past their flank and were well on their way to Klein-Cammin, where they dug themselves in.

Frederick now took up quarters in Tamsel, the little place where he had come a quarter of a century before to pay court to the lady Wreech. These agreeable memories were no compensation for the inconvenience of being stranded beyond the Oder so far from the other theatres of war. Frederick knew that his presence was urgently needed in Saxony, where Prince Henry faced the combined forces of Daun and the *Reichsarmee*, and it was galling not to be free of the Russians, even after the bloodletting of 25 August. The 31st brought a further frustration when Captain Wendessen and a raiding party failed to deliver a blow which Frederick had aimed at the large Russian depot at Landsberg.

At last on 1 September Frederick learnt that Fermor had begun to retreat. It was true that the Russians now fell back only as far as Landsberg, that they were in good order, and that they had the capacity to renew their advance, but Frederick could no longer delay his departure for Silesia and Saxony. He left Dohna in charge of the forces beyond the Oder, and on 2 September he set off to join Prince Henry.

The importance of the battle of Zorndorf lay not in the outcome of the day, which gave the advantage to neither side, nor in the very limited strategic results. Far more significant was what it revealed about changes in the character of the war. The Russian troops had begun to intervene in the main conflict, and the first encounter with these folk had engendered a combat of a ferocity which appalled every man who had survived the battle. Nobody in Frederick's experience had ever fought so obstinately, and Catt suspected that the king was now embarrassed by the scornful comments he had uttered about the Muscovites. A Prussian wrote that 'the terror which the enemy have inspired in our troops is indescribable. Most of our people speak without reserve about this condition of fear' (Herr von Goltz, in Immich, 1893a, 143).

The Prussian artillery had done well in the battle, and the achievements of the horse made Zorndorf 'the last great and glorious deed of the Prussian cavalry' (Dette, 1914, 71). Frederick told Catt of what he owed to some of his comrades:

That was a terrible day, and there was one moment when
everything seemed to be going to the devil. All would have been
lost, my friend, but for brave General Seydlitz and the courage
of my right wing, and especially the regiments of my dear
brother [Prinz von Preussen, 18] and Forcade [23]. I tell you,
they saved the state and they saved me, and my gratitude will
last as long as the glory which they have acquired on this day.
(Catt, 1884, 161)

However, the fine combinations of the 'Oblique Order', as applied at Zorndorf, demanded too much of the judgment of the generals, and of the endurance of the infantry, which went into battle already exhausted by hard marches, and faced an obstinate enemy on a day of crushing heat. The East Prussian regiments of Dohna's former army had wilted under the experience, and now that their homelands were lost to the enemy their reliability inspired still less trust. Indeed, the failure of the left wing had not only brought Frederick to the verge of defeat, but it aroused concern as to the steadfastness of the army in the face of similar ordeals.

It was with some urgency that Frederick wrote to Prince Henry: 'From what I saw on the 25th, I must tell you to keep your infantry under tight discipline. Mark my words, make them fear the stick! And take along with your army all the cannon you have time to collect, regardless of calibre' (PC 10265)

During Frederick's march against the Russians, Daun and the *Reichsarmee* had heaped up concentrations of no less than 100,000 Austrians and Germans in Saxony, a mass which threatened not only to engulf Dresden, but to endanger the Brandenburg heartland and Berlin as well.

On the Saxon theatre the Prussians had only some 45,000 disposable troops, namely the army of Prince Henry on the Elbe, and the 24,000 or so men of the Margrave Carl, who had moved into Lusatia. Frederick now came south with all possible speed with 15,000 or 16,000 troops detached from the Oder. 'The celerity with which the marches have been executed almost exceeds credibility. In five times twenty-four hours the army led by the king of Prussia has marched twenty [i.e. one hundred English] miles' (Mitchell, 7 September, in Mitchell, 1850, I, 445).

On 11 September Frederick joined his forces in Saxony, and entered Dresden under the eyes of the enemy hosts. He could see the rows of the tents of the *Reichsarmee* beyond the Elbe to the west, but he chose to establish his headquarters on the right bank of the river at Schönfeld, so as to be close at hand to the position of Daun's army amid the rocks at Stolpen. Frederick and his Austrian rival had in fact assumed the posture they were to maintain, with some violent intervals, for the rest of the war. 'The king held the plain, and Daun stayed in those hills which so frequently served as his refuge in this conflict' (Warnery, 1788, 278–9). There could be no question of turning Daun out of his camp by direct assault, and in this broken terrain the Prussians were too slow on their feet to be able to trap General Loudon, who was roaming about with an Austrian flying corps. Frederick therefore planned to put indirect pressure on Daun by threatening his eastern supply lines, which ran from Bohemia by way of Zittau, and from southern Silesia by way of Bautzen.

The Prussian army decamped on 26 September, and the next day Frederick detached Lieutenant-General Retzow with about 9,000 troops to hasten ahead in the direction of Bautzen and Weissenberg. Daun responded to this danger by abandoning the Stolpen position on 5 October, but instead of falling back into Bohemia, as Frederick had hoped, he moved laterally to another strong camp at Kittlitz, where he arrived on the 7th. In other words, the scene of the confrontation had merely been shifted thirty miles to the east.

It was now time for another attempt to get across the Austrian communications with Silesia. As a preliminary operation, Frederick ordered Retzow, who now commanded 10,000 men, to seize the dominating Strohm-Berg, which lay within artillery range of the right wing of the Austrian camp. Retzow got under way early on 10 October, but when the mist rose at 11 a.m. he found that the Austrians had anticipated him on the hill with heavy artillery and four companies of grenadiers. Retzow was disinclined to attack, and Frederick placed him under open arrest.

At the same time the first bound of the 30,000 troops of the royal army took them to Hochkirch, where Frederick intended to stay only until provisions arrived from Bautzen and enabled him to resume the eastward march. Meanwhile he arranged the army in a straggling camp which faced generally east in the shape of a shallow 'S'. (See Map 19, p. 366.) The centre extended from Rodewitz to the neighbourhood of Hochkirch, and was well emplaced above the Zschorna-Kohlwesa hollow. The nine battalions on the left wing were reinforced by a battery of heavy artillery standing in an earthwork, but their position was an isolated one, since Frederick was using them to facilitate his communications with Retzow's camp at Weissenberg.

It was, however, the arrangement of the southern, or right, wing around Hochkirch that excited the most interest. Eleven battalions of regular infantry and twenty-eight squadrons were positioned in the locality, of which three battalions and fifteen squadrons under the command of Zieten formed a salient projecting to the west. Hochkirch was a village of narrow streets, but its splendid new church resembled a small cathedral in size, and the massive churchyard wall was set with a palisade. South of the churchyard a low redoubt contained a battery of guns (twenty 12-pounders and six lighter pieces). Three battalions of grenadiers guarded the battery and two adjacent works, and beyond them again the free battalions of Angelelli and Du Verger were stationed on the far side of a birch wood.

All of this would have been eminently defensible if it had not been located so close under the dominating ridge of the Kuppritzer-

Berg, which was swarming with the enemy Croats. Again and again
the eyes of the anxious Prussian officers turned to the dark mass of
that hill, with its serrated outline of massive conifers.

If the Austrians lacked the elemental ferocity of the Russians,
they were accumulating a great fund of technical expertise. Daun
had 80,000 troops at his command, which was well over double the
force immediately available to the Prussians, and his gifted chief of
staff, Lieutenant-General Franz Moritz Lacy, persuaded him to employ this superiority in an attack by multiple columns. The weight-
iest blow was aimed against Hochkirch itself – the main army was to
approach over the Kuppritzer-Berg in two massive columns, while
Generals Loudon and O'Donnell led two further columns (mostly of
cavalry) against the flank and rear of the village respectively. The
tightly packed regimental columns were calculated to bring a great
concentration of force to bear on an objective in a short time. The
attack of the main army promised to be particularly effective, for on
this side the Austrians could take advantage of the cover offered by
the tongues of woodland which reached into the Wuischke hollow.
When the woods finally gave out, the Austrians needed only to cross a
short stretch of open fields before they entered dead ground, screened
by the further hill slopes from the view of the Prussians around
Hochkirch. The two Prussian free battalions were badly positioned to
see anything of interest, and they were isolated from all support.

The night of 13 October was damp, misty and starless. At five in
the morning half a dozen signal rockets streaked through the murk,
and the Austrians began to drive in the Prussian pickets. Frederick
was still resting in his headquarters at Rodewitz, and the battle
around Hochkirch was well under way before he was aware that
anything was amiss. The king had grown all too accustomed to the
noise of early-morning skirmishing around his camps, and though he
had spent the night half-dressed, his adjutants had been unable to get
him to stir. Finally a number of spent musket balls began to slap
against his lodging. He got up cursing, and in his bad temper he
smashed a pane of his bedroom window with his stick. Outside he
walked along the front of his troops, still repeating the formula 'They
are only Croats!'

The firing increased in force. Captain von Troschke now came up
with the report that the Austrians had taken the redoubt to the south
of Hochkirch:

'How can you possibly think that?' retorted Frederick. 'I am sure
of it,' said Troschke, 'and it won't be long before they start firing
at us with our own cannon.' He had scarcely finished when the
Austrians opened up with the 12-pounders from the redoubt

south of the churchyard. They were aiming at our camp, and the shot stormed over our heads. Frederick now exclaimed: 'Troschke, you are quite right! Lads, take up your muskets! Somebody find my horse!' (Barsewisch, 1863, 72)

Meanwhile the individual Prussian generals were bringing their forces into action as best they could. The right wing of the cavalry was battling to hold off the columns of Loudon and O'Donnell and intervene against the left flank of the Austrian infantry attacking the village. The Schönaich Cuirassiers (C 6; see Map 20, p. 368) had been stationed at Pommritz in the rear because there had been no room for them in the first line of the camp, and now they were standing at the disposal of Major-General Krockow, who had served in that regiment up to the rank of major. Krockow was unabashed when Zieten came up to him and delivered the startling order: 'General, you are to wheel to the right and attack the Austrian army!' Krockow summoned his officers to him. 'Gentlemen', he said, 'we have known one another for a long time. Today we must show what kind of people we are!' (Kalkreuth, 1840, IV, 167). The troopers formed a column on a one-squadron frontage, and after passing through the Prussian infantry they pressed home their attack against the Austrian grenadiers south of Hochkirch. Krockow was mortally wounded, but the regiment returned with a captured colour and a rich haul of Austrian prisoners.

The Prussian infantry around Hochkirch had ceased to exist as formed units, except for the second battalion of Margrave Carl (19), which emplaced itself behind the churchyard wall under the command of Major Simon Moritz von Langen. Meanwhile battalion after battalion of the unengaged centre was being rushed south in order to stave off the collapse of the right, and Field-Marshal Keith sent an officer to Frederick with the message: 'Tell the king I shall hold out here to the last man and give the army a chance to assemble. We are in the hands of God, and I doubt whether we shall see each other again!' (Paczynski-Tenczyn, 1896, 47).

Keith was directing a counter-attack by the regiment of Prinz von Preussen (18) when he received a musket ball in the stomach. Very shortly afterwards a second shot plucked him dead from his horse. At about the same time Moritz of Anhalt-Dessau was incapacitated by a bullet wound, and he had to be carried away. Prince Franz of Brunswick, the young brother of the queen, was beheaded by a cannon shot, just to the west of Hochkirch, and his riderless horse galloped in a panic up and down in front of the Prussian lines.

By now a mass of Prussian infantry was heaped up in front of the Austrian guns. In one of the streets, the notorious Blutgasse, as it was later called, the troops were jammed so tightly that the blood flowed in a veritable river, and the dead were held upright by the press of their comrades. This massacre was occasioned by the confusion in command, by the inadequate space for the infantry to deploy between Hochkirch and the Prussian cavalry to the west, and by the effects of the near-impenetrable fog and smoke.

More dangerous still, for the tenure of the position, was the attack which one of the columns of the Austrian right delivered against the north-eastern salient beyond Rodewitz. The grenadier battalions of Wangen and Heyden (St. gb 1; 19/25) for a time put up a brave fight, but the rest of the infantry melted away, and the Austrians stormed into the great battery that was the key to this flank.

Frederick was twice observed among the troops battling for Hochkirch. He was under musket fire with the regiment of Wedel (26) and suffered the loss of his fine brown English horse, and when daylight came he was seen with the cavalry of the right, covered with dust and earth from a cannon shot which had fallen nearby. By about 8 a.m., however, the king had to give all his attention to the business of forming a new rearward line north-east of Pommritz.

In front, the cool and capable Lieutenant-Colonel Saldern had reassembled the regiment of Alt-Braunschweig (5) and elements of five other battalions into an improvised rearguard, and he was now executing a zig-zag retreat that was calculated to throw the Austrian gunners off their aim. On the right flank Frederick received very welcome support from the corps of Retzow, who had seen the flashes and flames from Hochkirch, and dispatched Prince Eugene of Württemberg to assist the royal army with four battalions and fifteen squadrons. Württemberg spurred ahead with the cavalry, and he averted the very considerable danger that was presented by the division of O'Donnell, which might easily have cut across the path of retreat.

From Pommritz the king fell back to another temporary position on the heights north-west of Klein-Bautzen. He was in as much physical disorder as any of his men. His sash was stained with the blood from his horse. The order of the Black Eagle was torn from his chest, and his coat was blackened with mud and powder smoke. The subaltern Barsewisch reached him with three colours and thirty soldiers of the regiment of Wedel. The young man had had his hat knocked from his head by an Austrian cuirassier, and he had cast off his new sash in an attempt to divert his pursuers. Others arrived without coats, breeches or footwear.

The gallant Major Langen was one of those who had failed to make good their escape. He and his battalion had tried to break out of the back gate of Hochkirch churchyard at bayonet point. The troops were cut down in the alleyway outside, and Langen himself was now in the hands of the Austrians, dying of eleven wounds.

Having reassembled what was left of his army, Frederick established a camp in the evening at Doberschütz. That night, in his new headquarters, he was gripped by the full comprehension of his losses. The army had clearly suffered very heavily (its casualties and missing reached 9,097, or nearly one-third of the effectives). He was probably little affected by the end of Franz of Brunswick, once described as 'a lovable, gentle, courteous and benevolent prince' (Latouche, in Volz, 1926–7, I, 274), which was not Frederick's style at all. However, the king was reduced to tears by the death of Keith, in whom he saw a fellow spirit as well as an accomplished soldier.

Prince Moritz of Anhalt-Dessau never returned to the service. He survived his wound, and the experience of being intercepted on the way back to Dessau by the Austrians, but a lesion on his lip finally developed into a cancer which killed him before the end of the war. It had been impossible for Frederick to live on terms of companionship with this savage eccentric, but Moritz had been the soul of the infantry at Leuthen and Zorndorf, and his untutored intelligence had always been at the king's command.

Frederick talked of these losses with Catt on the same night:

> 'Just look at how many brave men I have lost! How I loathe the trade to which I am condemned by the blind chance of my birth! But I have something on me which can bring this episode to an end, if it becomes intolerable.' He undid his collar, and from beneath his shirt he drew out a ribbon, to which was attached a little oval golden box which had been resting against his chest. 'My friend, this is all I need to furnish the conclusion for my tragedy.' He opened the little box, and we counted out eighteen pills. 'These are opium', he explained, 'and the dose is more than enough to consign me on that dark journey from which nobody returns.' (Catt, 1884, 190)

Frederick successfully concealed the deepest injury of all, which was to his pride. No other defeat was ever attributed so directly to his miscalculations, and in no other action were his words and responses recorded so minutely. Frederick now bitterly regretted his separation from Retzow and one-quarter of the army on the morning of the 14th: 'At Hochkirch I saw and experienced the sad fate which overtakes an army when it weakens itself excessively by detachments' (PC 10658). The lack of vigilance was such as Frederick would not have forgiven in any of his commanders, as Warnery pointed out (1788, 281), and in general terms Mitchell concluded that the outcome of the day was 'owing to two causes, the very great contempt he had of the enemy, and the unwillingness I have long observed in him to give any degree of credit to intelligence that is not agreeable to his own imaginations' (Mitchell, 1850, I, 455). Four days after the battle Frederick received a hurt that was no less painful for having been long expected. He had already written to Prince Henry of his peculiar concern for their ailing sister Wilhelmine, explaining that he had been brought up with her since his earliest infancy. News of her death reached him on 18 October, and for some time his sobbing rendered it impossible for him to speak.

In the context of Frederick's life, the word 'heroic' has been devalued by over-use. However, it is not easy to think of a more suitable adjective to apply to a man who, after the ordeals which he had undergone, could now present a face of outward confidence to his army, and snatch the initiative from his enemies.

Frederick believed that he should linger no more at Doberschütz, facing Daun, at a time when the Austrians were feeding 20,000 troops into his beloved Silesia and had begun to lay siege to Neisse. After the losses at Hochkirch, Frederick sent word to Prince Henry to detach reinforcements from the Elbe, and he was delighted when his brother arrived in person on 20 October, bringing with him eight battalions and five squadrons. For the first time since the battle Frederick began to talk openly about military affairs, and he was cheered by the realisation that Daun was doing nothing to exploit the Austrian victory.

On the evening of 23 October the Prussian army slipped away from Doberschütz and began its swift and stealthy march on Silesia. The details were executed by the dour Lieutenant-Colonel Saldern, and on 26 October the Prussian advance guard gained the important road junction of Görlitz. Three days later Daun gave up all hope of anticipating Frederick at Neisse, and resolved instead to double back to the Elbe, where the Austrians might now have the chance to reduce Dresden and Torgau undisturbed, and the *Reichsarmee* under the Prince of Zweibrücken could reduce Leipzig. For the next week, therefore, Frederick and Daun recoiled in opposite directions. The Austrian siege corps under General Harsch decamped from before Neisse on 5 November, and Frederick entered this town two days later, having reached the eastward limit of his march.

The Austrian light troops swarmed across the routes between Silesia and Saxony, which left Frederick for some days uncertain of Daun's whereabouts. Only on 13 November, two days after the event, did Frederick learn that Daun had arrived before Dresden. Fortunately the commandant, Count Schmettau, won a useful span of time for his master by defying every call to surrender, and as a sign of his resolution he cleared the field of fire by burning the suburbs in front of the Altstadt fortifications – 'the whole circuit of the town appeared to be in flames, ruins and smoke' (Mitchell, 1850, I, 459).

Frederick turned back west in response to the threat to Dresden. He passed the field of Hochkirch, which aroused some melancholy reflections, but on 20 November he reached Dresden with an advance guard of cavalry. Daun fell back into his hills. Frederick was further gratified to learn that the *Reichsarmee* had retreated from before Leipzig, and that Haddik's corps of Austrians had abandoned the enterprise on Torgau.

Frederick stayed in Dresden for nearly three weeks, and then travelled to Silesia to spend the winter in Breslau. He dispatched each day's work as early as his could, and devoted the rest of the time to reducing his tumultuous memories to some kind of order. He was disturbed by the growing technical expertise of the Austrians, and by the certainty of a continuing war against near-overwhelming odds. There was a new savagery of temper, occasioned by the experience of the battle of Zorndorf. There was also satisfaction that the brilliant campaign which closed the year had effaced the memory of his humiliation at Hochkirch.

A notable air of deliberation attended all of Frederick's doings in the first months of 1759. He had renounced all ambition of taking the royal army once more on adventures south of the border hills, and for the first time since the Hohenfriedeberg campaign he was content to let the enemy carry the war to him, hoping to win 'a good decisive battle, which will render it safe for me to send detachments to where the need is most urgent' (*PC* 10812). Fortunately the mild winter and the late opening of the campaign enabled Frederick to restore the field army to a well-found 130,000 men, despite some initial shortages of remounts and clothing. He intended to hold the main force of 44,000 in Lower Silesia and apportion the rest among Henry in Saxony, Fouqué in Upper Silesia, and Dohna on the Polish flank. Meanwhile Frederick maintained an easy routine in Breslau, allowing himself ample time to join Quantz in the evening concerts, and to talk over his excursions into prose and verse with Catt.

In April Frederick drew the main army together in cantonments around Landeshut, and he sought to gain himself some time by sending small raiding corps across the border. Fouqué ruined the magazines at Troppau and Jägerndorf in Austrian Upper Silesia, while Henry launched a similar expedition from Saxony into north Bohemia, where he destroyed magazines to the worth of 6,000–700,000 thaler:

> Whilst they [the Austrians] expected to have been attacked in
> the centre, the extremities of their army at Troppau and
> Leitmeritz (distant from each other upwards of two hundred
> English miles) have been defeated, and their magazines ruined
> nearly in the same moment, His Prussian Majesty remaining all
> the time quiet in his quarters at Landeshut; with such justness,
> ease and ability does he guide this vast machine. (Mitchell,
> 1850, II, 55–6)

In May Prince Henry turned west against the upper Main and
wreaked similar destruction at the expense of the *Reichsarmee*,
compelling the Germans to fall back towards Nuremberg.

The main Austrian army finally left its quarters on 2 May, but
instead of obliging Frederick by crossing the hills to do battle, Daun
merely hung about on the Bohemian side of the border, drilling his
troops. Austrian officers were occasionally to be seen on the summits,
reconnoitring the Prussian position, but they invariably withdrew
again as soon as the Prussian hussars put in an appearance. 'Would
you have believed', Frederick remarked to Catt, 'that I would have
been capable of staying quiet so long?' 'Not at all, Your Majesty.'
'Neither do my enemies. They still do not know me very well. They
imagine that I am unable to stay put, that I must always be on the
attack. But I know how to remain on the defensive when I have to'
(Catt, 1884, 239). This waiting game was, however, very uncongenial
to Frederick's temperament. He was plagued by toothache, he continued to weep for Wilhelmine, and he wrote to d'Argens that he
feared that his fire and his good humour had gone for ever.

At the beginning of July the allied intentions at last made
themselves known. Daun with 75,000 troops was moving on Lusatia,
as if to draw Frederick to the south-west, while General Saltykov
completed the concentration of 60,000 Russians at Posen undisturbed
by Dohna, and he made ready to move against the Oder by the back
door:

> It is feared the King of Prussia's project of cutting [off] the
> Russian army has failed by the slowness of his generals. This has
> put His Prussian Majesty in very bad humour; and it is truly a
> hard case to be under the almost fatal necessity of executing in
> person the projects he has formed. (Mitchell, 1850, II, 74)

Frederick got the Prussian army on the move on 4 July. He made it
his first priority to guard the Bober crossings on the most direct route
between Daun and Saltykov, and to this end he planted himself in the
exceptionally strong position of Schmottseiffen on 10 July. He hoped
to fix the Austrians in Lusatia, while retaining the freedom of action

to move against Saltykov, or bring support to Henry in Saxony, or to Fouqué, whom he had left behind to guard Landeshut.

The Schmottseiffen camp extended over a luxuriant landscape of bold grassy bluffs, divided one from another by steep little valleys where oak, spruce and lime grew in profusion to a great height. It was admitted to be far more powerful than the position at Hochkirch, and Frederick later categorised it as one of those camps 'where the enemy is reduced to attacking one or two points' (Article VII, 'Éléments de Castramétrie et de Tactique' (1770), *Oeuvres*, XXIX, 13–14). The general conformation was that of a horseshoe, open to the north-west, with the salients of the Stein-Berg and the Kalten-Vorwerk reaching out towards the direction of the enemy approach. 'His Prussian Majesty is extremely vigilant; he reconnoitres the enemy's posts every day, attended sometimes with a body of horse and foot, and sometimes only with a very small escort of hussars, exposing his person to the greatest hazards, in a country formed by nature for ambuscades, and in the face of an enemy that abounds in light troops' (Mitchell, 1850, II, 78–9). The king wrote that he would soon know his bearings as well as in the garden of Sans Souci.

Between his expeditions, Frederick spent the time in his head-quarters in the lonely farm of Dürings-Vowerk, which formed an observation post in front of the centre of the position. He took the opportunity to correct some of his verse, and read French translations of Tacitus, Sallust and other classical authors. 'He was fond of saying, "You will often find me engrossed in reading and writing. I need this diversion at a time when I am preoccupied with gloomy thoughts. I see the dark clouds gathering, and before long a frightful storm will be visiting its destruction on some locality or other" ' (Catt, 1884, 243).

Events moved more quickly in the last ten days of July than over the previous seven months. Frederick was appalled to learn that Dohna was retreating in the face of the Russians, with his supply arrangements in a state of collapse. The king therefore bestowed dictatorial powers on his favourite young lieutenant-general, Kurt Heinrich von Wedel, and he sent him to assume command of the 28,000 troops beyond the Oder. Frederick gave him a twelve-point instruction, of which the most important articles read:

(a) First of all hold the enemy up at a good position
(b) Then attack them after my style [i.e. in the 'Oblique Order'].
    (*PC* 11238)

In the event the Russians were the ones who took up the 'good position'. Displaying unsuspected adroitness, Saltykov made a rapid circuit of the Prussian force and planted himself at Paltzig, astride Wedel's communications with Crossen on the Oder. Wedel knew nothing of the quality of the Russian army, and precious little more of his own, 'but he was convinced of one thing, and that was that he would unfailingly be called to personal account if he failed to obey the repeated orders from the king, and suffered General Saltykov to advance any further without bringing him to battle' (Gaudi, in Bethcke, 1907, 198). The Prussians duly attacked on 23 July, and they were repulsed with losses of up to 8,000 men, which made this battle of Paltzig (Kay) almost as costly as Hohenfriedeberg and Soor together.

Frederick had hoped at every moment to receive good news from beyond the Oder, but on the afternoon of the 24th Wedel's adjutant Bonin galloped up and told the story of how the army had been 'crushed by the terrible fire of the Russian artillery' (Catt, 1884, 245). Frederick gave vent to some harsh expressions concerning Wedel's stupidity, but he held no lasting grudge against him, for he knew that his general had acted in accordance with the spirit of his instructions.

Tall pillars of dust soared into the sky above the Silesian plain as column after column of troops now set themselves in motion. In essence Frederick was marching north to confront the Russians on the Oder. There were, however, some rather complicated processes at work, and it is perhaps worth setting them out in schematic form (see also Map 21, p. 369):

(a) Prince Henry had broken free of the Austrians in Saxony, and he had brought 19,100 troops to Sagan in central Silesia.
(b) Frederick in person assumed command of the Sagan corps on 29 July, and he made ready to move to the support of the approximately 19,700 survivors of Wedel's force on the Oder. Henry was left in charge of the 44,000 or so troops of the main Prussian army, which stayed in the Schomottseiffen camp.
(c) Daun simultaneously dispatched two corps of his own to link up with the Russians, namely Loudon with 24,000 men, and Haddik (who had followed Henry from Saxony) with 17,300.
(d) Saltykov and his 41,000 Russians were about to occupy Frankfurt-an-der-Oder.
(e) Fouqué with 19,000 Prussians was facing the 38,500 Austrians of Harsch in southern Silesia.

Frederick left Sagan on 31 July, and strove to overtake Loudon and Haddik before they could reach the Russians. By forced marches Frederick reached Sommerfeld on 1 August, and the next day he veered westwards and captured Haddik's baggage train at Markersdorf. The king did not appreciate that Haddik had already given up the race and was intent only on luring the Prussians away from the direct route to Frankfurt. Loudon therefore enjoyed a clear run to the

Oder. He crossed at Frankfurt on 5 August and joined Saltykov, so forming a Russo-Austrian army of about 64,000 men.

The Prussian concentration was also taking shape. Frederick made a camp south of the Friedrich-Wilhelms Canal at Müllrose, where by 6 August he had completed the union with Wedel's force. By now the king was something of an expert in the art of incorporating beaten armies. At first he kept Wedel's troops (like Bevern's after Breslau) in moral quarantine in a separate camp, lest the atmosphere of defeat should infect the whole, but meanwhile he was all graciousness and encouragement to the defeated troops. Frederick's own spirits were cheered by the news that Ferdinand of Brunswick had won a great victory over the French at Minden in western Germany.

On 9 August Frederick was joined at Wulkow by Lieutenant-General Finck with a corps of troops which had been covering Berlin, which gave the Prussians a total force of 49,000 men. The king planned to deal the blow against the Russians in exactly the same style as in the campaign of Zorndorf one year before. Once again he planned to pass the Oder downstream, or to the north of the Russian army. If all went well he would gain an undisputed passage, and then he would march south to the attack, trusting that speed and surprise would help him to discover some weakness in the enemy positions.

A regiment of Prussian fusiliers was ferried across the Oder at Göritz on 9 August, and the troops established a bridgehead which permitted two bridges to be constructed in safety the following day. One of the bridges was built with material from the nearby fortress of Cüstrin, and the other was formed of the army's pontoons. The infantry crossed the bridges on 10 August, which was a beautiful summer night, and the cavalry waded the shallow water at Ötscher. On the far bank the army advanced to a position just short of the village of Bischofsee, and when daylight came Frederick began to orientate himself in this singularly barren terrain of swamps, ponds, thickets and grassy heaths.

A certain Major Linden was found to have been in the habit of hunting in the locality, but he proved to be completely incapable of giving a tactical appreciation of the ground. Nor could any information be obtained from a senior forestry official, who was reduced to incoherence by the sight of the king, even though Frederick spoke to him in a gentle and friendly fashion.

Frederick made a personal reconnaissance in the afternoon, and from the low Trettiner Spitz-Berg he gained his first clear view of the enemy. As he looked south he saw that these people had entrenched themselves along the length of a row of hillocks, which rose like a sandy shoreline from the yellow reed-covered levels of the Hühner-

Fliess. These wetlands could be traversed only by two narrow cause-ways, and Frederick decided that it would be sufficient to keep the enemy amused on this side by bringing up Lieutenant-General Schorlemer with forty squadrons and Lieutenant-General Finck with the eight battalions of the reserve corps. The king had something more ambitious in mind for the main army, which he resolved to take on a wide left-handed circuit through the woods of the Neuendorfer-Heide around to the south-eastern or far side of the allied camp, which he assumed to be unfortified. Again the parallels with Zorn-dorf are very close.

How capable were Frederick's troops of responding?

> The heat and the dust were frightful . . . the soldiers had put
> their weapons in good order, and now they had thrown
> themselves down on the grass and the burning sand and given
> themselves up to sleep. The horses were lying round about.
> They were tormented by mosquitoes and flies, and they were
> just as spent and exhausted as the men. It was usual in such
> circumstances for the men to do their cooking, but this time
> hardly anyone availed himself of the opportunity – the heat,
> dust and exhaustion were all too much. (Lojewsky, 1843, II,
> 252)

The evening air brought a little coolness, but it also carried the sound of church bells from distant villages, awakening melancholy thoughts among those soldiers who were still awake.

Between 2 and 3 a.m. on 12 August the two columns of the main Prussian army began their silent march along the woodland paths. The tracks were obstructed by roots, undergrowth, ditches and mud-dy patches, and Frederick did what he could to cheer the troops as they were struggling forward. The Westphalians of the regiment of Puttkamer (9; see Map 22, p. 370) were two hours into the woods when they encountered Frederick, who was standing at the wayside. 'As we marched past he greeted us with a "Good morning, lads!" He added in Low German: "A good plate of beans would be nice just now, wouldn't it?" "Yes!" we replied. "Well then, wait a bit and we'll see what we can do" ' (Dominicus, 1891, 50).

The king reached the edge of the woods beyond Kunersdorf village in daylight, and he found that he had made two terrible miscalculations. First, the undulating ground along the south-eastern side of the enemy camp was far more heavily fortified than the northern side (only Loudon's corps near Frankfurt was looking north) – in other words Frederick had obliged the Russians by taking his army on an exhausting march just to attack them where they were strongest. Second, it appears that Frederick only now discovered that the frontage available for the assault was severely cramped by a chain of ponds which extended from the south into Kunersdorf village. In this context it was probably significant that the Dorf-See, the most considerable of these meres, lay concealed from view in a sunken bed.

Lacking the opportunity for a further reconnaissance, Frederick seems to have decided on the spur of the moment that the whole weight of the attack must be delivered to the east of the ponds against the salient of the Russian position on the Mühl-Berge. This (according to Tempelhoff) occasioned some delay and confusion while the heads of the columns retraced their steps and the drivers of the teams of the 12-pounders manoeuvred their pieces around on the narrow tracks between the trees.

Finally at 11.30 a.m. the Prussians opened a prolonged bombardment with an overwhelming force of at least sixty heavy guns. 'The heat was hideous. The rays of the sun were burning like jets of flame, and the dust and the scorching sand made the torture quite intolerable' (Lojewsky, 1843, II, 259).

The Prussian pieces were arranged in three batteries (on the Walk-Berge, the Kloster-Berg and the Kleiner-Spitzberg) and their concentric fire embraced the Mühl-Berge salient like siege guns destroying a hornwork in an attack on a fortress. The forty or more Russian heavy guns were beaten down, and the ordeal broke the morale of the five super-large regiments of the Observation Corps who were holding the position.

At 12.30 the nine battalions (about 4,300 men) of Frederick's advance guard marched to assault the Mühl-Berge. Just short of this position the Prussians disappeared from the sight of the enemy into a hollow in the ground, which gave the officers an opportunity to dress the lines. The leading four battalions of grenadiers then crashed through the abatis and routed the Observation Corps in a matter of minutes. 'The Russians made no attempt to defend themselves. The men of this splendid formation simply lay on the ground and let themselves be massacred by the Prussian bayonets, and all in honour of their patron saint, Nicholas' (Warnery, 1788, 312).

The Russians had lost more than one-quarter of their position together with perhaps as many as eighty pieces of all calibres, and Frederick was told by Finck, and probably also by Seydlitz and several other generals, that the enemy would surely abandon their camp during the night without any further sacrifice of Prussian blood. However, the king was determined to continue the attack, despite the heat of the day and the exhaustion of the troops.

There was a delay while the heavy batteries were brought

forward, and four of the new 'Austrian' 12-pounders were dragged through the sandy soil to the conquered Mühl-Berge. When the process was complete, the guns opened fire once more and enveloped the troops and the woods in a dense smoke.

The cannon smoke of Kunersdorf not only obscured the battle-field, but has ever since made it almost impossible for historians to determine how much more of the enemy position fell into Prussian hands, and when and where the formations of Prussian cavalry came into action. Only the outlines of this second phase of the battle are at all clear.

Unknown to Frederick, a sandy little valley called the Kuh-Grund snaked north-west from Kunersdorf village and served to isolate the Mühl-Berge from the main allied positions. Here Saltykov formed a new line of defence. Now that the Prussian attack had declared itself on such a narrow sector he could safely draw on the unengaged men and guns in the direction of Frankfurt, and feed them into the defence of the Kuh-Grund and the adjacent earthworks.

The Prussian infantry closed in from three sides. The eight battalions of Finck struggled across the swamp to the north, and launched repeated and vain assaults in the teeth of an Austrian battery and the massed Shuvalov- and unicorn-howitzers of the Russians. One of the most determined attacks was pressed home by a battalion of Hauss (55) under the command of Major Ewald Christian von Kleist, the celebrated poet of the Prussian army. He had already been injured in the right hand, and 'he received a further wound in the left arm from a small bullet . . . and ultimately was able to hold his sword only by the last two fingers and the thumb. He continued in command, and he came to within thirty paces of his next objective, a further battery, when three canister shot shattered his right leg. He fell from his horse' (Pauli, 1758–64, V, 216–7; Kleist died after the battle).

Frederick meanwhile brought up the main army. The right wing wheeled to the left in the tracks of the advance guard, and at the same time the centre and left marched through and around the smoulder-ing remains of Kunersdorf and piled up against the south-eastern salient in dense ranks:

> Both sides were putting up the most bitter fight . . . on the
> Kuh-Grund, and this part of the field was covered with bodies
> . . . Our infantry had been marching through sand on a very hot
> day. They were tormented with thirst, and could scarcely drag
> themselves along. On our side it was always the same battalions
> which went into action, whereas the enemy kept bringing up
> fresh troops. (Retzow, 1802, II, 113; Warnery, 1788, 306)

For most of the afternoon the Prussian cavalry arrived on the scene in small and badly co-ordinated groups. Manfred Laubert (1900) has identified a number of episodes. First, the Kleist Hussars (H 1) and the Jung-Platen Dragoons (D 11) moved around to the north-western flank of the Kuh-Grund position and attacked in support of the initial assaults of the infantry. Eleven squadrons of enemy horse arrived on the scene and drove them back.

In response to a call from the king, Seydlitz then descended from his viewpoint on the Kleiner-Spitzberg and brought the regiments of the left wing through the reassembled infantry of the advance guard. He scattered the allied cavalry, but on the far side of the Kuh-Grund he was thrown back by the fire of three newly arrived regiments of Russian infantry – the Azov and Second Moscow regiments and the First Grenadiers.

Some time after this attack a musket ball or canister shot hit the guard of Seydlitz's sword and lodged in his hand. The wound was very painful, and the command of the cavalry passed to Lieutenant-General the Prince of Württemberg, who was a brave man but suffered from poor eyesight. Württemberg rode ahead on reconnaissance with a single regiment (probably the Meinecke Dragoons, D 3). He believed that he could detect a way around the north-western flank of the Kuh-Grund position, but when he turned to give the signal for the attack he found that his men were already riding for their lives.

With ill-timed courage Major-General Puttkamer (a favourite of the king) sought to exploit Württemberg's initiative by throwing in his own regiment of White Hussars (H 4). These men were promptly engulfed by Austrian dragoons and Russian Tartars and Cossacks. For a time Puttkamer defended himself successfully with his sword, but then a shot rang out and he fell dead with a bullet in his chest.

By about 5 p.m. the efforts of the Prussian infantry were spent, and now that Seydlitz and Württemberg were both wounded the command of the cavalry passed to Lieutenant-General Platen. Without reference to the king Platen sought to bring the battle back to life by advancing the united cavalry between the ponds south of Kunersdorf and wheeling it against the hitherto inviolate earthworks to the west. The leading regiment, the Schorlemer Dragoons (D 6), sought to attack the formidable bastion of the Grosser-Spitzberg, and was annihilated by the Russian guns. The rest of the Prussian cavalry was still trying to form into line when it was hit by Lieutenant-General Loudon with the combined Russian and Austrian horse. The Prussians were caught at a fatal disadvantage, with their backs to the lakes and marshes, and their regiments were broken into fragments.

All the time the Russian guns rained down canister impartially on the struggling mass.

The heat, the exertion and the enemy gunfire had by now reduced the Prussian infantry to defenceless mobs. Morale and discipline finally collapsed at the sight of the survivors of the cavalry streaming back from Kunersdorf. 'They were gripped by the ridiculous fear of being transported to Siberia, and there was no means of stopping them' (PC 11345). Frederick experienced as much when he seized a colour of Prinz Heinrich (35) and called out: 'If you are brave soldiers, follow me!' Nobody responded.

Six hundred paces further to the rear, probably on the Mühl-Berge, Frederick sought to make another stand with six hundred men of the regiment of Lestwitz (31), but the Russian Shuvalov howitzers made the position untenable with their blasts of canister cutting horizontally to the ground. When the battle was already well past saving the Diericke Fusiliers (49) arrived at Frederick's command from the rear, where they had been guarding the artillery park. These men had only just been converted from pioneers, but they stood their ground in square like veteran infantry until they were overwhelmed.

During this final catastrophe Frederick and a few members of his suite were standing just behind the heroes of Diericke.

> A horse had already been shot under him. His second horse received a ball in the chest, and it was already in the process of collapsing when *Flugeladjutant* von Götz and an NCO helped Frederick from the saddle before the animal reached the ground. Götz gave him his own horse. The king had scarcely mounted before a musket ball penetrated between his coat and his hip, and it was stopped only by a gold snuff box which he carried in his pocket. (Retzow, 1802, II, 113)

Prussia nearly lost its king again when the royal party was overtaken by the crack Chuguevskii Cossacks, and Frederick had to be rescued by his small escort of Zieten Hussars under the command of Captain Prittwitz.

The army swarmed over the Hühner-Fliess amid scenes of total confusion. As he left the field Frederick was able to gather only 3,000 men under his direct command, and he was forced to send word to Major-General Flemming to bar the passage to the west bank of the Oder to all except the senior officers and the wounded. All of the rest of the army was left milling about in terror on the 'Russian' side.

The ensuing night was a hideous one. Lightning sprang from cloud to cloud in a rainless thunderstorm, illuminating the battlefield, and between the peals of thunder the Prussians could hear the screams of wounded comrades who were being done to death by the

Cossacks and Tartars. Frederick himself was in safety on the left bank in the Dammhaus at Reitwein. Here he formally delivered the command into the hands of Lieutenant-General Finck, instructing him to obey the overall directions of Prince Henry as *Generalissimus* (an appointment dating from 4 December 1758), and to swear in the army to his nephew and heir (*PC* 11338). The king wrote to Finckenstein, his foreign minister:

> My coat is riddled with musket balls, and I have had two horses killed beneath me. It is my misfortune to be still alive. Our losses are very great, and I have only 3,000 men left out of an army of 48,000. At the moment that I am writing everybody is in flight, and I can exercise no control over my men. At Berlin you ought to be thinking of your safety.
>
> I shall not survive this cruel turn of fortune. The consequences will be worse than the defeat itself. I have no resources left, and, to speak quite frankly, I believe everything is lost. I shall not outlive the downfall of my country. Farewell for ever! (*PC* 11335)

Frederick re-crossed to the east bank on 13 August. On that day his officers succeeded in forming about 18,000 men into regiments and battalions. In all probability he played little active part in the process, but one at least of his officers derived comfort from the apparent composure with which the king took his rest in for the night a peasant house at Oetscher.

> The building had been destroyed by the Cossacks and there was no roof remaining, but he was lying in a deep and peaceful sleep on a little scattering of straw, as if he was in perfect safety. His hat was tilted over his eyes, his drawn sword was at his side, and his adjutants were snoring on the bare floor at his feet. (Anon., 1787–9, I, 26–7)

On the 14th Frederick led his shaken army across the bridges to the west bank.

More than 6,000 of the Prussians had been killed outright, and their total casualties amounted to about 19,000 men, or nearly two-fifths of their army. Three generals were dead or dying, Seydlitz was speechless with shock, and some of the regiments were left with only two unwounded officers. These losses, terrible though they were, bore less heavily on Frederick than the catastrophe which seemed to hang over the Prussian state. The victorious allies were massed on the Oder, only fifty miles from Berlin, and the beaten royal army had no support nearer than the forces of Prince Henry at Schmottseiffen.

What had gone wrong? One of the officers talked with Catt about their master: 'He was doomed by his overconfidence, and by his scorn for an enemy who is, in fact, by no means to be underestimated. He is a remarkable and resourceful man, but I must say that I cannot imagine how he is going to extricate himself from all of this' (Catt, 1884, 280). It now seemed that Frederick's overhasty reconnaissance had impelled the army into attacking along a narrow frontage which denied the cavalry the means of acting in concert, and which had the effect of heaping up the infantry as a static target in front of the strongest sector of the allied positions. Frederick was also aware that he was being criticised for having prolonged the battle needlessly after he had captured the Mühl-Berge salient. He told Catt that he was justified in wishing to exploit his first success and the high morale of his troops, but he claimed that the leading battalions had 'plunged into the ravine [the Kuh-Grund] with excessive zeal and too little order. The other battalions came up too quickly and too close behind, and they ran into difficulties' (ibid., 255).

These were matters of detail. The outcome was determined above all by the advances which the Russians and Austrians had made in the art of war, and by the decline in the quality of Frederick's army. He wrote to Finckenstein: 'I would fear nothing, if I still had ten battalions of the quality of 1757. But this cruel war has killed off our finest soldiers, and the ones we have left do not even measure up to the worst of our troops at the outset' (PC 11345).

On 16 August Frederick's spirits recovered enough to enable him to resume the active command. He summoned up a train of fifty 12-pounders which had been left behind in Berlin, and by gathering in the fugitives and the lightly wounded he managed to assemble about 33,000 men by the end of the month. He told Catt: 'This would be quite enough, if I had my best officers with me, and those buggers wanted to do their duty. To be perfectly candid, I must say that I fear my own troops more than the enemy' (Catt, 1884, 494). The restoring of discipline was therefore a matter of the highest priority. Frederick ordered the Duke of Bevern, as governor of Stettin, to arrest all the unwounded officers who had found their way to his fortress, 'and you are to mete out forty blows with the stick to such men as are unwounded and who have thrown away muskets' (PC 11349).

Meanwhile the enemy were closing in to participate in what Frederick firmly believed would be 'the last scene in the play' (PC 11374). Loudon's Austrian corps crossed to the west bank of the Oder on 15 August and Saltykov's army followed the next day. Haddik reached the Müllrose position with 19,000 Austrians, and Lieutenant-General Beck was nearby with a further 9,000. Most significantly of all, Daun was marching north with the 25,000 men of the main Austrian army. He reached Triebel on 18 August and opened a dialogue with Saltykov.

On the same day, 18 August, Frederick fell back to a position on the right bank of the Spree at Fürstenwalde, and, rejecting all thoughts of a passive defensive, he steeled himself to fight a last great battle in the open field in front of Berlin. He suspected that the outcome would be determined by chance: 'This is the most frightful crisis in which I have ever been. Now we must conquer or die' (to Prince Ferdinand of Prussia, 24 August, PC 11368).

For some time Frederick could ascertain little of the doings of the enemy, but on 28 August there came the reliable and immensely heartening news that instead of pushing on for Berlin, the Russians, Haddik and Loudon had turned south in the direction of Lieberose. The king wrote to Henry announcing 'the miracle of the House of Brandenburg' (1 September, PC 11393).

Frederick tracked the Russians from a distance, and on 31 August he positioned himself at Waldow. He thereby covered the routes to Berlin and Saxony and denied the Russians all access to fertile Lower Lusatia, from where they could have drawn fodder for their horses. However, it was no great comfort to him to reflect that the lifespan of Prussia was now to be estimated in weeks rather than days (PC 11451).

The second stage of the Brandenburg miracle was represented by the astonishing failure of the allies to join their forces south of Berlin. In part this was the product of the discord between Daun and Saltykov, but it was also the consequence of a brilliant strategic counter-stroke on the part of Prince Henry, who commanded the 40,000 men whom Frederick had left behind in the south-west corner of Silesia. After receiving news of his brother's disaster, Henry took a powerful force from Schmottseiffen and advanced initially to Sagan. Upon reflection he decided that the most effective blow he could deal the allies would be to get astride Daun's communications through Lower Lusatia. He accordingly turned up the right bank of the Bober, and on 12 September he planted himself at Görlitz, on the principal Austrian supply line. Daun at once abandoned his intended march on Berlin.

Saltykov asserted with justice that his army had borne nearly all the burden of the campaign, and, now that he despaired of all help from Daun, he left his camp at Lieberose on 15 September and fell back east to the Oder. Here he hoped to seize some useful strategic point for the Russians before the end of the year.

Detachments had reduced Frederick's army to 24,000 men or less, but by a sequence of forced marches Frederick anticipated the greatly superior forces of the Russians on the heights of Baunau. This bold move saved the fortress of Glogau nearby. On 1 October Frederick discovered that the Russians and the corps of Loudon had retreated to the far bank of the Oder. He followed them across the river on the night of 7 October, and established himself on the far side in the camp of Sophienthal, where he spent most of the remainder of the month. It was evident that he was regaining a moral ascendancy over the allies. Finally on 24 October the Russians marched away to winter quarters.

By now the accumulated tensions of the campaign had reduced Frederick once more to a state of collapse. He wrote to Henry on the 27th: 'What is wrong with me is a rheumatism in my feet, one of my knees and my left hand. I have also been in the grips of an almost continual fever for eight days now . . . I feel so weak and exhausted that I will not be able to leave here for another fifteen days' (PC 11551).

Meanwhile a new campaign took shape in Saxony, where the *Reichs-armee* had been reducing the strongholds one by one. Frederick had sent a first reinforcement in that direction under that bourgeois adventurer Major-General Johann Jakob 'von' Wunsch, and Lieutenant-General Finck followed with a second contingent. By 13 September the Prussians had recovered Wittenberg, Torgau and Leipzig.

Wunsch and Finck were, however, far too weak in numbers to contemplate any attempt to regain the great prize of Dresden. The commandant, Count Schmettau, had defended the same place with great spirit in 1759, but now he was in receipt of a letter which Frederick had penned on 14 August, under the immediate impact of Kunersdorf. This message gave him the freedom to give up Dresden, if he could obtain good terms, and Schmettau accordingly capitulated to the *Reichsarmee* on 4 September. The garrison of 3,350 men marched out four days later, and one-third of the troops immediately defected to the enemy. Frederick afterwards put Schmettau under arrest, and dismissed him from the army with a miserly pension. Schmettau uttered a protest and received the reply: 'You ought to be glad you still have your head on your shoulders!' (Retzow, 1802, II, 132).

The rival forces made their way to Saxony in ever greater numbers. Prince Henry had deliberately drawn the attention of Daun upon himself, as we have seen, and towards the end of September the two main armies moved west into the electorate. Henry united with the Finck-Wusch corps on 4 October, and on the 16th he fell back to a camp near Torgau. This position was very well chosen, and Henry directed a number of counter-moves which frustrated every enterprise of Daun against his flanks and rear.

Now that operations on the Oder were at an end, Lieutenant-General Hülsen set out from Glogau for Saxony with 16,000–17,000 troops on 5 November. Hülsen's arrival brought the army in the electorate to a strength of 60,000 men, which was by far the highest concentration of force which the Prussians had effected during this year. Frederick followed at a more leisurely pace, since he was too ill to accompany the troops in person, and on 13 November he joined his brother on the west bank of the Elbe near Meissen.

Daun appeared to be every bit as unwilling to renew Frederick's acquaintance as Saltykov had been, and it was regarded as a personal triumph for Old Fritz when on 14 November the Austrians abandoned their position at the Katzenhäuser. Frederick at once pushed his army forward, and that night he slept better than at any time since the battle of Kunersdorf. Three days later a further retreat carried Daun to the immediate proximity of Dresden, where he arranged his army behind the Plauensche-Grund.

Frederick was confident that he would soon have the Austrians out of Dresden and the small area of Saxony remaining to them. The winter promised to be early and hard, which would block the navigation of the Elbe with ice, and since the neighbourhood of Dresden was thoroughly eaten-out Daun was heavily dependent for his supplies on the long and vulnerable route which stretched from Bohemia through the Erz-Gebirge. Frederick concluded that the Austrians would be very sensitive to any threats against their communications.

The little raiding corps of Colonel Friedrich Wilhelm von Kleist ('Green Kleist', not to be confused with the dead Ewald Christian) roamed destructively around north Bohemia, wrecking the magazine at Aussig, and disturbing the Austrian officers at their ablutions at Teplitz spa. More important still, the king dispatched Lieutenant-General Finck with a corps to the immediate rear of the Austrian army, for the purpose of threatening the route which led from Bohemia by way of the Nollendorf passage and Berggiesshübel. Friedrich August von Finck had actually commanded the royal army after Kunersdorf. He now had 15,000 troops with him, and he enjoyed the support of distinguished major-generals like Rebentisch and Wunsch.

On 18 November Finck took up station on the plateau of Maxen, which formed a number of small bare hillocks rising eerily from a tangled country of forests and steep valleys. The extensive and nearly trackless Tharandter-Wald separated him from the king's new headquarters at Wilsdruff, and the dangerous avenue of the Müglitz ran past his rear – all of which rendered him vulnerable to any counterstroke from the Austrian army nearby along the Plauensche-Grund. Prince Henry and many other officers of the royal army dreaded this eventuality, but with perhaps affected unconcern Frederick sat down on the afternoon of that same 18 November to write a verse parody of Voltaire's *Ecclesiaste*. His reader Catt entered at four o'clock, and Frederick indicated the position of Finck's corps on the large map which invariably hung in his room. With a pounding heart Catt told his master of the criticisms he had heard. The king replied: 'No, my friend, you have nothing to fear. You will see that our man with the papally blessed hat [i.e. Daun] and his minions will be only too happy to return to Bohemia, where they can scratch their balls at their ease. Now I'll read my verses over to you again' (Catt, 1884, 260).

Events now passed beyond Frederick's control. Daun maintained his first line intact above the Plauensche-Grund, but meanwhile he assembled a total of 32,000 Austrians and troops of the *Reichsarmee* around Maxen. Three of the groups had specific local tasks: Lieutenant-General Prince Stolberg with 4,500 Germans, together with Croats and two regiments of Austrian hussars, positioned himself to the east to prevent Finck escaping down the Müglitz valley to the Elbe; Brentano and 6,000 men descended from the north; finally the main Austrian force of 17,000 troops approached from Dippoldiswalde in the south-west. The Austrians had to march over ice and snow, but the valleys enabled them to concentrate close to their objective without being seen, and the heights to the north, west and south of Hausdorf offered them excellent sites for their artillery.

The battle began on all sides at 3.30 p.m. on 20 November, and it lasted scarcely three hours. For the principal attack from the south the Austrians were formed in four columns on single-battalion frontages, and they delivered their assault against the centre of the position. Finck soon discovered how unreliable his troops were. The battalions of Grabow and Zastrow contained large numbers of pressed Saxons, and they offered little resistance. The lone battalion of the Willemy Grenadiers counter-attacked from the east of Maxen and drove the Austrians from the village, but the regiment of Rebentisch, instead of lending support, began to disintegrate. The conscripted Austrian and Russian prisoners were now coming over to their friends *en masse*, and altogether the uncontrollable desertion deprived Finck of half of his infantry during this action.

As night fell the Prussians abandoned Maxen and a general flight set in. Wunsch and twenty squadrons of cavalry gained the authorisation to break out, but the troopers had to dismount and lead their horses in the darkness, and they progressed no great distance before they were told that they were embraced in a general capitulation of the corps.

On the evening of 19 November a Green Hussar had reached Frederick with a not altogether reassuring message from Finck. The king could not bring himself to believe that the corps was in serious danger, but as a precautionary measure he sent Lieutenant-General Hülsen with a detachment in the direction of Dippoldiswalde to lend support. Hülsen's march was delayed by the deep snow, and the battle was fought and lost before he approached any nearer the scene than Nieder-Colmnitz.

By the 21st it became clear to Frederick that something terrible had happened to Finck. When the details were finally known, it emerged that 500 officers and 12,500 NCOs and private soldiers had survived to enter Austrian captivity. Austrian casualties amounted to just 934. In round numbers the Prussian losses at Maxen were the equivalent of a Kolin or a Zorndorf. In some respects, however, the cost was higher still. The Austrians were no longer interested in exchanging prisoners, and so Frederick was deprived of the force as effectively as if the whole body had been struck dead. The captured leaders amounted to one-tenth of the officer corps, and the loss in cavalry was so great that Frederick had to recall the ten squadrons of Prussian dragoons who were doing service with Prince Ferdinand of Brunswick in western Germany. The king wrote to Henry in October 1760: 'Our resources are so depleted and scanty that we will be unable to oppose the huge numbers of the enemies who are ranged against us. If we go under, we must date our fall from the disastrous adventure of Maxen' (*PC* 12404). The enduring memory of the affair helped to paralyse Frederick's operations on the upper Elbe in July 1778 (*PC* 26590).

The shame of this event seemed to Frederick to be without parallel, for, as he indicated to Finck, 'It is something hitherto completely unknown for a Prussian corps to lay down its arms to an enemy. Up to now it did not seem possible that such a thing could happen' (*PC* 11620). Frederick held the 'Maxen regiments' in perpetual aversion, and after the war he instituted a series of courts-martial which cashiered Finck and the major-generals Gersdorff and Rebentisch, and sentenced them to fortress arrest.

Was the disgrace justified? Probably not. It was Finck's judgment that was really at stake, not his courage, for the king maintained that Finck should have seen the danger in good time and got out of the way. Finck certainly enjoyed a full theoretical freedom of action, but there were physical and psychological barriers to his escape. Already on 19 November the Austrian reserve corps under O'Donnell had moved to Dippoldiswalde, which cut the most attractive path of retreat west to Freiberg. Also it was unfair of Frederick to blame Finck for 'untimely firmness' when the ideal of *Contenance-Halten* was part of the code of the Prussian officer. On the larger issue – the advisability of placing a corps of any kind so close to the Austrian rear

– the well-informed staff officer Gaudi suggests that Frederick believed that he had a complete moral superiority over the Austrians after Daun had abandoned the Katzenhäuser position so speedily on the 14th (Bethcke, 1907, 200–1).

Thirteen days after the catastrophe of Maxen the Austrians annihilated yet another isolated Prussian corps, albeit a much smaller one than the vanished host of Finck. The victim was Major-General Diericke, who commanded a detachment which was guarding the Elbe communications downstream from Dresden. On 3 December he was caught with three of his battalions at Meissen, and after a lively action he was forced to surrender with his 1,500 survivors.

Meanwhile Frederick and Daun faced each other across the Plauensche-Grund. This was classic defensive terrain in the Austrian style, and Frederick played a waiting game, still hoping that the shortage of provisions would compel the Austrians to fall back into Bohemia. It was dismal work in the snow and bitter frost, and the frozen soldiers lay piled in heaps in their tents in search of animal warmth. Frederick himself was low in health and spirits. He wrote to Henry on 1 January:

> My heart is eaten away by sorrow, and what depresses me most
> of all is the knowledge that I have come to the end of my
> resources – we have nothing left. I do not wish to plunge you
> into gloom on this New Year's Day, but I have to speak frankly,
> and this terrible prospect is evident to all who do not shut their
> eyes to it. (PC 11731)

In 1757 there had been no fast-moving and victorious end to the campaign which might have carried the army into the next year at a high pitch of elation. Not only did the disaster of Kunersdorf stand forth undiminished, but the surrender at Maxen, the misfortune at Meissen and the cold and disease of the winter eroded the resources of the army, and undermined confidence in Frederick's generalship. 'He plunged us into this cruel war', wrote Henry, 'and only the courage of the generals and soldiers can get us out again' ('Note', c. 15 December, PC 11673).

Frederick's skill as a re-maker of shattered armies was never shown to greater effect than in 1760. It was a lengthy process, which was completed in the material sense with surprising speed, but extended in the moral dimension into August. The lack of good officers was felt at every level of command. Boy *Junkers* came out to take the place of the officers who had been killed at Kunersdorf or made prisoner at Maxen. Seydlitz was still incapable of doing service after his wound, though to the king's surprise he found the energy to marry the vicious seventeen-year-old Countess Susanne von Hacke.

For all of the king's efforts the number of troops in the field never exceeded 110,000, and this figure was raised only by dint of a promiscuous impressment of Austrian and Saxon captives, and by making heavy drafts on the Prussian cantons. The forces of the enemy alliance amounted to about 230,000 men, and Frederick could not believe that he would be able to withstand these vastly superior numbers before July. In the meantime, however, he decided to hold his main army of 55,000 troops in the Camp of Meissen, which offered direct protection to the Elbe magazines, Brandenburg and Berlin, and from where he could move if necessary to Silesia or Pomerania. Lieutenant-General Fouqué was standing guard with about 12,000 men in southern Silesia in the area of Landeshut, and in April Prince Henry gathered another 35,000 or so in the central position of Sagan, so as to deter the Austrians from raiding into Silesia and discourage the Russians from pushing across the Oder.

On 13 June the *Reichsarmee* began its ponderous march from Hof in central Germany to the theatre of war in Saxony, where it was going to bring Daun's force at Dresden to a strength of 100,000 men. In the short interval remaining to him Frederick aimed a pre-emptive blow at the isolated Austrian corps of Lieutenant-General Franz Moritz Lacy, on the east bank of the Elbe. This Lacy was a man of mixed Irish and German Baltic blood, and a kinsman and protégé of the Field-Marshal Browne who had been mortally wounded at Prague. He was the founder of the Austrian staff corps, and he was also making his name as one of the quickest-moving of those excellent young field officers who were emerging in the enemy army at this stage in the war.

Frederick crossed to the right bank of the Elbe, and on 19 June he was at Radeburg, ready to launch his attack, when he learnt that Lacy had vanished during the night. He remarked to Catt: ' "My blow has fallen on thin air. How very sad! I really ought to go off and hang myself. Have you ever felt that urge?" "No sir, I cannot say that I have." "My bad luck seems to be hounding me everywhere. I would have beaten Lacy, but he got away" ' (Catt, 1884, 426).

After the blow at Maxen few people were ever bold enough to mention the word 'detachment' in Frederick's hearing. Now, at the start of the campaign of 1760, Frederick experienced the loss of another force of the same kind in peculiarly painful circumstances. Lieutenant-General Henri-Auguste von Fouqué, Frederick's old companion from the Rheinsberg days, had been ordered to reoccupy the post of Landeshut and thereby secure an important road junction that would facilitate any return of the royal army to Silesia. On 23 June the little corps was overwhelmed by the Austrians in its scattered hill-top positions south and east of Landeshut town. Fouqué was captured along with 8,051 of his troops, and nearly 2,000 of his men lay dead on the field. This was the doing of the dour and craggy-faced Gideon Ernst von Loudon, who was Lacy's great rival in the Austrian camp. Frederick had once rejected him as unsuitable for admission to the Prussian service.

The first report of some reverse came from an Austrian officer who addressed himself to the Prussian outposts, probably on 24 June. Frederick stood as if paralysed, and stared speechlessly for some minutes at the adjutant who brought him the news. The king's only consolation was that Fouqué had battled to the last against over-whelming odds, displaying a courage worthy of the ancient Romans.

Frederick moved his army to Gross-Dobritz on 26 June, so as to cling closer to Daun, who had meanwhile moved to the east bank of the Elbe in support of Lacy. The king was gloomy and bad-tempered, and it was with no enthusiasm that he decided that he must shift the greater part of his army into Silesia, where Loudon had the opportunity to wreak great damage after his victory at Landeshut.

At midnight on 3 July the royal army set off from Gross-Dobritz. The Prussians moved with all possible speed across the forests and hills, but Lacy adroitly decamped from his position at Lichtenberg just before Frederick could pin him down. The Prussians reached the abbey of Marienstern on 5 July, and on the 6th they crossed the headwaters of the Spree to Nieder-Guriz. These two days were re-membered for the appalling heat, and the burning, clogging sands, and the 105 Prussians who died of exhaustion on the second march.

On 7 July, a desperately needed day of rest, Frederick learnt that in spite of all his efforts the main Austrian army had drawn ahead of him in the race for Silesia. He therefore turned to the usual expedient of commanders who found themselves outmarched on this theatre, namely to double back along the way he had come, and do what damage he could before the enemy returned to the scene.

Frederick made his about-turn on 8 July, and on the 13th he established himself around Dresden in very favourable circum-stances. The Prince of Zweibrücken had withdrawn the *Reichsarmee* of about 19,000 troops behind the Müglitz valley, and he was joined there by the 19,700 men of Lacy's corps.

Meanwhile Frederick had a free hand at Dresden. He began on that same 13 July by sending his jaegers and the free battalion of Courbière to clear the Croats from the extensive Grosser-Garten, which gave rise to a bizarre battle among the avenues and the statuary. He then opened his attack on the city behind. He did not have the time or patience to carry out a sit-down formal siege, and chose instead to bombard the place with a train of ten 12-pounder cannon and four 50-pounder mortars, which were shipped upriver from Torgau.

The bombardment of Dresden opened on 19 July. Some of the mortar bombs were directed at the slab-like tower of the Kreuz-Kirche, and the wooden pinnacle at the top caught fire and toppled over, spreading flames among the neighbouring houses. Street after street was then consumed in a conflagration which destroyed a large area of the city. None of this made the slightest impression on the powerful garrison of 13,900 men under the Austrian major-general Macquire.

This episode was remembered even among Frederick's admirers as an example of the horrors of modern warfare (Archenholtz, 1840, II, 49; Mitchell, 1850, II, 184; Lehndorff, 1910–13, I, 247–8). The Prussians claimed that they had seen Austrian observers, or even cannon, on the Kreuz-Kirche tower, and the royal secretary Eichel wrote a confused and embarrassed letter to the foreign minister Finckenstein, trying to persuade him that the artillery had been aiming at the fortifications, not the city, but that it had been difficult to observe the fall of the bombs (PC 12257). Frederick was neither a saint nor a pyromaniac. In all probability he had ordered the city to be bombarded, never expecting, after the limited effects of the bombardment of Prague in 1757, that Dresden would prove to be so inflammable.

It was too dangerous for the Prussians to maintain the siege of Dresden much longer, for on the evening of 18 July Daun and the main Austrian army had reached the heights to the east of the Elbe and established contact with the city. On the dark night of 21 July the Prussians were evacuating their guns from the batteries when they came under attack from a body of Austrian troops which Daun had pushed across the river. The covering force (a battalion of Prinz Ferdinand, and the first and second battalions of Anhalt-Bernburg) was put to flight, and only with difficulty were the survivors able to break through to the Grosser-Garten.

Frederick held the army close under Dresden for seven days more, hoping in vain that Daun would come out to fight. Meanwhile his ire fell on the Bernburgers. The soldiers had to yield up their swords and the officers and NCOs were made to cut the lace from their hats. Likewise Frederick heaped rebukes on the cringing necks of the engineers and the officers of the artillery. All the time the real blame rested with the king, as Retzow points out: 'A simple bombardment was powerless to compel a strongly garrisoned fortress to surrender, especially when an enemy army of relief was at hand. Frederick must have known as much from a number of historical examples, and more particularly from what happened at Prague in 1757' (Retzow, 1802, II, 223).

As happened in 1759, the unfathomable combinations of geography and strategies produced a great convergence of rival forces in Silesia in the high summer of the year. So it was that in July and August 1760 Frederick was drawn eastwards once more by the threatened collapse of his affairs in that part of the world. Saltykov and his Russians were moving slowly forward from Posen. Worse still, the all too familiar sound of Austrian victory salutes announced another triumph for Loudon, who on 29 July took the fortress of Glatz by a brilliant *coup de main*. The Austrian forces on the eastern flank now had a clear run through the passes of Silberberg and Wartha to the Silesian plain. Frederick wrote: 'We have striven to charm away the storm but all our efforts have proved vain and useless . . . There is nothing left but to try our luck in combat, but even this comes down to a question of dying four weeks sooner or later' (*PC* 12291).

Frederick decided that he must leave a corps under Hülsen in the old Meissen camp to guard the Elbe, and take the rest in person to Silesia. Once again it will probably be convenient to enumerate the armies and corps which were coming together:

(a) Frederick was making eastwards from Saxony to Silesia with 30,000 men.
(b) Prince Henry had about 38,000 troops under his command. He left his blocking position beyond the Oder at Landsberg, and on 5 August he relieved Breslau, which had been under attack by Loudon.
(c) Now that the way to the Oder was clear Saltykov was moving south from Posen with 60,000 troops; of these, 25,000 were detached under Lieutenant-General Chernyshev to reach out to the Austrians in Silesia.
(d) Daun and Lacy (altogether about 90,000 troops) were also on the march, and they hoped to be able to reach Silesia before Frederick did.

Frederick disengaged from his positions near Dresden on the wet and stormy night of 29 July. He passed the Elbe at Zehren on 1 August, and a first bound of continuous marching carried him the ninety miles to Bunzlau by the 7th. The pace was literally lethal. Many troops died from heatstroke on the way to Arnsdorf on the 5th, and hundreds more deserted in the woods around Rothwasser the next day.

The army rested at Bunzlau on 8 August 'after those almost incredible marches' (Mitchell, 1850, II, 191). Frederick intended to continue his progress to Schweidnitz or Breslau, but first he had to overcome the obstacle of the Katzbach. This was 'a small rivulet with steep banks, resembling an ordinary ditch' (ibid.), but the passage of the bridges and fords was a matter of some delicacy now that the enemy were in the neighbourhood. The army was on the move again on the 9th, and Frederick discovered that the Austrians had anticipated him at Goldberg. In other words for the second time this year Daun had outmarched the Prussians, moving his larger forces with greater facility across higher and more broken country. The junction of Daun and Loudon was now assured.

On 10 August Frederick set off down the left, or western, bank of the Katzbach, hoping to slip past the Austrian right flank and reach the heart of Silesia, where he could unite with Henry, restore his communications with Breslau and Schweidnitz, and interpose himself between Daun and the Russians. The army set off in three columns, but 'no sooner did he begin to move, than the Austrians immediately decamped, and continued marching along the heights on the opposite side of the Katzbach; and so to the eye they appeared to make a fourth Prussian column, so small was the distance between' (Mitchell, 1850, II, 192). Frederick halted in the neighbourhood of Liegnitz. He could see that the Austrians were drawn up in battle array on the right bank of the river, barring his route to Jauer.

Frederick heard that the Austrians had proclaimed: 'We have opened the bag. Now all we have to do is to tie it up, and we have the king and his whole army inside.' Frederick laughed and commented: 'There is something in what they say. But I intend to make a great hole in this bag which will be difficult to sew up again.' What he had in mind was to double back upstream and effect a passage beyond the Austrian left.

Frederick made his attempt on the night of 10 August. At Goldberg he bumped into the corps of Lacy, who, unknown to the king, had been hovering in the Prussian rear. Frederick chased Lacy over the Katzbach, but on the far side his progress was checked by Daun, who had shifted the main Austrian army to the left. Frederick was left with the prize of Lacy's baggage at Goldberg, which contained the meticulous Irishman's portfolio of maps, and a very pretty Tyrolean kitchen maid. Frederick wrote to Lacy a few days later, offering to return the maps once the Prussian engineers had copied them out.

The lightness of the tone belies the magnitude of the crisis in which Frederick found himself at the time of the event, isolated from his magazines and from any support. His army had not been in such peril since the far-off day of Mollwitz. 'Half of Europe was at war with Frederick over Silesia, and the general opinion was that this drama was drawing to its eagerly desired close' (Zimmermann, 1788, 226).

The state of affairs was still more dangerous than Frederick knew, for Chernyshev was across the Oder with his 25,000 troops and was marching to join the Austrians.

Having failed in all attempts to force his way past the immediate flanks of the Austrian forces, Frederick could see no alternative but to march down the 'Prussian' side of the Katzbach as far as the confluence with the Oder near Parchwitz, and then seek to gain the roads to Breslau or Glogau as the occasion arose. The first stage of the process was to feed the army across the narrow, swampy-banked Schwarzwasser, a fitting younger sister of the Katzbach. The baggage train and the bakery were sent ahead, and at 8 p.m. on 14 August the army began to pass to the east bank by the crossings at Liegnitz town and further upstream. At this juncture a note of low comedy supervened with the arrival of a Lieutenant or Captain Wise, an Irishman who had been dismissed some time before from the Austrian service, but who continued to haunt the fringes of the enemy camps, picking up gossip. Wise reached Frederick in a state of advanced drunkenness, but after the administration of much tea and cold water he was able to report that Daun intended to attack the Prussians.

Frederick's move across the Schwarzwasser now appeared in a providential light. With any luck the Austrian blow would fall on the old camp site west of the stream, where the Prussians maintained their fires and kept their pickets in position. On the left side of the Schwarzwasser Frederick now arranged his army on a bushy plateau three miles north-east of Liegnitz. This feature was of insignificant height in itself, but it derived its importance from its position relative to the open meadows which extended to the Katzbach.

Upon consideration, the Prussian right wing appeared to Frederick to be over-extended and vulnerable. He therefore drew it in closer to the hump of the Reh-Berg, and formed it along a front facing south-west. He likewise brought the second line through the first, and ordered it to take up a position guarding the rear. This was a tedious process, because the move was executed in darkness and the second line was encumbered with the batteries of 12-pounders which were now attached to the brigades of infantry. 'Frederick had enjoyed no sleep for two days and one night. Now on this second night it was more important than ever for him to be awake. He rode between the scattered regiments, and dismounted wherever he considered his presence useful' (Küster, 1793, 25). It was a serene, starry night, according to some accounts, but cold, damp and windy on the authority of others. Frederick settled down for what remained of the hours of darkness by a small fire in front of the Rathenow Grenadiers (1/23; see Map 23, p. 371). He was wrapped in his cloak, and he had his back against a tree.

Daun had also got his troops on the move and he trusted that the Prussian army would not survive long into the next day. The light detachments of Beck and Wied had the task of advancing direct on Liegnitz town and so fixing the attention of the Prussians on this stretch of the Katzbach. Meanwhile the main Austrian army was making ready to cross to the north bank of the Katzbach well upstream from Liegnitz at Dohnau. Once it had completed the passage it was to form a line of battle facing east, and attack the supposed Prussian camp on the near side of the Schwarzwasser. Simultaneously Lacy was to fall on the enemy flank, having completed a long circuit to the north.

Daun had no intention of providing the Prussians with a 'golden bridge' for their escape, in the milder traditions of eighteenth-century warfare. He assigned to Loudon the important responsibility of passing the Katzbach downstream from Liegnitz, and moving west against Frederick's rear. In other words, Loudon was to form the 'anvil' for Daun's 'hammer', and the Prussians were to be crushed between them in a process of annihilation more complete than Frederick ever designed for any of his enemies. It was an ambitious and well-thought-out scheme, and it provided for every eventuality except Frederick's eastward change of position during the night.

At a strength of 24,000 men Loudon's corps by itself was not far short of that of the entire Prussian army (30,000). Daun, Lacy and the rest brought the total Austrian numbers to about 90,000.

In the darkness of the early morning of 15 August Major Hundt and his two hundred Zieten Hussars were patrolling the lower Katzbach when, in the neighbourhood of Bienowitz, they ran into Loudon's infantry already in full march on the north bank. Hundt galloped back to the army. The first sensible man he encountered was Saldern, who rose from his camp chair to meet him. As a newly promoted and ambitious major-general Saldern had kept himself constantly informed of Frederick's whereabouts during the night, and he was able to point Hundt in the right direction. It was about 3 a.m. when he reached the Rathenow Grenadiers:

> Major Hundt came up at speed, yelling, 'Where is the king? Where is the king?' He was heard by Major-General Schenkendorff, who had dismounted some time before, and was now engaged in poking the king's fire with his stick. 'Here he is', he called out softly to the major. Frederick's attention was aroused, and he asked, 'What's going on?' 'Your Majesty,' said Hundt, 'as God is my witness the enemy are here!' 'Well then,' the king replied, 'hold them up as long as you can. I must have a horse!' (Anon., 1787–9, X, 32–3)

Frederick instructed Lieutenant-General Zieten to keep the greater part of the right wing in position looking south-west. The king in person then took charge of the rest of the army (about 14,000 troops), and began to arrange the infantry brigade by brigade ih a new front facing east against the advancing Austrians.

Frederick went first to Schenkendorff and, looking towards the first light of dawn, he told him to plant his battery of 12-pounders on the Reh-Berg and place the battalions of his brigade on either side. Schenkendorff's line was prolonged to the right by the Alt-Braunschweig regiment (5) and the second battalion of Wedel (26) (making up the brigade of Saldern), and to the north by the regiments of Prinz Ferdinand (34) and Bernburg (3) (brigade of Anhalt-Bernburg) which came up from the rear.

This further redeployment of the Prussian infantry was still far from complete when the left flank of Frederick's new position threatened to collapse under the impact of the cavalry of Loudon's right-hand column, which emerged from the Katzbach meadows between Pohlschildern and Bienowitz. The Zieten Hussars (H 2) and the Krockow Dragoons (D 2) streamed back in some disorder, but the Prussian cuirassiers stood their ground and pushed the Austrians back. The highly excited troops of the Bernburg regiment joined in this counter-attack with their bayonets, one of the few occasions in military history in which infantry have ever taken the offensive against cavalry.

Loudon was astonished to find that the Prussians were already in possession of ground which, he had been assured, was free of the enemy. His right wing was being repulsed, as we have seen, and the left-hand column was unable to advance far beyond Panten in the face of the Prussian artillery. However, there could be no question of breaking off the combat now that he was committed to the attack, and the weight of the battle came to rest upon the infantry of the Austrian centre, who pushed valiantly up the bushy slopes until they were checked by musketry and blasts of canister.

At 4 a.m. the Prussian left wing spilled from the low plateau in a counter-attack. At Frederick's command Lieutenant-General Wied advanced with the battalions to the right of the Reh-Berg (Alt-Braunschweig, and the Rathenow (1/23) and Nymschofsky (33/42) Grenadiers) and drove the Austrians from Panten. On the left the men of the Bernburg regiment rushed forward to the deafening chant 'Sieg oder Tod!' and, together with the musketeers of Prinz Ferdinand and the Prinz Heinrich Cuirassiers (C 2), they broke through the first and second lines of Loudon's infantry. With just 14,000 troops under his command, Frederick was probably able to exercise a large degree of personal control during these events:

In this action the king of Prussia exposed his person to the
greatest dangers. A grape shot pierced the skirts of his coat; the
horse he rode was wounded by a musket ball; one of his pages
had a horse killed by a cannon shot; and his ecuyer, and one of
his grooms, were both mortally wounded. (Mitchell, 1850, II,
201)

The Austrians executed a fighting retreat in very good order, and
before they reached the Katzbach their cavalry dealt a vicious
counter-blow which rode down the Stechow Grenadiers and hewed
into the exposed left flank of the Bernburg and Prinz Ferdinand
regiments. Loudon left about 3,000 casualties and prisoners on the
field, and after 6 a.m. he brought the engagement to an end by
withdrawing to the south bank of the Katzbach.

The battle of Liegnitz had been fought and lost by Loudon
without the Austrian main force ever having come into action. Lacy's
corps had indeed reached the upper Schwarzwasser in good time, but
nowhere could it find a suitable passage. Only a few squadrons of
dragoons and hussars availed themselves of a ford at Rüstern, and
these folk were beaten off when they tried to attack the baggage of
Frederick's headquarters at Kuchelberg. Meanwhile Daun's army had
been very slow in crossing to the north bank of the Katzbach. It was
5 a.m. before the Austrians were in position on the high ground
between Weissenhof and Lindenbusch, and even then Daun refused
to plunge across the Schwarzwasser valley before he knew more
about the progress of the action which had broken out so unexpectedly on Loudon's front. Word of Loudon's defeat came two hours later.

According to patriotic legend Frederick rode to the survivors of
the Bernburg regiment immediately after the battle. Nobody was sure
whether their impetuous bravery had effaced the impression of that
disastrous night in the trenches before Dresden:

The officers uttered not a word, in the silent expectation that
the king would render them justice. But four old soldiers rushed
to his stirrups, clasped his knee and begged him to restore them
to favour in recognition of how well they had done their duty
this day. Frederick was moved. He answered: 'Yes, lads,
everything will be given back to you. All is forgotten!'
(Archenholtz, 1840, II, 68)

No time remained for further congratulations. Frederick got the
army on the move again with a speed that was the best evidence of the
continuing urgency of strategic affairs. Saldern saw to the business of
collecting up the transportable wounded and the captured Austrian
guns and muskets, and already at nine o'clock on the morning of the

battle the left wing set out on the road to Parchwitz.

The triumph of Liegnitz was not complete until the evening of 16 August, a day which Frederick described as the most anxious of the whole campaign. He feared that the troops of Chernyshev were emplaced on the road to Breslau. Now came the blessed news that the Russians had fallen back across the Oder. A cloud of dust to the south seemed to indicate that Daun too was on the march to Breslau, but on this same day the Austrians turned towards southern Silesia, where Daun now intended to reduce Schweidnitz and establish himself in the wooded border hills. When this news reached Vienna, Maria Theresa appreciated at once how far Daun had fallen short of the main objective, which had been to accomplish the union with the Russians.

At Liegnitz king and army had regained their confidence in each other, and Frederick had more than won back all the esteem he had forfeited after a year of uninterrupted misfortune. The British ministry believed that 'The superior genius of that great prince never appeared in a higher light than during this last expedition into Silesia. The whole manoeuvre is looked upon here as the masterpiece of military skill' (Lord Holdernesse, 9 September, PRO SP 90/76). In the Austrian camp the French military plenipotentiary Montazet sighed: 'I know that people were fond of saying that the king was practically finished, that his troops were not as good as his old ones, and that he had no generals left. That could be true, but his spirit, which brings everything to life, is the same as it always was – and so, unfortunately, is ours' (Gr. Gstb., 1901–14, XII, 226).

The battle had been lost for the Austrians by the unaccustomed failures of their reconnaissance and staff work. Here it was perhaps significant that Lacy was preoccupied with his responsibilities as a corps commander, and that his highly esteemed young compatriot, the *Generalquartiermeisterlieutenant* Major-General James Nugent, had fallen into the hands of the Prussians during the 'Bernburg' action at Dresden (Mitchell, 1850, II, 176; Lehndorff, 1910–13, I, 252–3).

As for the credit for the victory, Mitchell records that Frederick awarded it to the bravery of his troops and claimed that everything else was due to the operation of chance:

'Had I remained in the camp of Liegnitz, I should have been surrounded on all sides. Had I arrived one quarter of an hour sooner on the field of battle, the event would not have happened, and a few days would have put an end to the whole affair' . . . I took the liberty to reply, that it was plain to me, if Providence had not given His Majesty a better understanding than his enemies, he would not have been victorious that day.

He answered, with good humour, 'I know we are not in agreement on that point, but your mind is made up, and I am not disposed at the moment to argue with you.' (Mitchell, 1850, II, 203–5)

From 19 to 29 August 1760 the royal army rested at Hermannsdorf near Breslau, while Frederick made ready for the new campaign that was to bring the Austrians to battle in southern Silesia. Now that the Russian army appeared to be withdrawing into Poland, Frederick sent word to Prince Henry to leave about 14,000 troops on the far side of the Oder and bring all the rest to the royal army. This reinforcement arrived on the 29th, which gave Frederick a total of 50,000 men under his command, and he at once moved against the 80,000 Austrians who were grouped in the neighbourhood of Schweidnitz.

The Prussians marched all day on 30 August and all through the following night, and this first push of twenty-two miles most effectively turned the flank of Daun's position to the west of the Zobten-Berg. He raised his blockade of Schweidnitz, but rather than accept battle in the open field he recoiled to a new camp in the hills between Burkersdorf and Freyburg.

Frederick was therefore denied the decision he had been seeking. He shifted a little way to his right and spent the period between 3 and 10 September at Bunzelwitz, making arrangements to re-provision the army. The release of tension produced its usual effect on the mind and frame of the king, and he was gripped by onsets of pain which made it difficult for him to breathe. 'For two years now I have been exposed to sorry and endless anxiety. This is an ordeal calculated to undermine and overthrow the most robust constitution' (PC 12350).

On 11 September Frederick resumed his westward march. He progressed no further than Baumgarten before he found that the Austrians were enclosing him in a semi-circle of positions. Daun had moved sideways in the direction of Freyburg, while Loudon's corps gained the rounded heights south of Reichenau and headed off the Prussian advance.

The increasingly impatient Frederick resorted to the last move that was left to him, namely to march around to Daun's right or eastern flank. The three columns of the Prussian army set off in great silence at 3 a.m. on 17 September. The first miles of the march were across flat country, and Frederick hoped to gain a start on Daun by making rapid progress under cover of the morning mists. However, the army was still well short of its objectives when the veil lifted, and the Austrians were now able to bring their cavalry and guns into action against the enemy who were trailing past them on the plain below. 'All the people around the king were afraid of being shot, or of losing their master. The danger was in fact very real, for a sutler woman was brought down not far from him. But Frederick remained as cheerful as ever, and encouraged his suite to follow coolly in his tracks' (Anon., 1788–9, III, 17–18; see also Seidl, 1781, III, 310).

By 4 p.m. the advance guard had turned south towards the wooded hills and reached the Schweidnitz–Waldenburg road. Lieutenant-General Wied went ahead to anticipate the Austrians on the heights of Hoch-Giersdorf, and the army joined him there after clearing an abatis on the road. The cannonade had lasted without intermission from daybreak until 7.30 p.m. 'The noise carried as far as Breslau, and it was so considerable that the officers of the garrison believed there had been a battle. It was just a march, but it occasioned more cannon fire than had been fired in more than one open combat in times past' (Oeuvres, V, 75).

A last brief push on 18 September served only to lodge the Prussians a little deeper in the hills between Hoch-Giersdorf and the Münsterhöhe south-east of Reussendorf. Frederick wrote that he had been able to beat some Austrian detachments, but 'so far the only effect has been to make Daun more cautious than ever, and encourage him to hold onto a series of absolutely impregnable positions in the hills' (PC 12366).

The initiative passed to the allies. Away in the Russian headquarters the French liaison officer Marc-René de Montalembert suggested that an allied raid on Brandenburg and Berlin might force Frederick to break up his concentration south of Schweidnitz. The Russians responded with enthusiasm, and in the first week of October Major-General Totleben and Lieutenant-General Chernyshev descended on Berlin with two raiding corps from the Russian army, totalling 17,600 men. The first Russian attacks were beaten off by the garrison of Berlin, aided by 16,000 men who had raced thither from Saxony and the inactive theatre of war against the Swedes in Pomerania. On 7 October, however, Lacy reached the neighbourhood with 18,000 Austrians and Saxons from Daun's army. In the face of the now overwhelming forces of the allies, the Prussians abandoned Berlin, and the governor of the city surrendered to the Russians on the 9th.

For three days Berlin and Potsdam lay at the mercy of the allies. Lacy sent Prince Emeric Esterhazy with the Kaiser regiment to stand guard over Sans Souci and the Potsdam Schloss. Esterhazy held Frederick in holy awe, and he contented himself with removing a royal portrait and two flutes as souvenirs of the great man. No such restraint was exercised at Berlin, where the Austrians, the Cossacks and the vengeful Saxons made free with the palace of Charlottenburg, smashing the celebrated collection of classical statuary which

Frederick had purchased from Cardinal Polignac.

The essential damage to Frederick's interests could have been much worse. A Prussian courtier wrote on the 10th: 'The fall of Berlin signifies a frightful loss. All the resources to sustain the war are gone at a single stroke. The enemy have possession of our magazines, our factories, our powder mills and countless other stores' (Lehndorff, 1910–13, I, 270). The Austrians certainly broke up the machinery and the stored weapons in the small-arms factory at Spandau. However, no great harm was done to most of the objects of strategic importance. The cloth factory was spared, and the activities of the Russians in the Berlin Arsenal, the bronze foundry and the immense magazines amounted to little more than minor vandalism (Warnery, 1788, 535; Ligne, 1795–1811, XVI, 46).

The allies streamed away from Berlin on 11 October, upon the report that Frederick was on the move. The Austrians tried to drag the famous 'Mollwitz Grey' from Potsdam as a last trophy, but the old creature stood its ground in the Lustgarten under repeated blows, and it was left to live out its days in peace.

By 4 October Frederick had been convinced that his western flank and his capital were in the greatest danger. He knew of the departure of Lacy's corps, and he believed that it was making for Saxony, where the Prussian forces under Hülsen had retreated from Torgau in the face of the *Reichsarmee*. Alarming news also came from Lieutenant-General von der Goltz, who commanded the troops who had been left by Prince Henry to observe the Russians. Not only had the main army of the Russians advanced once more to the Oder, but at headquarters they were talking quite openly about some great blow they were going to deal at Brandenburg.

Ever since 18 September the Prussian army had been immobile in the Waldenburg Hills around Dittmannsdorf, while Frederick watched in vain for some opening that might enable him to catch the Austrians at a disadvantage. Now he saw that he must retreat to the plain, where at least he would gain the freedom to move into Saxony or Brandenburg, wherever the need proved greater. Frederick provided the army with enough flour, bread and biscuit to sustain it for a full month, and on the night of 6 October the Prussians abandoned the Dittmannsdorf position in the greatest silence.

The strategic deadlock had been broken on terms dictated by the enemy. Nobody could have guessed as much from Frederick's cheerful demeanour when he marched his army north-west towards the borders of Brandenburg and Saxony. He exchanged good-natured insults with his soldiers, and he talked as an equal with the company womenfolk, who helped with the cooking and laundry. He was amused when a soldier's wife blew sparks from a cooking fire into his face. Another of these ladies halted for a few minutes at a barn to give birth to a son, and when the march resumed she announced that the infant was to be called Fritz, in honour of the king.

In the middle of October Frederick veered west out of the direct path to Berlin, upon receiving reports that the enemy had evacuated the capital and that the main Russian army was motionless at Frankfurt. A little later it became clear that the Austrians were building up a powerful concentration in Saxony – Lacy made his way there after he abandoned Berlin, and Daun was marching with the principal army from Silesia to join him on the middle Elbe.

On 26 October the rival Prussian and Austrian armies completed their concentrations on the west bank of the Elbe above Magdeburg. Frederick had written that he was hoping for a decisive battle which might bring this exhausting war to an end (PC 12435), but people like Prince Henry and the gossipy ex-cavalryman Warnery could never understand why the king was so set on a confrontation. Long afterwards one of the royal ministers (probably Finckenstein) even claimed that the Russians had made some kind of underhand deal with Frederick, and that they required him to fight a battle in order to give them an excuse to retreat (Toulongeon, 1881, 103–4).

On 27 October Frederick set out from Dessau and went in search of the enemy. He first struck out for Düben, where he expected that Daun and the Reichsarmee intended to join forces. The 30,000 Germans made off by way of Leipzig, however, rather than endure another Rossbach. At Eilenburg, on 30 October, Frederick learnt that the Reichsarmee was out of the reckoning, which left the Austrians without support, and on 2 November he established that Daun was in position hard by the little town of Torgau.

Torgau was known as the most strategically important crossing of the middle Elbe. The permanent bridge had been demolished, but the Austrians had built three bridges of boats to take its place. Military men were also aware of the tactical value of the low ridge that extended to the north-west of the town. From here Prince Henry had bidden defiance to Daun's 60,000 Austrians in 1759, and here also Lieutenant-General Hülsen had held the Reichsarmee at bay earlier in the present campaign. Frederick was therefore acquainted with the general features of the Torgau position, if not with the precise location of the Austrian units.

In the course of his search for Daun, Frederick had actually worked himself around to Langen-Reichenbach, six miles to the south of the Austrian army. He knew enough of the Torgau camp to deter him from delivering his main assault against the southern, or nearer, side of the Austrian army. In this direction the slopes of the plateau were at their steepest, particularly to the west of Süptitz, and the access was impeded by the marshy and steeply banked channels of the Röhr-Graben, which ran by way of the two Sheep Ponds (Schaff-Teiche) and the village of Süptitz to the Great Pond (Grosser Teich), a large lake stretching to the south-west of Torgau.

A 'left-flanking' circuit around to the west of the position was all the more attractive to Frederick since he could march through the wooded Dommitzscher-Heide and with any luck arrive unseen at the rear of the Austrian army, from where he could ascend the gentle northern slopes of the plateau to the attack. The ridge was scarcely eight hundred paces broad at the top, which opened the agreeable prospect of the Austrians sinking into confusion when they tried to rearrange their densely packed forces to meet the assault.

Frederick was going to pit about 48,500 troops against 52,000–53,000 Austrians. He owned a train of no less than 181 howitzers and 12-pounder cannon, which gave him a superiority in heavy ordnance over the Austrians, with their 58 howitzers and heavy cannon. However, the king was outmatched in the total number of barrels of all calibres, which amounted to 246 pieces for the Prussians and 275 for Daun.

Frederick was used to being outnumbered in his battles. What made the plan for the combat at Torgau so remarkable was that the king, already inferior in troops and guns, was inspired by the lie of the ground to divide his army into two parts, of which Zieten was to lead 18,000 troops (11,000 infantry and 7,000 cavalry) against the southward-facing front of the Austrian position, while Frederick made his way to the Austrian rear to launch the principal attack with the remaining 30,500 (24,000 infantry and 6,500 cavalry). (See Map 24, p. 373.) Frederick's instructions for Zieten were private and verbal, and we know nothing for certain about the nature of Zieten's task, the intended timing of his movements, or what arrangements, if any, were made for communication between the two elements of the army, once they had separated.

The main force was to make its way through the Dommitzscher-Heide in three columns. Frederick in person accompanied the leading column of just under 16,700 troops. Fifteen battalions of columns comprised the striking head, and the 1,000 Zieten Hussars provided an immediate escort of cavalry. The reliable old Lieutenant-General Hülsen was to bring up the second column of twelve battalions, or about 6,300 men. Finally Lieutenant-General Prince Georg Ludwig of Holstein-Gottorp led the third, cavalry-heavy column of thirty-eight squadrons of horse (about 5,500 men) and four battalions (2,000). From the wording of the relevant *Disposition* (PC 12458) it is evident that Frederick wished to deliver an 'oblique attack', with the heaviest weight falling on the rear of the eastern wing of the Austrian army, which, he assumed, extended all the way to the bluffs adjoining Torgau.

Frederick set his column in motion at about 6.30 a.m. on 3 November, a day of almost symbolic gloom. He had a route of some twelve miles to follow, which on this ground was the equivalent of about six hours of marching. At Weidenhain (Mockrehna or Wildenhain, according to some accounts) the royal column clashed with the Austrian light corps of Ried a little before noon. The sound of the cannon fire carried to the ears of Daun, and shortly afterwards the Croats and the Austrian fugitives brought him news that strong Prussian columns were moving through the woods against his rear. Daun, collected and efficient as always, began to form a new line facing north.

A chapter of accidents and miscalculations rendered it impossible for Frederick to bring his army simultaneously onto the field. First of all the senior forester of Weidenhain misdirected the king's column along the path towards Elsnig, instead of by way of Neiden as the *Disposition* had laid down. The second column therefore found the king's column blocking its way, and Hülsen had to re-route the tail of his column down an unauthorised track, recall the head and send it along behind. Holstein's force was the slowest of all. The prince tarried overlong at his breakfast, or so it is alleged. His squadrons then made an extremely slow passage of the street and stream at Schöna, and the further march was prosecuted along narrow tracks of soft sand.

Towards 1 p.m. the head of Frederick's column reached the edge of the woods north-west of Neiden. The Austrian light troops abandoned the crossings of the little Strie-Bach, and Frederick rode out with an escort of the Zieten Hussars to take stock of the Austrian position. He was forced to make some radical reappraisals by what he saw and heard. Not only had Daun, contrary to expectations, found the time to rearrange his troops into a kind of hollow square, of which one side challenged the intended Prussian attack, but the east wing of the main Austrian army reached not to the vineyards near Torgau, but only as far as the area of the plateau north-west of Zinna. Here the Austrians had a heavy concentration of artillery, which probably deterred Frederick from any thought of turning that flank.

Instead of attacking with his left and 'refusing' his right, Frederick was compelled to shift the whole weight of the first attack further to the right or west, and assail the plateau on the sector to the north of Süptitz. Some of the Prussian battalions had already wheeled into line along the frontage originally assigned for the attack, and these troops now had to make a right turn and march in column to the west. The rearward battalions, in order to save time, made straight for the new positions by a diagonal movement from column.

Frederick did not believe that he was justified in delaying his attack until Hülsen and Holstein had reached the scene of action. The lowering sky discharged showers of snow and icy rain, reminding the Prussians that they had but a few hours of daylight left to them. Furthermore the Austrian baggage had been sighted crossing the Elbe at Torgau, which seemed to indicate that the enemy were about to make good their escape. Lastly, the strong south wind carried sounds of what appeared to be heavy firing from the far side of the ridge, and Frederick concluded that Zieten had already begun his attack.

At about 2 p.m. Frederick ordered the ten leading battalions of his grenadiers to advance to the attack. The march of the grenadiers was obstructed by the woods, where there was an old abatis, and the troops could shake themselves into order only when they emerged into open ground 850 paces from the Austrian position – in other words, under effective range of the enemy guns. The progress of their own artillery was impeded by the trees and the passage of the muddy Strie-Bach, and the grenadiers had 'marched so speedily that not a single cannon was able to follow them. But it was essential to attack' (Gaudi, in Koser, 1901, 282). The Austrian gunners took deliberate aim, secure in the knowledge that the Prussian troops were too distant to reach them with musketry, and 'Daun received the Prussians with a cannon fire more intense than any known in land warfare since the invention of gunpowder . . . The oldest veterans of the two armies had never seen such a display of fireworks. The king himself repeatedly exclaimed to his adjutants: "What a frightful cannonade! Have you ever heard anything like it!" ' (Archenholtz, 1840, II, 106–7).

Frederick in person was behind the grenadiers. A branch of an oak tree was severed by a cannon shot and fell nearby, and every minute the sights about him and the reports of casualties brought home to him the realisation that his first ten battalions of elite troops were being massacred. Two-thirds of the grenadiers were killed or wounded in a matter of minutes, and the survivors fled through the ranks of the regiments that were coming up behind.

Many of the forces of the royal army were still trailing through the woods, but rather than lose further time Frederick put in a fresh attack with the sixteen or so battalions that were most immediately at hand. These comprised the rearward brigades of the first column, and the six leading battalions of Hülsen's column. The Prussians reached the plateau, but they were unable to sustain themselves there under the fire of the massed Austrian guns. Daun burst out: 'My God, why is the king throwing so many men away? Doesn't he know it will do him no good?' The Prussian infantry made back to the woods.

Frederick's cavalry too was quickly put out of action, once Holstein emerged from the trees. The Schmettau Cuirassiers (C 4; see Map 25, p. 374) overcame a regiment of Austrian dragoons, then together with the Bayreuth and Jung-Platen Dragoons (D 5, D 11) they veered to their right and crashed into the infantry of the Austrian left. The Prussian troopers rode down the regiment of Durlach and engaged the regiment of Kollowrat, but the Austrian general Löwenstein brought up fresh battalions from the reserve line and drove the Prussians back.

Most of the remainder of Holstein's cavalry appears to have inclined to the left, to the east of the Zeitschken-Graben, and it ran into the main force of the Austrian cavalry, which Daun had concentrated on his east wing during the change of front. Here the Austrian commander General Carl O'Donnell counter-attacked with three of his regiments and put the Prussians to flight.

To all appearances the effort of the royal army was spent by about 4.30 p.m. For some minutes it had seemed that the king himself was numbered among the casualties. Frederick's adjutants had stayed close to their master during the assaults on the plateau. 'I looked towards the higher ground', writes Georg Heinrich von Berenhorst, 'and saw that the king had let slip his reins and was in the process of sinking backwards. I hastened up in time to prevent him falling . . . Our next priority was to remove ourselves from danger without the slightest delay. The groom led the horse to the wood, while I supported the unconscious king in my arms. And so we brought him back' (Berenhorst, 1845–7, II, 22). The adjutants tore aside Frederick's coat and shirt and found that a musket ball had penetrated the clothing but not the royal person. 'At that moment the king came to himself, and said with perfect composure *ce n'est rien!*' (Nicolai, 1788–92, II, 221–2). Frederick explained afterwards that the bullet had struck him on the breastbone, leaving him completely stunned, but that most of the force had been absorbed by his coat with its double layer of velvet, and by a fur vest which he wore beneath.

Berenhorst believed that he had saved the king's life, and he was affronted that Frederick never showed the slightest recognition of this service. We may be sure that Frederick only wanted the episode to be forgotten – he was notoriously unwilling to appear vulnerable, he disliked being under obligations, and with his marked prudishness he must have loathed the thought that his shabby underclothing and his body had been exposed to view.

Many more hours passed before Frederick was aware that he had gained the bloodiest victory of his career. This unexpected outcome was due to one last push by the remnants of the royal army to the north of the plateau, which we shall review presently, and to the action of Zieten's wing from the south.

In the morning Zieten's troops had separated from the main army beyond Audenhain. The corps had a much shorter distance to cover than did Frederick's men, and because Zieten did not wish to declare his presence to the Austrians needlessly early he marched his 18,000 troops slowly along the woodland paths and reached the open ground towards 2 p.m. It came as a surprise to Zieten to discover that the Austrian line on this side had been prolonged to the south-east by Lacy's corps, which had arrived during the morning and was now drawn up behind the Grosser-Teich.

There was a noisy clash between the advance troops of the two corps (see p. 213), but Zieten held back his main force and was content to exchange artillery fire with Lacy until, some time before 4 p.m., he marched against Daun's army. We shall never know what impelled him to move – whether messages had reached him from the king, urging him to attack, whether he was acting on his own estimation of the course of the battle, or whether perhaps the timing had been prearranged with Frederick. In any event Zieten managed his shift to the left with some skill. He set the brides of Tettenborn and Saldern in successive motion around the rear of his corps, like the links in a caterpillar track, and he maintained the brigades of Zeuner and Grumbkow in position facing Lacy until it was their turn to move as well.

Zieten arrived in front of the position of the main Austrian army, but his first attacks turned out as badly as did the assault by Frederick's grenadiers north of the ridge. Tettenborn's brigade was able to clear the village of Süptitz only as far as the Röhr-Graben. Further to the left, or west, the five battalions of Saldern's Garde brigade suffered heavy casualties when they forced the passage of the upper reaches of the same stream beyond Süptitz, and while darkness was falling they were repulsed by the point-blank canister fire of the Austrian cannon on the plateau behind.

The inspiration for a new attack appears to have come from an officer who was riding to Zieten's corps on some mission from the king. On the way he noticed that there were no Austrian forces guarding a route which led across the causeway between the two Sheep Ponds and up to the heights on the western flank of Daun's position. He reported his interesting discovery to Lieutenant-Colonel Möllendorff of the Garde. Möllendorff in turn addressed himself to his brigade commander and old friend Major-General Saldern, and the two of them agreed that it was practicable to attack the plateau from this direction. The scheme appeared all the more attractive since the flames of the burning village of Zinna revealed that the Austrians were concentrating their forces on their far, or eastern, flank.

Saldern's brigade and a battalion of Grumbkow's brigade filled across the causeway and climbed the slopes beyond. Zieten moved up the rearward elements of his corps in support (Tettenborn's brigade forded the stream nearby), and the Prussians were able to establish themselves on the plateau. No effective counter-attack came from the enemy, for Daun was wounded and had been carried from the field, and in the darkness the Austrians knew little of what was happening on their distant western flank.

On Frederick's side of the plateau, just as in Zieten's battle, some quite junior officers seem to have had the power to breathe fresh life into their seniors. The means of delivering one last attack were at hand in the shape of the uncommitted regiments of Schenkendorff (9) and Dohna (16), which had marched with the cavalry column, together with 1,000 fugitives who had been rallied by Major Lestwitz of the regiment of Alt-Braunschweig. The Prussians could see that the enemy were feeling the impact of Zieten's intervention, and the staff officer Gaudi, according to his own account, persuaded old Lieutenant-General Hülsen that he must make a final attempt on the Austrian position, though Frederick's admirers find it difficult to believe that such an important initiative could have come from anybody but the king.

Hülsen was determined to accompany the attack in person, in spite of the darkness and the loss of all his horses. 'His age and his wounds prevented him from going on foot, and so he planted himself on a cannon and had himself pulled into the enemy fire' (Archenholtz, 1840, II, 110). The drummers were kept hard at work, to keep the men together, and when Hülsen's troops encountered Zieten's the Prussians had the equivalent of about twenty-five battalions on the summit, which rendered the rest of the position untenable for the enemy. As Daun's successor, General O'Donnell withdrew the Austrian army as best as he could over the Torgau bridges.

Thousands of Austrians were left wandering on the muddy plateau, and they mingled with the Prussians, many of whom had also lost their bearings and were equally ignorant of the outcome of the day. Möllendorff himself was taken prisoner by four Austrian hussars whom he mistook for Prussians. Likewise the Austrian general Migazzi gave orders to an astonished Prussian battalion, which took him into custody without more ado.

Frederick had meanwhile made his way from the field, apparently in search of some quiet spot where he could write out his orders and dispatches. He dismounted a couple of miles away at Elsnig. At first he intended to stop at the parsonage, but on finding the rooms full of wounded officers he repaired to the village church, where he spent the rest of the night on the brick step of the diminutive altar, writing by candlelight. Frederick had most probably reached Elsnig at 9 p.m. at the earliest, by which time the battle had been convincingly won (Koser, 1901, 274–5; Herrmann, 1912, 590–1). Warnery, however, draws our attention to a hostile account according to which Frederick had abandoned the field after the first repulse of the royal army: 'He believed that all was lost. People saw him in tears at the very time when, unknown to him, Zieten had gained the heights of Süptitz' (Warnery, 1788, 439).

Early on 4 November the royal adjutant Berenhorst assembled six dragoons outside Elsnig church, each bearing a captured Austrian colour, but Frederick came out of the low door in 'a gloomy and earnest mood, and he mounted horse without casting so much as a glance in the direction of those dearly won trophies' (Berenhorst, 1845–7, I, xv).

Frederick's ill-humour was occasioned by what he knew must be the appalling cost of the battle. He pressed Berenhorst for an accurate computation of the butcher's bill, 'and finally, several days after the battle . . . Berenhorst finished his sums and carried the completed list to the royal chamber. Frederick emerged from behind the stove and snatched the paper from his hand. He reviewed the numbers of the losses . . . and told him sharply "It will cost you your head, if this figure ever gets out!" ' (Berenhorst, 1845–7, I, xv).

It was said that Berenhorst's assessment exceeded 20,000, which accords with Hans Bleckwenn's figures of 24,700 for the total Prussian dead, wounded and missing (Bleckwenn, 1978, 203). Even Curt Jany's much more modest estimate of 16,670 exceeds the Austrian losses by 1,000 men, and the disproportion in actual casualties was greater still, for the Austrian total comprised 7,000 prisoners left alive in the hands of the Prussians. The king had certainly pushed the Austrians from their position, 'but this success was purchased by huge sacrifices, and Frederick failed to attain that decisive triumph which alone might have offered a compensation' (Anon., 1886, 42). More than anything else Frederick must have regretted the virtual destruction of his first ten battalions of grenadiers.

Torgau emerges as a mid-eighteenth-century Borodino, which was huge in scale and bloodletting but left the two embattled parties with a sense of having fallen well short of their objectives. In Vienna, the chancellor Kaunitz despaired of being able to recover even so little as the County of Glatz for the Austrians, and he began to consider the advisability of making peace. The court of Versailles was disconcerted by the news of the defeat of their allies, 'and nobody more so than the Dauphiness [a Saxon princess], who is inconsolable, as it destroys all the hopes she had of seeing Saxony delivered from the Prussians' (report to the Duke of Newcastle, 17 November, British Library, Add. MSS 32,914).

Torgau has left us with probably more unanswered questions than any other of Frederick's great engagements. As we have seen, Frederick's contemporaries harboured doubts, which have still not been fully put at rest, concerning the motivation for the battle, Frederick's part in the management, and the number of casualties. The official relation was singularly uninformative, as the king himself admitted (*PC* 12505).

In particular we remain in ignorance of the task assigned to Zieten, and speculation on this head has therefore ranged unchecked. Napoleon, for example, declared that Frederick deserved to have been beaten for splitting his forces, whereas Clausewitz, Hans Delbrück, Walter Elze and Eberhard Kessel have deduced that the king was exploring a new form of dispersed battle (Kessel, 1937, 1; see also p. 314 of the present work). For the same reason we shall never know whether Gaudi was right when he claimed that Frederick had ruined the plan by attacking one and a half hours before an agreed time (Koser, 1901, 287).

Warnery was probably mistaken in his belief that Frederick left the battle when the issue was still in doubt. However, Frederick's role in the last stages was an unusually passive one, and the division of the forces into two parts prevented him from exercising his usual style of leadership. The Garde had been assigned to Zieten's wing, and the men could not understand why they had not seen the king at their head during the battle. The next day Frederick stopped at one of their outposts:

> After a little while the king unbuttoned his blue overcoat, since the heat of the watch fire was making him uncomfortable. During this process the grenadiers saw a bullet drop from his clothing, and they noticed that a shot had grazed his chest. Now they were seized with admiration and they called out: 'You are the same Old Fritz! You share all our dangers! We shall willingly lay down our lives for you! Long live the king! Long live the king!' (Anon., 1786, IV, 349)

Only on 6 November, three days after the battle, did the Prussian army march up the Elbe from Torgau to Strehla. The next day Frederick nearly caught Lacy's corps on the west bank of the Elbe at Meissen. However, this expert gentleman made his escape in the nick of time and the main Austrian army made an undisturbed retreat to Dresden, where the enemy stood fast and reoccupied the celebrated position of the Plauensche-Grund.

Frederick had to be content with leaving Dresden in the hands of the Austrians, and he distributed his troops in winter quarters across central Saxony and southern Silesia: 'This is all the advantage we have derived from that dangerous and bloody battle. I suspected what was going to happen, and I am very sorry to have been proved right' (PC 12511).

Frederick spent the winter of 1760–61 in Leipzig, rebuilding the strength of his person and his state for the continuing war. For the sake of quiet recreation he sent to Berlin for his orchestra and for his friend, the Marquis d'Argens. His companions found the king melancholy and withdrawn, and looking much older than his forty-nine years.

All hopes of peace came to nothing. The Austrians continued the war with a dull persistence, and the Duc de Choiseul breathed fresh life into the French, after all their recent reverses. The Russians had a new commander, Aleksandr Borisovich Buturlin, and they had by now completely familiarised themselves with the conditions of Western warfare.

For the next campaign the Austrians planned to maintain 60,000 troops in Saxony under Daun, and to reinforce Loudon in Silesia to no less than 72,000 men, who were to undertake offensive operations in concert with the main Russian army. Frederick rightly prophesied that Silesia would be the most active theatre of operations, and here he intended to concentrate his best and most complete regiments, comprising about 55,000 men. Henry was to take charge of the 28,000 poorish troops remaining in Saxony. Another 14,000 were posted in Pomerania, where the most important task was to hold the port of Colberg against the Russians.

In the third week of March 1761 Frederick began to assemble the Prussian forces in the camp of Meissen, and on 4 May he set out with the royal army to join the corps of Lieutenant-General von der Goltz in Silesia. It is not at all certain what kind of a war he intended to fight. In the spring he rated his chances of victory in battle at no more than even (PC 12822), and on 24 May he wrote to Henry that he would attack the Austrian fortified camps only in the case of absolute necessity (PC 12904). Henry nevertheless feared that his brother still hankered after bloody *Batailliren*, and he tried to persuade the king that the soundest strategy would be to maintain equal numbers on all sides, and hold off the enemy by *expédients*. This challenge stirred something of the old Frederick of 1757. It was wrong, he rejoined, to allow yourself to be pushed tamely back. Rather you should concentrate your forces, move fast, and gain the precious commodity of time by fighting (27 June, PC 12995).

From 15 May to 6 July Frederick held his army on the long, low and open ridge of Kunzendorf, just to the west of Schweidnitz, waiting for the allies to declare their intentions. He had hoped to anticipate the Russians by sending 12,000 men to attack their columns as they marched up through Poland, but on 29 June he heard that the Russians had already set out from their forward depot at Posen. Frederick also learnt that Austrian reinforcements were on their way to join Loudon, and from all of this he deduced that the allies intended to execute a pincer movement, and that the jaws would meet in the south-eastern corner of Silesia. He accordingly abandoned the Kunzendorf camp on 6 July and took up a position on the eastern side of Schweidnitz at Pilzen, where he was on the excellent road to Frankenstein.

On 19 July Loudon advanced boldly from the border hills and gained the Silesian plain by way of the Eulen-Gebirge passes at Silberberg and Wartha. Frederick had only 32,000 troops immediately at hand, but by dint of forced marches he beat Loudon to the heights of Gross-Nossen on 23 July. He thereby interposed himself between the Austrians and the upper Oder, and barred their way to the Russians. On 29 Frederick continued his move into south-eastern Silesia, and from 31 July to 3 August he occupied a new blocking position at Oppersdorf behind the line of the Biele. Loudon was not tempted to try to break through to his Russian friends, and he fell back west to the Eulen-Gebirge. This successful campaign had so far cost the Prussian army just eight fatalities – namely two hussars, and six of the men of the free battalions (who hardly counted as human beings). With his attention still fixed on Upper Silesia, Frederick withdrew his army on 5 August to the central position of Strehlen, which was within a single march of the upper Oder, and equidistant from his fortresses at Breslau, Neisse and Schweidnitz.

By the middle of August, however, the state of affairs changed rapidly to Frederick's disadvantage. Effectively, while the king was still looking north and east, the allies reached out to one another behind his back. On 12 August the Russians passed the middle Oder at Leubus, and three days later they united with forty squadrons of Austrian horse, which had advanced from the Eulen-Gebirge. On the 15th Frederick went in search of the Russians, and now at last he found them strongly emplaced near Liegnitz. He was disinclined to attack them, after the Prussian experiences at Zorndorf, Paltzig and Kunersdorf. Frederick forfeited his last chance of defeating the allied armies in isolation when, on 19 August, Buturlin executed a bold march by way of Liegnitz and reached the main body of the Austrians.

Frederick had failed in the purpose of his campaign, which had been to hold the allies apart, and for the first time in this war the Austrians and Russians had succeeded in uniting their principal armies. The combined allied force amounted to about 130,000 troops, of which Loudon's Austrians constituted some 72,000 men, and the Russians 47,000 regulars.

Amid this sea of enemies, Frederick constructed a secure refuge for his little army of 55,000 men. This was the entrenched camp of Bunzel-witz, which extended to the north-west of the fortress and depot of Schweidnitz: 'Frederick, by judiciously protecting the final issue, effected his extrication. Instead of acting offensively and committing all to hazard, as he had done more than once in the preceding campaigns, he seems to have exchanged qualities with his antagonist, and to have adopted the phlegm as well as the caution of Daun' (Wraxall, 1806, I, 204).

Work on the Bunzelwitz camp began on 20 August, and for this purpose the army was divided into two shifts, which took it in to labour around the clock. Fortunately the soil was a light, greyish-brown substance, and within three days the position was in a defensible state. The perimeter was about 15,000 paces in extent, and described the shape of an irregular oblong:

> In this location the Prussian army stood on a series of low and mostly gentle eminences, which were utilised in a masterly fashion. The approaches were by no means physically insurmountable, but what rendered them difficult to reach were the little streams, the swampy meadows, and the enfilading and grazing fire from the batteries on every side. (Tielke, 1776–86, III, 84)

The line was discontinuous, by deliberate intent. Frederick had about 460 guns at his disposal thanks to the pieces he borrowed from Schweidnitz, and he mounted the heavier calibres in well-sited batteries. 'Each of these works was protected by a couple of fougasses, or by ditches which were dug just outside and filled with gunpowder, shot and shells, ready to be touched off at any moment by means of powder trains running through tubes' (Archenholtz, 1840, II, 170). Outlying villages and commanding sites were also palisaded and entrenched. Between the various strongpoints, however, wide gaps were left to permit the defenders to sally forth in counter-attacks, 'which is the essential – though often misunderstood – secret of the art of field fortification' (Tielke, 1776–86, II, 84).

It will perhaps be of interest to make a brief anti-clockwise tour of the position (see Map 26, p. 376). Frederick was forced to conform in general terms with the lie of the land, which dictated that the southernmost sector (Works XVII–V) projected in a naturally vulnerable salient, deriving little benefit from the enfilade fire of lateral works. Frederick accordingly made the artificial defences of this area the strongest of all. Beyond the camp proper he emplaced one free battalion, three hundred detached infantry and ten pieces near the top of Wickendorf village in an almost complete circuit of palisade and breastwork (I), commanding an open field of fire over the ground which descended to the willows of a branch of the Freyburger-Wasser, just out of musket shot to the south. This garrison was expected to identify and delay an initial attack.

Frederick expected a more serious resistance to be offered to the rear of Wickendorf at Alt-Jauernick, which had a fortified churchyard mound. The village street, which was in a slight depression, was swept from III at the upper end, and Lieutenant Tempelhoff (the future historian) commanded five *Brummer* (heavy 12-pounders) in IV immediately to the north-east.

Continuing our circuit to the east we discover that V contained six howitzers, as well as six *Brummer*, and that it had the task of setting fire to Alt-Jauernick and Bunzelwitz if these villages fell to the enemy.

The Würben Hill (IX) formed the south-eastern extremity of the camp, but it was by nature much stronger than the corresponding southern salient. 'This hill is the highest in the whole position, and very difficult to attack on account of the very broken terrain roundabout. It is also worth mentioning that the breastworks were very skilfully designed to correspond with the slope of the hill' (Tielke, 1776–86, III, 93). Six new 12-pounder cannon were in position here, though Frederick considered that there was no necessity to keep this formidable post under a strong permanent guard.

The broad north-eastern side (X–XVII) had no marked geographical features, but its evenly spaced batteries offered a wide base of fire, and the existence of the Striegauer-Wasser, two miles to the north, deprived the enemy of any great depth for mounting an attack. Frederick wrote that he had a masked battery (XIV?) ready to receive the Austro-Russian forces of Brentano and Chernyshev if they sought an entry by way of the little valley leading from Peterwitz, and a path was cut through the woods to permit Lieutenant-General Platen to intervene with the Prussian cavalry, most of which was massed behind this sector.

A short but strong line, looking towards Tschechen, extended across low, arid hills from XVIII to the corner bastion of XXIII, and from there a long, straight and important front ran south-east to XXVII, which completes the circuit. This last sector looked south-west towards the main Russian army and the Austrian light corps of

Beck, and it was afforded some very necessary protection by the swampy meadows of the Freyburger-Wasser, and the abatis which had been cut in the Nonnen-Busch, where the Prussian jaegers skirmished daily with the Croats.

The life in the Bunzelwitz camp was an arduous one. The sun beat down on the unshaded works, and towards the end of the night, when the men on the day shifts might have been sleeping soundly, the entire army stood under arms in its battle positions around the perimeter. 'Officers and soldiers alike had to live on bread and water. So as to set an example to the soldiers, the king made a point of staying every night in one or other of the batteries, where he had a bale of straw brought up to serve as his chair' (Warnery, 1788, 474). In fact the circuit was rather long for the 36,000–38,000 infantry at Frederick's disposal, and so every battalion was absorbed in holding the line, leaving him with no reserve except the cavalry massed in the south-eastern corner.

The main Russian army arrived outside the Bunzelwitz camp on 25 August, and the Austrians came up the next day. The main Austrian army was massed opposite the southern sector near Wicken- dorf, as Frederick had almost certainly anticipated, and he took the precaution of planting his night-time headquarters tent on the little bump of the Farben-Höhe, just to the west of Alt-Jauernick. From here, when the sun began to reveal the landscape, Frederick could observe almost every object of interest for miles around. To the left the royal gaze swept over the smooth elongated pyramids of the Zobten-Berg range, the scarred hill of Würben closer at hand, and finally in the immediate foreground the gently sloping plain to the north of Alt-Jauernick which offered such a magnificent field of action for the Prussian cavalry grouped in the interior of the camp. As he turned to his right Frederick took in the boxy tower of Alt- Jauernick church, the onion dome of Wickendorf, the distant pin- nacle of Schweidnitz, and then the bulky blue lumps of the Glatz mountains shading into the long curtain of the Riesen-Gebirge. Lastly the spire of Hohenfriedeberg and the low hills beyond Striegau brought reminders of how often he had carried his armies to this part of the world.

Frederick was certain that the allies were going to attack, and equally confident that he would give them a bloody nose. His assur- ance derived partly from the tactical strength of the works, and also from his location, so near his fortress-depot of Schweidnitz (PC 13153, 13156, 13160; Mitchell, 1850, II, 233).

Such an assault was indeed being debated in the allied camp. Loudon's first proposals were rejected by the Russians on 27 and 29 August, but he returned with an extremely well-thought-out plan for a joint attack that was to take place on 1 September. On the north-eastern or 'Peterwitz' sector Berg's corps of Cossacks and Russian hussars were to skirmish in the area of Saarau, while Chernyshev (12,000–13,000 troops) and the Austrian corps of Brentano (6,000) crossed the Striegauer-Wasser and advanced through Puschkau as if to attack Tschechen. Meanwhile the main Russian army was to deploy on an impressively wide frontage between Stanowitz and Zirlau, so as to fix the attention of the Prussians who were on the south-western sector.

The genuine attack was to be the work of the Austrians, and for his target Loudon selected the point of the southern salient. The assault was timed for 3.30 a.m. (the sun rose at 5.16 a.m.), and was to be led by an advance guard of two columns, namely:

(a) a left-hand column of 6,000 under Major-General Amadei, supported by Lieutenant-General Ellrichshausen with a reserve of 10,000, and

(b) a right-hand column of 7,000 under Major-General Brincken.

The chosen sector was undoubtedly the weakest of the position, and the Austrians, once established on the Farben-Höhe, could have begun to roll up the south-western and south-eastern fronts of the perimeter, exploiting to the full the lack of any Prussian infantry reserve, and the fact that the Prussian heavy guns, now facing the wrong way, could have been extricated from the batteries only with some difficulty. Much would have depended on the completeness of the surprise at Wickendorf and Jauernick, and the extent to which the Prussian cavalry allowed itself to be bemused by Berg, Chernyshev and Brentano. Platen, the cavalry commander, was a man of great enterprise, who would probably have intervened against the Austrians without waiting for orders, but we must not discount the influence of Major-General Ramin, a steady but literal-minded officer, who had the immediate command of the 'Peterwitz' sector, and who might well have been influenced by the allied demonstrations.

All of this remains a matter of speculation. The allied army was at a high pitch of excitement on the night of 31 August, awaiting the order to attack, when Buturlin suddenly gave way to the pressure of his generals and withdrew his consent to the enterprise. Frederick still expected an attack from one day to the next. At last, on 9 September, Buturlin decamped, pleading lack of provisions. To encourage him on his way, Frederick sent Platen with a corps of 10,000 troops on a raid against the Russian base areas in western Poland.

Buturlin retreated beyond the far side of the Oder on 14 September, but he had assigned one-third of his infantry to Austrian command, which left Loudon with a respectable force of 80,000 or more regulars, emplaced on the hill slopes at the southern edge of the Silesian plain. Frederick had by now conceived a very low opinion of Loudon's abilities, and he judged it safe to leave the Austrians in their camp and move closer to Neisse, where there were ample provisions. On 26 September the Prussian army abandoned the Bunzelwitz position and began the leisurely march to the east. Frederick wrote to Henry: 'I think you need have no further anxiety on our account. Basically the campaign is over, for neither the Austrians nor ourselves are capable of taking any initiatives' (PC 13185).

It seemed scarcely possible, after the bloodless Prussian triumphs of the summer of 1761, that a series of reverses in the autumn and winter could have brought Frederick's army and state to the verge of collapse.

On the night of 30 September the sound of cannon fire carried from the west to Frederick's camp at Gross-Nossen. The report then arrived that Loudon had taken the fortress of Schweidnitz 'in an almost incredible manner' (PC 13195) by open assault, without bothering to dig trenches or establish siege batteries. The loss of this place deprived Frederick of his best-placed depot, magazine and refuge on the Silesian theatre of war. No event since the rout of Kunersdorf induced such consternation in the Prussian army. The king was thunderstruck, the private soldiers deserted in droves, and the senior officers were in the grip of horror (Mitchell, 8 October, PRO SP 90/78; Warnery, 1788, 480; Archenholtz, 1840, II, 184; Catt, 1884, 446; Möllendorff, in Volz, 1926–7, II, 94).

The wintry weather set in very early that year, and on 6 October Frederick established his despondent army in cantonments between Strehlen and Brieg. His headquarters at Strehlen were so negligently guarded that at one time Frederick's life was actually in danger from a plot engineered by Baron Warkotsch, an Austrian sympathiser. The conspiracy was discovered shortly before the intended event, and the Austrian generals hastened to dissociate themselves from this infamous scheme. Finally on 9 December Frederick planted himself for the winter in the royal Schloss at Breslau. He was uncommunicative and plagued with headaches, and the palace was in a condition corresponding with his mood, full of wreckage from Loudon's bombardment of 1760.

Never before had the Prussian army been forced to take up its quarters so deep inside Silesia, and for the first time in the war the Austrians were able to establish their troops in cantonments on the Prussian side of the border. The tidings from Saxony were scarcely more encouraging. Daun had manoeuvred Henry out of the Meissen camp in the course of October, and the Prussians could barely maintain a foothold in the electorate for the winter.

Beset by so many misfortunes close to home, Frederick was perhaps less disturbed than he ought to have been by the news that Prime Minister Pitt had resigned on 5 October. Only in 1762 did he come to see that his successor Bute was 'a man who ought to be broken alive on the wheel' (Marcus, 1927, 52).

Just when it seemed that the year could have no further blows in store, Frederick received the terrible news that Colberg had fallen to the Russian corps of Rumyantsev on 16 December, after a six-month blockade and siege. The ownership of this little place, isolated on the sandy coast of Pomerania, was an issue of some magnitude in the history of the war. The Russians (who were denied the free use of neutral Danzig) now at last had a port where they could land supplies close to the theatre of operations. Moreover, with Colberg as flank protection, the Russians were able to hold themselves for the winter at the gates of Brandenburg, instead of retreating to Posen and beyond as in previous years, and by establishing an effective cordon along the border they cut off for the first time the cereals which Frederick had been accustomed to draw from Poland.

There was at this period a touch of irrationality in Frederick's thinking, engendered by the desperate condition of his affairs. In all seriousness the king clung to the thought that the Prussian state might yet be saved by Muslim intervention from the east. Henry was surprised at the credit which Frederick gave to the reports of his envoy Rexin, who was in Constantinople to arrange a commercial treaty, to the effect that the Turks were preparing to open war against Russia and Austria in the spring. Frederick exclaimed that he would do anything to obtain a diversion from those folk. More outlandishly still, Frederick was entranced by the appearance in his headquarters of a representative from the Khan of the Crimea, and he began to spin schemes for a joint Prusso-Tartar cavalry raid into Hungary and eastern Austria.

Frederick got his favourite adjutant, Major Wilhelm Heinrich von Anhalt, to work out a plan of campaign based on the happy assumption that the allies would be so disconcerted by the irruption of the Turks and Tartars that they would be unable to resist Prussian invasions of Bohemia and Moravia. This interesting document (*Project zur künftigen Campagne*, undated December 1761, PC 13368) was sent to Henry, who reasonably asked what would happen if the Turkish help did not materialise.

Frederick's reply was not of a kind to set his brother's mind at rest. In that case, he wrote, he would combine all the Prussian forces in a single mass and fall on one or another of his enemies. 'I can already hear the kind of difficulties and objections you will offer. But just consider – to die bit by bit or to die all together, don't they amount to the same thing?' (9 January, *PC* 13390).

It was a different Frederick, more realistic, more concerned to secure some kind of existence for Prussia over the long term, who had meanwhile been in correspondence with his foreign minister Finckenstein. He outlined to him the advance of the allies in Silesia, Saxony and Pomerania, and frankly owned how much the continuance of the struggle depended on Turkish help: 'Quite simply, we are lost without their assistance' (10 December, *PC* 13332). This, he admitted on 6 January 1762, was not something which could be relied on:

> If such aid is not forthcoming, our courage and our armed forces will be unequal to sustaining the next campaign, let alone restoring our affairs. It seems to me that we ought to open negotiations, so as to rescue all we can from the wreckage of my cause, and preserve the interests of my nephew from the greed of my enemies. I leave it to your judgment to decide whether to embark on these negotiations through the English, or whether the situation is so urgent that you must address yourself directly to France, Vienna or St Petersburg. (*PC* 13383)

Frederick's spirit was overcome, at the close of 1761, not just by the strategic implications of the loss of Schweidnitz and Colberg, but by processes that were ravaging the structures of army and state.

Interestingly enough, Frederick's good management spared Prussia from financial crises of the kind which caused a slackening of the Austrian military effort in 1761 and set France on the path to revolution. Frederick's achievement was all the greater when we reflect that he embarked on the conflict with a treasury of a little over 13,500,000 thaler at his disposal, that the war cost a total of 140,000,000 (Johnson, 1975, 184), and that he had nevertheless contrived to amass a surplus of 14,500,000 by the end.

How had he done it? Only a small proportion of these sums derived from conventional sources like the produce of the royal domains, or the taxes and loans raised from the provinces. However, the British subsidy, made over at £670,000 *per annum*, yielded the equivalent of 27,500,000 thaler between the first payment in July 1758 and the termination in 1761. No less than 48,000,000 more were raised by force in Saxony, and further contributions in money and kind were exacted from the neighbouring German states: 'An important note concerning the Mecklenburg contributions! Take some hostages, and threaten the stewards of the duke that you will start burning and plundering unless they pay up promptly' (to Dohna, 4 December 1758, *PC* 10582).

No less reprehensible, to the moralists' way of thinking, was the debasement of the currency which Frederick undertook in association with the merchant concerns of David Itzig, Moses Isaac, and Ephraim & Sons. Soldiers, public servants and foreign creditors were forced to accept the debased *Ephraimiten* at full face value, which occasioned the rhyme:

> The outside is silver, the inside a sham,
> Outside Frederick, inside – Ephraim.

Likewise, economy in the strategic dimension helped to redress the imbalance which in purely numerical terms pitted a population of 4,500,000 souls against the 90,000,000 or so of Austria, the *Reich*, Russia, France and Sweden. On the central theatre Frederick's strategy of interior lines successfully postponed the union of the main Austrian and Russian armies until the late summer of 1761, while Hülsen, Henry or other detached commanders held the *Reichsarmee* in check in Saxony. The French never got to grips with Frederick at all, except briefly and disastrously in November 1757; for the rest of the war they were kept at arm's length by the Protestant German and British army of Prince Ferdinand of Brunswick, a force which contained only a small proportion of Prussians. Ferdinand never let the enemy get within striking distance of his master, even during the supreme effort by 160,000 French in 1761.

The Swedish campaigns in northern Pomerania were farcical, except in the contest for the navigation of the Oder estuary, which the Prussians desired to keep open for British merchantmen. On the water the Swedes owned a superiority in speed, manoeuvrability and firepower, and on 10 September 1759, at Neuwarp in the Stettiner Haff, they destroyed most of the Prussian flotilla of converted fishing boats and timber carriers. By 1761, however, the Prussians had rebuilt their naval forces, and on land their moral ascendancy was not seriously in dispute. The Swedes rarely put more than 15,000 men into the field, and they were held at bay by the hussar officer Wilhelm Sebastian von Belling and his little force of light cavalry and Pomeranian provincial militia. In 1762 Frederick was amused to see the Swedish envoys approach him with a view to ending hostilities. ' "Have I really been at war with the Swedes?" In all seriousness the envoys replied in the affirmative. "Oh yes, I remember now," answered Frederick, "my Colonel Belling had some dealings with them" ' (Hildebrandt, 1829–35, III, 140).

At the same time no brilliant calculations, no sarcastic wit, could stay the losses that Frederick was suffering in his contest with his two genuinely formidable enemies, the Austrians and the Russians. He estimated afterwards that the Prussians had run through

180,000 men in the course of the war, and that scarcely one hundred men per regiment remained of those who embarked on campaign in 1756 – which indicates a rate of survival of about one in fifteen (for a more detailed study of the nature of the losses and combat stress at this period, please see the author's forthcoming *Experience of War in the Age of Reason*).

What accounts for damage on this scale? About 106,000 men were killed, wounded or missing in open battle. The losses amounted to 33 per cent of the Prussian combatants at Zorndorf, about 40 per cent at Kunersdorf, and 30 per cent or possibly much more at Torgau. There is nothing unlikely in the story that at Silberberg in 1778 Frederick met a widow who had lost six of her sons in the last war.

To the losses in open battle we must add the erosion occasioned by small-scale actions, exhaustion, disease, and especially by desertion. The ex-Saxon soldiers were still more likely to make off than were the Catholics from Glatz and Upper Silesia, and the army as a whole was thinned out whenever it prosecuted forced marches through broken country, as on the way to Liegnitz in 1760.

Whole regiments at a time were temporarily removed from the order of battle whenever detached corps or garrisons surrendered to the enemy. The campaign of 1759 was particularly destructive in this respect, and cost the Prussians no less than twenty-eight battalions and thirty-five squadrons. Another twenty-six battalions were lost in this way in 1760. A few of the officers eventually came back to the army by way of exchange (Frederick effected the return of Möllendorff two days after Torgau), but many others remained in captivity until the end of the war, and the less patriotic of the soldiers were never seen again.

Indirectly, the army was weakened by the progressive encroachment of the allies on the native recruiting grounds. East Prussia and the Prussian Rhineland were lost to the enemy outright, and Silesia, Pomerania and the Neumark became active theatres of war, where normal recruiting was difficult. The morale of the East Prussians, even when they were serving in the army, was undermined by the knowledge that their homeland was under Russian occupation.

Seeking to maintain the numerical strength of his army, Frederick was forced into taking measures which told heavily on morale and proficiency. Enemy prisoners and deserters were enrolled without hesitation in the full knowledge that these folk would make themselves scarce as soon as they escaped the eye of their NCOs. The best of the remaining troops – the grenadier battalions and the regiments of Brandenburg and Pomeranian musketeers – were retained as far as possible with the royal army, while the detached corps were filled out with a higher proportion of second-grade troops like the homeless East Prussians, the little Catholic fusiliers from Upper Silesia, and the brigand-like scum of the free battalions. Here we must be all the more careful to do justice to the excellent mixed free corps of 'Green' Kleist, and the long-suffering Pomeranian *Land-Regimenter* who helped to sustain the prolonged *kleiner Krieg* against the Russians and Swedes.

The Prussian officer corps was now paying dearly for its privileges. There were some 5,500 holders of commissioned rank at the beginning of the war; by the end, 1,500 or more had been killed, and another 2,500 or so were wounded. Whole noble families were significantly diminished in the slaughter. The prolific tribe of Kleist could afford its two dozen sacrifices, but the Kameckes lost nineteen of their number, and the Bellings forfeited twenty out of their twenty-three males. Ultimately Frederick was compelled to recruit large numbers of boys and bourgeois as officers, which is itself a significant indication of how far the ranks of the corps were being thinned.

Thirty-three generals died in the first four years of the war alone, and by the end of 1758 an entire generation of senior commanders – Schwerin, Winterfeldt, Keith and Moritz – had passed from the scene. Frederick lamented: 'You know how rare good generals are, and how few I have at my disposal . . . It seems as if the Austrians are immortal, and that only our own people are dying. My generals are passing the Styx at a furious rate of knots, and soon there will be nobody left' (to Henry, 9 August 1758 and 16 July 1759, *PC* 10195, 11212). Zieten survived and he was retained with the royal army, but Ferdinand of Brunswick was beyond recall in western Germany, and Prince Henry and (when his health allowed) Seydlitz were usually absent on detached commands.

The discontented Prussian general and officer, unlike the Frederician private soldier, could not change his conditions of life by deserting. Instead 'we owned a formal opposition in the Prussian army in the Seven Years War. Whatever Frederick did was certain to evoke denigration and disapproval in this quarter. The opposition maintained a correspondence between its members in the various armies, as Frederick was well aware . . . Occasionally he intercepted the letters and laughed at the contents' (Zimmermann, 1790, II, 317).

Prince Henry emerged as the hero of all those who harboured reservations about Frederick's conduct of affairs. He was bookish and misogynistic, like his brother, but the two were separated not just by thirteen years of age but by important matters of principle. Henry challenged the tenets of the existing Prussian society, which held the nobles in a kind of military servitude and excluded the middle classes from honour (see p. 330). More important in the present context, he questioned the justice of the war and believed that Frederick was conducting it in an irresponsible way.

What gave Henry's opinion its weight was his undeniable professional skill. 'He was an educated soldier, in the best sense of the term' (Massenbach, 1808, I, 14), and two qualities in particular impressed his contemporaries. He followed the tradition of Schwerin in maintaining orderly administration and effective discipline. Indeed, a Saxon landowner once exclaimed that 'he would rather see Prince Henry march through his estates with 50,000 men than another general with one-tenth of that number' (Lehndorff, 1910–13, I, 229). Second, when it came to the conduct of operations, Henry excelled at exploiting every opportunity offered by terrain and the passage of time:

> The positions which he took up always answered their purpose. They were always secure, and they always corresponded to the difficult situations in which he often found himself. He made an accurate study of the character of his opponents, and he invariably punished them when they were careless enough to offer him an opening. (Retzow, 1802, I, 333)

Nowhere could Frederick find a fellow spirit after Winterfeldt was killed in 1757. The king enjoyed the great advantage of the concentration of political and military authority, but by the same token the burden of the conflict weighed far more heavily on him than on any other statesman or general. He was isolated in the army, as we have seen, and also within the circle of his own military family. The adjutant Berenhorst testifies:

> By the fourth and fifth years of the war Frederick no longer commanded love, respect or even fear among the nearest and most intimate members of his suite. I can say this because I saw it with my own eyes. When we rode behind him there was a mischievous young brigade-major of the cavalry, called Wodtke, who set out to amuse us by going into comic contortions behind his back, imitating the way he sat in the saddle, pointing at him and so on. Wodtke bestowed on Frederick the nickname 'Grave-Digger'. Later on he abbreviated it to 'Digger', and this is what he called the great hero when we came together in private and engaged in jokes and malicious talk. (Berenhorst, 1845–7, I, 181)

The strain on the king was manifest in physical and psychological symptoms – the haemmorrhoids, the rheumaticky pains, the headaches, the hankering after a release by suicide – and in an alteration of character that was noted by his admirer the British envoy Mitchell:

> I am very sorry to observe . . . that I think the king of Prussia's temper considerably ruffled and grown more harsh since the battle of Zorndorf; to this I impute his keeping the Russian officers still at Cüstrin, the burning of Count Brühl's house, etc. . . . I cannot think of the bombardment of Dresden without horror, nor of other things I have seen. Misfortunes naturally sour men's tempers, and the continuance of them at last extinguishes humanity. (12 December 1758, 31 July 1760, Mitchell, 1850, I, 476; II, 184)

The change in appearance was shocking to Frederick's reader Catt, who saw the king after a period of absence, and knew him only by the fire in his eyes. The king himself was alive to the processes that were at work. He wrote in 1760 to his beloved 'Mama', the old Countess Sophie Caroline de Camas:

> I tell you, I lead a dog's life, and I suspect that only Don Quixote has ever known this kind of existence, with its endless disorders. It has aged me so much that you would scarcely recognise me. My hair is completely grey on the right side of my head. My teeth are breaking and falling out. My face is as deeply folded as the flounces on a lady's skirt, my back is bent like an archer's bow, and I go about as gloomy and downcast as a Trappist monk. (Oeuvres, XVIII, 145)

These were afflictions which Frederick was prepared to sustain indefinitely. What impelled him to ask Finckenstein to open negotiations, on 6 January 1762, was not his personal distress, and not even the bloodletting among his troops, but the collapse of the Silesian and Pomeranian frontiers, and the approaching disintegration of the fabric of the army and state.

The scale of acceptable losses is not a mathematical constant, but something which must be continuously and closely redefined in a military, political, social and economic context. The two concerns that mattered to Frederick more than anything else were the welfare of his core of 'useful, hard-working people', and the maintenance of military discipline. Both were now in danger.

Frederick knew that about half a million of his subjects were refugees. He was also aware that the system of military administration threatened to crumble as completely as that of the civilian officials, who had been abandoned to their own devices since the beginning of the war. In the winter of 1761–62 the captains for the first time failed to receive the monies with which to fit out their companies for the next campaign. Möllendorff wrote to a friend:

> The soldier does not have the wherewithal to live, and he lacks
> the most basic commodities. He resorts to robbery. Now a thief
> is a man devoid of honour, and a man who lacks honour is a
> coward. The consequence is the decay of discipline, which is
> the basic and ultimate support of the army. The officers are in
> the same condition. Things are so bad with them that they no
> longer understand the meaning of the words 'honour' or
> 'reputation'. (12 December 1761, in Volz, 1926–7, II, 95; see
> also Frederick to Wied, 15 May 1762, in Wengen, 1890, 355;
> Riesebeck, 1784, II, 137; Warnery, 1788, 441)

Prussia entered the New Year of 1762 with her army approaching ruin
and her king resembling nothing so much as a demented scarecrow. It
is curious to reflect that if one lady had lived for a very few weeks
longer, historians would by now have analysed in the most convincing detail the reasons for a collapse as 'inevitable' as that which
overtook the Sweden of Charles XII.

The female in question was one of Frederick's most implacable
enemies, Empress Elizabeth of Russia, who died on 5 January 1762.
The first tidings reached Frederick on 19 January, by way of his envoy
in Warsaw. Frederick was too inured to disappointments to be able to
believe that such an event could work any dramatically favourable
revolution in his affairs. Much more heartening was a letter from
Finckenstein, who wrote to the king from Magdeburg on 27 January,
announcing that news had come that the new Russian Emperor Peter
III had commanded all his forces to cease hostilities and had ordered
General Chernyshev to withdraw his corps from the Austrian army in
Silesia. Frederick exulted: 'This is the very first ray of light. May
Heaven be thanked! Let us hope that the storms will give way to fine
weather, God willing!' (to Finckenstein, 21 January, PC 13439; the
king was strikingly given to pious exclamations at this period).

Frederick resorted to the grossest flattery in the hope of securing
the active friendship of Emperor Peter, an eccentric individual who
was known to be besotted with things Prussian. He sent the Order of
the Black Eagle to the pug-nosed monarch, he made him Chef of the
Berlin regiment of Syburg, and he awarded him high nominal rank in
the Prussian army. Indeed, 'Peter believed that he was more honoured
by the title of a Prussian general than by that of Emperor of Russia'
(Warnery, 1788, 495).

Frederick's personal envoy, the young Baron von der Goltz, was
able to conclude a treaty of peace and friendship on 5 May, by virtue
of which the Russians undertook to evacuate the Prussian territories.
The Swedes too came to terms, on 22 May. Finally on 1 June Goltz and

the Russians made an actual treaty of alliance. The Prussians promised to support Peter's claims in Schleswig, and they gained in return the assistance of Chernyshev's troops for the war in Silesia.

Frederick was disappointed only in respect of his scheme for the grand Turkish and Tartar intervention. He posted the Hungarian-born Lieutenant-General Werner in Upper Silesia with a corps of about 10,000 men, ready to move across the Beskids and join a force of up to 26,000 Crimean Tartars. This bizarre assemblage was then supposed to execute a sweep through Hungary against Vienna, 'and so as to compel the Austrians to fall back to Vienna, you could usefully arrange to have the Tartars (but not our men) commit far more atrocities in Austria than elsewhere. You could burn a number of villages around Vienna, and especially the ones belonging to the highest aristrocracy, so that the flames may be seen from the capital and the lords will utter loud screeches, which will plunge everything into confusion' (to Werner, 13 April, *PC* 13606). In the event nothing more was heard of the Tartar host, or the Turkish war against Austria, and Werner did no more than make a brief and unsupported foray into Austrian Silesia.

For the continuing war against the Austrians the king entrusted Henry in Saxony with about 30,000 troops, and gathered between 66,000 and 72,000 under his own command in Silesia (the estimates vary greatly). These armies were respectable only in terms of numbers. The regular troops comprised burnt-out and disorderly veterans of Frederick's last campaigns, along with reinforcements from the theatre of war against the Swedes, men returning from Russian captivity, and recruits who began to arrive from the newly recovered north-eastern provinces. An unusually high proportion of the total was made of light troops – free battalions of infantry, squadrons of irregular hussars, and the super-large regiment of mounted Bosniaks. Morale was low throughout the army, but for once Frederick owned a very un-Prussian advantage in the *kleiner Krieg* of raids and skirmishes, all the more so because the Austrian Croats were in poor condition, and the enemy cavalry had been heavily cut back for reasons of economy. Uniquely in this war, Frederick also had the leisure to concentrate his attention on a single objective – to prise the Austrian army from its positions around Schweidnitz, and regain this fortress and with it the possession of southern Silesia.

Daun opposed the Prussians in Silesia with about 82,000 men. Like Frederick, he knew that whoever was the master of Schweidnitz at the end of the campaign could effectively dictate the terms of peace between Austria and Prussia. In the middle of May 1762 the Austrians left their quarters and took up positions to cover Schweidnitz and the Eulen-Gebirge passes leading to the County of Glatz. Daun emplaced

the main force on an arc to the north and east of Schweidnitz, with
the right resting on the Zobten-Berg (which gave its name to the
whole position) and the left extending to the Striegauer-Wasser.
Loudon hovered in front of the Eulen-Gebirge, and there was a corps
under Beck in Upper Silesia.

Frederick knew that his army was quite unequal to the ordeal of
taking the Austrian camp by head-on assault. Instead, with ample
time at his disposal, he was content to wait until his reinforcements
reached Breslau and the grass was growing high in the fields, and then
force the Austrians off their positions by manoeuvre and diversion.
For detached command he now had the services of the Duke of
Bevern, who had returned from the 'war' against the Swedes. Bevern
had lost the royal favour after the battle of Breslau in 1757, but he was
'a worthy man and a great officer, beloved by the whole army'
(Mitchell, 4 February 1761, PRO SP 90/77).

Reinforcements of an altogether more curious nature arrived in
midsummer, in the form of 15,000–20,000 of Frederick's former enemies the Russians. An advance guard of 2,000 Cossacks crossed the
Oder on 25 June, and the regulars made the passage at Auras on the
30th. Frederick was wearing the Russian order of St Andrew in their
honour. He greeted Chernyshev and his staff on the left bank, and
took them to dine with him in Lissa Castle of happy memory.

The Russian corps reached the army south of Breslau on the night
of 1 July, and Frederick at once initiated the move against Daun. He
intended not just to uncover the way to Schweidnitz, but to anticipate the Austrians on the hill slopes behind. Lieutenant-General
Wied was therefore detached with 18,000 men (twenty-five battalions and twenty-six squadrons) to make a right-flanking hook
south-west by way of Freyburg around Daun's left, while the main
army executed a frontal advance behind a wide screen of Cossacks,
Prussian hussars and Bosniaks as if to make a direct assault.

The device succeeded only in part. Daun got wind of the plan
through a deserter. He evacuated the Zobten-Berg position on the
same night, but fell back only as far as another well-prepared camp on
the hills between Ober-Bögendorf and Kunzendorf.

Frederick moved first to his old camp at Bunzelwitz, then re-
newed the two-pronged advance on 5 July. On the next day Wied ran
into the corps of Lieutenant-General Brentano, on the far side of the
Adelsbach valley, and was beaten off with 1,331 casualties. However,
the Austrians were so impressed by the threat to their western flank
that they abandoned the Kunzendorf position, and moved to their
right-rear to the *Ne Plus Ultra* of their 'Camp of Burkersdorf' in the
Waldenburg Hills, the last emplacement from where Daun could
keep up the communication with Schweidnitz.

Once again Frederick looked to Wied's corps as the key with which to unlock the Austrian positions. He reinforced Wied to a strength of more than 20,000 men, and told him to continue his advance as a grand diversion into north-eastern Bohemia, where Daun had his magazines. On 9 July Wied moved across the border at Friedland, and he sent Lieutenant-General Reitzenstein in the direction of Königgrätz with a swarm of light cavalry. These gentry soon ran amuck, and Reitzenstein had to report that 'the disorder among the Cossacks is so great that no honest man could be associated with these men without losing his honour and good name' (Wengen, 1890, 405). Many of the Cossacks made back to Poland with their plunder and were never seen again. The raiders ruined a small depot at Jaromiersch, but Brentano managed to interpose himself between Wied's main force and the magazine at Braunau. This little adventure appeared to have produced no effect on Daun's host, and Frederick recalled all but 5,000 of the force to the Silesian plain. On 13 July Zieten and part of the main army pushed to Hoch-Giersdorf, in the immediate proximity of the Austrians, but Frederick had come to the end of his repertoire of feints and diversions, and Daun was entrenched as immovably as ever in the Burkersdorf camp.

If the Seven Years War had been a story, no respectable novelist would have dared to raise tension at this stage of affairs by a device as crude as that now arranged by Providence, which decreed that Frederick must now be deprived of nearly one-third of his army. On 18 July Chernyshev came to him with the news that his new-found friend Peter III had been dethroned in a palace revolution and that the Russian corps was under orders to leave the theatre of war. There were even indications that Peter's formidable wife Catherine, the leader of the *coup d'état*, was ready to resume hostilities against the Prussians.

Frederick engaged Chernyshev in an earnest private conversation, and the Russian came out of the room weeping. 'What a wonderful man is your king,' he exclaimed, 'and that would I not give to be in his service! He is utterly irresistible when he speaks!' He had agreed to postpone the departure of the Russian corps for three days, and meanwhile to allow it to fill out the line of battle, though in a non-combatant role. The royal secretary Eichel noted: 'His Majesty must be extremely pleased with the conduct of Count Chernyshev, for he is going to give him a rich present' (PC 13880).

Frederick could no longer put off a direct assault on the Burkersdorf camp, since it was vital to make use of the three days in which Chernyshev remained with the army, and he could not be sure how long the Austrians would remain in ignorance of the revolution in Russia.

The Prussians and Austrians had confronted one another on this same ground on many occasions in the past, and Frederick was acquainted with every detail of the terrain. Even now he shrank from attacking the main emplacement of the Austrian army, which was drawn up behind the deep valley of Dittmannsdorf and Reussendorf, facing north-west. Frederick therefore arranged a programme of entertainment to hold Daun's attention in this sector. The Russians promised to maintain an impressive display on the near side of the valley. The Prussians kept their unoccupied tents standing, and the Lossow Hussars and the red-coated Bosniaks leant a touch of animation to the scene. Ahead of the Russians, on the far western flank, the brigade of Ramin extended itself in a two-rank line of battle with wide intervals. The intention was for it to endow itself with a formidable appearance as it emerged from the valley of Seitendorf, where the Austrians knew that Frederick had his headquarters. Likewise on the right centre of the Prussian army the jaegers of the brigade of Manteuffel were to skirmish forward from Hoch-Giersdorf, while the howitzers on the plateau there began to lob shells over the woods and take the Austrian right wing in the rear.

Only about a dozen battalions were devoted to these diversions in the Dittmannsdorf-Seitendorf sector. Conversely Frederick concentrated more than thirty in the plain for the principal blow, which was to come from the north-east against the isolated right wing of some 5,000 troops, standing under the command of Lieutenant-General William O'Kelly. The Irishman had two battalions in position on his far eastern flank on the Leutmannsdorfer-Berg, whose slopes were devoid of cover and slippery with recent rain. O'Kelly's remaining ten battalions, or about 4,000 men, were disposed to cover the ground above Burkersdorf. Here the bosky valley of the Weistriz offered a scene of idyllic beauty, for the little stream rushed loudly towards the light green Silesian plain, which was framed like an opera set by wooded headlands reaching forward on either side. In military terms, however, the Weistritz valley presented a potentially dangerous re-entrant, and the Austrians took the precaution of closing it off by four redoubts – one at the entrance from the plain, one each on either side of the stream further up the valley, and a powerful work, surrounded by a deep abatis, sited in a commanding position towards the head.

The diversions of the previous weeks had been more effective than Frederick knew. The Austrians had 16,000 troops in Upper Silesia, 9,500 at the Eulen-Gebirge passes, 21,000 guarding the communications on the Bohemian side of the hills, and Brentano returned from his operations around Braunau only after the Prussian assault had already begun. Altogether Daun's force in the Burkersdorf camp had been whittled down to less than 30,000 men, and he conceded both the overall and the local superiority to the Prussians.

Frederick devoted much attention to the business of bringing his main force into its attacking position. Wied had prosecuted two overnight marches in streaming rain from the border hills, and on the night of 19 July he made a third march of the same kind around to the north and east of Schweidnitz to the foot of the Burkersdorf and Leutmannsdorf hills. He was accompanied on the circuit by the brigade of Möllendorff, which marched from Hoch-Giersdorf with a train of heavy artillery. The brigade of Knobloch in turn marched straight from Ober-Bögendorf and halted on Möllendorff's right.

On the evening of 20 July four battalions of the Möllendorff brigade seized the village of Burkersdorf, and after a hard fight they expelled a picket of Austrian grenadiers from the nearby castle, a strong old work surrounded by tall poplars. During the night a force of workers built a breastwork to the east of the castle, behind which the bombardiers and gunners arrayed no less than fifty-five pieces (forty-five 7- and 10-pounder howitzers, and ten heavy 12-pounder cannon) wheel to wheel in a single line. This mass of ordnance stood at the extreme range of 2,000 paces from its designated targets. The howitzers were to plant their shells in the redoubts, while the solid shot of the 12-pounders were directed at the Weistritz valley, which would have to be traversed by any reinforcements coming from the Austrian main army.

The three formations of the infantry were assigned precise timings and objectives. Wied, on the left or eastern flank, was to initiate the attack by assaulting the Leutmannsdorf position, from where the Austrians could otherwise sweep the avenues to the Weistritz sector. Once Wied had begun his advance, Möllendorff was to open fire with the great battery at Burkersdorf Castle and ascend the Weistritz valley, supported by Knobloch on his right.

Frederick reached Möllendorff's brigade at 3.30 a.m. on 21 July. The rain had ceased, after the third wet night in succession. He inspected the battery, greeted the troops, and re-emphasised to Möllendorff that he must await the sounds of Wied's attack before setting himself in motion. Frederick then rode off at a gallop to the corps of Wied, who had been waiting for the sky to lighten behind the Zobten-Berg.

Wied advanced as soon as Frederick arrived. The attack was not begun a moment too soon, for Brentano's corps was beginning to arrive on the summit of the hills. Major-General Prince Franz of Anhalt-Bernburg brought three battalions of Wied's left wing through the village of Leutmannsdorf, clearing the Croats from the gardens, but on the steep slopes beyond he was bloodily repulsed by the leading battalions of Brentano. Wied sent two battalions in support, and Bernburg was now able to push over the crest and drive back Brentano's right wing.

Meanwhile, on Wied's left, Colonel Lottum ascended the heights near Ludwigsdorf with the regiments of Schulenburg (22) and Mosel (10). (See Map 27, p. 378.) The troops knew that they were under the king's eye, and the Pomeranians of Schulenburg hauled each other up the slope in their eagerness to get to the top. Lottum cleared the work to the north of Ludwigsdorf, and with the help of the regiment of Ramin (25) he forced back Brentano's left towards Michelsdorf.

With deep satisfaction Frederick saw the colours of Lottum's battalions appear on the captured fortification, and he sent an adjutant to tell him that he had been promoted to major-general. The king then turned his horse around and made for the west, where Möllendorff's battle had been opened by the great battery. An enemy officer records that two regiments of Austrian cavalry, the Württemberg Dragoons (D 38) and the Nádasti Hussars (H 11), had been feeding their horses at the exit of the Weistritz valley, and 'the first impact was terrible. I have seen few actions which began with such a blow . . . The shot and the howitzer shells wrought terrible devastation. The horses broke their halters and ran for half a league' (Ligne, 1795–1811, XVI, 132).

The infantry attack was a most scientific affair. Instead of bludgeoning his way into possession of the Weistritz valley redoubts, Major-General Möllendorff explored a narrow path through the woods with the help of a forester, and then, undetected by the Austrians, he carried his brigade clear of the lower three fortifications and all the way to a position opposite the eastern flank of the work at the top. Two hundred volunteers led the assault across the narrow Kohl-Bach valley, and up through a growth of hazel bushes and oak saplings against the redoubt. An enterprising grenadier named Wolf set fire to the surrounding abatis and cleared a way through, but the moment of triumph was not survived by First Lieutenant Cunno Friedrich von der Hagen, who was one of the most distinguished junior officers of the army. 'A ball drilled his head above the left eye. He fell to the ground without a sign of life, and took his newly won laurels to the grave' (Pauli, 1758–64, IX, 305).

The Austrians abandoned their fortifications in the lower valley, which were now untenable, and the advance of Manteuffel's brigade from the north persuaded O'Kelly to evacuate his position altogether. Frederick called off the intended attack of Knobloch's brigade, and he ascended the Weistritz valley in person. According to one story he encountered a wounded musketeer on the way:

> 'How goes it?' asked the king. 'Very well, thank God! The enemy
> are on the run and we have really beaten them.' 'I see you are
> wounded, my friend,' continued the king, and he proffered his
> handkerchief. 'Bandage yourself with this.' Count Chernyshev
> was riding with the king. 'Now I see,' he exclaimed, 'why men
> serve Your Majesty with such zeal. You are so kind to your
> soldiers!' (Anon., 1787–9, IV, 71)

At the top Frederick saw the body of Hagen, lying in a pool of blood,
which was the last of the several occasions on which this young man
had come to the king's attention during the war. Early in the
afternoon Daun ordered a general retreat.

Altogether the Prussians had suffered about 1,600 casualties in
the course of the Burkersdorf action. The Austrians lost at least as
many in dead and wounded, as well as 550 men taken prisoner, but the
magnitude of Frederick's success was evident only on 22 July, when
Daun abandoned his communications with Schweidnitz and retreated to the highest summits of the hills. The Russians departed on
the same day, but they had by now done everything that Frederick
desired of them. On the 30th came news that Catherine would abide
by the peace, and that her husband Peter had died of a gastric
disorder. 'It is not difficult to guess what kind of seizure this must
have been' (Frederick to Finckenstein, 1 August, PC 13938).

The standard histories of the period devote scarcely a line to the
events at Burkersdorf. They were nevertheless of the greatest political
and strategic importance (more important, indeed, than the results
of a bloody day like Torgau), and they indicate new directions in
Frederick's tactical thinking:

> In the description of this action we fail to hear the trumpets of
> Rossbach, or the march that was sounded during the attack at
> Leuthen. In the first years of the war combat was an affair of
> long lines of battle, which stood under unitary command, and
> advanced through the powder smoke like long ocean waves.
> Burkersdorf was quite different. There the formations were
> assigned operational tasks, just as in the conditions of modern
> warfare. (Jany, 1907, 90–1)

During the remainder of the Silesian campaign Frederick's attention
was divided between the siege of Schweidnitz and the need to keep a
watch on the exits from the Eulen-Gebirge passes, by which Daun
might attempt to break through to the relief of the fortress from the
County of Glatz.

The operation against Schweidnitz took much longer than
Frederick had expected. The fortifications were not particularly

strong, but the garrison was very powerful, at 10,000 troops, and the quality of the men and technicians was excellent. The fortress did not yield until 9 October.

Meanwhile Frederick had summoned up Bevern with 9,000 men from Upper Silesia to the heights of Peilau, near Reichenbach, and told him to guard the avenues from the Eulen-Gebirge. On the night of 15 August Daun emerged near Silberberg with 45,000 troops, and he sent 25,000 of them hastening ahead with the intention of overwhelming Bevern, and gaining the Költschen-Berg as a *point d'appui* on the way to Schweidnitz.

Bevern first came under attack at 5 a.m., and Frederick at once rushed to his support with whatever forces he could first gather in his camp at Peterswaldau. The Brown Hussars and the Czettritz Dragoons strode out ahead, and the Bosniaks and the rest of the cavalry were streaming behind. Frederick was mounted on the little Cossack horse Cäsar, which was going like a rocket. 'It was splendid to see the Prussian cavalry arrive at a gallop from the camp of Peterswaldau, and especially the Bosniaks, who gave their horses their heads' (Ligne, 1795–1811, XVI, 152). After a spectacular but almost bloodless cavalry battle the Austrians withdrew from the field before Frederick's main force could come into action.

Daun now gave up Schweidnitz entirely for lost, and retreated into the County of Glatz. Frederick was not inclined to pursue him through the fortified passes, 'but we can acquire an equivalent by recapturing Dresden. As the price of recovering the electorate of Saxony the allies will have to restore Glatz and the territories of Cleves and Gelders' (*PC* 14095).

Frederick sent a reinforcement to Saxony on 17 October, but he was still in Silesia when news reached him that Henry and Seydlitz had crowned a very active campaign against the *Reichsarmee* and the Austrians by a victory in open battle at Freiberg on 28 October. Frederick wrote to his brother that the news made him feel twenty years younger. The king reached Torgau on 7 November, but he was disappointed to discover that the enemy were too strongly entrenched behind the Plauensche-Grund to permit him to recover Dresden.

On 29 November a certain Baron Fritsch, a slight acquaintance of Frederick's, arrived at the royal headquarters at Meissen bearing a first proposal from Maria Theresa for a 'reasonable and dignified' peace. Frederick's response was harsh and sarcastic, but a threatening message from Catherine of Russia put him in a more amenable frame of mind for a second interview. Active peace negotiations opened on 30 December in the devastated royal Saxon hunting lodge at Hubertusburg.

The enemy were still in possession of the Prussian territory of Glatz, and it took heavy pressure from Frederick, and appeals to the military judgment of Daun, before the Austrians agreed to return to the borders of 1756. Effectively, Glatz was traded for the Prussian evacuation of Saxony. A treaty of peace was signed on 15 February 1763, and thus terminated 'this cruel war, so costly in blood, anguish and devastation' (Frederick to Henry, 2 February 1763, *PC* 14417).

After the war Frederick attributed his survival to the lack of harmony among the allies, the short-sighted stratagems of the Austrians, who placed the chief burden of the war on their friends, and the death of the Empress Elizabeth, which brought about the collapse of the Austrian alliance system (*Oeuvres*, V, 229). Posterity must add that Frederick's generalship and the performance of the Prussian army were not without some influence on the outcome.

The decidedly un-resonant name 'the Seven Years War' did not enter usage until the early 1780s, by which time the term 'the last war' was no longer applicable. All the dramatic connotations derived from the realities of the event, which was 'more remarkable, bloody, important and instructive than any other war in the history of the world' (Müller, 1788, 92).

The emotions engendered by the war served to give a powerful impetus to the literary cult of 'sensibility' in the German lands (Brüggemann, 1935, *passim*), and endowed the Prussians with a sustaining myth directly comparable with the one that the Frontier came to represent for the Americans. Men of letters rejoiced that Prussia was now decked out with a pantheon of heroes to rival any in antiquity (Pauli, 1758–64, I, '*Vorwort*'; Seidl, 1781, III, 388–9; Haller, 1796, 93).

Warnery was probably mistaken when he wrote that the war had left 400,000 people dead without the slightest advantage to any of the parties (1788, 533). Britain made important conquests overseas, as Frederick pointed out in his history of the war. Negatively, Prussia had gained a defensive victory of the first order. The Danish minister Bernstorff had indicated in 1759: 'This war is being fought not for some passing interest, not for a couple of fortresses or small provinces, but for the existence or extinction of the new [Prussian] monarchy' (Koser, 1921, III, 161). Without setting up Frederick as a proto-Bismarck or Hitler, we must agree with his biographer Koser that 'The Seven Years War did not indeed create Prussia's position as a great power, but, in the face of all opposition and doubts, it consolidated that position and won it a general acknowledgement' (*ibid.*, II, 383).

Frederick was not at all impressed to learn that he himself was now regarded as a figure of European renown. The admiration of the

British public was documented in broadsheets and decorated pottery; American colonists named one of their little towns 'King of Prussia'; French civilians laughed at the defeats which their armies suffered at his hands. Elsewhere the respective causes of Frederick and Maria Theresa were taken up with such enthusiasm as to occasion outbreaks of violence among Venetian monks and gondoliers, and awaken fears of a civil war in Switzerland (Meyer, 1955, 145). Frederick reflected:

> Our military glory looks very fine, seen from a distance. But if you had witnessed the distress and hardship with which it had been acquired, in what physical deprivations and struggle, in heat and cold, in hunger, filth and destitution, then you would have learnt to think quite differently about this 'glory'. (Koser, 1921, III. 165)

Frederick returned to Berlin by way of Silesia and the Neumark. He was expected in the capital on 30 March 1763, and the companies of urban militia were waiting outside the Frankfurter Tor to greet him. Frederick, however, had stopped for a time on the field of Kunersdorf, with its gloomy landscape and gloomier memories, and the citizens began to murmur when the bleak afternoon wore on and nothing was yet seen of the king. The indignation was shared by Frederick's friend the Marquis d'Argens, who burst out: 'I wrote to him that he owed it to his people to acknowledge their appreciation. It is quite unforgivable for him not to put in an appearance!' (Nicolai, 1788–92, I, 49).

Frederick arrived in his shabby campaign coach at eight in the evening, by which time darkness had fallen, and he drove on to the Schloss by a roundabout route. It is said that the early hours of the next day found him back at his desk, working.

CHAPTER SIX
In Search of Old Fritz

Now that we have spent so long in Frederick's company, we need not be surprised at the ways in which he responded to the sudden relaxation of the stresses of wartime. Once he had alleviated the immediate hardships of the people of Berlin, he returned to Sans Souci to rejoice in the daily transformation that spring was working in the face of nature. In the middle of May 1763 he visited the former theatre of war against the Russians in the Neumark and Pomerania, but he was overcome by a physical collapse so complete that he had to be driven around in a carriage. It seemed scarcely possible that he had more than a short span of life left to him.

Frederick's labours to make good the ravages of war have been given the general title the *Rétablissement*. This process ranged from the rebuilding of damaged houses and farm buildings (12,000–14,500 by the end of 1766) to the reform of the debased currency, the restocking of the fields with cattle, experiments in agricultural improvements, and the peaceful conquest of internal colonisation. Up to 500,000 souls had died or fled from Prussia during the war, which was a severe diminution in a population of only some 4,500,000. Foreign immigration made up for less than 60,000 of the losses, but a disproportion of 30 per cent in births over deaths made Prussia the fastest-growing state in Germany in terms of population, and helped to bring the total up to 5,430,000 by 1786.

It is not altogether easy to determine the purpose and character of the *Rétablissment* (for a modern estimate see Johnson, 1975). If the coal and iron industry in Upper Silesia grew significantly from 1777, the manufactures and trade as a whole languished, thanks to the system of monopolies and the duties on exports – 'a piece of wrong politics of so flagrant a nature, that would make one think his abilities were those of a warrior alone' (Marshall, 1772, III, 274). Frederick looked upon industry, as much as anything else, as a means of keeping people at work, and he regarded taxation primarily as a regulator of the economy (Zottmann, 1937, 167). In fact most of the

244

state revenues came directly from the produce of the royal domains.

Frederick's quirkiness was, however, most evident in the *Rétablissement* of the army. His achievement was certainly great, in the gross material sense. By the end of 1777 the arsenals were stuffed with 140,000 muskets and 1,376 re-cast pieces of artillery, and the supply magazines held enough cereals to sustain two armies of 70,000 men each for two years. In 1768 Frederick raised the peace establishment to 161,000 troops, and the annexation of West Prussia in 1772 made it possible for him to increase this figure to some 190,000, which made the Prussian army the third largest in Europe after Austria (297,000) and Russia (224,000).

The character of the army had by then undergone a profound change, which was the consequence of the strictness, amounting almost to contempt and hatred, which Frederick displayed towards his officers and men. Frederick believed that only harsh measures were capable of restoring discipline, and Curt Jany detects the working of the Seven Years War on the king's character: 'His judgments of men became harder and more bitter, and their inner qualities became of less interest to him' (Jany, 1903, 9). The army which had been destroyed in the war was effectively the one he had inherited from his father. The army of Frederick the Great, properly speaking, came into existence only from 1763, and it was to be inferior in almost every respect to its predecessor.

The tone of this new institution was set by the instructions for the commanders of the regiments of cavalry and infantry, which were signed on 11 May 1763. Here we find the celebrated passage: 'Generally speaking the common soldier must fear his officers more than the enemy.' In that same year of 1763 it was determined that foreign recruits were no longer to be raised for individual companies, but thrown into a common pool and allocated by the central military bureaucracy. Recruiting parties therefore lost their interest in the kind of men they were raising. The quality of the native soldier probably also declined. A cumulatively great number of exemptions freed many of the steadier young folk from the cantonal obligations, and in 1780 Frederick actually established military service as one of the punishments for crime.

No gratitude was extended to the corps of officers for its sufferings in the Seven Years War. Frederick continued to exercise a terrifying degree of personal control in the springtime reviews and the autumn manoeuvres, and Berenhorst could write at the end of the century: 'Everybody used to tremble under his gaze. Nowadays there must be many veterans who start from their sleep, whenever this vision appears in their dreams' (Berenhorst, 1798–9, I, 126). Indirectly, Frederick enforced discipline and uniformity of standards by dividing the regiments into groups, or 'inspections', and delivering them up to the mercy of Inspectors, the first of whom he appointed in 1763.

A marked social reaction could be seen in the treatment of the many middle-class officers who had been commissioned during the war emergency. Frederick now evicted these people wholesale from the army, or transferred them to the hussars, and he made up the gaps by resorting to 'noblemen from foreign lands . . . who give evidence of intelligence, ambition and a genuine inclination towards the service' ('Instruction für die Commandeurs der Cavallerie-Regimenter', 11 May 1763, Oeuvres, XXX, 280).

There was a corresponding tactical reaction which accorded very strangely with the huge experience which the Prussian army had accumulated in the Seven Years War. Frederick enforced a needless complexity of manoeuvres, and an extraordinarily high rate of infantry fire (up to six rounds a minute) which made a great impression on the drill square, but which would have been impossible to sustain in real combat (but see p. 318). When they were not on parade, the young officers were expected to attain the higher reaches of the military art through a diligent application to their books.

Frederick believed that his army began to attain the desirable degree of order and precision from 1770 onwards. Significantly enough, some commentators trace the decay of military morale to about the same period. In the view of the old drummer Dreyer, who had served since the days of Frederick William, the decline of the army, already evident in the Seven Years War, was prolonged and accentuated afterwards. This he ascribed to the complications in the drills, and a loss of true respect for authority that he linked with 'a hunger after the good life which gripped all classes of society, giving rise to the excessive imbibing of coffee and spirits, to prostitution and a decline in religion' (Dreyer, 1810, 21). Georg Heinrich von Berenhorst, who belonged to a younger generation, nevertheless had much the same thing to say about the harmful influence of luxury, and he added that the new emphasis on pedantry had engendered two kinds of officers: namely limited and practical-minded men who believed that the new theories were altogether too difficult for them, and young 'little masters' who excelled in all the paperwork. 'Both sorts neglected the essential point of their calling, which was to see to the welfare of the common soldier, and thereby win his trust' (Berenhorst, 1798–9, I, 130).

Meanwhile Prussomania raged unabated through military Europe. In services like the French, Spanish and Austrian (and under Peter III and Paul I also in the Russian) the imitation of things Prussian extended not just to the details of what was known as *das preussische Costum*, but to the spirit of the discipline and some of the fundamentals of military institutions. According to the Prince de Ligne: 'In relation to military affairs Prussia has acquired the same reputation as did Versailles for fine manners. Soon our armies will become unrecognisable – they all want to be like Frederick's' (Ligne, 1795–1811, I, 162–3). This enterprise was based on nothing better than a sketchy acquaintance with the crippled army of the later years of Frederick's reign, and therefore stood at two removes from the force which had won Rossbach and Leuthen.

Wiser heads appreciated how absurd the attempt was. Simply by watching parades and manoeuvres it was impossible for the foreigner to detect either the moving principles of the tactics, or 'certain minor details . . . which may easily escape the attention, but which are nevertheless all-important' (Riesebeck, 1784, II, 139). As Christian Garve indicated, the Prussian army was the product of a cumulative education which it had received over the years from Frederick, who had shaped it through formal instructions, letters to individual officers, and the comments that he passed on campaign and at the reviews and manoeuvres (Garve, 1798, 140). In 1770 Frederick himself tried to dissuade Prince Karl of Sweden from constructing an army on the Prussian model: 'My army has been thirty or forty years in the making, and it is still far from perfect. How can you hope to work an overnight transformation in a force as undisciplined as yours?' (Volz, 1926–7, II, 232–3; see also Guibert, 1778, 131; Seidl, 1781, III, 335).

It will perhaps be of interest to accompany the foreign pilgrims on their attempts to penetrate the secrets of our hero. They usually made the journey to Brandenburg as an extended excursion from Saxony. On leaving the fertile open fields of the electorate the travellers entered a vast zone of woodland. 'The rivers are bordered by extensive swamps, and the frequent and dense woods of conifers are not calculated to give the landscape a cheerful aspect' (Riesebeck, 1784, II, 80–1).

Eight or ten hours driving along sandy roads brought the tourist to the royal capital Berlin, where something of the character of the Prussian monarchy began to emerge. It was a large city, of great outward splendour, 'as well from the breadth of the streets, their cutting each other at right angles, as for the magnificence of the buildings' (Yorke, 1913, III, 228). The population increased by one-third during Frederick's reign, from less than 100,000 in 1740 to nearly 150,000 in 1786. A number of imposing edifices began to rise before the Seven Years War, most notably the Opera House (1741), the Catholic church of St Hedwig (1747, modelled on the Pantheon in Rome), and the palace of Prince Henry (1748). This work was completed after the war, and the re-shaping of the Unter den Linden, and the addition of further buildings, like the Library and the Playhouse, gave unity to the whole.

The two royal palaces were mostly the work of earlier times. The Berlin Schloss was an assemblage of different periods, and it held little appeal for Frederick, who disliked its position in the centre of the city. However, a pleasant walk through the avenues of a park led to the river Spree and the palace of Charlottenburg, which was originally built for Sophie-Charlotte of Hanover, the second wife of Frederick I. In the early 1740s our own Frederick had considered spending a good deal of time there, and he commissioned Knobelsdorff and the painter Antoine Pesne to fashion an elegant new east wing. Much devastation was caused here by the allies in 1760, and after the war Frederick used Charlottenburg only as a base from which to supervise the reviews and manoeuvres in the nearby open country.

The Prussian military identity was expressed more directly elsewhere. In the secluded Wilhelmsplatz there arose commemorative statues of Seydlitz, Keith, Winterfeldt, and of Schwerin at the moment when he was killed at Prague. This ensemble was considered to be a unique compliment for a king to pay to his generals. On the main axis of the Unter den Linden the Great Elector's splendid Arsenal still served an immediate military purpose. The ground floor held all the field artillery for the Berlin and Potsdam forces. The upper storey ran around all four sides of the building, and its broad, well-lit halls were stacked with mountains of drums, piles of swords, huge chests of ramrods, and stands of more than 100,000 muskets. No space was given to antique weapons, and there was 'nothing but what is ready for immediate service' (Marshall, 1772, III, 281).

Frederician Berlin succeeded least well in matters of detail. Scarcely a traveller failed to notice the disparity between the intentions expressed in the regular streets and impressive stucco façades, and the reality which obtruded in the vandalised statues, the shoddy brickwork showing through the plaster, and the common character of most of the inhabitants.

For most of the year the air of Berlin was notoriously keen, but the summers were short and hot and in that season the mosquitoes swarmed in from the lake water round about, and the wind propelled great clouds of troublesome dust. The moral climate was at once louche and invested with an element of authorised violence. By Frederick's admission, 'the way of life at Berlin is pretty wild' (Taysen, 1886, 81). Observers were scandalised by the toleration of atheism, prostitution and worse, and in his guide-book of 1758 Johann Peter Willebrandt warned the traveller to be on his guard not just against perils of the Parisian kind, but a danger unique to Berlin.

Frederick had forbidden the forcible enlistment of foreign recruits, but nothing could deter the Prussian officers from making off with any well-set-up young men who fell into their power. It was therefore only prudent for the tourist to shun 'the guzzling of wine and those other excesses . . . which so often impair the understanding and the will' (Willebrandt, 1758, 225). Visitors almost invariably made the journey through fifteen miles of woodland to Potsdam, where Frederick by preference spent the greater part of his time when he was not absent on his tours or campaigns. The isolation and the military character of this town were accentuated by the presence of no less than twenty-two of the field regiments, and by the great loop of the Havel which made the place into a virtual island, placed under heavy guard. All the reservations harboured by the foreigners about the streets of Berlin were here felt with greater force. There was still less sign of animation in the streets, and all the more contrast between the external dignity of the buildings, and the ignoble way they were treated. Already in the last years of Frederick William I Potsdam had begun to expand north and west from its modest red brick core into new streets with stucco façades. This labour was continued by Frederick after the Seven Years War, and the rustications and the pediments indicate that Old Fritz was striving after something digni-fied and impressive. However,

> to one's question 'Who lives in these palaces?' One hears that
> they are all empty space, or only occupied by goods never
> wanted, or corn there is nobody to feed with . . . when one sees
> the copies of antique bas-reliefs, in no bad sculpture, decorating
> the doors whence dangle a shoulder of mutton or a shoemaker's
> last, it either shocks one or makes one laugh. (Piozzi, 1789, II,
> 356–7)

Nobody could deny that Potsdam, like Berlin, was fitted out with public ornaments worthy of ancient Rome. Indeed the inscriptions and ornaments might have led the stranger to 'suspect that the Christian religion was exploded from the Prussian dominions, and old Jupiter and his family restored to their ancient honours' (Moore, 1779, II, 171).

The main axis of this public Potsdam (Map 13, p. 356) ran across the Havel loop. At the eastern end, the massive quadrilateral of the Stadtschloss formed the largest single edifice in Potsdam. It was the product of successive stages of construction from 1664, but under the direction of Frederick (1744–52) the interior was redecorated, and the exterior was given a modern and uniform treatment and painted in a startling scheme of red and yellow. The bulk of this building was alleviated by lines of those colonnades which represented Frederick's favourite and most successful architectural device. One such colonnade ran west to the long low range of the rebuilt Stables (*Marstall*). Another colonnade (prolonged by an elegant balustrade) reached south to the Lustgarten and the Havel. All of this served to enclose the Parade Platz. Frederick was frequently discovered there in the morning, drilling the troops, and on Sundays this great square drew every visitor:

> At the stroke of ten there began to unfold a mighty spectacle, putting an end to the chatter of the crowd, which had sounded like the murmur of the sea or merchants at an exchange. It seemed scarcely possible that so many thousands of troops could be so directed as to become like toys led by a string, or puppets at the end of a wire . . . The colonel, who commanded the parade, had a terrifying demeanour as he rode along the front and between the ranks, and all the time the men stood as immobile as a wall. Then eighty drummers and forty fifers sounded at the same instant, making a frightful din. (Sanders, 1783–4, II, 209, 192)

Leaving the parade, the tourist walked just over two hundred paces to the west and found himself at the Garnison-Kirche (1731–5), whose tall, slender tower was the symbol of Potsdam. Here everything was designed to

> raise the Prussian soldier in his own estimation above those of other European states. No relics, saints, or shrines are there to be found: the music, ornaments and decorations are all military, and all appropriate. Trophies and ensigns, gained in battle, float from the roof in every part of the edifice. (Wraxall, 1806, I, 99)

Frederick never went near the place.

Continuing his promenade, the foreign traveller turned right at the impressive military orphanage (*Waisenhaus*) and exited by way of the Brandenburger-Tor (rebuilt 1770), which formed one of the openings in the excise wall which embraced all the landward sides of the town. Four hundred and fifty paces to the north, where the road to Bornstedt began to curve uphill to the left, the tourist arrived at the obelisk with fantastic 'Egyptian' hieroglyphs which signified the entrance to the long and narrow royal park of Sans Souci. More than Berlin, more than Potsdam town, these sandy acres were associated with the character of Frederick.

It was immediately obvious that this was the residence of no ordinary sovereign. There was no attempt to stun the stranger, no grand stony courtyard à la Versailles or Schönbrunn, and indeed little means of orientation until the central axis of the park was opened up after the Seven Years War. Without a guide or map, the foreigners needed some time to discover that the most interesting establishments were arrayed along a ridge which followed the northern side of the park.

The palace of Sans Souci proper (1745–7) was readily accessible to strangers when the king was not in residence. For the pedestrian it was normally reached by the steps which led to the right up the hillside, which had been reworked into six broad terraces. These were retained by walls ten feet high, which were at first furnished with glazed niches for exotic fruit trees, and then in 1773 entirely encased in continuous greenhouses 'so that the palace, seen from below, seems to float in an amphitheatre of glass. It is one of the most extraordinary sights you can conceive' (Toulongeon (1786), 1881, 126). At the top the visitor encountered what was essentially a single-storey pavilion, set back a little way from the crest. Knobelsdorff, the nominal architect, would have preferred something higher, standing at the very edge so as to make a greater impression, but Frederick was intent on pleasing nobody but himself.

Generals and other grand folk reached the pavilion from the rear, driving up a ramp through a double colonnade to the modest entrance, which lay on the northern side. A coolly decorated vestibule led on to the central hall, an oval chamber which was floored and walled with marbles of the most delicate vein and hue. Corinthian columns of Carrara marble reached up to the central cupola, and the excellence of the proportions and the subtlety of the treatment conspired to make this space seem much bigger than it really was. The king who commissioned and supervised this work was a man of exquisite taste.

In warm weather Frederick liked to dine in the central hall, and favoured guests needed to take only a few steps to join him from their rooms in the western wing. The most famous of these chambers, the so-called 'Voltaire Room', owed its cheerful decor to the work that was carried out, almost as a fumigation, after that sage's disastrous visit of 1751–3.

Frederick himself lived and worked in the eastern wing. Much of the business of army and state was conducted from a small drawing room, which represented the first of the range of apartments leading from the central hall. A dirty old sofa contrasted with the rococo elegance of the decoration, and an open fireplace was standing where the stranger might have expected one of those great earthenware stoves of Central Europe. Frederick loved the liveliness of an open fire.

The adjacent concert room (Plate 22) was given over entirely to recreation. On the walls the inset paintings alternated most effectively with mirrors and panelling, and the ceiling was decorated with representations of tendrils of vines, spreading over a gilded pergola. On the floor of the room the harpsichord, the music stands, the flutes and the manuscripts waited only for the return of their master to bring them to life. The sole reminder of a harsher world was represented by a fine portrait of Emperor Joseph II of Austria, which Frederick set up by the entrance to his bedchamber 'lest this great and enterprising man should escape from his sight' (Zimmermann, 1788, 40).

Visitors were rarely prepared for what they found when they passed through this further door. Sherlock writes:

> I enquired of the Swiss attendant 'Well then, where is the king's bedroom?' 'Here it is, sir', he replied. I looked for some magnificent bed. There was a passably fine cabinet at the end of the chamber, but there was no bed inside. 'Where is the bed?' said I. 'Over here, sir!' Behind a small screen, in the corner, stood a very narrow bed with curtains of green silk. I asked my guide about the location of the king's wardrobe, and received the answer 'He wears all his clothes on his back!' (Sherlock, 1779, 20–1)

Beyond the bedchamber Frederick had his innermost sanctum in a tiny circular library, or rather reading cabinet. This was a comforting refuge, and the decorations of gilded bronze sat most agreeably upon the warm brown of the cedar panelling.

In the summertime orange trees in large tubs were ranged along the terrace outside, and Frederick liked to take the air under the eyes of the long-suffering caryatids who supported the heavy entablature of the pavilion. The view in front extended over the formal gardens to Potsdam town and the Havel landscape, but at either end the terrace was terminated by hedges and those little grass plots where Frederick had the tombstones of his dogs.

Sans Souci shared its hillside with two large single-storey buildings. The New Chambers (*Neue Kammern*) to the west were remodelled from an orangery (1747) to serve as guest apartments. Hard under the eastern end of the Sans Souci pavilion the massive single vault of the Picture Gallery (*Bildergalerie*) housed the Flemish and Italian canvases which Frederick bought in such quantities in the final decades of his reign.

The gardens and park were copiously adorned with statuary, many of the pieces depicting maidens writhing in the grasp of bearded and muscular fellows who were clearly up to no good. Among the architectural set pieces the most notable was the Chinese Tea House

(1754–7, Plate 23), a fanciful circular pavilion designed by Frederick in collaboration with Johann Gottfried Büring. This folly was set in a shady grove and furnished with deep verandahs, and on very hot days Frederick was fond of taking his guests there for lunch. Dogs were included in the invitation, and extra portions of roast veal were set aside for their enjoyment.

The park was closed at its western end by some constructions that were a world removed from the spirit of Sans Souci. The Neues Palais (1763–9), with its great façade and tall central cupola, was built to give employment to native craftsmen, and to serve as a *Fanfarronade*, or gesture of defiance, on the part of the Prussian monarchy after the ordeal of the Seven Years War. To the rear, the pompous *cour d'honneur* formed an architectural ensemble with the heavy colonnade and two box-like houses of the Communs,which were built to accommodate the palace servants and visiting officers, and to screen the boggy wastelands which extended beyond the park. Within the palace, the Marble Hall and other chambers were impressive to an intimidating degree, but we detect little of the distinctive influence of Frederick. Neo-classical detailing, like the medallion busts set above some of the doors, ran counter to the king's rococo tastes, and we know that he detested the kind of activity celebrated in the *Jagdkammer*, with its representations of defunct herons, deer and wild boar.

Significantly, the Neues Palais was not allowed to dominate the Sans Souci park, and only the merest glimpse of the façade could be sighted at the end of the slot-like central avenue once the trees had grown to a respectable height. In inspiration and purpose the Neues Palais was a public building. It was never intended for prolonged periods of residence, but it provided a magnificent setting for the receptions, balls and operas that were held on the occasion of the manoeuvres and the annual gathering of the royal family.

At Sans Souci, on the other hand, everything was calculated for convenience and privacy. No guest came there uninvited. No provision was made to accommodate the queen or the ladies of the royal family. There was no chapel royal, no pompous retinue of officials of the household, and no glittering bodyguard. A corporal and four soldiers arrived from Potsdam town every evening, and their principal duty was to stand watch over the king's peaches and apricots overnight.

In peacetime Frederick led a regular life which made it possible for contemporaries to establish the externals of his existence with great precision. The New Year found him in the Berlin Stadtschloss, enduring what was for him the tedious commotion of the Carnival. Etiquette decreed that he must remain there for the anniversary of his coronation, on 18 January, but as soon as possible thereafter he stole back to his winter palace, the Potsdam Schloss. Here he spent the month of February, drawing up the schemes for the coming reviews. His favourite room was a strategically placed chamber at the south-east corner, which gave him prospects over the Havel bridge, the Lustgarten and the tree under which his petitioners took their station.

The military year opened in May, with the reviews of the regiments of the Berlin, Potsdam and neighbouring garrisons, which were usually held in the Berlin Thiergarten or on the plain outside Charlottenburg. As in the previous reign, the narrowly focused 'special reviews' enabled the king to make an informed assessment of the quality of his troops:

> It is incredible with what accuracy and minute attention he did
> examine them, the colonel of the regiment walking along with
> him, to answer any question and hear his directions and
> remarks. By this exactness he not only knows the condition of
> the army in general, but the appearance, degree of discipline
> and strength of each regiment. (Moore, 1779, II, 135)

The 'general reviews' were grander assemblies of mixed arms, and culminated in a three-day exercise staged outside Berlin in the third week of May.

Immediately the Berlin reviews were over, Frederick betook himself to the similar gatherings in Pomerania and outside Magdeburg. In the middle of June the king was back at Potsdam to fix the state budget for the coming financial year. He counted the next two months as a holiday to be spent at Sans Souci, and then in the middle of August he departed for the extremely important manoeuvres in Silesia. These were intended to educate the officers and generals, and the scale of the forces and the element of contest brought these exercises much closer to reality than did the spring reviews.

The Silesian manoeuvres rival the campaigns of the Seven Years War as a source of anecdote. There were the blistering messages addressed to individuals as august as old Tauentzien, the inspector of the Silesian infantry. There were displays of physical violence, which might lead to Frederick chasing an officer through the ranks with raised stick. There were the brutal terminations of long military careers.

On 20 September or thereabouts the regiments of the capital and the residence assembled for the final event of the military career, the Potsdam manoeuvres. Frederick made this gathering an occasion for celebrations, and he summoned all the generals to table at the Neues Palais. The ensuing evolutions, however, were secret and experimental, and were closed to all but a very few invited strangers. Foreign governments were disturbed by the gathering of such a force at the traditional season for opening a war, after the harvest was gathered in, and military men could only speculate as to what tactics were being explored inside the sealed perimeter of the Potsdam peninsula.

Frederick's daily routine followed an equally predictable train. He was up in his little chamber at four in the morning in summer, and five in winter, and if he slept any longer his servants were under orders to awaken him, if necessary by force. A cup of coffee, laced with a little mustard, helped to dispel any lingering drowsiness. While still in bed he drew on his stockings, breeches and boots (if indeed he had ever bothered to take them off), and had himself shaved by the first attendant who came to hand. He powdered his hair himself, and protected his clothing with a dirty old dressing gown.

The working day began immediately. Frederick received reports from the First Battalion of the Garde concerning the states of Potsdam town and garrison and the royal *Leibkompagnie*. Over breakfast he sorted through the packet of correspondence which had been assembled for him on the previous evening. Many of the letters ended up on the fire. Some were handed to the secretaries with pithy marginal notes, or other terse indications as to the reply. The rest occasioned a full dictated or written letter from Frederick in person.

After breakfast the cabinet officers and the heads of the various departments of state were called to render accounts and receive instructions. Much of the detail of government was determined on these occasions through the famous Frederician 'cabinet orders', which were autocratic decrees written on small pieces of paper. Once the bureaucrats had been sent on their way, Frederick devoted about sixty minutes to interviewing such officers and petitioners as had been invited into his presence.

One of the secrets of the great length of Frederick's active life undoubtedly lay in the five or more hours he set aside for recreation in the middle of the normal day. Late in the morning he liked to ride into Potsdam or Berlin town, and he returned to the palace for lunch with a selected company. 'This monarch eats well and in a leisurely fashion' (Guibert, 1778, 9).

The courses were modest in appearance, but carefully prepared. There were dishes in the French and Italian styles, bowls of excellent home-grown fruit, and plates of the hotly flavoured food beloved of the king. 'He scorched his innards daily with dishes laced with condiments of quite incredible fieriness' (Zimmermann, 1788, 29). Frederick downed champagne and burgundy in great quantities, though he had a pronounced aversion to the German product. 'If you

want to know what it is like to be hanged', he once declared, 'just
take a drink of Rhenish wine' (Volz, 1926–7, III, 205).

The Frederician lunches were an undeniable ordeal for the
guests, on account of the king's revolting table manners, and those
dreadful royal monologues that reduced his officers and brothers to
an overawed silence, tormented Mitchell in the course of the Seven
Years War, and consigned the Austrian generals to sleep during the
conference at Neisse in 1769.

Late in the afternoon Frederick got down to a final hour's work
with his secretaries and heads of department, and he made sure that
all his messages and letters were sealed and dispatched by six. There
was no supper, and Frederick did not share Maria Theresa's addiction
to cards. In the evening he betook himself to the music room, and
played through a short programme in private with his orchestra. He
might walk alone for some time in the open air, and then, usually
before ten at night, he retired to his bedroom. He chatted with his
reader Catt (who read aloud to him) or other intimate friends, and
before taking to his bed he summoned his household officials and
argued through the next day's menu and the accounts of the stables
and palace.

The filthy state of Frederick's surroundings, clothing and personal hygiene was a matter of public knowledge. The youthful dandy was
long dead. Now the interior of the king's coach resembled the prover-
bial *Zigeunerlager*, and his little greyhounds were allowed to rip up
cushions and commit still worse atrocities in the royal apartments.

On the evidence of the royal attendant Schöning we know that
Frederick stood about five feet five inches tall, and that he was of
average proportions (and therefore probably not as thin as he is
usually depicted). His head inclined slightly to the right, from
playing the flute for so long, and his back was humped, but he was an
expert and hard-riding horseman, and his gait on foot was easy,
natural and rapid. 'The pitch of his conversation was a most pure and
agreeable tenor. When he commanded his troops his voice was loud,
and carried with the utmost clarity to a considerable distance'
(Anon., 1787–9, I, 7).

All of this detail, and a good deal more, was readily accessible to
the foreigner who read the travellers' tales, interrogated the gossips of
Berlin, or caught a glimpse of the king on parade. However, the
moving principles of Frederick's life, and the lineaments of his character, were things that escaped his contemporaries, and which have
remained impenetrable to historians ever since.

The foreign soldiers naturally looked first at what military
literature could tell them about the great man. Some of the most
celebrated sources were not yet available to them. The first volume of

the earliest systematic history of the Seven Years War (*Geschichte des siebenjährigen Krieges in Deutschland*) appeared only towards the end of the reign in 1783, and then merely in the shape of an annotated translation of the exceptionally arid account of the Austrian general Humphrey Evans Henry Lloyd. Much the best features were the commentary and continuations by the translator, the distinguished Prussian gunner Georg Friedrich von Tempelhoff. Frederick was already dead by the time of the publication of the earliest schematic and detailed study of the Prussian army, by the French diplomat Mirabeau, or rather his collaborator Jakob Mauvillon (originally part of *Sur la Monarchie Prussienne sous Frédéric le Grand*, 1787, then published separately in London in 1788).

In Frederick's lifetime the most celebrated of the foreign commentators was undoubtedly the young French officer Jacques-Antoine Hippolyte de Guibert, author of the celebrated *Essai Général de Tactique* of 1770. Guibert came to Prussia in the summer of 1773, and he was received by Frederick in the Picture Gallery at Sans Souci. Guibert was too overwhelmed by this first encounter to be able to form a clear impression of the king, but in August he had the opportunity to observe Frederick and his army during the Silesian manoeuvres. Guibert's notes formed the basis of his *Observations sur la Constitution Militaire et Politique des Armées de sa Majesté Prussienne* (1778). This book was probably known to most of the intending military pilgrims to Prussia in the later years of the reign, and it became the subject of intense debate within Frederick's dominions. Patriotic men were scandalised by what seemed to them to be the superficiality of Guibert's writings, and indeed of the whole genre.

For the stay-at-homes, a flavour of things Prussian was brought direct to Paris by one of Frederick's former pages, the scapegrace Johann Ernst Pirch. While on parade in Prussia he had let a red juice dribble from his mouth, to convince the authorities that he was dying from consumption, and he then betook himself to France as a major in the hired regiment of Hesse-Darmstadt. 'He introduced a truly Prussian discipline to this regiment, which made a great sensation at that time, and drew the particular attention of the court of Versailles' (Thiébault, 1813, III, 326). Pirch wrote an influential *Essai de Tactique* in collaboration with a French officer, but he died in 1783 at the age of thirty-eight of a *polype au coeur*. This time he gave a definitive performance.

When the foreign officer sought out his Prussian counterparts, he found that some of the more articulate of these men were severely critical of Frederick's generalship and his management of the army. A good deal of what they had to say was published only long afterwards,

if indeed it was ever printed at all, but their opinions were well
known in the officer corps, and some of their memoirs were circulated
widely in manuscript form. The military diarist Henckel von Donnersmarck and the staff officers Friedrich Wilhelm Ernst von Gaudi
and Georg Heinrich von Berenhorst were associated in the public
mind with the circle of Prince Henry. Then again Captain F.A. von
Retzow and Friedrich Wilhelm Carl von Schmettau were respectively
the son and nephew of generals who had been harshly used by
Frederick. The old hussar colonel Charles-Emanuel von Warnery had
been banished from active service in 1758, but it is more than possible
that his astringent comments represented at second hand the opinions of Seydlitz, his friend and neighbour in Silesia. The resentments
of Friedrich Adolph von Kalkreuth also dated from the middle of the
Seven Years War, when as a young Garde du Corps he had been
disciplined by the king. He dictated his recollections in 1818, and they
gave the impression of having been 'distilled through poison and gall'
(Janson, 1913, 209).

Sentiments of revenge were harboured by Frederick's own intimate, that man of letters and unwilling free-corps brigand 'Quintus
Icilius' (Colonel Carl Gottlieb Guischardt). At once attracted and
humiliated by the king, Quintus Icilius assembled great quantities of
material with a view to compiling a history that would reveal the
dominant role played by accident and blunder in the Seven Years War
(Guibert, 1803, I, 21). He died in 1775, and Frederick at once bought
up his books and papers. They were never seen again.

Foreigners and natives alike were tempted, as we must be, by the
ambition to form a rounded and convincing view of Frederick as
soldier, king and private man. For a number of reasons, this enterprise
is probably hopeless. For a start, Frederick was lacking in basic
'integrity', when we use this word in the strict sense of the force
which binds together public and private conduct. Maria Theresa
owned this integrity when Frederick patently did not. Old Fritz once
advised his nephew concerning *la politique particulière*:

> when I was crown prince I showed little inclination towards
> military things. I was fond of my comforts, good food and wine,
> and I was often frantic with love. When I became king I put on
> the guise of soldier, philosopher and poet. I slept on straw, I
> camped among my soldiers eating ration bread, and I affected to
> despise women.
>
> Here is how I carry on. On my journeys I dispense with an
> escort, and I travel night and day. My suite is tiny and well
> chosen. My carriage is simple, but it is well sprung and I can
> sleep in it as well as in my bed. I pay little apparent attention to

the way I live, and my kitchen train consists of an attendant, a chef and a pastry cook. I arrange my own menu, and in fact I see to myself quite well. I know the country and I know where the best game, fish and meats are to be found. When I arrive at my destination I affect to be tired, and I always show myself to the public wearing a dreadful overcoat and an unkempt wig. Such trifles often make an extraordinary impression. (Toulongeon, 1881, 147)

It was also of some relevance that Frederick's tastes and eccentricities were of a kind to disengage him from some of the enthusiasms that were beginning to move his contemporaries. In peacetime he professed an indifference to public opinion, and he seemed to go to earth in Potsdam 'as savage, bitter and hostile as a lion in his den, who employs his leisure to lap up the blood of his victims' (Count Karl Gustav von Tessin, in Volz, 1926–7, II, 194). He rejected all attempts at ingratiation, even from his fellow Freemasons.

Likewise every impartial biographer has drawn attention to the king's preference for the French language and culture, and his indifference towards the men of the new German literature, who did everything they could to gain, if not Frederick's active approval, at least a sign of attention. Frederick was not attracted by the Anglomania of the 1770s and 1780s, for he disliked the English for their stiffness and gloom, their political faction, and their inclination towards physical violence. He did not feel impelled by the writings of Rousseau to go about on all fours, eating grass. *Sturm und Drang* was contrary to his nature, and so, at the other extreme, were the cold, pompous neo-classical forms of Winckelmann's rediscovery of the architecture of ancient Greece. His visual world remained that of the rococo. In their lightness, colour and movement the interiors of Sans Souci surpass anything in that style at Schönbrunn, and, long after fashions had changed, he insisted that the Berlin porcelain factory must continue to set before the public the decorative floral patterns of his youth. The paintings of Watteau continued to attract him, even when he was purchasing a more representative selection of great canvases for his Picture Gallery.

Frederick judged all music by reference to the Italianised German masters of the earlier part of the century. He disliked what little he knew of Gluck, and Haydn and Mozart remained virtual strangers to him: 'Good things remain good, and even when you have heard them before it is still nice to hear them again' (to Electress Maria-Antonia of Saxony, 8 January 1778, *Oeuvres*, XXIV, 292).

Traits of character such as these help us to construct a wider context for the military reaction which was so pronounced in

Frederick's later years, but they do not take us far along the way to understanding the whole man. We are left with those extraordinary paradoxes which render the present study as unsatisfactory as all the rest.

While phenomena like 'Prussian military discipline', 'the oblique order' and so on might have led us to suppose that their creator was a man of cool precision and detail, Frederick emerges as a creature of intense emotions and artistic temperament. His grasp of finance, like his allocation of strategic resources, was instinctive in character. He maintained to Voltaire that geometry dried out the wits, and in his writings he took little trouble over the accurate reproduction of dates, numbers, names and all the other minutiae which mean so much to little people. He was only too glad when picturesque weeds grew up to disturb the symmetry of the Sans Souci gardens, and he forbade his gardeners to uproot them.

The king was writing for himself, as much as for any of his generals, when he urged the vital necessity of preserving military secrets. A French diplomat observed:

He is indiscreet by nature, and in this respect he commits
blunders which are unpardonable in such an intelligent man
. . . The difficulty for the listener comes in sorting out the king's
true opinion from the host of contradictory utterances which
fall from his lips, especially after he has noticed that he has let
slip something which he should have kept to himself. (Lord
Tyrconnell, in Volz, 1926–7, I, 263)

Frederick expressed contempt for mankind in general, and he was notorious for the hurt he inflicted on people who failed to live up to his arbitrary standards of military excellence, or from whom he desired to extract information or ransoms. At the same time there are grounds for believing that Frederick was not a particularly cruel person – indeed, it is not extravagant to claim that many of his instincts were milder than those generally allowed in the Western world for decades or centuries to come. He deplored hunting, not just for the waste of time and money, but for the cruelty inflicted on innocent creatures. He counted prize-fighting as one of the objectionable habits of the English. He replied with angry sarcasm to one of his customs officials who asked for leave for his brother, a Bordeaux merchant, to go slaving under the Prussian flag:

I have always been of the opinion that the trade in negroes is a
blight on the human race. Never shall I do anything to
authorise or promote it. However, if this business is so attractive
to you, you have only to go back to France to be able to indulge

your taste. May God keep you in his holy and fond care! (Preuss, 1832–4, IV, 296)

The detailed business of killing, whether on the battlefield or by way of discipline or judicial punishment, was something that Frederick found repulsive. No punishment was inflicted on dishonest or careless servants of the royal household, or on those officials who administered East Prussia for the Russian enemy in the course of the Seven Years War. Frederick had a low opinion of humankind, and he was never shocked when it lived down to his expectations.

None of this detracted from the terror evoked by Frederick's presence. Countess Henriette Egloffstein describes how as a little girl she heard a troop of horse riding past her family coach as it waited at one of the gates of Potsdam:

I at once put my head out of the window, and saw that this body of cavalry was led by the mummy-like figure of an old man in a shabby uniform. A large plumed hat was jammed at an angle above the face, which was deformed by a huge nose, a small caved-in mouth and great bovine eyes. This frightening creature rode so close to me that his arm . . . literally brushed my upturned nose. The king glanced back, and those terrifying eyes bored through me, compelling me to draw my head inside. Only after he had passed did I pluck up the courage to alert my companions to the presence of the king. They thought I had let my imagination run away with me. (Volz, 1926–7, III, 198)

Amid so much that is uncertain, the loneliness of Frederick's later years is transmitted with all the greater force. We know from the many biographies that Frederick remained a stranger to his queen, and that the table circle of Sans Souci was never reconstituted in its old glory after the Seven Years War. The survivors and the newcomers bore the character of victims as much as of companions. Maria Theresa delivers the terrible verdict: 'This hero who has everyone talking about him, this conqueror, does he have a single friend? Must he not distrust the whole universe? What kind of life is it, from which all humanity is banished?' (to Joseph II, 14 September 1766, in Volz, 1926–7, II, 213).

Among the famous military men, there was a tincture of reproach in the physical and mental distance they held between themselves and the king. Prince Henry, who was probably the most gifted of them, maintained at Rheinsberg what was virtually a rival court, the focus of some of the most rancorous and resentful elements in the officer corps. Fouqué received gracious messages and presents of fruits from the king, but nothing could tempt him to make the twenty-mile journey to Sans Souci from his place of retirement in Brandenburg town.

Prince Ferdinand of Brunswick resigned from the Prussian service in 1766. He was at odds with the king over the new frenchified tax system, and the undue favour which Frederick was extending to the young Count 'Wilhelmi' Anhalt. However, the reasons for their falling-out were more fundamental: 'Above all we must consider that in Ferdinand the king saw a rival to his glory, and a man to whom (as he himself confessed) he and the whole House of Hohenzollern owed an extraordinarily great amount. It simply was not in Frederick's character to put up with seeing such a person day after day, and having to be suitably polite to him' (Mauvillon, 1794, II, 379–81).

Seydlitz meanwhile ruled the Silesian cavalry from Ohlau, and he had his own circle of friends who delighted in his company in his new house nearby at Minkowsky. This great man was ultimately brought low by a stroke, and he was already nearing his end when Frederick came to see him at Ohlau on 27 August 1773. They talked for over an hour, and Frederick more than once exclaimed: 'I cannot spare you! I cannot manage without you!' (Varnhagen von Ense, 1834, 229). Seydlitz died on 8 November.

The passing of Seydlitz left Zieten as the one survivor of the group of generals most closely associated with Frederick. The old hussar learnt to endure the repeated criticisms of the loose discipline among his men, but at one manoeuvre the king went too far: 'The regiment of Zieten carried out a first attack, and Frederick was so dissatisfied that he told our general: "I don't want to see you any more! You may remove yourself from my sight!" Zieten at once took him at his word, causing a considerable sensation' (Blumenthal, 1797, 255).

Within a few years Zieten could no longer be considered for independent command in the field, but he could be assured of a warm welcome at Potsdam. Frederick now treated him with invariable solicitude and respect. Once, when Zieten nodded off at table, the king refused to have him disturbed: 'He is a brave old man. Let him sleep on. He has stayed awake long enough on our account' (Hildebrandt, 1829–35, II, 136).

CHAPTER SEVEN

Public Affairs, and the War of the Bavarian Succession, 1778–9

Frederick discerned a rough correspondence between the exhausted state of the Continent after the Seven Years War, and his own desire for rest. For a span of fifteen years, the chief threat to this repose seemed to reside in the instability of eastern Europe, where some terrible Austro-Russian conflagration might be occasioned by the anarchical condition of Poland, or by Catherine II's growing appetite for conquests at the expense of the Turks. To Frederick's disappointment the connection between France and Austria survived the war, and it was only in order to rescue himself from complete isolation that he concluded a defensive alliance with the Russians in 1764.

Frederick drew up the second of his secret *Political Testaments* in 1768. This was a stock-taking still more comprehensive than the first essay in 1752, and it showed how the intervention of the state was capable of promoting the physical, educational and moral welfare of the subject. In so far as this document touched on international affairs, it indicated that Frederick believed that he had survived the Seven Years War, rather than won it, and that only constant preparedness would permit Prussia to exist in the same world as the genuinely first-class powers of Austria and Russia. He wrote with satisfaction of what had already been achieved in the way of accumulating revenues, cereals and munitions, but he added that the Austrians had by now become so formidable that any campaign against them must be conducted with the greatest caution: 'it is easier to crush 15,000 men than to beat 80,000, and you attain more or less the same result by risking less. By multiplying small successes you gradually heap up a treasure for yourself' (Frederick, *Politischen Testamente*, 163).

A shortened and updated edition of the *Testament* (*Exposé du Gouvernement Prussien*) was prepared in 1776 for the benefit of Prince Henry, but probably never actually shown to him (Hintze, 1919, 3–8).

The note of caution recurs in Frederick's *Éléments de*

Castramétrie et de Tactique, which was completed on 12 November 1770, and printed in German translation in 1771 as *Grundsätze der Lagerkunst und Taktik*. Frederick composed the work with two ends in mind: to widen the mental perspectives of his generals beyond their immediate arm of service, and to draw attention to the dominant role played by positions in modern war:

> Warfare . . . has become more refined, difficult and dangerous, because we are now fighting against something more than men . . . We must get it into our heads that the kind of war we will be waging from now on will be a question of artillery duels and attacking defended positions. (*Oeuvres*, XXIX, 3, 4)

Copies of the *Grundsätze* were given to the Inspectors, and circulated by them in conditions of secrecy among the generals and the regimental and battalion commanders.

Frederick developed his strategic ideas in his private *Réflexions sur les Projets de Campagne*. These were finished on 1 December 1775, and the note *scriptum in dolore* refers to an onset of rheumaticky pains which afflicted him at the time. The *Réflexions* were cast in the form of a wide-ranging survey, exploring possible responses to the cases of:

(a) offensive war with the help of Russian auxiliaries
(b) war between equally balanced forces
(c) a vigorously conducted defensive war

It is evident that the wary circumspection of Frederick's new tactical schemes did not apply in the same measure in the strategic sphere. The offensive war against Austria was intended to carry off the prize of Bohemia, and among the various strategies 'the most sure in its effect, and at the same time the most difficult to carry out, will be to transfer the theatre of war to the Danube, so as to compel the court of Vienna to withdraw its main forces from Bohemia. This will facilitate the task of the Prussian army which is due to invade that kingdom' (*Oeuvres*, XXIX, 76).

By now the military power of Austria had become identified with the ambitions of Maria Theresa's eldest son, Joseph II, who was made Emperor and co-regent in 1765. Frederick had hoped to be able to renounce the active trade of arms, but in Joseph he was confronted as if by the spectre of his own youth, come to trouble him in his old age. He was only too well aware that 'young princes are more difficult to decipher than the most dissembling of private individuals' (to Maria Antonia of Saxony, 10 August 1766, *Oeuvres*, XXIV, 120).

In 1769 Frederick responded most willingly to Joseph's desire to arrange a meeting. Old Fritz was eager both to take the measure of his new neighbour and to demonstrate his independence of the Russians. Joseph and his unpretentious suite accordingly travelled to the Upper Silesian fortress-town of Neisse, and at noon on 25 August he reached the episcopal *Residenz*. Frederick was at the foot of the stairs to meet him, 'and after mutually gazing at each other for a single moment, they embraced, with demonstrations of reciprocal pleasure' (Wraxall, 1806, II, 450–1).

The visit extended over three full days. In the mornings Frederick and Joseph used to ride out to view the troops. Joseph showered Seydlitz with compliments, which did not please the king greatly, and the Austrian cavalry general Joseph d'Ayasasa took the opportunity to tour the ranks of the Seydlitz Cuirassiers, examining every item of uniform and equipment. On these occasions Joseph found that Frederick was full of consideration: 'He has made a fundamental study of the art of war, and read virtually everything that has been written on the subject. It is quite enchanting when he speaks. Everything he says is vigorous, solidly reasoned and deeply instructive' (to Maria Theresa, 25 September, in Volz, 1926–7, II, 215).

In the afternoons the Austrians made the acquaintance of the longueurs of the Frederician lunch, and they noted that the king was the only one of the Prussians to speak. Evening entertainment was provided by a wretched company of German comedians, whose feeble jokes seemed to cause Frederick a disproportionate amount of amusement.

In 1770 it was Joseph's turn to repay the hospitality. He invited Frederick to come to him at Mährisch-Neustadt, on the edge of the plain of Olmütz, where the open ground and a couple of small hills offered an excellent theatre for moving and viewing the Austrian troops. Frederick arrived on 3 September, wearing a uniform of snuff-stained Austrian white which must have presented one of the more curious sights of the eighteenth century. Old Fritz had ridden all the way from Breslau on horseback, which in itself gave him a certain moral advantage over the much younger Joseph, who had travelled to Moravia by coach. Frederick had been looking forward to renewing the acquaintance of this lively and intelligent prince in whom he saw something of a fellow-spirit, but this time the element of competition was sustained throughout the visit.

Frederick's obsequiousness was altogether too artificial. Not only did he hold the bridle of the Imperial horse when Joseph was hoisting himself into the saddle, but he inserted the august boot into the stirrup. At table he refused to allow himself to be served before the Emperor, and if the Austrians at Neisse had cultivated Seydlitz, so now Frederick was full of attention for Loudon. 'His politeness nearly had a painful ending. The Emperor was accompanying him out of the chamber, and when Frederick was making his obseisances he would have fallen backwards down the steps if somebody had not grabbed him in time' (Duke Albert of Sachsen-Teschen, in Koschatzky and Krasa, 1982, 92).

In the military displays, the splendid Austrian grenadiers helped to efface the impression that had been made by the Seydlitz Cuirassiers of the year before. It was unfortunate that the grand review, which was held on the third day, was marred by a terrible deluge which soaked the two monarchs and the 30,000 troops to the skin, but afterwards the Austrians were amused to see that Frederick had to stand in a cloak while his coat and breeches were left steaming in front of the fire in a peasant hut.

Politically, the Mährisch-Neustadt conference passed off rather better than we might have expected, from these descriptions, because Frederick and Joseph agreed that the Russian conquests from Turkey represented a threat to the balance of power. Less than two years later the notorious First Partition of Poland helped to assuage the appetites of the three great monarchies of eastern Europe, and so helped to prolong a peace of sorts. The first signal had already been given by Joseph, who in 1769 had made off with the 'Thirteen Towns' of Zips, a Polish territory on which the crown of Hungary had ancient claims. Prince Henry, on a visit to St Petersburg, suggested on his own initiative that something of the sort might be arranged for the benefit of Prussia and Russia. Catherine and Frederick were responsive to the idea, and chaotic Poland lost one-quarter of its surface and more than one-quarter of its population in virtue of a Prusso-Russian accord of 5 January 1772, and a further agreement embracing Austria on 5 August.

Frederick made what justifications he could to Voltaire, claiming that the partition had helped to avert a general war, but Enlightenment Europe persisted in regarding the deal as 'an act that revolted every mind not insensible to the distinctions of right and wrong' (Wraxall, 1806, I, 106).

The Austrians gained three million new subjects, and the Russians 1,800,000. In numerical terms Prussia did the least well, acquiring 20,000 square miles (36,000 square kilometres) and 5,000–600,000 people of very diverse racial stock. In most other respects, however, Frederick won by far the greatest relative advantages. As master of West Prussia, he now owned a wide bridge to the hitherto isolated territory of East Prussia, and he advanced the eastern strategic borders of his state to the Vistula and the Netze. Frederick controlled both the mouth and the middle reaches of the Vistula, and by constructing the Bromberg Canal to the Oder he integrated the Vistula with the inland waterways of the old dominions. Thus the city of Danzig remained independent only in name, and Frederick exercised control of the Polish foreign trade, and especially the export of grains, which could now be diverted to Prussia in the event of shortage.

West Prussia was a barren and backward territory, but it yielded annual revenues of 1,700,000 thaler, of which 1,200,000 were devoted to maintaining the locally raised troops (five new regiments of fusiliers, one of hussars, four garrison battalions, and two battalions of artillery). A visit to West Prussia was now incorporated into the routine of the royal year, and Frederick had a half-timbered cottage built at Mockrau, near Graudenz, to serve as his headquarters for the reviews.

Frederick commissioned many young West Prussians as officers in the new regiments, without looking too closely into their ancestry, but he failed entirely in his ambition to make some military use of the considerable Jewish population:

> They vainly remonstrated to His Majesty, that war was neither analogous to their native genius, nor agreeable to their private feelings. But such was found to be on trial, their insurmountable disinclination to bear arms, that after many vain endeavours, they were finally broken and disbanded. (Wraxall, 1806, I, 219)

The peace, or rather the temporary satiation of appetites induced by the Polish Partition, ran for only five years before Frederick was faced with the prospect of dragging his old bones off to a new war.

Austria had failed in the great enterprise of recovering Silesia, but now in the later 1770s Joseph and Chancellor Kaunitz snatched at the opportunity of gaining a more than adequate compensation in southern and western Germany. The last of the direct line of the Bavarian electoral House of Wittelsbach died on 30 December 1777, and his successor, the dissolute Carl Theodor, agreed to sell Lower Bavaria to the Austrians outright, and surrender to them the reversionary title to the Upper Palatinate. All of this might appear to be the small change of eighteenth-century diplomacy. However, if the deal had gone ahead unchallenged, Austria would have been strengthened so mightily in territory, population, and above all in its Germanic character that the Prussian state would have been put at a permanent disadvantage.

Joseph had gained an ascendency in the counsels of Vienna over his mother Maria Theresa, who dreaded a new war, and he dismissed all Frederick's offers of negotiation as so many signs of weakness. Maria Theresa herself joined in the laughter at the ludicrous spelling mistakes in Frederick's letters.

On 26 January 1778 Frederick set in train the process of a lengthy mobilisation. The impoverished electorate of Saxony was now a strategic satellite of Prussia, and in March the king sent Colonel Johann Christoph von Zegelin to Dresden in order to work out a detailed scheme of military co-operation. In the subsequent talks the Saxons agreed to allow the Prussians free access to their territory, and to support their operations with about 20,000 Saxon troops. The Prusso-Saxon force on this western flank amounted to 85,000 men, and Frederick chose Prince Henry for the command. Another 87,000 troops were to constitute the royal army in Silesia.

The plan of operations was based closely on the case of an offensive war against the Austrian monarchy, as outlined in the *Réflexions* of 1775. The objective in both schemes was to conquer Bohemia by means of a careful balance of invasions across widely separated sectors of the Austrian frontiers. (See Map 28, p. 380.)

The grand diversionary thrust into Moravia was the responsibility of the royal army, and before it got under way Frederick planned to make a smaller demonstration, or reconnaissance in force, by a mass of cavalry moving from Glatz into north-east Bohemia in the direction of Königgrätz. Frederick knew nothing for certain about the location of the Austrian forces, but he was confident that they would be sucked eastwards by the programme of diversions, leaving Henry with a clear run from Saxony to the neighbourhood of Prague. Frederick hoped that the element of Russian support, which was an important feature of the plan of 1775, would be provided by an auxiliary corps of 30,000 troops operating against Austrian Poland. (He retained his trust in Russian help until 1 October, by which time active hostilities were nearly over.)

There were soon indications that all was not going to go well with the war. Unlike the Austrians, Frederick had made no arrangements to assemble the nucleus of a supply train in peacetime, and now with the approach of active operations he was forced to reconstitute the whole apparatus from the beginning. In the event, the arrangements for moving not just the supplies, but the immense artillery train of 915 pieces, began to collapse even before hostilities broke out. Goethe enthused at the scenes of lively commotion in the capital, but to a military eye the gathering of the Berlin artillery resembled nothing so much as 'the bringing together of a caravan . . . intended to transport a multitude of tradesmen's goods to some market place or other' (quoted in Jany, 1928–9, III, 114).

Prince Henry predicted that 'these enormous masses which are piling up on either side will reduce each other to a defensive . . . If one or other of the parties tries to force the issue it will acquire a certain amount of glory – and lose one-third of its troops in the process' (to Frederick, 10 March, *PC* 26085). Frederick was aware that endless trains of Austrian artillery were reported to be moving into Bohemia, but he believed that the Prussians must respond by building up powerful local concentrations of their own ordnance, so as to effect a breach in the enemy positions (*PC* 26399, 26433, 26458).

On 12 April Frederick established his headquarters in the village of Schönwalde, hard under the hill fortress of Silberberg and a couple of marches from the Bohemian border. Weeks of negotiation came to nothing, and he wrote to his foreign minister Finckenstein: 'those Austrian buggers are laughing at us . . . press them hard to give us a categorical reply, or these swine will play us along until winter comes, which does not suit my purposes at all' (9 June, *PC* 26445).

On 4 July 1778 the advance guard of the royal army made the ascent of the stony roads leading from the County of Glatz. Next day the Prussians made for the little stream near Nachod which marked the Bohemian border, and Frederick ordered all the regiments to pass this new Rubicon with beating drums and sounding music. 'The king was standing quite alone on the Austrian side of the bridge which leads over the river . . . As the troops marched across he examined them with the same calm confidence and sharpness of eye as if he had been on the Parade at Potsdam' (Anon., 1884, 35). The new West Prussian regiments were greatly impressed.

On 6 July and again the next day Frederick rode out with his light cavalry to make his long-meditated reconnaissance in force. He encountered no opposition as he moved west over the lightly wooded country around Skalitz, but he discovered that the Austrians were heavily emplaced on the avenue between the two great primeval woods of this corner of Bohemia – the Königreich-Wald to the north, and the near-trackless Königgrätzer-Wald to the south. He knew this area very well indeed, and he grasped at once the significance of the transformations which the Austrians had worked in the neighbourhood since he had last passed this way in 1758. Not only had the enemy planted a permanent fortress at Königgrätz, which, as he already knew, gave added force to the southerly barriers of the Adler river and the Königgrätzer-Wald, but a considerable number of troops were now throwing up field works along the far, or western, bank of the upper Elbe, thus denying his only access to the open country of Bohemia beyond.

During the first ride, the inquisitive young hussars had crowded around the king:

Frederick was no longer the monarch whom the older hussars remembered from the Seven Years War. Sixteen years had passed since that time, and their effect was all too evident in his bearing, his features, and still more in something peculiar to

very old men – a gloomy, almost morose disposition of mind.
(Hildebrandt, 1829–35, III, 129)

Frederick decided to bring his advance guard up to about 3,000
paces from the enemy lines on the sector to the north of Jaromiersch.
On the morning of 8 July he rode out once more, and came close
enough to the Austrian outposts to draw skirmishing fire:

> To begin with he appeared gentle and good-natured, and he
> joked in a very relaxed way with several people who were about
> him. But he grew impatient after he had waited two hours in
> vain for the columns to arrive. His gaze became dark,
> threatening and fearsome, and his face betrayed signs of mighty
> and barely containable anger. (Schmettau, 1789, 34)

The Prussians remained thirty-seven days in their Camp of Welsdorf. In other circumstances the neighbourhood would have been an
attractive one, with its gentle hills, verdant valleys and scattered
woodland. The troops soon came to hate it. 'Already by the second
day we were short of everything. Not only were we running out of
food, but we suffered from lack of tobacco, spirits, salt and even water
and straw for our camp. You would scarcely have recognised our poor
men. All good humour and cheerfulness had vanished' (Anon., 1884,
39–40).

Frederick made himself at home in a hut of squared logs in
Ober-Welsdorf, an open village of cabins, scattered along either side
of a little stream. To the north, a plain extended to the tall, close-
packed trees of the Königreich-Wald. Southward, a low rounded ridge
separated the Welsdorf hollow from the valley of the upper Elbe. The
vandalism of the soldiers ranged around him unchecked. The huts
were broken up for firewood, and the agricultural instruments and
the seed corn were senselessly destroyed.

Daily Frederick rode up and down the heights of the left bank,
looking for some gap in the enemy positions on the far side. These
were the equivalent of the defences of the Bunzelwitz perimeter of
1761, uncoupled and arranged in line along six miles of the upper
Elbe, complete with batteries, palisades, mines and abatis. The
strongpoints of this 'Camp of Jaromiersch' (Map 29, p. 381) were
carefully sited to take full advantage of the salients and re-entrants
formed by the low hills. The left or northern flank was anchored on
the bastion presented by the palace or monastery of the *Barmher-
zigen Bruder* at Kukus, which had been built to the prescriptions of
the old Austrian cavalryman Count Sporck. The house was garrisoned, and when Frederick looked at the gardens, he could detect
several pieces of artillery, as well as the baroque statues of the Virtues

and Vices gesticulating at him from the terrace. Upstream from Kukus and Schurz the hills of the right bank were very densely wooded, and the Austrians had cut an abatis there which made all movement absolutely impossible.

The river Elbe presented the least of the obstacles. It was only a stone's throw wide, and so shallow at this season that the Croats were able to wade across without difficulty and make a nuisance of themselves in the bushes on the Prussian side.

The check at Jaromiersch had an important strategic dimension. Joseph's chief military adviser, Field-Marshal Lacy, has been derided as a practitioner of a vicious type of strategy called the 'cordon system', which is supposed to have had the effect of scattering troops evenly over long stretches of ground, rendering them vulnerable to attack at any one point. The cordon system, if it ever existed, was never brought into play in the war of 1778. Instead, at considerable cost in effort and money, Lacy held the bulk of the 100,000-strong *Elbe-Armee* in a single mass, ready to match any concentration which Frederick might form against the otherwise thinly held line of the upper Elbe. The king could not possibly have left this powerful army unwatched, so close to his borders, and thus his intended reconnaissance in force became a confrontation between the two royal commands. Frederick ordered up the uncommitted reserve from Nachod, which increased his infantry in the Camp of Welsdorf from twenty-five battalions to forty.

In the middle of July Baron Thugut arrived with a private message from Maria Theresa begging Frederick to join her in bringing a negotiated end to the hostilities. Frederick replied in courteous terms, but he could not entirely persuade himself of Maria Theresa's sincerity or of the reality of the differences of opinion between her and the warlike Joseph: 'We will have to beat these buggers if we want to bring them to a more reasonable frame of mind' (*PC* 26611).

Frederick did not believe that he could beat any of the buggers at Jaromiersch, and so he turned the original plan of campaign on its head and looked to his brother Henry to provide the diversion with the Prusso-Saxon army. Henry at first responded most magnificently. His task was to turn the strategic flank of the second Austrian army, under Loudon, which was positioned on both sides of the middle Elbe close to the Saxon border. Henry made his most important moves behind the screen of the border hills. First he transferred his army to the right or eastern bank of the Elbe, and then, having been joined by the Saxon contingent, he forced the Upper Lusatian/Bohemian border by way of a number of 'impracticable' passes. Leaving the Saxons at Gabel, to guard his communications, he pressed through the rocky woods to Niemes, just short of the Iser valley.

All of the Austrian plans for the defence of northern Bohemia were overthrown at one stroke. Prague was abandoned by the garrison and the aristocracy, and the Austrian tenure of the whole of Bohemia now hung upon the troops who were re-grouping along the line of the Iser. Joseph betook himself to what was now called the *Iser-Armee*, and he found an atmosphere of despondency reigning in Loudon's headquarters at Münchengrätz. The Emperor did what he could to stiffen Loudon's resolution before he had to return to the *Elbe-Armee* at Jaromiersch. 'I am setting off today', he wrote on 14 August. 'I leave most unwillingly, because I fear that the slightest alarm will occasion our retreat' (Koser, 1910, 524). Three days later Lieutenant-General Möllendorff proposed to Henry a push which, as we can now appreciate, would certainly have unseated Loudon from the Iser. Henry rejected the idea, because he feared for his communications in this wild country, and he believed that the possible rewards from Möllendorff's scheme were not commensurate with the risks.

Frederick was quite unable to persuade Henry to advance to the Iser, and he had to be satisfied with getting his brother to move to the left bank of the middle Elbe, from where he could threaten Prague. Henry hung around dejectedly in the neighbourhood of Lobositz, and then on 24 September he began a retreat on Saxony.

Meanwhile Frederick had got the royal army on the move while the Austrians were still alarmed by Henry's original excursion. He planned first to consume all the cereals and fodder in the Welsdorf area, so as to deny the Austrians a base from which to invade Silesia. He would then disengage the army, take it on a wide circuit to the north and west through the wooded valleys, and reinsert it on the uppermost reaches of the river near Hohenelbe (Map 30, p. 382), where the ground began to rise more than 4,000 feet to the summits of the Riesen-Gebirge. This march would carry the army clear of the densely wooded hills along the right bank of the Elbe between Schurz and the Bradl-Berg, and Frederick hoped that the Austrians would not have time to occupy the Hohenelbe sector in any strength. Any opposition would be cleared away by a mighty concentration of howitzer fire.

On 16 August the royal army decamped from the devastated surroundings of Welsdorf and marched to a new camp at the Bohemian Burkersdorf, on the site of the battle of Soor. Now that speed was imperative, six days were lost while working parties cleared the paths for the further advance of the artillery by way of Trautenau, Wildshütz, Mohren, Leopold, and Hermannseiffen.

At last, on 22 August, the main army and the cumbersome train of artillery began the march on Leopold, while Frederick took off with four hundred hussars to join the detached corps of the Hereditary Prince Carl Wilhelm Ferdinand of Brunswick, who was making direct for Ober-Langenau, within sight of Hohenelbe. The royal party progressed along a valley of woods, meadows and rushing brooks – ideal country for an ambush – and for some minutes Frederick was almost engulfed by the Austrian hussars who were swarming around the column. 'The situation was made still more dangerous by the physical weakness of the king. He could ride only at the walk, being no longer capable of galloping or tolerating any kind of rapid movement' (Schmettau, 1789, 112).

Frederick was in a bad temper when he broke through to Brunswick's troops on the broad and open Langenau heights. Now at last he caught his first sight of the objective, and it was only too evident that the enemy were arriving simultaneously with him. As he looked hard left, or to the south, several detachments of three or four battalions each were visible on the low, narrow but continuous ridge which extended in the direction of Arnau. About 3,000 paces to the king's front, and beyond the diminutive channels of the Elbe, some 15,000 Austrians were shaking themselves into line on the Fuchs-Berg and the other easily accessible heights on the sector between Pesldorf and Hohenelbe. To the right rear of the royal party, the forest-clad slopes of the Riesen-Gebirge soared black and inaccessible. As far as Frederick's companions could tell, the royal gaze never settled on the great mounds of the Wachura-Berg, which rose to his right between Hohenelbe and the Riesen-Gebirge slopes. The Austrians had not yet had the time to occupy this vital ground, which was the key to the left flank of their new position. Frederick observed the gathering Austrians for two hours, but the officers could not determine whether he had noticed his opportunity. By this stage in the king's career 'nobody dared to contradict him, or even put forward objections. People went about in more fear of him than they did of the enemy' (Schmettau, 1789, 22). Frederick returned with his escort to Leopold, where the leading elements of the main army were arriving.

Joseph had indeed arrived at Hohenelbe at the same time as Frederick, and, since the Prussians did not disturb him at his work, he was able to complete his defensive arrangements along the whole front from Arnau to the Riesen-Gebirge. On 23 August Frederick was back at Ober-Langenau with his hussars. He stared in bad-tempered silence at the Austrians, who could be counted almost man for man and cannon by cannon.

Frederick was not yet ready to renounce his enterprise. Speed and surprise had failed him, but he still believed that it might be possible to evict the Austrians by force. He intended first to secure his right flank, by sweeping the corps of Siskovics from the Wachura-Berg, and then establish a battery of forty-five howitzers near Hohenelbe to open a way for a push across the Elbe. Once the Prussians had established themselves on the hills on the far side, between Branna and Starkenbach, the whole of the Austrian position would become untenable.

The main army rested at Leopold for three full days, and only on the 26th did Frederick bring up the troops to support Brunswick's corps. Frederick made a further reconnaissance the same day, and on returning to his headquarters at Lauterwasser he pronounced: 'I am sorry to say it, but I don't think there is anything more we can do here' (Schmettau, 1789, 155). His infantry and cavalry were in position, but the artillery, and especially the howitzers, was still lagging miles behind.

The rest of the war is quickly related. Frederick talked about evicting the five Austrian battalions from their post on the near side of the Elbe on the Hartaer-Berg near Pelsdorf, as if to persuade his own army that he was still intent on active operations. His true objective, however, was now simply to draw back gradually to his borders, eating out the grain and fodder of the countryside as he went, so as to interpose 'a kind of desert' (PC 26640) between the Austrian forces and Silesia during the winter.

In the event, the chief destruction was worked on the Prussian army. Cold wet weather set in on 31 August, and from 1 September the crests of the Riesen-Gebirge were covered with snow. The Prussian troops were ravaged by dysentery and unparalleled desertions. Frederick's own intestines were badly disordered, and he was increasingly depressed by his surroundings – the steaming pinewoods, the muddy hollows, the bestial peasants, the barbaric place names, the wayside religious statues – all of which accentuated his isolation from the civilised world.

Frederick abandoned the Lauterwasser camp on 8 September and fell back initially to Wildschütz. He moved to Trautenau on the 15th, and up the border hills to Schatzlar on the 21st. The marches were frequently plagued by Austrian detachments, and every hillside track became a Via Dolorosa for the artillery.

In the middle of October the last Prussian troops withdrew into Silesia. Even now Frederick was unwilling to allow them much rest. The Austrian lieutenant-general Ellrichshausen had a corps which seemed to threaten Upper Silesia, and Frederick still believed in the possibility of a winter campaign on the part of the young and ambitious Joseph. Frederick detached successive reinforcements from the main army to Upper Silesia, and on 23 October he arrived in person at Jägerndorf. By the middle of November he was satisfied that the cordon was secure for the winter, and he returned to Silberberg and Breslau to prepare for the next campaign and keep himself informed of the course of the political negotiations, which were beginning to take an interesting turn.

Frederick was still revolving ambitious plans of offensive war for the next season. The gulf with Prince Henry ran deeper than ever, and in December Frederick agreed to his brother's request to be allowed to resign from the command of the army in Saxony. He was probably only too glad to replace him by the Hereditary Prince Carl Wilhelm Ferdinand of Brunswick, for whom a brilliant future was predicted. On 16 January 1779 the king furnished Brunswick with his plan for the next campaign. The army from Saxony was to invade north Bohemia and come at the line of the Upper Elbe from the rear, while the royal army executed the cherished design of the sweep through Moravia towards Vienna.

Henry protested against his brother's emphasis on offensive action (*PC* 27140), and in fact it is doubtful whether the Prussian army, or Frederick's physical or mental constitution, were in any way equal to the kind of effort which the king had in mind for 1779. It was the Austrians who made all the running when mild weather in February and March made it possible to resume the skirmishing along the borders. Thus on 18 January the Austrians descended on two weak Prussian battalions which were stranded at Habelschwerdt, due south of Glatz town. Captain Capeller and one hundred men offered a heroic resistance from a blockhouse until the wooden structure was set on fire by howitzer shells and he was forced to surrender. Frederick moved up with his reserve to Silberberg, so as to be able to lend support along the frontier as necessary.

This march was the last one that Frederick ever undertook in command of forces in the field. The very names of the leaders of the Austrian raiding parties, Clerfayt and Wurmser, are a reminder that a new generation of officers was at hand, and there was something senile and querulous in the way Frederick protested: 'These men are the kind of people we call "glory-hunters". For the sake of gaining decorations and distinctions from their court they harass us by every conceivable means, and sacrifice their soldiers regardless of the cost' (*PC* 27185).

By now the course of the war was being overtaken by political developments. The Austrian treasury had been plunged ever deeper into debt by the very success of Joseph and Lacy in outmarching the Prussians in troops on the Elbe. The Austrians had only 175,000 soldiers under arms on the eve of hostilities, but 297,000 men stood ready to take the field in 1779 (Peters, 1902, 347), and the issue of rations for men and horses far exceeded that for the campaign of 1760, which was the period of greatest effort in the Seven Years War. Maria Theresa had always been opposed to the war, as we have seen, and the peaceful accommodation, which she had failed to achieve through the missions of Baron Thugut, was finally accomplished by the mediation of France and Russia in the spring of 1779. An armistice came into effect along the borders in the second week in March, and on 13 May the Peace of Teschen brought hostilities to a formal end. Out of all their gains in Bavaria, the Austrians retained only the little 'quarter' between the rivers Danube, Inn and Salzach.

Thus a diplomatic triumph for Frederick succeeded a defensive victory for the Austrians in the field. His demoralised army streamed home, its ranks depleted by more than 30,000 men through disease and a desertion greater than in the whole of the Seven Years War.

Any passably serious book which sets out to trace Frederick's career will always be a lengthy one; the temptation must be, as the monarch's life draws to its close, to pass rapidly over the months of the War of the Bavarian Succession. The narrative-minded biographer finds nothing to compare with the sustained excitements of the Seven Years War, and the seeker after military sensation is unmoved by a positional confrontation in which combat casualties were numbered in their hundreds, instead of by the tens of thousands who fell on the single day of Torgau. Likewise professional historians prefer to fix their attention on the war that was proceeding on the far side of the Atlantic, or to set the scene for the cataclysm that was going to overtake Europe in the 1790s.

Frederick's admirers have needed little prompting to take their cue from the old king, who could write in 1781 about the lack of promotion 'during a long period of peace like the present one, which has lasted nearly twenty years' ('Instruction für die Inspecteurs der Infanterie', Oeuvres, XXX, 361). In other words, he liked to think that no real war had ever supervened in 1778. It seemed almost blasphemous to Cogniazzo and others to suggest that the feeble motions of the Prussians could have been determined by anything other than political considerations (Pilati di Tassulo, 1784, 136; Cogniazzo, 1788–91, IV, 307, 331).

This convenient explanation does not correspond to the earnestness of Frederick's tactical schemes, which were the culmination of a line of development which originated in the middle of the Seven Years War (see p. 315). If we did not have a great battle, it was simply because Frederick was so slow at getting his howitzers into position.

Nor does the notion of 'armed negotiation' (Ranke) accord with the aggressive plans of campaign, which were at least as ambitious as anything which Frederick hatched between 1756 and 1758. We may cite not only the strategy for the opening campaign, but the *Instruction* to Brunswick on 16 January 1779, and the further set of *Réflexions* of 28 September of the same year, which again made the Danube the objective in the event of peace breaking down (*Oeuvres*, XXIX, 132–44). All the restraints were on the Austrian side, as when Thugut's negotiations prevented Joseph from falling on the Prussians as they shuffled from Welsdorf to Burkersdorf.

The reasons for the Prussian failure must therefore be of a military character. It was only too evident that every branch of Frederick's army was in a state of decline. If the demoralisation among the infantry was regrettable, the indiscipline of the cavalry was a matter of still greater concern, for the native troopers had always been counted as the most reliable element in the service. Much had also been expected of the artillery, and yet 'at the time of the invasion of Bohemia, the artillery train was already reduced to the kind of condition you would normally have seen only by the end of a campaign' (Kaltenborn, 1790–1, II, 137). The officials of the commissariat proved to be every bit as rapacious as Frederick feared they were going to be, but the extent of the collapse of the medical services remained unknown to him until Dr J.G. Zimmermann told him about it in 1786 (Zimmermann, 1788, 125). The army as a whole was unresponsive and painfully slow-moving, and it needed three or four days to recover from a single march.

Frederick bears the ultimate responsibility for the shortcomings in 1778, in the same way as he has the credit for the brilliant campaigns of 1745 and late 1757. Observers returned to Berlin to report that

His Majesty has experienced a great diminution of that
confidence in his abilities, and enthusiasm for his person, which
inspired the troops at their onset. That his age and infirmities
make him unable to transport himself with his usual expedition
to the different scenes of action, where he wishes to preside, and
opportunities are thus lost which might be improved into
decisive advantages. (H. Elliot, 1 December 1778, PRO SP 90/
107)

This is confirmed by the evidence of Friedrich Wilhelm von Schmettau, who was in the immediate proximity of the king for most of the campaign. Schmettau was certain that Frederick was serious about his war, and he finds the reasons for the disappointing outcome in the mental as well as the physical failings of the king, who concentrated in himself an authority which he was no longer capable of wielding (Schmettau, 1789, 1–2, 5).

13 May 1779 was the date for the signing of the Peace of Teschen, and also, as Frederick knew, the birthday of Maria Theresa. The provisions of the treaty were not supposed to take immediate effect, but in honour of the empress-queen Frederick ordered his troops to evacuate all the townships of the Austrian border before the day was out. In itself this little courtesy will nowadays appear of little account, but it signified a great deal when it proceeded from somebody as austere and demanding as Frederick. It was the salute of one old warrior to another, and it was acknowledged as such by Maria Theresa.

CHAPTER EIGHT
Final Years and Immortality

If we except Catherine of Russia, Frederick entered the 1780s as the single figure of heroic stature on the stage of Europe. Maria Theresa had died on 29 November 1780, but Frederick could find no satisfaction in his victory of physical survival: 'She did honour to her throne and to her sex. I waged war against her but I was never her enemy.'

Free of the restraints which had been exercised by his mother, 'Monsieur Joseph' now sought every opportunity to exalt the Austrian state at the expense of Prussia. In 1781 he made a defensive alliance with Catherine, finally killing off the already moribund Prusso-Russian connection, and in 1785 he negotiated for an exchange of the Austrian Netherlands for Bavaria. Frederick was once again faced with the immediate prospect of a new and hostile Catholic superpower arising to his south. This time, instead of resorting to war, he enlisted the support of Saxony, Hanover and a number of the smaller states of the Empire in a *Fürstenbund*, or League of Princes, which was constituted on 23 July 1785. Joseph thereupon saw fit to abandon his scheme. The *Fürstenbund* was in no way the precursor of a united Germany, for it was conceived in the narrow interests of Prussia, and made effective only through the indirect support of the French, but it ensured that Frederick lived out his days bathed in the sunset glory of a pan-German hero.

Frederick's health had actually improved for a time after he returned from the war of 1778–9. He resumed the strenuous routine of the reviews and manoeuvres, and he called in on Zieten whenever his journeys took him near Wustrau. 'It was most agreeable to see how that great man, who was now into his seventies, used to travel in his snow-covered coach to visit his . . . servant, casting aside the burden of his years and dignities' (Blumenthal, 1797, 586).

The last occasion on which Frederick presided over the grand Silesian manoeuvres was in August 1785. The Duke of York, Lord Cornwallis and more than two dozen other British officers were present as guests, as well as their old opponent the Marquis de

Lafayette. Frederick lodged more unassumingly than any of them, in a peasant house at Gross-Tinz near Nimptsch.

After having followed the exercises for several days, most of the foreigners chose to absent themselves when bad weather descended on 24 August. Frederick carried on as normal:

> He was in no way dressed to withstand the cold rain, wearing neither overcoat nor cloak, and yet his activity was unflagging. He was seemingly oblivious of the downpour, but the beautifully trimmed uniforms of the Duke of York and the Marquis de Layfayette were sacrificed to the rain, along with the less handsome garb of the other folk. It rained so hard that individual battalions had scarcely three muskets that were in a condition to fire, and ultimately they had none at all. The loading and drilling went ahead regardless. (Warnsdorff, in Volz, 1926–7, II, 289)

This last show of bravado proved to be too much for the seventy-three-year-old Frederick. He was prostrated by exposure, and he had to give his adjutants the responsibility of directing the secret Potsdam manoeuvres in September.

The *Parole*, and other public orders, were now issued to the officers indoors. At one such gathering, on 22 December, Frederick invited Zieten to come up from the rear of the company, and he summoned up a chair for the old hussar. He inquired after his health, his hearing, and so on. Finally he told him: ' "Farewell Zieten! Take care not to catch a chill. I know you are old, but carry on as long as you can. I want to have the pleasure of seeing you many times yet!" At this the king turned about. He spoke with nobody else, nor did he follow his usual custom of progressing to the other rooms, but betook himself to his solitary chamber' (Blumenthal, 1797, 595).

Frederick spent an uncomfortable winter, for he had suffered a slight stroke, and his legs were swelling with dropsy. Lafayette found him in this reduced condition when he visited Potsdam on 8 February 1786:

> I . . . could not help being struck with the dress and appearance of an old, broken, dirty corporal, covered all over with Spanish snuff, with his head leaning on one shoulder, and fingers almost distorted by the gout; but what surprises me much more is the fire, and sometimes the softness, of the most beautiful eyes I ever saw, which give as charming an expression to his physiognomy as he can take a rough and threatening one at the head of his troops. (Lafayette, 1837, II, 120–1)

Frederick's mental activity was unimpaired, and he kept up an energetic correspondence on all affairs of army and state. Amongst other business he arranged to set up three permanent battalions of light infantry, as a partial substitute for the wretched free battalions which used to be constituted afresh at the outbreak of every war.

In May and June Frederick was still too weak to be able to attend the reviews. He had as little faith in medical science as he did in religion, but it was probably this continuing immobility which persuaded him to call on the services of the famous doctor J. G. Zimmermann. The physician came to Sans Souci on 22 June:

> The king was sitting in a large armchair, with his back against the side of the room by which I had entered. On his head he had a large, old and plain hat, which was suffering from the passage of time. Its old white plume was in the same condition. He wore a dressing-gown of light blue satin, with heavy stains of yellow and brown from the snuff he had spilled down the front. He still had his boots on, though one of the legs was terribly swollen and resting on a stool . . . And yet all the intelligence and greatness of his best years gleamed in his eyes. (Zimmermann, 1788, 3)

In a final gesture of independence Frederick managed to get himself into the saddle of the long grey Condé on 4 July, and he rode at speed through the gardens. He collapsed when he returned, and never ventured out of doors again, except when on sunny afternoons he was carried out to the Sans Souci terrace. For the rest of the time he stayed in his room, and between spells of coughing and sleeping he read through the piles of letters on the table beside his settee, and signed, documents with a trembling hand. He sent the following message to the head of the Cadet Corps: 'Take it from me, if I lost half my monarchy, and yet was able to put myself at the head of my Pomeranians and Brandenburgers, and keep my composure, I could still drive the very devil from Hell!' (Taysen, 1886, 70). The sun now hurt his eyes, but he refused to have the curtains drawn: 'No, no!' he protested, 'I have always loved the light!' (Zimmermann, 1788, 103).

Frederick the Great died at twenty minutes past two on the morning of 17 August 1786.

How has posterity chosen to judge our hero? One of the better-founded observations was current in Frederick's lifetime and shortly afterwards, namely that the king had concentrated authority in himself to an excessive degree, and that, when he was aware that his successor was his uncharismatic nephew Frederick William, he had made no provision for his work to be carried on other than by the sovereign. Reservations like these were, however, the province of the intellectuals and the political commentators. For many years yet the memory of Frederick was a matter of awe and fascination for the ordinary public, and it was for a receptive audience that the veteran J.W. von Archenholtz penned his *Geschichte des Siebënjahrigen Krieges in Deutschland* (1791), a compound of unpedantic history and personal recollection.

The Frederician age was abruptly terminated in the years 1806–7, when the Prussian forces went to their defeat at the hands of Napoleon Bonaparte, and the army and people suffered a near-total collapse of will. This new soldier-sovereign was in the habit of passing a number of not very well informed comments on the generalship of the old king. He doubted, for example whether the 'oblique order' had ever really existed. Frederick's observations on Napoleon, if we can imagine such a thing, are perhaps of more interest, and they had to do with his grasp of the potential of the French nation, and its responsiveness to leadership. The Europe of the *ancien régime* was familiar with the notion that despised French soldiers, if commanded by somebody like Frederick, would have been capable of great things (Guibert, 1778, 129–30; Warnery, 1788, 235; Archenholtz, 1840, I, 115–16). As early as 1743, writing to Voltaire, Frederick scored a prophetic hit that was more impressive, because better considered, than Rousseau's famous statement about something remarkable coming out of Corsica. He expressed his liking for the French nation, and added:

> Broglie and others more incapable still have to some extent tarnished its ancient splendour. Yet this is something which may be restored by a king who is worthy to command that nation, who governs with wisdom, and who gains the admiration of the whole of Europe.
>
> A prince like this will find it a task worthy of his talents to make good what other people have damaged. There can be no glory greater than that which is acquired by a sovereign who defends his subjects against their embittered enemies, and who proceeds to change the face of affairs and compel his foes to come to him to beg for peace.
>
> I would be prepared to express my humble admiration for what this great man may do. Nobody among the crowned heads of Europe will be less jealous of his achievements. (15 September, *Oeuvres*, XXII, 140)

Inside Prussia, after the disasters of 1806–7, Old Fritz seemed to have died twice over. In historiographical terms the breach in continuity ran very deep, for the Romantics, the Neo-Classicists and the Nationalists were inclined to associate the memory of Frederick with a dispensation that was dry, artificial and non-German. Thus the retired major Carl von Seidl conceded in 1821 that it would be thought eccentric of him

> to write about Frederick at a period when he no longer offers fashionable reading-material . . . I accept the risk of being consulted by just a couple of grey-haired veterans of Frederick's school, or a few of his last contemporaries . . . If Athens and Rome exiled so many of their great men, or put them on trial, at least they remembered them after their deaths, and honoured them in histories or monuments. There must be, there *will* be a time when it will once more be acceptable to call to mind the great deeds of Frederick. (Seidl, 1821, v–vi)

Within less than twenty years Seidl's wish was amply fulfilled. The credit goes largely to the labours of the provincial schoolmaster J.D.E. Preuss, whose multi-volume *Friedrich der Grosse* was published as nine volumes of narrative and supporting documentation between 1832 and 1834. This work signalled the awakening of a genuinely historical interest in Frederick. It also encouraged the Prussian bureaucracy to compete with the National-Liberal movement in its newly professed admiration for Old Fritz, who was beginning to emerge as an all-German hero-figure. Preuss, as a loyalist and conservative, was accordingly commissioned by Frederick William IV to supervise the publication of the great series of Frederick's *Oeuvres* (30 vols, 1846–57).

By that time Frederick had recovered his place in the public imagination. This process was to a great extent the work of the skilful populariser Franz Kugler, who brought together anecdotal tradition and the findings of Preuss in his *Geschichte Friedrichs des Grossen* (1840).

In 1842 a young and largely self-taught Silesian artist, Adolf Menzel, engraved the illustrations for a new edition of the Kugler biography. These pictures were widely acclaimed, and they encouraged Menzel to embark on the celebrated setpieces of *The Round Table at Sans Souci* (1850), *The Flute Concert* (1852), *Frederick the Great on his Travels* (1854), *The Night of Hochkirch* (1856) and *The Interview of Frederick and Joseph II* (1857). Menzel's career was a long and active one, and it was as the most celebrated artist of Germany that he made the magnificent plates that appeared early in the twentieth century in the German edition of the *Oeuvres*. Menzel exerted a powerful influence on his near-contemporaries Robert Wartmüller, Arthur Kampf and Wilhelm Camphausen, and we still see Frederick and his times through the 'primal image' established by this remarkable man. His draftmanship was informed by precise observation, and his sympathy for the rococo style was of a different order from that expressed in the ormolu-laden knick-knackery of the apartments of the nineteenth-century millionaires.

Menzel's feeling for the individuality of characters, events and landscapes has its counterpart, in the medium of historical literature, in Thomas Carlyle's *History of Friedrich II of Prussia* (1858–65). Carlyle despised the professional historians, and these prickly gentlemen have repaid him in similar coinage, but his work represented a triumph over the inadequacy of the sources, the absence of reliable maps, and the miseries of contemporary travel. Carlyle set out to visit the sites of all of Frederick's major battles, and his record of the landscape of pre-Industrial Revolution Europe is enough by itself to make his book of enduring value.

Much of what we know about Frederick, in a more 'scientific' sense, derives from the extraordinary flowering of historical studies in the later decades of the nineteenth century.

One element in the new Frederician historiography was given wide prominence by Theodor von Bernhardi, whose *Friedrich der Grosse als Feldherr* (2 vols, 1881) became the standard military biography. Broadly speaking, Bernhardi and the other historians of the Prussian 'establishment' liked to represent Frederick as the practitioner of a style of warfare which corresponded closely to the energetic campaigning of Napoleon Bonaparte and von Moltke the Elder. Thus the invasion of Bohemia in 1757 was hailed as a prefiguring of the events of 1866 and 1870 (Bernhardi, 1881, I, 2; Ollech, 1883, 28).

Another school, predominantly civilian, and headed by Hans Delbrück, maintained that Old Fritz was a creature of his times and that he chose as he saw fit from the whole arsenal of weapons available to him, ranging from ambitious schemes of destruction, down to the *Ermattungsstrategie* of waiting and attrition. Reinhold Koser (the future author of the most scholarly and balanced of the biographies of Frederick (effected a compromise of sorts, and in 1912 the retired *Generaloberst* Count Schlieffen made a study which indicated that the opening of the campaign of 1757 indeed fell short of what was required for a strategy of annihilation (see Boehm-Tettelbach, 1934, 24).

Delbrück, however, was one of those people who draw their vital force from confrontation and controversy, and the argument about matters of detail was prolonged into the 1920s. The debate had been given a new lease of life by the alleged shortcomings of the usually excellent history of the wars of Frederick the Great, by the Second Historical Section of the German Great General Staff. The first volume appeared in 1890, and the rest followed at irregular intervals until the outbreak of the Great War killed the series at a nineteenth tome, just short of the battle of Torgau. One of Delbrück's pupils, Rudolf Keibel (1899), sought to overthrow the Staff's version of Hohenfriedeberg, and the Austrian historian von Hoen proceeded to make heavy revisions of the accounts of Prague and Kolin (1909 and 1911).

Nowadays the quarrel between Delbrück and his opponents wears something of the character of a period piece, but its effect has been a damaging one, for it presents the student with a great mass of monographical and periodical literature which remains as much a deterrent to inquiry as an aid to our understanding of Frederick the soldier. We must regret that the antagonists took up their entrenched positions before the publication of the full run of the *Politische Correspondenz* (which is mainly on military affairs) made it possible to take in a broader overview of Frederician warfare. Who finally got the better of the argument? Delbrück and his school have the credit for illuminating aspects of Frederick's strategy which would otherwise have escaped the readers of the patriotic histories. Subjectively, Bernhardi and the like were better at grasping the essence of Frederick, who pursued the offensive option with the more overt enthusiasm than any other commander of the time.

A further controversy was fuelled by those politically minded historians who recalled the work of Frederick in order to persuade Germany of the reality of Prussia's mission of leadership and unification. Frederick's campaigns were now seen almost in the light of holy crusades, which began the process of excluding the Popish and half-Slavonic and Magyar Austria from the German body politic. In 1871 an old Protestant theologian, Dr Ewald, was actually consigned to prison for suggesting that Bismarck had followed Frederick in waging unjust wars against the Austrians (Sagarra, 1974, 32).

This bitter feud was revived towards the end of the century by Max Lehmann, who claimed (1894) that the clash of 1756 proceeded from the collision of two offensive schemes – not just the design of the allies to humble Prussia, but also Frederick's ambition to conquer and hold Saxony (see p. 83). Lehmann gained the support of Delbrück, but he was rejected by the more narrowly nationalistic of the German historians.

Rudolf Augstein concludes: 'The king's mentality lends support to the case of Lehmann and Delbrück, but the sources speak for the opposition' (1968, 176). This documentary material, or rather the lack of it, lay at the heart of the problem, for the unwillingness of the Prussian archivists to open up their collections served to create the impression that they indeed had something sinister to hide. The papers of Quintus Icilius disappeared without trace into the royal library, as we have seen, and likewise the revealing diaries of the staff officer Gaudi were published only in extract. It was therefore no coincidence that Frederick's *Exposé du Gouvernement Prussien* (1776) slipped into print in the revolutionary year of 1848: 'At that time people probably had little consideration or respect for the kind of objections which, only a few years earlier, had appeared quite dangerous and insurmountable' (Hintze, 1919, 5). This comment refers to the decision which had been taken in 1843, on the advice of Ranke and Alexander von Humboldt, not to publish the two *Testaments Politiques*. In the second half of the century, when order had been re-established, only a few scholars of unimpeachable loyalty were allowed to make verbatim notes of the sensitive 'Rêveries Politiques' of the *Testament* of 1752, and the complete documents appeared in a complete edition only in the year 1920, which again coincided with a period of political upheaval.

After the collapse of the old Western civilisation in 1918, the record of Frederick was appropriated or rejected by ideologies and racialisms without overmuch regard for the realities of the eighteenth century. Old Fritz, or rather a certain vision of Old Fritz, was undoubtedly incorporated into the heart of National Socialism. In *Mein Kampf* Hitler expressed his admiration for the old Prussian sense of discipline, and he and his followers hailed Prussia as the germ cell of the new order. The old Holy Roman Empire and Austria had been too weak to strike deep roots, but Frederick was seen as the man who re-founded the *Reich*, laying the foundation on which Bismarck and Hitler could build (Baeumler, 1944, 44). 'Therein resides the importance of Frederick in historical perspective. We accordingly remember him with veneration. We date the construction of the Third *Reich* from the ceremony in the Potsdam Garrison Church on 21 March 1933, and we lead the Hitler Youth every year to the sarcophagus of the great king' (Wolfslast, 1941, 165).

The deposed Kaiser telegraphed to Hitler from Doorn, in the triumphal year of 1940: 'The Anthem of Leuthen is resounding in every German heart' (Augstein, 1968, 8). Likewise in the catastrophe of 1945 Josef Goebbels could turn to Carlyle and draw encouragement from the description of how Frederick's Prussia was repeatedly rescued from the blackest disasters: 'Why should we not also pin our hopes on a similarly miraculous transformation in affairs?' (Mittenzwei, 1979, 211).

It is historically absurd to ask what Frederick would have made of the Third *Reich*, otherwise we would have imagined his surprise at the Danubian accents of the Führer, or the physical dangers he might have undergone from his association with Masons and Hebrews. The monarch who slipped into Berlin by a figurative back door in 1763 would not have recognised himself as the same individual who, in the film *Der Grosse König* (1942), presided over a victory parade of the homecoming veterans. This question of style is not without some importance, for the genuine old Prussian military tradition was one of understatement. Hans Bleckwenn recalls the fate of the mortal remains of Frederick's court dancer Barbara Campanini, which were re-buried with full military honours in 1857 in mistake for the body of Winterfeldt. 'It is only too evident that Prussia is not the right setting for displays of bombastic romanticism. Winterfeldt himself, who was not averse to jokes and charades, would probably have found it extremely funny' (Bleckwenn, 1978, 190).

In the decades following the Second World War, the name of Frederick was repeatedly invoked in the debates as to whether it was possible to discover elements of continuity between the old Prussian state and Hitler's new order. In West Germany these arguments engaged the attention not only of the professors but of mass communicators of the calibre of Rudolf Augstein and Marion Dönhoff. It is relevant to call to mind that the population of the *Bundesrepublik* embraces large numbers of refugees from the historic lands of the Prussian monarchy, and that these folk and their descendants form a significant part of the leadership of army and state. In 1967 the 'Prussians' comprised almost exactly half of the officer corps of the *Bundeswehr* (Nelson, 1972, 73). Frederick himself, and his father, now rest in the castle of Hohenzollern in Württemberg, whither the bodies were removed in 1945.

The other Germany has inherited more of the physical legacy of the royal regime (Mittenzwei, 1979, 212), and every year brings fresh evidence of the search for formulae that will reconcile Marxism-Leninism with the growing popular interest in Frederick and his Prussia. In the German context every historical statement is inevitably a political statement, and it was not possible for the East German authorities to take a course as simple as the one adopted by the Soviets, of warming up an entire nineteenth-century school of nationalistic historiography. Instead we have the process of 're-historisation', by which Luther, Bismarck and other figures are found to have displayed tendencies that were 'progressive' by the standards of their time.

In the East German popular mind the standing of Old Fritz is directly associated with the fate of the great equestrian statue by Christian Daniel Rauch, which was first unveiled in the Unter den Linden in 1851. This monument escaped the destruction which overtook the Berlin Schloss and Arsenal, but the symbolism of the eastward-striding figure was so strong that in 1950 it was banished to a remote corner of the Sans Souci park. Those who made the effort to track it down used to find Old Fritz lying on his side behind a wooden fence, and the sight of those brazen eyes, staring so fiercely at such a short distance, produced an effect directly comparable with that of the human original.

In 1963 Frederick took the short journey to the Sans Souci Hippodrome, where he was put on open display. Finally in 1980 he was declared by the Politburo Secretary-General Erich Honecker to be 'one of those works to whom the people have a right', and he was restored to his place in the Unter den Linden. Ingrid Mittenzwei's biography of Frederick had just been published, the first of its kind in the GDR, and the public was told that there had been elements of compromise and flexibility, even in the way that Frederick had set out to preserve the old order. In the eastern provinces of Germany today the dialectics of the thing are of little interest to those quiet, decent and friendly folk who were the root stock of Frederick's musketeers and grenadiers. However, the fire and the enthusiasm enkindled by the very mention of Old Fritz, who has been dead these two hundred years, will give the traveller some inkling of what it was that made these people the terror of Catholic Europe.

CHAPTER NINE
Frederick and War

Frederick's theory and practice of war are of unique interest in the annals of military history. He was, like Napoleon, supreme director of army and state, but he was also a genuine intellectual who brought to his trade the detachment of an outsider.

It was natural in Frederick to consider his profession in the widest possible context. In religious matters he moved from a Calvinistic determinism (which he probably adopted just to annoy his father) to a deism which he was prepared to uphold in the face of the outright atheism which became fashionable in some intellectual circles in the 1770s. He believed that Christianity in its various forms, of which Protestantism represented the least objectionable, served a useful social purpose, but Frederick's God remained a distant one, who could have no conceivable interest in the outcome of wars, let alone the welfare of the individual (*PC* 14288; Catt, 1884, 110).

Frederick had an acute awareness of the place of his own time in the unfolding of history, and on the whole he was encouraged by what he read and observed. Material and intellectual conditions had certainly improved in recent centuries, and he traced this betterment to the gradual diffusion of the wealth of the New World, to the invention of printing, and to the establishment of an efficient system of posts. He conceded that the eighteenth century was perhaps mediocre in comparison with more heroic periods, 'but I must say to its credit that we see none of those barbaric or cruel acts which disfigure earlier ages. Nowadays we have less trickery or fanaticism, but more humanity and good manners' (to Voltaire, 13 October 1742, *Oeuvres*, XXII, 115).

When war did break out, Frederick explained that a certain regulative process came into effect. 'Europe divides into two great factions . . . The consequence is a certain balance of forces which ensures that any one party, even after great initial successes, is hardly any further forward by the time we conclude a general peace' ('Pensées et Règles', 1755, *Oeuvres*, XXVIII, 124).

Moreover the powers of Europe had adopted the system of regular, standing armies which had been perfected by Louis XIV in the 1680s. This phenomenon had been made possible by centralised government, and the ability to levy taxes (Kann, 1982, 30–1), and Frederick was convinced that the effects were almost wholly beneficial. The regular armies gave occupation to the unemployed, without troubling the useful workmen or the tillers of the field. They promoted the circulation of money, and their very cost served to curtail the length of wars.

What was the general character of the leadership which Frederick gave to the state and the institution of the army? The expression 'Enlightened Absolutism' was first employed in the correspondence of Diderot, first put into print by Raynal in 1770, and introduced to historical terminology by W. Roscher in 1847. It was intended to describe the efforts of those monarchs who, ruling despotically but not tyrannically, sought to ameliorate the condition of their subjects by rational reforms. Frederick was familiar with the guiding principle of 'Enlightenment' from his sympathetic reading (in French translation) of Christian Wolff's *Vernünftigen Gedanken von gesellschaftlichen Leben der Menschen* (1721). Wolff broke with the biblical formulae of the old German political scientists. He adopted the 'natural' and the 'rational' as his guides instead, and declared that the purpose of the state was 'the promotion of general welfare and security'. Voltaire was acquainted with the nature of Frederick's reading, and he wrote to him in 1736 of his joy when he

> saw that the world holds a prince who thinks like a human
> being – a philosopher prince who will be good for mankind . . . I
> assure you that the only truly happy kings are those who have
> begun, like you, with a process of self-education, learning to
> know mankind, loving truth, and detesting persecution and
> superstition . . . Under your rule Berlin will become the Athens
> of Germany, and perhaps of the whole of Europe. (Undated,
> *Oeuvres*, XXI, 7, 23)

Frederick, as reigning king, in some ways lived up to the expectations of the *philosophes*. Soon after his accession he decreed the abolition of torture, and reappointed Wolff to his university post. He delighted in the gradual retreat of superstition to the peripheries of Europe; he tolerated, or rather remained indifferent to, the criticisms of his person, and he adhered to an unassuming style of kingship that was as far divorced from the baroque pomp of Louis XIV as it was to be from the trappings of the bloated Caesarism of the Napoleonic age (the idea of Frederick wearing a crown is quite ludicrous). It would be difficult, however, to maintain that Frederick's notion of the ruler amounted to anything more pretentious than the idea of responsible stewardship that he presented in his *Essai sur les Formes de Gouvernement et sur les Devoirs des Souverains* (*Oeuvres*, IX).

Frederick was neither particularly effective as a despot, nor 'enlightened' in all his actions. The first of these statements may seem to be contradicted by the atmosphere of bleak servitude which oppressed so many of the foreigners who found themselves in Prussia. Likewise Frederick's interventions in the most detailed matters of army and state, and his accessibility to private petitioners, appear to indicate an extraordinary degree of personal control.

All of this presents only the most superficial resemblance to a militaristic totalitarianism on the twentieth-century model. If 70 per cent of the revenues were devoted to the army, it was because the state had so little else to spend its money on – education, the care of the sick, and the management of law and local administration were largely funded from local sources (Bleckwenn, 1978, 61–2). The number of state officials was small, amounting to only 2,100–3,100 functionaries of all kinds in 1754, of which about 640 made up the central bureaucracy, from ministers down to copy clerks. The officialdom was also unresponsive to royal control, for there were opportunities for obstruction at every level, from the conservative Colleges at the centre, to the local *Kriegs- und Domänen Kammern*, where the interests of the nobility were often paramount (Guibert, 1778, 54–5; Küster, 1793, 154; Johnson 1975, 152–3). Frederick rarely travelled to see the far western territories or East Prussia. Silesia more than any province counted as his personal domain, and yet even here he acquiesced in the frauds that were being practised against him by the minister of state von Hoym.

The military machine itself escaped despotic control. The officers were the soul of obedience in operational matters, but they never allowed themselves to be overborne by the king in weighty matters of conscience (see p. 334). An appropriate tip or bribe was enough to secure the foreigner ready access to the Berlin Arsenal, or to the arms factory and the state prisoners at Spandau. The plans of the Prussian fortresses, which were counted as a great secret, were shown to Guibert in 1773 by Major Prince Hohenlohe.

Likewise Frederick's 'Enlightenment' knew some important limitations. He could never bring himself to believe that mankind was basically good, or that an increase in knowledge would bring with it an advance in virtue. Moreover he dashed some of the most cherished hopes of the *philosophes* when he embarked on war in 1740. The relationship with Voltaire was kept up, with some notorious interruptions, until Voltaire died in 1778,

But the myth of Frederick as philosopher-king had been
destroyed and the intellectuals who followed the lead of
Voltaire would come, step by step, to reject the concept of
enlightened autocracy . . . Frederick earned their admiration
for his patronage of the arts and sciences and for his religious
toleration. But the grim side of the king's personality and
accomplishments, particularly his military record, prevented a
further theoretical development of the concept of the
philosopher-king. (Johnson, 1982, 15)

The notion of Frederick as an 'Enlightened Absolutist' does not
survive a close examination. Should we extend more charity towards
another concept, also much used in connection with Frederick and
his times, namely that of 'Limited War'?

By 'Limited War', we understand a kind of warfare which is
waged within a framework of deliberate or enforced restraints. This
idea has become part of the currency of modern strategy, where the
constraint is exercised by the fear of nuclear incineration. Historians
have received all the greater encouragement to explore the workings
of checks in past ages, and the eighteenth century appears to most of
them as a classic age of such 'Limited War', delineated clearly from
the more full-blooded style of warfare waged in the Revolutionary
and Napoleonic periods.

Almost certainly the dividing line has been too sharply drawn. If,
however, we do not equate a measure of restraint with something
that is totally devoid of importance, interest and energy, then the
wars of the middle of the eighteenth century do measure up well to
most of the definitions of such 'Limited War'.

We must first consider one of the most fundamental limitations
of all, that of objectives. Something of consequence began to brew in
Europe in the middle 1750s. Indeed, just before the outbreak of the
Seven Years War the Lisbon earthquake of 1755 worked as great a
shock on the optimistic complacency of society as did the sinking of
the *Titanic* in 1912. The aims of the hostile alliance, if they had been
accomplished in that war, would have reversed the progress which
the new Prussian monarchy had made in Europe (see p. 242), and
exercised the most profound effects on the history of the continent.

It is therefore easy to ignore the restraints that were still being
observed. Most important, the allies never intended to overset the
regime in Prussia, let alone impose a new form of government or a
new ideology. It was significant that in 1761, when victory appeared
to lie within her grasp, Maria Theresa wrote to Daun that her purpose
was just 'the reduction of the house of Brandenburg to its former state
as a rather secondary power . . . comparable to the other lay elec-
torates' (Ingrao, 1982, 59).

From the pen of Frederick we know of the limiting effects produced at this period by the cost of the great standing armies, and the working of the balance of power (see p. 288). With specific reference to the conduct of the Seven Years War the veteran Warnery adds:

> The allies left Poland at Frederick's disposal, and this country furnished him with an abundance of recruits, horses, cattle and cereals. Every winter they allowed him the time to restore his army, and the Austrians, instead of harassing him at that season, concluded various conventions which all worked to his advantage. Moreover, the enemy corps which penetrated to Berlin and Potsdam only went through the motions of ruining the factories that produced the weapons and other commodities. (Warnery, 1788, 535)

Nor should the narrow and shaky foundations of the coalition be overlooked, or the lack of single-mindedness with which the combatants pursued their aims. Austria and France disliked the thought of Russia intervening in Central Europe as a full belligerent power. They were anxious lest the Russians should establish themselves permanently in East Prussia, and with the support of the Saxon-Polish authorities they dissuaded the Russians from taking the free city of Danzig by force of arms – a venture that would have greatly alleviated the supply problems of the Russian army (e.g. Brühl to Riesedel, 21 December 1760, in Brühl, 1854, 169).

Such political and grand-strategic limitations as these by no means excluded a lively conduct of the actual campaigns. In this respect the Seven Years War was different in kind from anything that Europe had experienced before (Pauli, 1758–64, IV, 303–4). Lossow drew attention to the forced marches, the winter campaigns, and to the bloodiness of the battles even in Napoleonic perspective (Lossow, 1826, 10), and Christian Heinrich von Westphalen, secretary to Ferdinand of Brunswick, believed he could detect the consequence of the massing of the rival armies on the north German plain, as compared with the more dispersed operations in earlier wars. 'But this higher rate of activity is not simply the result of the working of numbers and the constriction of space. It also derives from changes in the conduct of war, which in turn may be ascribed to refinements in the military art, and the particular genius of the commanders' (Westphalen, 1859–72, I, 131–2).

No direct relationship exists between the degree of humanity with which a war is waged and the totality of the conflict. Indeed, some of the most 'limited' wars are the dirtiest of all. It is therefore a matter of no great consequence that the celebrated 'politeness' and 'humanity' of eighteenth-century warfare cannot always be detected in the contests over Silesia. The possible reproach of barbarism did not deter Frederick from giving serious consideration in 1761 to the idea of employing a flame-thrower, proposed by a Captain Henry O'Kelly in England. If the device was never employed in war, it was almost certainly because O'Kelly could not guarantee to propel the jet to three hundred paces, as Frederick demanded (*PC* 12755).

The goods, the liberty and occasionally the lives of the civilians were by no means sacrosanct. In the context of the Seven Years War, the word 'atrocity' is usually associated with the ravages of the Cossacks in Pomerania and the Neumark. However, the Cossacks behaved no better when they came under Prussian control in 1762, and one can only guess at the kind of destruction that would have been worked by the Crimean Tartars if, as Frederick had intended, they had descended on Hungary and the countryside around Vienna.

Plundering and vandalising of property became almost a matter of routine when some of the Prussian armies passed through inhabited areas, or quartered themselves there (*PC* 10702, 12504; Mitchell, 1850, I, 319; Bräker, 1852, 143; Catt, 1884, 352). In Moravia in 1742 Frederick employed this practice as an instrument of strategy, and in general the habits of the royal army were usually compared unfavourably with those of Schwerin and Prince Henry, which observed strict discipline (see p. 231). We reproduce without comment two extracts from Frederick's correspondence:

> Among his possessions Count Brühl has two or three estates in the neighbourhood of Leipzig and Nossen. It would be nice if you could detach Lieutenant-Colonel Mayr with some of his free companies to beat up those places a little – only I don't want to know anything about it. (To Keith, 12 December 1757, *PC* 9580)

> Madam, I am in receipt of your letter of the 15th. As regards the subject matter, I can only declare that all the information I have is that some troops, as they were passing by Nischwitz, were told that there were some weapons concealed in the house there. They entered the establishment to carry out a search and ascertain the truth of the story. All the damage on this occasion was done by the local people, whom nothing could dissuade or divert from assuaging their anger at the expense of those who, they declared, were the cause of their misfortune and that of Saxony in general. (To Countess Brühl, 28 February 1758, *PC* 9799)

Altogether the eighteenth century offers no exception to the general rule that 'war is hell'. Its reputation for moderation comes from the fact that atrocities in other times were generally worse, and that the civilian peoples were more often the incidental victims of careless brutality than the deliberately selected targets of military operations.

The plundering of Saxony had a justification of sorts in Frederick's desire to limit the extent to which the material resources of his own state were committed to the war. In the event, Saxon money and fodder made a very significant contribution to the Prussian effort. Manpower was another commodity which Frederick was anxious to conserve, for Prussia was thinly peopled in proportion to the extent of its territories, and he equated the size of the population very closely with the inherent strength of the state. Hence he made up the ranks of the army with foreigners, and he wrote what has become a celebrated passage in his *Political Testament* of 1768:

Society and government would perish, if the labour of the peasants did not render fertile the arid heart of our countryside. These useful and hard-working men are the apple of our eye. We must accordingly spare them, and draw recruits from the land only on occasions of utmost necessity. (Frederick, 1920, 140)

Frederick was also driven to limit the military involvement of the mass of his subjects by his hierarchical instincts, and his love of categorisation. Few people, in his estimation, were capable of grasping what was at stake in matters of policy. He reckoned that in a given state of 10 million people, there would perhaps be about 50,000 who were not fully engaged in working for their daily bread. Out of these, just 1,000 would be men of education and intelligence, and this tiny number would embrace many disparate talents.

Similarly, Frederick regarded the business of fighting as entirely the concern of the regular army, and he discouraged the intervention of all other elements. A cook of the Margrave Carl once captured an enemy, and brought him proudly before the king. Frederick inquired:

'Who are you?'
'A cook.'
'Well then, stay in your kitchen!' (Anon., 1788–9, II, 10)

He could find nothing praiseworthy in the conduct of a woman who had served bravely through several campaigns of the Seven Years War in the guise of a soldier:

It's contrary to nature. I don't want to have any women soldiers in my army. There might be some advantage from them in wartime, but the disorder would be all the greater in time of peace. The women have always had a hankering to wear men's pants, which would give rise to all sorts of confusion. (Anon., 1788–9, III, 43)

Early in the Seven Years War Frederick once ordered Lehwaldt to arm the civilian population against the Russians, but, with this solitary exception, he set himself firmly against the principle of popular resistance to invaders. When he enlisted large numbers of men of military age into the Land Militia in 1757, he intended chiefly to deny recruits to the enemy and secure an *Augmentation* of manpower for the regular army (Dette, 1914, 77). He turned down the request of the islanders of Borkum, in Ost-Friesland, to be allowed to offer resistance to the French in 1757 (Wiarda, 1792–1817, VIII, 392), and in 1759 he rejected a proposal from Prince Henry to revive the project of arming the men of the eastern provinces against the Russians.

From a superficial reading of Frederick's works and correspondence, we might therefore conclude that eighteenth-century warfare corresponded to what some historians have represented it to be – a mechanical parade of armies which went about their murderous business unmoved by emotion, and which killed each other off beneath the impassive gaze of the civilians. However, it is impossible to ignore the existence of deeply felt loyalties and patriotisms of the people, any more than the grudges, blood feuds and racialisms of the battlefield. Most powerful of all was the influence of religious faction, which was associated largely, if not exclusively, with the Seven Years War, after the Diplomatic Revolution had produced an alignment of forces which corresponded roughly with the sectarian divisions of Europe. The Seven Years War, if it was not a struggle about religion, became a war with an important religious content, during which well-informed people, and Frederick himself, were at times tempted to believe that the survival of one or other of the confessions was at stake (Riesebeck, 1784, I, 125; Lehndorff, 1910–13, I, 124; Schlenke, 1963, 231–56).

The massacres at Hohenfriedeberg, Kolin, Rossbach and Zorndorf were powered by the bitter antagonisms among the soldiers. In the same spirit civilians put up armed resistance to the Prussians around Neisse in 1741, in the Moravian-Bohemian border hills in 1742, and possibly also at Domstadtl in 1758. Passive opposition could be more effective still. Simply by denying food and information the civilians could imperil any army which operated in enemy country far from its base (as Frederick experienced in Bohemia in 1744), and he allowed that assistance from the people was one of the advantages of campaigning in one's own land ('Principes Généraux', 1748,

Oeuvres, XXVIII, 49–50; 'Pensées', 1755, *Oeuvres*, XXVIII, 133; 'Des Marches d'Armée', 1777, *Oeuvres*, XXIX, 113–14). Throughout the wars, the Catholics of Glatz and Upper Silesia remained an element of instability in the Prussian army, on account of their loyalty to their religion and to the Habsburgs. These folk were still unreconciled at the end of the reign.

British public affairs were recognised to be a unique phenomenon in the Europe of the time, and it is by no means incompatible with the more conventional interpretations of 'Limited War' that Frederick should have set out to manipulate British political opinion in his favour. He found a receptive general public for the accounts of the victorious Prussian battles and campaigns, and, when the need arose, he sought to move politically active people in specific directions, as in favour of continuing the subsidy to Prussia in 1758 and 1759, or against the ministry of Bute in 1761.

More surprising, perhaps, is the extent to which Frederick and his enemies thought it worth their while to maintain a favourable climate of opinion in continental Europe, where the political tradition was much more authoritarian. Frederick wrote to Voltaire: 'I wage war on my enemies by all possible means' (24 February 1760, *Oeuvres*, XXIII, 70). His weapons embraced official relations, political tracts, outright forgeries, and little satires at the expense of targets like the pope, Daun, Kaunitz and the Pompadour. The narratives were given a certain credibility by the sobriety of the style, and Frederick took care to have them published in foreign newspapers as well as in the Prussian gazettes. In fact much of the undesirable detail was suppressed, 'for some things are better left unsaid' (*PC* 12505), and the style and the timing of the release were conceived 'so as to make the greatest impression on the public in general, and especially abroad' (*PC* 12441), as when Frederick desired to accentuate the allied vandalisms in Berlin in 1760, after the unfavourable publicity given to his recent bombardment of Dresden.

Frederick was not insensible to the opinions of his own subjects. Anxious to disguise the appalling realities of the battle of Zorndorf, he commanded the *Te Deum* to be sung in the churches throughout the Prussian lands. Mitchell found that the officers themselves were kept as far as possible in ignorance of the extent of military failures, like the disastrous end to the campaign of 1761:

His Prussian Majesty very rarely communicates to the Secretary of State (Finckenstein) his plan of military operations. If the attempt succeeds, he sends [him] a *Relation* . . . but when the project miscarries, little or nothing is said of it, and every man is left to make his own conjectures, for His Prussian Majesty never chooses to write on disagreeable subjects. (25 November 1761, PRO, SP 90/78)

If Frederick was willing to join in the contest for opinions with enthusiasm and wit, he was much concerned to limit the spread of his wars into international dimensions which he could not fully control or understand.

Frederick's vanity, his contempt for mankind, and his confidence in his own army made him the worst of allies. He abandoned the French in 1742 and again in 1745. He began the wars of 1740 and 1756 without active partners, and his capacity to carry on the fight was not seriously disturbed when the British terminated their subsidy in 1761. Only the huge military potential of Russia had the power to make him look nervously about for friends.

Frederick's self-sufficiency, according to the Duc de Nivernais, was in part the product of ignorance:

He has a very full understanding of the interests, resources and means of his own power and state, but I believe that he has only a feeble comprehension of how these things relate to other powers. He is totally unaware of the influence which commerce and maritime trade now exert on the political system of Europe. (1756, in Volz, 1926–7, I, 286)

It was not Frederick but the Duke of Bevern who was responsible for the attempt to do battle with the Swedish flotillas on the Baltic estuaries and lagoons in the Seven Years War. Frederick himself renounced the ambition of building a navy, on account of the expense of construction and manning, the unsuitability of the geography, the indecisive nature of sea battles, and the unfamiliarity of the element – 'land animals like us are not accustomed to live among whales, dolphins, turbot and codfish' (to Maria Antonia of Saxony, 23 September 1779, *Oeuvres*, XXIV, 327; also *Political Testaments* of 1752 and 1768, Frederick, 1920, 101, 244).

In a famous passage the historian Macaulay condemned the conquest of Silesia: 'The evils produced by his wickedness were felt in lands where the name of Prussia was unknown; and, in order that he might rob a neighbour whom he had promised to defend, black men fought on the coast of Coromandel, and red men scalped each other by the Great Lakes of North America' (Macaulay, 1864, II, 253). In fact the reverse was the case. The colonial wars had an impetus of their own, and Frederick lived in perpetual fear that the red men would involve him in the Anglo-French quarrels over a wilderness like Canada, whose importance he 'rated at six hundred crowns' (Catt, 1884, 391). It was Galisonnière's fort-building and other causes of friction between the British and French in Canada which more than anything else set in train the process of the Diplomatic Revolution. Writing of East Prussia, Count Lehndorff observed:

> This poor land became a chance victim of the quarrel between the great powers. It certainly offers a wide field for philosophical rumination when you consider that a war which began in America about Nova Scotia should have led . . . through a strange concatenation of circumstances, to the devastation of a kingdom in the far north of Europe. (Lehndorff, 1910–13, I, 137)

Frederick kept himself informed of the course of the consequent struggle in the Channel, North America and India, as far as his maps allowed, but he never relaxed in his determination to distance himself as far as he could from 'those wretched wars about dried fish' (*PC* 8352, 8416, 12287). At least twice he was seized by the vision of an uncontrollable, apocalyptic conflagration that anticipated by two centuries the 'helter skelter' conceived by the evil lunatic Charles Manson (*PC* 13395; Catt, 1884, 110).

In 1778–9 Frederick was only too delighted when he succeeded in divorcing his new quarrel with Austria from the War of American Independence. He wished to know nothing of what the British had to say about North America, and he sent word to the rebel emissary William Lee that it would be a useless gesture for him to enter into any kind of treaty of commerce or recognition with the United States, since he had no navy with which to protect the American trade (*PC* 26195, 26300). Frederick wrote to his old correspondent, Maria Antonia of Saxony: 'In olden times our good-hearted Germans used to believe that they had to take up arms in Europe, when the war trumpet sounded in Mexico or Canada. I now believe we have totally disabused ourselves of this delusion' (23 September 1779, *Oeuvres*, XXIV, 326–7).

It is time to focus more narrowly on Frederick's views about the nature and conduct of war. Frederick, as the somewhat tarnished philosopher, was willing to pretend to Voltaire, Maria Antonia and others that war was a 'scourge', a recurring 'onset of fever', waged by 'bandit chiefs' and 'privileged murderers' who sent men from their homes to cut the throats of strangers in another country.

We should not expect to find too close a correspondence between these admirable sentiments and the practice of Frederick's wars. As a soldier and statesman, he distrusted any declaration of pacific intent that was not inspired by financial exhaustion or the fear of destruction. Frederick believed that a perpetual peace of the kind proposed by the Abbé de Saint-Pierre (1713) could obtain only in an unreal world, where 'mine' and 'yours' did not exist, and mankind was devoid of passions (*Oeuvres*, IX, 129). He was one who was eminently qualified to pronounce on the subject. His own motives for going to war may be summarised as:

(a) the need to anticipate potential invasions of the Prussian monarchy, with its open, indefensible borders;
(b) the ambition for territorial aggrandisement;
(c) that desire to astonish and excel which transformed Frederick the artist and scholar into Frederick the soldier.

In Frederick's view, the study of the conduct of war was an exercise that was essential and intellectually valid: 'The art of war owns certain elements and fixed principles. We must acquire that theory, and lodge it in our heads – otherwise we will never get very far' (Catt, 1884, 214).

In part such principles were to be deduced from a continuous evaluation of one's own experiences, and the officer who failed to make this effort would end his days like the pack mule who followed Prince Eugene on his campaigns, and remained just as ignorant as when he set out. The other fund of information was military history. Voltaire once wrote to Frederick that war must indeed be something frightful, since the enumeration of all the details was so boring. Frederick replied that his friend should not confuse the mere enumeration of facts with true military history, which established the relations between cause and effect and identified fundamental principles (22 February 1747, *Oeuvres*, XXII, 164).

Frederick was himself a historian of some stature. His first accounts of the Silesian Wars were written very soon after the event, in 1742 and 1746, and ultimately re-worked in 1775 as part of the *Histoire de mon Temps*. The Seven Years War was still in progress when Frederick began to assemble the documentary material for another narrative, and he made the writing of a full-scale history one of his first priorities after the peace. A disaster of some kind appears to have overtaken the first draft – it was set on fire by a spark from a chandelier, according to one account, or dragged into the fireplace by the royal dogs – but Frederick is said to have re-written it all again from memory. The preface set out the motivation for the work in some detail. Frederick wished in the first place to show that he had been forced into the war by his enemies. Next, he hoped that his successors would be able to consult his history for useful lessons if war ever broke out on the same theatre again: 'On occasions like this it is possible that some use can be made of the camps in Saxony and Bohemia (which I have discussed in detail), which will shorten the work of the men who direct the armies.' He did not intend that this chronicle or any other should be read in a spirit of servile imitation, for no two situations were ever exactly reproduced: 'Past events serve to feed the imagination and stock the memory. They are a fund of ideas which provide the raw material which can then be refined and tested by the exercise of judgment' (*Oeuvres*, IV, xv, xvii).

On the whole, Frederick's historical works reflect very favourably on his honesty and competence as a writer. His reproduction of numbers and dates is admittedly cavalier, and his treatment of diplomacy is, as we might have supposed, somewhat less than candid. At the same time he is just and generous to his enemies, merciless towards many of his own military mistakes, and ever alive to his obligations as a story-teller.

Frederick's knowledge of the campaigns of the remoter military past was derived from his reading of the wars of Caesar, Gustavus Adolphus, Montecuccoli, Turenne, Luxembourg, Eugene, and above all Charles XII of Sweden, whose meteoric career was replete with dreadful warnings.

Frederick began the process of making war when he drew up one of his 'projects of campaign'. He never varied in the matter of fundamental principles. He claimed that in schemes of this kind the commander must take due account of the nature of the theatre of operations, and the numbers and quality of the rival troops. Military calculations alone were insufficient, for the belligerents might be able to call on the help of allies: 'Hence these projects of campaign are of value only so far as they are in accordance with the political scene' ('Essai' for the Chevalier de Courten, 28 February 1745, *PC* 1738; see also 'Article II, Des Projets de Campagne', in 'Principes Généraux', 1748, *Oeuvres*, XXVIII, 8; 'Pensées', 1755, *Oeuvres*, XXVIII, 123). The commander must conceive his operations on a grand scale, like Prince Eugene, which in the case of Prussia indicated an ultimate drive to the Danube near Vienna. However, it was prudent at every stage to project oneself into the mind of the hostile commander, and face the question 'What design would I be forming if I were the enemy?' ('Principes Généraux', 1748, *Oeuvres*, XXVIII, 41).

Frederick also adhered throughout his military career to the maxim he established for himself in the *Antimachiavel*: 'It is an incontestable truth that it is better to forestall the enemy, than to find yourself anticipated by him.' In part Frederick wished to avert the danger of being overtaken by an enemy offensive, and reduced to fighting a defensive war on his own territory, which was unsuited for the purpose. More positively, he desired to make use of the unique war-readiness of the Prussian army.

Whereas in peacetime the Austrian and Russian troops, and especially their regiments of cavalry, were scattered in distant quarters for the sake of ease of subsistence, Frederick had it in his power to effect sudden concentrations of force in Brandenburg and Silesia, and reach the heart of Saxony or Bohemia before the enemy could mobilise. He was under no obligation to consult ministers or allies, and his regiments were expected to be able to march within six days of receiving the appropriate order, 'the consequence of which is, that the Prussian army is the best disciplined, and the readiest for service at a minute's warning of any now in the world, or perhaps that ever was in it' (Moore, 1779, II, 147–8). Frederick never lost the great advantages he gained from being the first into Silesia in 1740 and the first into Saxony in 1756.

Frederick wrote frequently and eloquently about the advantages of offensive action, and never more so than when he was seeking to instil energy into his commanders: 'One of the falsest notions in war is to remain on the defensive and let the enemy act offensively. In the long run it is inevitable that the party which stays on the defensive will lose' (to the Hereditary Prince of Brunswick, 8 January 1779, PC 27005; see also PC 8352, 8770, 9781, 9823, 9839, 11357, 27140; 'Principes Généraux', 1748, Oeuvres, XXVIII, 8–9, 14, 61, 73, 76; 'Réflexions', 1775, Oeuvres, XXIX, 85; Warnery, 1788, 313).

How was it possible for the Prussians to wage war in such an aggressive style when they laboured under an overall inferiority in numbers? Frederick had a ready answer in his younger years, which was to concentrate his forces and reach a speedy decision by battle (see p. 309). This doctrine was clear and forceful, and Frederick sought on many occasions to put it into effect in the Seven Years War, as the veterans and the patriotic historians pointed out (PC 11150, 11274; Warnery, 1788, 343, 536–7; Retzow, 1802, I, 102; Bernhardi, 1881, I, 17; Gr. Gstb., 1901–14, VI, 57).

However, Frederick's emphasis on the offensive was neither exclusive nor absolute. The Austrian generals certainly never talked about the attack with such enthusiasm as did Frederick, and yet they were the ones who took the initiative at Chotusitz, Soor, Moys, Breslau, Hochkirch and Maxen, and who at Liegnitz planned to bring about the complete destruction of the royal army. It is significant that in the Seven Years War, when Frederick wrote about 'ridding myself of an enemy', or 'a good decisive battle' (PC 9393, 10812), he had in mind no longer 'the total annihilation of the enemy' ('Principes Généraux', 1748, Oeuvres, XXVIII, 79–80), which was now scarcely possible, but winning the time and freedom to redress a deteriorating state of affairs at the other end of the theatre of war.

By the evening of 18 June 1757 Frederick knew that the war was going to be a long one, and that he would have to take drastic measures to stave off his defeat at the hands of the gathering enemy alliance. His celebrated strategy of interior lines was first put into effect in the campaign of Rossbach and Leuthen. It was a potent multiplier of forces, and Frederick could not have survived without it (*PC* 9393, 10559, 10910, 12961, 12995, 13390; Massenbach, 1808, I, 117), but he never regarded it as anything more than an undesirable expedient, corresponding directly to the unfavourable case of a war against a powerful alliance, as outlined in the *Principes Généraux* of 1748:

> in such an eventuality we must know . . . when it is timely to cede ground, sacrificing a province to one of our enemies, while marching with all our forces against the others, and putting forth our ultimate effort to destroy them. Afterwards we can make our detachments. Wars of this kind ruin our armies through exhaustion and hard marching, and if they last for any length of time they will bring us to a bad end. (*Oeuvres*, XXVIII, 16; see also 'Réflexions', 1758, *Oeuvres*, XXVIII, 164; *PC* 12995; Catt, 1884, 148)

In some further strategic dimensions, the Frederician battle fell short of the Napoleonic practice, and indeed of some of the maxims he laid down in his own writings. He stipulated in the *Principes Généraux*: 'It is an ancient rule of war, and I am just repeating it – if you separate your forces you will be beaten in detail. When you give battle you must concentrate all the troops you can – you cannot find a better use for them' (*Oeuvres*, XXVIII, 36). Through miscalculation he had already allowed himself to be surprised by the Austrians at Chotusitz and Soor when his forces were divided. The lesson appeared to have sunk home, and yet in the Seven Years War we discover that Keith was left in command of powerful detached forces while Frederick was fighting at Lobositz, Prague and Kolin. Retzow was absent when Frederick came under attack at Hochkirch, and Prince Henry remained with nearly half the army at Schmottseiffen when his brother was being routed at Kunersdorf. Accident and carelessness account to some degree for this startling gulf between theory and practice. Laubert (1900, 119) goes on to suggest that the value of numerical superiority was not appreciated at this period in warfare, which seems to go against the clear message of the *Principes*. More likely, as Caemmerer indicates, there was no point in heaping up more and more men in a single locality, at a time when armies were not yet broken down into handy semi-permanent corps and divisions in the Napoleonic style:

when you consider that a contemporary army was a unitary force, without organic articulation, you must concede that the difficulty of employing it grew in proportion to its size. Thus, in relation to the conditions of the period, Tempelhoff was quite correct to write about 'burdensome strength', however much scorn Clausewitz pours on the idea. (Caemmerer, 1883, 37)

Sixty thousand troops were about the maximum that could be managed by the command and control machinery of the time.

The divorce between what Frederick taught and what he did was still more evident in the matter of the pursuit: 'Exploit your victories, pursue the enemy to the utmost, and push your advantages as far as they will go' ('Castramétrie', 1770, Oeuvres, XXIX, 92; see also 'Principes Généraux', 1748, Oeuvres, XXVIII, 80; 'Pensées', 1775, Oeuvres, XXVIII, 120–2; 'Instruction für die Cuirassier-, Dragoner- und Husaren-Regimenter', 1778, Oeuvres, XXX, 339). Only the pursuit after Leuthen came at all close to this ideal, and even here Zieten moved so slowly on the trail of the Austrians that he had to be replaced by Fouqué. After his other victories Frederick was held back by the physical and moral exhaustion of his army, the shortage of provisions, or the need to race back to the far extremity of the theatre of war.

Not even the Prussian army could spend its whole time marching and fighting, and Frederick twice saw fit to entrench himself in fixed positions that were as strong as anything of the kind that were fashioned by Field-Marshal Daun. He bided his time at Schmottseiffen in 1759 until the allies declared their intentions, and at Bunzelwitz in 1761 he dug himself in for the sake of physical survival.

Still less to Frederick's liking, in the strategic context of the war, were the increasingly frequent episodes in which the momentum of the campaign was halted on terms dictated by the enemy. The marching-power of the Prussian infantry, and the manoeuvrability of the Prussian cavalry, could be deployed to the best effect only on the plains of Silesia and northern Saxony, 'a terrain where we are assured of victory' (to Henry, 24 March 1759, PC 10797; see also 'Refléxions', 27 December 1758, Oeuvres, XXVIII, 164–5; 'Political Testament', 1768, in Frederick, 1920, 155; Fouqué to Frederick, 2 January 1759, in Fouqué, 1788, I, 77–80; Nivernais, 1756, in Volz, 1908, I, 286; Kunisch, 1978, passim). Simply by withdrawing to the hills which overlooked the plains, Daun was able to nullify the Prussians' chief advantages and bring his own powerful artillery into play.

Frederick was forced to recognise the change in the character of warfare which had been wrought by the Austrian guns and spades, and the result was a new cautiousness in his minor-strategic outlook that was first evident in 1758, and which became more pronounced in the final decades of the reign:

> A general will be mistaken if he rushes to attack the enemy in hilltop positions. The force of circumstances sometimes compelled me to resort to this extremity, but in a war waged between equal forces you can be more certain of gaining the advantage by the employment of deception and speed, while exposing yourself to fewer risks. (Preface, 3 March 1764, to 'Histoire de la Guerre de Sept Ans', *Oeuvres*, IV; see also 'Réflexions', 1758, *Oeuvres*, XXVIII, 163; 'Castramétrie', 1770, *Oeuvres*, XXIX, 5; 'Réflexions sur les Projets de Campagne', 1775, *Oeuvres*, XXIX, 83, 91–2; 'Political Testament', 1768, in Frederick, 1920, 163, 173; *PC* 12904; Lossow, 1826, 11; Kalkreuth, 1840, II, 150)

Utterly irreconcilable with the viewpoint of some of the historians of the German General Staff was the idea that Frederick could ever have made the possession of territory his objective, rather than the violent overthrow of the enemy main force (Gr. Gstb., 1890–3, III, 327). In fact, considerations of territorial control were often paramount in the thinking of Frederick and his opponents, for they related directly to the motive power of the cavalry, artillery and transport, namely the horses (see p. 67). By Tempelhoff's reckoning, a theoretical army of 100,000 men would be accompanied by no less than 48,000 horses. In winter quarters these ravenous creatures were sustained by dry fodder – hay, straw and grain. The great difficulty came when the army went to war, since the dry fodder was so bulky that it could be readily transported only by water. Campaigning did not normally begin 'before the green grass grows' (*PC* 1809, 10725), which permitted the army to avail itself of the fresh fodder on the theatre of war; and, as a matter of routine, powerful foraging parties were sent out during every lull in operations to gather in the hay from the fields, and raid the barns of the peasants for whatever dry fodder might be found.

Both Frederick and the Austrians were adept at exploiting the other's need for the constant intake of fodder. By eating-out the enemy border regions, you could secure yourself against invasion for weeks or months to come, and by penning up the hostile forces in a single area, until it was thoroughly foraged-out, you could make them decamp without the necessity of taking their positions by force. This contest for fresh fields and pastures new provides the motive for decisions that are otherwise inexplicable, and makes sense of many of the long intervals in the campaigns in which nothing in particular seemed to be happening (*PC* 12345, 13332; Stille, 1764, 191; Mitchell, 1850, I, 359).

The greater part of Frederick's instructions to his generals were concerned not with battles or the higher reaches of strategy, but with the routine of feeding, moving and encamping the army.

Whereas the historian can cover the campaigns in superficial narrative sweeps, Frederick had to ensure that the army could be fed from one day to the next. The question of fodder had an important strategic dimension, as we have seen. As for feeding the men, the king never allowed himself to be bound by a rigid system of magazines and convoys. To save time he sometimes took the risk of dispatching the bakery, the supply train and the pontoons ahead of the army to the intended destination. Likewise, when he was executing his rapid marches across the northern plain, he sent word to the commandants of the Elbe or Oder fortresses to have flour, transport and other commodities ready for his use as he hurried by.

The normal marching formation of the army comprised an advance guard, the four columns of the main force, and a rearguard. The advance guard was a corps of picked troops, mostly hussars and grenadiers, and Major-General Yorke explains that this formation had a special place in Old Fritz's scheme of things. In most localities the people were against him, and furnished him with no news of the whereabouts of the enemy:

> He has no remedy for this but to push large corps of troops
> forward as near the enemy as possible in order to see with his
> own eyes their positions. For this purpose, in the beginning of
> the campaign, he names a certain number of battalions and
> squadrons . . . which form the vanguard of the army, and with
> whom he marches in person. This force is sufficient to enable
> him to maintain a post till his army can join him, and in the
> meantime he makes himself master of the advantages and
> disadvantages of the country round about him. (Yorke, 1913,
> III, 224)

During his marches Frederick sought as much as possible to avoid woodland, to minimise the dangers of desertion and being shot up by the Croats, but the cross-country mobility of his army was a remarkable one, as will be noticed by anybody who has tried to follow his tracks for any distance on the ground today. Tempelhoff remarks: 'I took part . . . in all the campaigns of the Seven Years War, and yet I never saw the Prussians deterred by the badness of the roads' (Tempelhoff, 1783–1801, I, 135–6). If all the roads were poor, then any one route was as good as any other. River crossings occasioned little appreciable check to the army's progress, for rivers and canals ceased to present significant obstacles after the French had devised the copper pontoon in the 1670s.

In a normal, unhurried march the Prussian army could cover between twelve and fifteen miles per day, and Frederick accumulated a detailed knowledge of the relations between time and distance on the various theatres of war – three days, for example, were allowed for the eight *Meilen* (forty miles) from the effective head of Elbe nagivation at Leitmeritz to Prague, and four days for the twelve *Meilen* (sixty miles) from Ratibor in Upper Silesia to Olmütz in Moravia. Frederick maintained his superior mobility over the Russians to the end, though by 1758 he could no longer guarantee that he would not be outmarched by Daun.

Every time the army halted during the campaigning season, it was arranged in a 'camp', a word which at that period was synonymous with 'defensible position'. In degree of permanence and strength such camps ranged from simple overnight stops to locations like Schmottseiffen and Bunzelwitz, where the defensive role was paramount.

The camp was selected by the king or commanding general in person. He looked for ground that was high-lying, or at least not overlooked by hills. Woods, marshes, streams or ravines might offer useful flanking support, though most of the villages of Central Europe were lightly built and open, and therefore useless for this purpose. There was a limit to the number of sites which fulfilled all of these considerations as well as being of strategic consequence. 'We find that certain established posts, advantageous locations and temporary rest camps are occupied over and over again – this is the result of making war in the same theatre for some length of time' (Ligne, 1795–1811, XVI, 102). Thus the Austrian armies, like homeless hermit crabs, scuttled into the positions of Schmottseiffen and Torgau after they had been abandoned by Prussian corps.

The mechanics of taking up a position were explained to the regimental quartermasters by Frederick on 6 September 1756, when he established his first camp on enemy soil in the Seven Years War, at Roth-Schönberg in Saxony. He declared that in future he would merely indicate the limits of the two wings of the first line of the army, leaving all the rest to the staff officers and the quartermasters. All the camps, he said, were to be traced according to the lie of the ground, 'without attempting to dress several battalions or regiments on the same alignment' (Ludwig Müller's account, *Oeuvres*, XXX, 261).

The interiors of the Prussian camps were originally ordered in tidy company streets,

but towards the end of the Seven Years War this practice was
changed, for it betrayed the strength of our army to the enemy
from a distance. Frederick adopted a less decorative but more
suitable arrangement. The streets disappeared, and now the
armies encamped in three rows of tents, closely packed
together. This triple line could be changed, as the situation
demanded, into a double row or a single one. It was easy to
spread the army out, and in general devise all sorts of ways of
deceiving the enemy. (Archenholtz, 1974, 36–7)

Quarters of cantonment offered an intermediate resting place
immediately before a campaign began, or just after it had ended,
when it was safe to scatter the troops in the shelter offered by villages
and little towns. Frederick was capable of prolonging campaigns deep
into the winter when the face of strategic affairs demanded it, as in
1740, 1744 and 1759, but as soon as at all possible he withdrew the
army into outright winter quarters, leaving the guard of the frontiers
to a *Postirung* of hussars.

In accordance with the medical notions of the time, Frederick
took advantage of the season of winter quarters in order to have the
troops purged and bled. More usefully, he sought to prevent the men
from sealing themselves up hermetically in overheated rooms. Now
at last the generals could incorporate the recruits and remounts, and
clean up and drill the veterans, 'so as to restore the smartness which
they have lost in the field' ('Ordres für die Generale von der Infanterie
und Cavallerie', 1744, *Oeuvres*, XXX, 122).

Frederick's military life was a long one. As Crown Prince he heard
about the battle of Fehrbellin (1675) from men who had witnessed
the event. He saw his first campaign in 1734, guided by veterans who
were formed in the wars of Louis XIV. He directed his final operations
in 1779, and he died in 1786, less than three years before the French
Revolution. A study of the way Frederick shaped his battles must
therefore be an evolutionary one, taking some account of three
important processes that were at work over a period of years:

(a) the development of the famous Oblique Order,
(b) the very effective response of the enemy alliance in the Seven
     Years War, and
(c) Frederick's long search for countermeasures.

For the sake of convenience we shall accept the Oblique Order in
the wider sense of the term, as applied by Hans Delbrück and others to
the sum of the schemes which determined the character of the
Frederician battlefield until about the middle of the Seven Years War.

In its essence, the Oblique Order was the bringing together of a powerful concentration of force against a chosen sector of the enemy line. This tactic had been employed by Epaminondas when he defeated the Spartan army at Leuctra in 371 BC, and it fired the imagination of military men anew when the early modern world rediscovered the literature of anitquity. Montecuccoli, Folard and others explored this idea in their writings, and very likely the Old Dessauer conveyed the basics to Frederick when the Crown Prince stood under his military tutelage.

The germs of the Frederician Oblique Order are already present in two of the 'Seelowitz Instructions' of March 1742 ('Instruction für die Cavallerie', 17 March, *Oeuvres*, XXX, 33; 'Disposition für die sämmtlichen Regimenter Infanterie', 25 March, *Oeuvres*, XXX, 75), though there remains some doubt as to when Frederick began to put the notion into practice. The historians of the German General Staff maintained that Frederick explored the Oblique Order in a serious way only after the Second Silesian War, and that he did not give it full effect until the battles of 1757. The limited definitions and time-scale of the Staff Historians were, however, disputed by Otto Herrmann, who claimed that the king had sought to employ the Oblique Order at Mollwitz and Chotusitz. With perhaps more detail and conviction, Rudolf Keibel made the same contention on behalf of Frederick at Hohenfriedeberg (Gr. Gstb., 1890–3, I, Part 1, 163; *Urkundliche Beiträge*, XXVII, 278–84; Herrmann, 1892 and 1894, *passim*; Keibel, 1899 and 1901, *passim*).

The details of the thing certainly underwent some refinement. In the innocent 1740s it was still possible for Frederick to believe that the enemy could be dislodged simply by the moral effect of marching at him with shouldered muskets. At that time the Austrians seldom stood their ground. The advance with levelled bayonets appears to have been introduced in 1753 – 'a heroic evolution which presents a *coup de théâtre* unparalleled in the art of war' (Berenhorst, 1798–9, I, 246). However, the very heavy Prussian casualties at Prague in 1757 were directly attributed to the fact that the infantry had marched into the teeth of the Austrian batteries without opening fire, and thereafter firepower began to assume a much higher place in Frederick's scheme of things.

What were the ingredients of the fully-fledged Oblique Order? First came a lengthy march which was prosecuted overnight or from the early hours of the morning, and which was designed to place the army in an advantageous attacking position on the enemy flank or rear. Napoleon deplored such movements across the front of the hostile army, but here Frederick was using the strength of the opposing positions to his own advantage, for the more advantageously the enemy were sited, the less willing they were to come out and disturb him. Moreover, at Zorndorf, Kunersdorf and Torgau the extensive woodlands helped to screen the movement from view, while offering no great obstacle to the Prussian columns.

Once the heads of columns had gained enough ground, the army formed into lines. This was usually accomplished by the simple and almost instantaneous left or right wheel of platoons. The attack was then delivered by a powerful concentration of forces, comprising an advance guard, one or more lines of supporting infantry, a flank guard of cavalry, and up to thirty or forty heavy pieces.

The corresponding 'refused' wing was an impressively long, but actually rather thin line, which reached back from the attacking wing in a staggered formation of echelons (*Staffeln*), which at Leuthen consisted of units of two battalions at a time (the Oblique Order in the narrower sense). The task of the refused wing was to fix the enemy in position, and then, according as the battle went, to exploit the victory or cover the retreat (on the Oblique Order in General: 'Instruction für die General-Majors von der Infanterie', 1748, *Oeuvres*, XXX, 157; 'Instruction' for Lehwaldt, 23 June 1756, *Oeuvres*, XXX, 206; 'Ordre' to Dohna, 20 July 1758, *Oeuvres*, XXVIII, 159–60; 'Instruction für die General-Majors von der Infanterie', 1759, *Oeuvres*, XXX, 266–7; 'Castramétrie', 1770, *Oeuvres*, XXIX, 25; 'Testament Politique', 1768, in Frederick, 1920, 144; *PC* 10103, 10152, 11150, 11238; Anon., 1772, I, 71; Guibert, 1778, 127; Toulongeon (1786), 1881, 200; Warnery, 1788, 112–13; Scharnhorst, 1794, 117; Lossow, 1826, 336).

Two principles appear to have shaped the Oblique Order. First there was the ambition to concentrate overwhelming force on a vulnerable point, which would render it possible for a small army like the Prussian to gain a local superiority.

The second was Frederick's desire to exert the greatest possible control throughout the battle. In military affairs the divorce between intention and reality is notorious, and Frederick might have been speaking for all commanders at all times when he talked with Catt after Zorndorf:

Frederick: That was a diabolical day. Did you understand what was going on?

Catt: Your Majesty, I had a good grasp of the preliminary march, and the first arrangements for the battle. But all the rest escaped me. I could make no sense of the various movements.

Frederick: You were not the only one, my dear friend. Console yourself, you weren't the only one! (Catt, 1884, 162)

The management of large-scale battles was more than usually diffi-

cult in the eighteenth century, which was a period of unitary armies
and linear tactics. A force, once committed to an engagement, was
effectively lost to the control of the commander (Tempelhoff, 1783–
1801, I, 129). Through his time-consuming flank marches Frederick
therefore sought to extract the greatest possible advantage from the
marching-power of the Prussian troops before this degradation of
control set in. It was true that the striking wing was committed
beyond recall once battle was joined, but in his 'refused' wing
Frederick still had a force that was responsive to command – a
consideration that weighed importantly in what he wrote about the
Oblique Order.

The Oblique Order worked to near-perfection at Leuthen, and
Frederick held throughout his life to the ideal of attacking with a
single wing. However, it would probably be misleading to describe
the battle tactics of 1757 as the culminating form of Frederician
corpse-making. They accorded well enough with Frederick's temperament, but they were the product of a lengthy evolution, as we
have seen, and they were themselves to undergo profound changes.

Before long, Frederick had to take stock of some very significant
advances that the enemy alliance was making in the art of war. When
we look at the progress of his immediate enemies, the Austrians and
Russians, it is evident that the balance of military proficiency was
already swinging away from Frederick by the time of the outbreak of
the Seven Years War. Austria entered hostilities as a state whose
army and institutions had been radically changed by the lessons of
the Silesian Wars. The progress of the Russians was almost as dramatic, though it took longer for Elizabeth's armies to become fully
effective in the common struggle.

The allies, and the Austrians in particular, arrived at an astute
and very complete knowledge of Frederick and his army. In the
matter of fundamental institutions the Austrian chancellor Kaunitz
explored the advantages of Frederick derived from a military system
that actually promoted population and manufactures, and from a
nobility which could make its way only by merit and service ('Votum
über das Militare', in Bleckwenn, 'Zeitgenossische Studien', 1974, in
Altpreussischer Kommiss, 1971, etc.). Concerning war on the large
scale, the Austrian major-general Tillier explained to the Russian
ministry on 16 January 1759 that Frederick's seemingly miraculous
survival could be traced to recognisable assets like the internal
qualities of the army, the military character of the government, the
personal leadership of the king, and a strategic geography of rivers
and fortresses which made possible the strategy of interior lines.
'Taking these circumstances into account, we assert that his almost
invariable system is to make a sudden descent upon one or other of the

allied armies' (*Arkhiv Knyazya Vorontsova*, 1870–95, IV, 394).

Matters such as these were a subject of debate in the Viennese cabinet, as Frederick knew from his informants (*PC* 10701, 10838, 10906). The Emperor Francis Stephen, who was not renowned for his military perception, grasped the essentials of the Oblique Order when he told his brother Charles, before the opening of the campaign of 1757, that Old Fritz liked to attack with one wing only, and that his style of warfare demanded a great deal of his troops, who were not always of the most reliable material. All of this, he suggested, might be turned to good account (Arneth, 1863–79, V, 171–2). Finally a direct insight into Frederick's thinking was obtained from documentation like the copy of the *General Principia*, which was captured with Major-General Czettritz at Cossdorf in 1760.

On the practical side, the Austrians learnt to make effective use of their hilltop positions, their swarming Croats, their roving detachments, their French siege experts, their new staff system (which made possible the elaborate attacks at Hochkirch and Maxen), and their powerful artillery (and especially their medium 12-pounder cannon, which, when it fired canister, became the defensive equivalent of the machine gun of the Great War). The Russians too became enthusiastic diggers, and like the Austrians they acquired the techniques of moving their reserves about the battlefield. The necessary procedures were regulated by Fermor's *General Disposition* of 1758, and the points that Buturlin added in 1761, which together made provision for a third line or reserve, the fortification of the flanks of the army, and the dispatch of designated brigades to threatened parts of the position.

By the middle of the war, therefore, Frederick was beginning to encounter an informed and expert opposition. The consequence was the indecisive slaughter at Zorndorf, the disaster at Kunersdorf, and the negative and appallingly costly victory at Torgau. A number of inherent defects had now became evident in the Oblique Order.

First of all, the lengthy flank marches made heavy demands on the troops before they so much as came to grips with the enemy. 'In all the battles of this war, when the Prussians were on the attack, they invariably reached the enemy out of breath' (Warnery, 1788, 310). If Torgau was fought on a cold, wet and murky November day, all the other encounters were staged at the height of those exceptionally hot summers of the Seven Years War.

The strain of the flanking movements told most heavily of all on the train of heavy artillery, whose efforts were so vital for the success of the other arms. Again and again the absence of artillery support contributed to the defeat of the attacking infantry, as witness the destruction of Schwerin's first line after the passage of the swampy meadows at Prague, the failure of the assaults on the rearward Russian position behind the Kuh-Grund at Kunersdorf, and the massacre of the ten leading battalions of grenadiers at Torgau, which Gaudi attributed directly to the exhaustion of the teams which drew the Prussian guns.

Except at Leuthen, which was ground that was very well known to the Prussians, Frederick had been accustomed to plunging into the attack in almost total ignorance of the terrain and of the enemy positions. Now that the allies knew what Old Fritz was about, the Prussians encountered a series of increasingly unpleasant surprises, and a direct challenge to Frederician battlecraft, which had relied so much on the success of the opening gambit.

Where Frederick was able to keep the initiative, as at Leuthen, the geometrical plan of the Oblique Order was sustained to great effect. It was a different story when the enemy were waiting in prepared positions, as at Kunersdorf, or when they made prompt about-turns like Fermor at Zorndorf or Daun at Torgau. The Prussian assaulting wings were devoid of the physical and psychological support that was required to overcome opposition that was as stiff as this. Moreover, as Clausewitz noted, the natural instinct of the commanders was to try to re-establish contact with the rest of the army. Hence at Zorndorf the division of Kanitz veered to the right, out of the axis of the attack, leaving the advance guard to run into the Russians unassisted.

Once things began to go badly wrong, Frederick had no ready means of re-shaping the battle. The cavalry was the only element of the Prussian army which was capable of dealing successive blows on different parts of the field, as at Rossbach or at Zorndorf itself. The infantry of the 'refused' wing could be brought into action only with great difficulty, for it stood in a fixed relation to the striking force, and it lacked the mobility and independence which are the attributes of a genuine reserve.

We now proceed to the third or final stage of our story, in which Frederick went in search of fresh inspirations which might restore his advantage over his enemies. It is a long episode, which embraces not only the last campaigns of the Seven Years War, but the War of the Bavarian Succession. This quest took Frederick up to the very limits imposed by the constitution of his army and the technology of the time.

It is possible, but by no means certain, that Frederick was tempted to follow the example of the Austrians, who had devised a new form of combat, 'those fearsome attacks, *aiming at the total destruction of the enemy*, carried out by separate corps which have no direct communication with each other' (Cogniazzo, 1788–91, III,

276). This was the scheme of Hochkirch, Maxen and Liegnitz, and Cogniazzo writes about it in terms which suggest that it was a matter of general discussion among military men before the French Revolution.

Clausewitz was unaware of the ancestry of this phenomenon, and he attributes the idea to Frederick, citing the detachment of Finck's corps at Kunersdorf, a plan of 8 July 1760 for an attack on Lacy in three columns, and the widely separated offensives of Frederick and Zieten at Torgau (Kessel, 1937, 1). If we accept this reasoning, Torgau emerges as at once the last great stand-up battle of old Europe, and a kind of eighteenth-century Chancellorsville, in which a bold commander divided his already inferior forces. It must be said, however, that hard evidence to this effect is lacking, and that in the absence of documentary support we must be cautious about imposing systems of war on Frederick, who did so much on the spur of the moment. In any case the inter-operation of separated forces was subject to excruciating difficulties at this period, since the various corps and divisions were temporary *ad hoc* creations, and the communications depended upon slow and vulnerable mounted messengers. The Austrians discovered as much when they tried to annihilate Frederick at Liegnitz.

We must turn to Frederick himself for firmer confirmation of the new trends in his thought. During his period of reflection at Leitmeritz, in June and July 1757, he considered whether, instead of using his best troops to spearhead the assaults, he should actually engage the worst – 'for this purpose we can employ the free battalions or other bad units. We can shoot them up ourselves, if they fall back or do not attack with sufficient enthusiasm' ('Aphorismen', 1757, *Oeuvres*, XXX, 237).

The free battalions in question were 'detestable scum' (*execrables Geschmeiss*), raised for the duration of hostilities by cosmopolitan adventurers, and Frederick never regarded them as much more than low-grade infantry, destined to spare his respectable troops by operating in difficult country and secondary theatres of war, or, in the present context, by absorbing punishment in battle ('Réflexions sur la Tactique', 1758, *Oeuvres*, XXVIII, 162; 'Castramétrie', 1770, *Oeuvres*, XXIX, 41; 'Instruction für die Frei-Regimenter oder Leichten Infanterie-Regimenter', 5 December 1783, *Oeuvres*, XXX, 399–406; *PC* 7868, 10702; Jany, 1903, 13–15; Dette, 1914, 78–80).

In the event, nearly all of the free battalions were assigned to the command of Prince Henry, and Frederick did not spare his precious grenadiers the ordeal of inaugurating the attack at Torgau. Possibly his most recent victory at Liegnitz had encouraged him to believe that his troops were, after all, as solid as the men he had led to war in

1756. His troops in that battle were of untypically high quality for that stage in his campaigns, for the previous marches through the wooded hills of Upper Lusatia had afforded ample opportunity for the unreliable elements to desert. Perhaps Frederick had forgotten that his success at Liegnitz was a defensive one, determined by the effect of the 12-pounder cannon that were scattered among his infantry. It is significant that the regiments of Bernburg and Prinz Ferdinand, which took the initiative in the Prussian counter-attack, were mauled very heavily.

Frederick adhered with more consistency to another of the identifiable inspirations which struck him at Leitmeritz, namely that of using ordnance as a key to open the deadlocked battlefront. In earlier times no great importance had been attached to artillery in the general scheme of things, but this arm assumed an altogether greater significance in the Seven Years War, thanks to the labours of Piotr Ivanovich Shuvalov in Russia, and of Frederick's old friend and correspondent Prince Joseph Wenzel Liechtenstein in Austria. Frederick was no great lover of artillery, but the weight of the enemy firepower, and the strength of the Austrian and Russian positions (and those of the French confronting Ferdinand of Brunswick in western Germany), left him with no alternative but to strive to keep pace: 'If this war goes on a few years more, I believe that we shall eventually have detachments of 2,000 men marching with 6,000 cannon. This is ridiculous, I know, but we have to go along with fashion willy-nilly, otherwise we are lost' (to Ferdinand, 21 April 1759, PC 10888; see also 'Castramétrie', 1770, Oeuvres, XXIX, 4, 38; 'Testament Politique', 1768, in Frederick, 1920, 141–2; PC 10265; Warnery, 1788, 357; Catt, 1884, 37).

As a defensive measure Frederick distributed 12-pounder cannon among the battalions of infantry in 1759 and 1760 (PC 11299. He probably used the light 12-pounders made superfluous by his new 'Austrian' medium 12-pounders). This arrangement, as we have seen, stood the Prussians in good stead when they were attacked by Loudon at Liegnitz. For offensive purposes Frederick was much taken with the potentialities of the howitzer, with its high, arching trajectory, and its explosive shells: 'When we attack high ground, we must employ howitzers rather than cannon. When a cannon shot is fired at such a target, it seldom hits. When, however, a shell bursts on a hill, it causes immediate damage and considerable confusion' (Aphorismen', 1757, Oeuvres, XXX, 240; see also 'Instruction für die Artillerie,' 1768, Oeuvres, XXX, 310–11; 'Testament Politique', 1768, in Frederick, 1920, 144, 163; PC 9838, 26433; Mirabeau-Mauvillon, 1788, 156; Guibert, 1803, I, 189).

As a preparation for the artillery bombardments and infantry

assaults, Frederick strove by every means he could to disperse the
enemy concentrations from the hilltop posts. One of the first clues as
to the way he was thinking came from his conversation with Catt on
15 November 1759, when he talked about the means that were open to
him to persuade Daun to leave Dresden and its craggy heights (Catt,
1884, 257). Immediately afterwards, he sent Kleist coursing through
northern Bohemia, and he posted Finck on the plateau of Maxen in
the immediate rear of the Austrians.

The new strategies and tactics were exploited to almost their full
potential in the summer of 1762, when it was a matter of prising Daun
from his hilltop positions overlooking Schweidnitz:

> I am facing 82,000 men, and I have only 76,000 at my disposal.
> This would not be so embarrassing if the enemy (thanks to our
> succession of misfortunes) had not been given the opportunity
> to occupy all the advantageous ground. We cannot think of
> attacking them, without putting our fortunes rashly at stake.
> We must resort to the diversions. (To Henry, 31 May, PC 13742)

We have already seen how Frederick's elaborate programme of raids
and demonstrations persuaded the Austrians to abandon their outlying positions, and reduced their main concentration to a manage-
able size of less than 30,000 men. When it came to planning the
assault on the Austrian rearward position at Burkersdorf, Frederick
placed the corps of Wied and the brigades of Möllendorff and Knobloch in advance of the operation in front of the chosen sector of the
Austrian lines, and he did not require them to make the assault
immediately after a long and exhausting flank march. Likewise he
positioned his massive artillery reserve on a static site at the foot of
the hills, and told it to do all its work from there.

Finally, on the morning of 21 June 1762, the Prussian artillery
opened up to devastating moral effect, and the groupings of infantry
(which had been given precise timings and objectives) worked forward under cover of the re-entrants which led into the right flank of
the Austrian position. We have moved very far indeed from the
parade-like battles of the first campaigns of the Seven Years War (see
p. 240).

In his writings and correspondence after the war, Frederick held
to the artillery-based tactics and the strategy of diversion. Once again
he toyed with the idea of blanketing the enemy's initial fire with the
free battalions ('Testament Politique', 1768, in Frederick, 1920, 163),
and yet once more he did nothing about it in actual operations, when
hostilities returned in the War of the Bavarian Succession. The
problem had less to do with tactics than with the fact that the

Prussian military machine could not admit of infantrymen who might be able to fight out of sight of their officers – the wretched free battalions had as little in common with the loyal Croats of Maria Theresa as they did with the accomplished riflemen of Sir John Moore in the next generation.

Old Fritz was, however, still absolutely convinced of the value of massed artillery, and especially the howitzers. He wrote to Prince Henry on 11 June 1778 that the Austrians would have as many as fifteen pieces for every one of their battalions: 'But by concentrating our howitzers and cannon at a single point we will gain the local superiority, and perhaps be able to beat them. The real difficulty is to make the hole in the enemy line, but once we have done that we will overcome the remaining obstacles soon enough' (PC 26458).

In the same war, the element of diversion was represented by projects only slightly less ambitious than those of 1762. In place of the rampaging of the Tartars, Frederick reposed equally unfounded hopes in the proposed Russian invasion of Galicia, which would have drawn considerable Austrian forces to the far north-east of their empire.

If the Prussian campaign in 1778 was feeble and unsuccessful it was not just on account of the political limitations of the war, the sluggishness of the military machine, or the decline in Frederick's powers. It was also the consequence of the Austrians' grasp of military topography and their mastery of logistics. Ironically, Joseph and his advisers kept their troops so lavishly supplied that they ruined their state treasury in the process, and Frederick, as he began to suspect on 26 August, emerged as the man with the last penny in his pocket, 'and this decided almost as much as a battle' (PC 26640).

To sum up, a body of evidence appears to indicate that Frederick's notions on the battle underwent a continuous evolution, and that, after the Oblique Order failed to meet the demands of the time, he strove in his final campaigns towards two objectives. First, to tease apart the enemy concentrations by means of a programme of diversion, which at the higher level reached grand strategic and political dimensions; second, to employ his massed artillery to open a breach in a chosen sector of the hostile positions.

The Frederick who emerges is no longer the hero-king who existed in 1757, let alone the martyr-king of 1759, but a man of perception, and perhaps unsuspected adaptability and resource. It is odd to find such a close approximation to some of the military practices of Napoleon in a ruler whose views on society and the economy were so little susceptible to change.

In the matter of minor tactics Frederick always had a firm grasp of what was practical and essential (Guibert, 1778, 126; Toulongeon

(1786), 1881, 198; Kaltenborn, 1790–1, II, 55). He certainly put his troops through a series of artificial and demanding drills in peace-time, but his purpose was to sharpen the wits and responses. By learning to do complicated manoeuvres very well on exercise, the officers and men might be able to give a passable rendering of something much more simple in the stress of combat.

One of the fundamental problems of tactics related to the diffi-culty of changing a column (best for marching) into a line (best for firing). Two devices were available. The ordinary parallel march (*Alignements-Marsch, Aufmarsch*) brought the army onto the field in two or more columns of open platoons. The force continued on its way, across the front or around the flank of the enemy host, until a single word of command wheeled the component platoons into line. This stately but simple manoeuvre was the favourite of Frederick throughout his wars.

The *Deployiren* was a more dramatic affair, in which tight columns of closed platoons marched directly at the enemy, then branched out in sub-units which made off to right or left directly to their assigned places in the intended line. This was an invention of Frederick's, and it was thought to have important applications when the terrain was too cramped for the *Alignements-Marsch*, or the commander desired to conceal his strength or intentions from the enemy. The *Deployiren* was described by Frederick in 1748 ('Instruc-tion für die General-Majors von der Infanterie', *Oeuvres*, XXX, 157), and it became one of the most celebrated peacetime evolutions of the Prussian army.

The actual use of the *Deployiren* in warfare was much more limited. According to General Buddenbrock, the movement was first essayed in battle at Soor in 1745 (D. de G., 1767, 17). Thereafter it appeared only when its application was suggested by some peculiar conformation of ground or unpredictable turn of events – as in the narrow valley at Lobositz, the encounter battle at Gross-Jägersdorf, or the complicated deployment of the royal army at Torgau.

Frederick derived his infantry tactics from the Old Dessauer, who had himself observed the practice of Marlborough in the War of the Spanish Succession. Prussian parade ground drills were based on a rolling fire of platoons, each firing four rounds a minute (six from the later 1770s, after the invention of the 'cylindrical', or rather double-ended, ramrod). Once again the reality in warfare differed from the theory, for the scientific repartition of fire among the platoons usually degenerated into a general blazing-away, and the rate of fire sank to a sustainable two rounds per minute. However, the king was not a blind reactionary when he tried to hold as far as possible to the ideal of volley firing. Greater average accuracy could be obtained from smooth-bore muskets in volleys rather than in individual fire, as was shown by Prussian experiments early in the next century. Moreover, directed fire helped to conserve ammunition, and therefore postponed the blunting of the flints and the fouling of the musket barrels.

Again, the classic Frederician linear formations were a proper expression of the technical and social conditions of his time. It would be unhistorical to draw direct comparisons between the tactical forms that were valid in the eighteenth century, and those which were influenced by the development of cheap, rapid-firing rifles one hundred years later. In secret, Frederick deplored the fact that he had nothing in kind to match the Croatian skirmishers of the Austrians, but we should not reproach him for failing to convert his whole infantry into swarms of little men who would have gone scampering over the hills in coats of green. Light infantry was of marginal consequence in the warfare of the time, since only regular troops in dense formation had the firepower and solidity to resist cavalry in open battle, and conquer and hold ground against heavy opposition.

No less importantly, Prussia lacked an institutional base on which Frederick might have built an effective force of skirmishers. The small bodies of Prussian jaegers were recruited from the gamekeepers of the feudal estates, and their rifles, although very accurate, were much slower to load than the smooth-bore musket, which placed these gentry in some embarrassment when they faced anything more dangerous than a deer or a rabbit. The jaegers actually had their rifles taken away from them after some of their people were cut down by the Russians at Spandau on 9 October 1760.

Still less reliance could be placed on the ephemeral free battalions, who were not even composed of decent and steady men like the jaegers. Only at the end of his reign did Frederick lay the foundations of a regular light infantry, when he ordered the constitution of three permanent *Frei-Regimenter*. He had already outlined the tasks he had in mind for them. On campaign they were expected to perform outpost duty and the like. In battle, they could usefully cover the flanks of the army, by occupying any areas of woodland. More significantly, they might be told off to lead the attack, in which case 'they must rush blindly straight into the enemy. It will be absolutely forbidden for them to open fire before they engage in hand-to-hand fighting' ('Instruction für die Frei-Regimenter oder Leichten Infanterie-Regimenter', 5 December 1783, *Oeuvres*, XXX, 401).

This sacrificial role was far removed from that assigned to the Revolutionary or Napoleonic *tirailleurs*, who were to harass the enemy from a distance by skirmishing fire. To that extent, Frederick was still a man of the mid-eighteenth century. In 1761 he had encountered a jaeger lurking in the Nonnen-Busch, just outside the Bunzelwitz camp. The jaeger explained that he had been wounded in the arm by an Austrian, and that he was waiting to exact his revenge:

> Frederick was extremely angry and he replied: 'You ought to be ashamed of yourself! Do you want to be a highwayman, skulking in a ditch! Come out into the open and behave properly, like a Brandenburger and a real soldier!' (Hildebrandt, 1829–35, IV, 61)

The fluid, swift-moving and aggressive action of well-trained cavalry appealed mightily to Frederick's instincts. After the experiences at Mollwitz he made it one of his first concerns to create a force that had the will to carry through an attack upon every occasion without the slightest hesitation. He remarked before the Seven Years War: 'They were besotted with the idea of firing off their pistols. I finally had to make some straw dummies, and I was able to show them that all their pistol shots missed, whereas they cut down every single figure with their swords' (D. de G., 1767, 28–9). Eventually regiments like the Rochow Cuirassiers at Kolin were capable of attacking at a long gallop over a distance of 1,500 paces. Against infantry the Prussian horse advanced *en muraille*, in a solid wall. The formations for cavalry combat were more flexible, and able commanders (like Driesen at Leuthen, or Seydlitz at Zorndorf) sought to gain the enemy flank.

What made Frederick's cavalry better than that of all the other armies? In the first place he owed a great deal to some gifted commanders, among whom we must number people like Wartenberg, Driesen, 'Green' Kleist, Platen, Belling and Werner as well as the famous names of Zieten and Seydlitz. Individual regiments, like the Gens d'armes and the Bayreuth Dragoons, became models of excellence, and the headquarters of the Seydlitz (formerly Rochow) Cuirassiers at Ohlau was revered as the spiritual home of the European cavalry.

Frederick's cavalry was brought together in large bodies in peacetime much more frequently than the Austrian or Russian counterparts, and the sense of cohesion was further promoted by the cross-posting of officers. These circumstances made it possible for the salutary influence of the hussar service to be felt among the dragoons (medium cavalry) and the cuirassiers (heavy, armoured cavalry). These hussars were exceptionally versatile and dangerous folk, and one of their veterans wrote: 'The Seydlitz Cuirassiers may serve as an example to the cavalry of the rest of the world, and yet General Seydlitz himself, who was a great man, and my friend, confessed to me . . . that on a march of any duration he could not guarantee to withstand six hundred good hussars' (Warnery, quoted in Jähns, 1889–91, III, 2, 633). Seydlitz learnt his work as *Chef* of a hussar squadron in the Second Silesian War, and Frederick, throughout his reign, was in the habit of sending parties of the heavier cavalry on attachment to the hussars. Such an interchange was not possible in Maria Theresa's army, where the hussar service was the tribal speciality of the Hungarians.

The Prussian cavalry completed the victories at Hohenfriedeberg and Leuthen, it decided Rossbach almost unaided, and at Zorndorf it redressed the fortunes of the infantry. 'However the brilliance of the cavalry gradually dimmed from the end of the Seven Years War. It ceased to exercise the role which had been peculiarly its own since Rocroi – that of winning battles' (Anon., 1844, 11).

It is striking that Frederick identified himself so enthusiastically with the cavalry, whose greatest days belonged in the past, and accommodated himself so unwillingly to the artillery, which was growing in power with every decade. He could not bring himself to believe that the build-up in his ordnance represented a true advance in tactics. He sent the worst of the recruits to this arm, and he continued to write about its officers in terms of the most bitter contempt. He allowed the gunners no proper structure of command, no proper chief. As a young officer of the Hanoverian artillery, visiting Prussia in 1783, Scharnhorst was surprised at the lack of uniformity in the ordnance, which he correctly ascribed to the lack of supervision on the part of its royal master (Lehmann, 1886–7, I, 35). Indeed, in the matter of artillery design, Frederick did not have the Austrians' knack for striking a balance between the conflicting requirements of hitting-power and mobility. His heavy howitzers had a phenomenal range, but they were almost impossible to drag across difficult country. His celebrated horse artillery, which first appeared in 1759, raced ahead of the infantry but was too slow to keep up with the cavalry.

The business of military engineers in the eighteenth century was the design, building, attack and defence of fortresses. Frederick's relations with these folk were, if possible, still worse than his relations with his gunners. Scarcely one of the Prussian engineers escaped a period of disgrace during his career, and some underwent detention or the threat of physical attack.

There were many reasons why Frederick got on so badly with his technicians. He deplored the expense and weight of the artillery's equipment, and the slow action of fortress warfare accorded ill with his active and restless temperament. Frederick's general ideas on gunnery and fortification, and the strategic use of strongholds, are certainly of great importance and originality (see Duffy, 1985, for

Frederick as the inventor of ring forts), but he remained a military romantic, and in matters of practical detail he could not always impose his will on people who were better at drawing and mathematics than he was. We have lived with Frederick long enough to know how offensive it must have been to him to abdicate any control to others, let alone to men who claimed some acquaintance with the sciences. In August 1778 he sent an officer of his suite to determine the range for the artillery to the hills above Hohenelbe. This clever fellow returned unexpectedly early, having measured out a base line and reckoned the distance by triangulation. There ensued the following conversation:

Frederick: Have you actually been on the hills?
Officer: No, Your Majesty, but . . .
Frederick: And you want me to believe that you know the range?
Officer: With your Majesty's permission, may I explain that through
    a simple geometrical calculation . . .
Frederick: To hell with your calculations! Away with you!
(Schmettau, 1789, 159)

The perfect captain, according to Frederick, was an assemblage of 'contradictory virtues' ('Principes Généraux', 1748, *Oeuvres*, XXVIII, 39) – a man of honesty and a consummate deceiver, sparing his soldiers at one moment, and expending their blood at the next, and somebody who could establish the relationship between great affairs and the tiny details of which they were composed.

The fundamental military prerequisite of courage was of more than one kind. An instinctive bravery was appropriate to the soldier, but something more reflective ought to inspire the officer. Great leaders like Caesar, Condé and Charles XII were spurred on by an obsessive love of glory. 'Such are the different instincts which lead men into danger. There is nothing inherently attractive or pleasant about that state, but you hardly think of the risk once you are in action' (to Voltaire, 28 April 1759, *Oeuvres*, XXIII, 40).

In battle Frederick himself was a stranger to the icy detachment of the archetypal nineteenth-century commander, smoking his cigar on the *Feldherrnhügel*, as Augstein has pointed out. The king was highly receptive to the impressions of the moment (a characteristic he probably inherited from his mother), and often his eye was caught by the incidental details of combat – the moments of tragedy, and the episodes of dearly-bought comedy. A succession of untoward events would arouse him to a pitch of excitement in which the impulse to rush forward, colour in hand, was at one with the urge to betake himself to the rear in despair. One of his aides commented:

> He was masterful in the way he conceived his enterprises, but there was often something lacking in the final execution. He was defective in sang-froid, and he carried into warfare a poet's power of imagination. Thus we encounter excessive haste as at Kolin and Torgau, and panic fear as at Mollwitz and Lobositz, alternating with presumptuous underestimation of his enemies as at Hochkirch and Maxen. (Berenhorst, 1845–7, I, 180)

The air of Olympian serenity was an artifice, sustained by devices like the one noticed by Prince Henry, of preparing 'spontaneous' verses well in advance, so that they could be produced to general admiration at time of crisis.

Frederick's courage, in the gross physical sense, was undoubted. The horses killed under him, the bullet holes in his clothing, the snuff box that was flattened at Kunersdorf, all testify that he carried himself into the heaviest fire. Whereas Joseph II had to put himself in training for war by sleeping for a time on a camp bed, Frederick needed to make only the slightest adjustments in his usual habits whenever he went on campaign. He pursued this spartan, hard-driving way of life with all the more rigour because it sprang from principle rather than from his natural inclinations. He got up at three every morning, and he admitted to Catt, 'It costs me something, I tell you, to rise so early. I am so tired that I long to stay in bed a few minutes more, but I know my business would suffer' (Catt, 1884, 11–12; on this paradox see also Schwicheldt and Nivernais in Volz, 1926–7, I, 183, 284; also Yorke, 1913, III, 229; Zimmermann, 1788, 200–3; Guibert, 1803, I, 232).

As at Sans Souci, Frederick went about in the field clad in boots, black breeches, and the plain coat of the *Interims-Uniform* of the First Battalion of the Garde. He camped in the open field in the Silesian Wars, but in the Seven Years War he spent most of the nights of the military season in whatever house or hut came most readily to hand, assigning one room to his staff, and reserving another for himself. 'Very often the sutlers' tents were standing immediately outside his headquarters, and gambling, music and every kind of din was prolonged day and night. Immediately after table he liked to take a solitary stroll through the scene, and enjoy the happy tumult' (Kaltenborn, 1790–1, I, 30–1). During some of the longer interludes in the operations Frederick was fond of betaking himself to some monastery or noble palace, like those at Seelowitz, Leitmeritz, Camenz, Grüssau, Rohnstock or Kunzendorf, where he found spacious accommodation and the possibility of good talk. He shunned the vicinity of great towns until the campaign was safely over.

Frederick's remaining luxuries became of some importance to

him in the wars. He indulged his love of open fires by having holes knocked through the roofs of his lodgings; he was careful to compensate his landlords, and in 1778 he went so far as to buy a whole house at Schatzlar in Bohemia, which made him, he was amused to think, a subject of Maria Theresa and Joseph. He eagerly awaited the consignments of a fine young white cheese, called *Fromage de la Poste de Meaux*, which came to him regularly in its distinctive pots of white, glass-like earthenware, and 'on his campaigns he took more snuff than ever. He came into close proximity with his soldiers, as he rode, walked or stood among them, and he evidently needed some preventive against the foul stench of those common folk' (Büsching, 1788, 30).

Frederick always attached the first importance to his physical mobility: 'I am up and about when I am ill, and in the most appalling weather. I am on horseback when other men would be flat out on their beds, complaining. We are made for action, and activity is the sovereign remedy for all physical ills' (Catt, 1884, 90). On his campaigns Frederick took with him a considerable string of horses (no less than thirty-six at the beginning of the Seven Years War). These animals were schooled to be calm and responsive, and they derived their turn of speed from their English birth: 'The kind he uses is of the large sort, about fifteen hands or upwards, with strong bones and easy motions, and what he calls the ancient race of English horses (for he does not like the fine, delicate and slight kind)' (Mitchell, 1850, I, 403). Frederick kept a list of his horses on his person, and he all too often had to consult it after his mounts were killed in a battle. Out of consideration for his favourite Cerberus, a fine black horse with a white blaze and fetlock, he decided to ride Scipio instead on the day of Kunersdorf. In the event poor Scipio was killed, and so was a remount.

Frederick's choice of dogs also represented a considered judgment. His favourite kind of animal was a smallish greyhound, a breed of melancholy and nervous aspect, but a dog that was unmoved by gunfire and well able to sustain a day's marching (along with all the necessary canine excursions on the way).

Frederick was a fast if eccentric rider. He never wore spurs, and instead urged on his horse by tone of voice or (to the outrage of Seydlitz) by hitting it between the ears with his crook stick. Frederick wore his stirrups unusually short, by the standards of the time, but he slouched badly in the saddle, and he not infrequently fell off when his mind was on other things.

To the end of his campaigning days Frederick travelled in his coach only when absolutely necessary, and in his old age he could count on the aid of an experienced groom, whom he had inherited from Seydlitz. 'When the king placed his left boot in the stirrup this man was very clever at taking him under the arm in a discreet way, and helping him to swing up into the saddle' (Nicolai, 1788–92, IV, 47).

The one physical disability of Frederick in his prime was shortness of sight, as befitted a scholar. At Lobositz he was forced to ask Ferdinand of Brunswick what he could see of the second cavalry attack, and after the war he admitted his failing to the Prince de Ligne, and explained that he used his telescope as a corrective. However, by *coup d'oeil* the eighteenth century understood not sharpness of eyesight, but the capacity for rapid orientation, judgment and decision which enabled a commander to exploit all the potentialities of the ground. Frederick explained that 'it is possible to learn and perfect this talent, providing you have an innate aptitude for war. The foundation of this *coup d'oeil* is beyond doubt the art of fortification' ('Principes Généraux', 1748, *Oeuvres*, XXVIII, 25).

At the time of Frederick's wars a commander's personal knowledge of the terrain was of an importance which we can scarcely imagine at the present day. It was no coincidence that at Kolin the Austrians beat Frederick on the scene of their peacetime manoeuvres, or that the Prussians repaid them in the same coin at Leuthen. This knowledge was an attribute as valuable as skill in manoeuvre or the capacity to maintain discipline. The name of Fouqué was associated with the topography of the County of Glatz, just as Zieten and Hülsen were at home in the neighbourhood of Meissen. As for Frederick,

> He was no friend of geometry, and perhaps he did not know very much about it. But that defect was compensated for by the vivid impression that was made on him by the forms of visible objects, by the completeness with which his memory could conjure up that vision, and the accuracy and detail that remained in his imagination. All of this enabled him to select the plan of battle best calculated to seize on all the advantages of a given locality. (Garve, 1798, 135)

Second-hand information was no substitute. Frederick might require officers to draw up topographical memoranda, like the one he requested of Carl C. von Schmettau in the campaign of Chotusitz, and he consulted local foresters before the battles of Zorndorf, Kunersdorf and Torgau. At the same time he warned his officers that 'a peasant and a drover are not military men, and you will find that quite different descriptions of the same stretch of country will be given by an economist, a carter, a huntsman or a soldier' ('Des Marches d'Armée', 1777, *Oeuvres*, XXIX, 116).

In 1742 Frederick established a *Plankammer* in the Stadtschloss at Potsdam. This became the repository of highly secret maps, like the survey of Silesia which Major Wrede compiled between 1747 and 1753. The Wrede map was, however, the only one of the kind available to Frederick in the Seven Years War, and it had some distinct limitations. There was a gap in the coverage in the areas of Strehlen and Neumarkt. Moreover, while the slopes of individual hills were represented well enough by hachuring, Wrede gave no indication of the nature of extensive regions of high ground.

The most reliable map of all was therefore the one which Frederick formed in his head, over the course of his thousands of miles of campaigning (e.g. *PC* 12159). He could write in 1779: 'Lower Silesia, Bohemia, and Upper Silesia with Moravia are the areas of which we have a detailed knowledge. This will stand us in good stead if, in the event of new wars, these provinces again become the theatre of operations' ('Réflexions sur les mesures à prendre au cas d'une guerre nouvelle avec les Autrichiens', 28 September 1779, *Oeuvres*, XXIX, 131).

Frederick's staff was very small, and our myopic king became literally the eyes of the army when he rode out on reconnaissance with the advance guard or a little escort. He looked not only for the positions of the enemy troops but for signs like smoke from cooking fires and bakeries, which might tell him that the Austrians would shortly be on the move. This was dangerous work, for it brought Frederick into the zone of the enemy outposts.

Frederick devoted much effort and imagination to every aspect of what we now call 'intelligence': 'If we always had advance notice of the intentions of the enemy, we could, with a small army, hold a permanent advantage over a larger one' ('Principes Généraux', 1748, *Oeuvres*, XXVII, 46). He was probably at his most successful in the work of gathering intelligence of a long-term, strategic kind. The Jew Sabatky acted as his liaison with the more corruptible of the Russian officers, and Frederick had at least one spy in the heart of the Austrian headquarters (*PC* 8526). Personable and resourceful young men were told off as 'sleepers' to Vienna, where they melted into the local society and got on intimate terms with the serving girls of the great ladies. 'The discoveries made by these young Adonises were quite incredible. Some of these gentlemen maintained liaisons with the Viennese chamber maids for a couple of years on end, and they wrote reports which contained far greater and more important disclosures than all the dispatches of the envoys' (Zimmermann, 1790, I, 288).

Oddly enough, day-to-day operational intelligence was usually lacking altogether. Frederick interrogated enemy prisoners and deserters in person, but he seldom derived anything of value from them. The peoples of most of the theatres of war – the Bohemians, the

Moravians, the Wendish Saxons – were recalcitrant and unreliable.
Frederick's own spies were of little use to him, for he paid most of
them poorly, and he refused to believe them when they brought him
bad news (Archenholtz, 1840, I, 278; Mitchell, 1850, I, 419; Catt,
1884, 353; Yorke, 1913, III, 224).

Frederick, who was one of nature's chatterboxes, laid down some
stern rules for the guidance of himself and his army:

> The art of concealing your thoughts, or 'dissimulation', is
> indispensable for every man who has the management of
> weighty affairs. The whole army tries to read its fate from the
> countenance of the commander. It asks itself why he happens to
> be in a good or bad temper, and it tries to read some meaning
> into his behaviour – in fact nothing escapes this scrutiny. When
> the general is deep in thought the officers murmur among
> themselves 'Our commander must be hatching some great
> scheme.' If he appears sad or anxious, they declare 'Things must
> be going badly!' . . . All of this means that the general must
> behave like an actor, who assumes whatever expression best
> accords with the part he wishes to play. If the commander is no
> longer master of himself, he must give out that he is ill, or
> devise some bogus excuse that will deceive the public.
> ('Principes Généraux', 1748, *Oeuvres*, XXVIII, 40)

Frederick changed his cyphers as soon as he feared that they
might have been compromised, as after Soor and Landeshut, and he
reserved to himself the knowledge of the losses in battle, and the
effective strengths of the individual units and therefore of the whole
army (Mitchell, 25 November 1761, PRO SP 90/78). The British envoy
Mitchell was in Frederick's presence daily, and yet he had to report to
Holdernesse in London:

> I am sensible the accounts I send Your Lordship must appear
> very lame and defective. But will you please to consider there is
> but one person [i.e. Frederick] that knows everything, that he
> does not choose to talk of disagreeable subjects, and that his
> rank is such as exempts him from being importuned with
> questions. As for the general officers of the army, they know
> only what passes in their own bodies, but seem not in the least
> informed of the general plan of operations. (4 May 1760, PRO SP
> 90/76)

Frederick was no less attentive in his management of ruses or
'disinformation'. He wrote: 'When we are at war we must put on the
skin of the lion or the skin of the fox, as the occasion demands. A ruse
can succeed where brute force might fail' ('Principes Généraux',

1748, *Oeuvres*, XXVIII, 43). In 1745 he lured the Austro-Saxon army from the hills by a feigned retreat and drew it into the strategic ambush of Hohenfriedeberg. In 1758 he matched his wits with Daun, who was a man as wily as himself, and he got his army into Moravia, and successfully out again, by giving deceptive signals as to his designs. A great number of devices lay at Frederick's disposal for this kind of work – double spies, planted messages, showy concentrations of troops or transport, or simply the way he arranged his forces in camp ('Castramétrie', 1770, *Oeuvres*, XXIX, 46).

All of this might encourage one to read into the eighteenth century the degree of responsiveness that was made possible by the technology and disciplines of the twentieth century. We must therefore return to the question of control, which we have already explored with respect to Frederick as the manager of the bureaucracy, and Frederick the designer of battle tactics. How effective was it possible for our hero to be in the present context, as strategist and commander in the field?

Frederick liked to appear as a creature that was omnicompetent, infallible and invulnerable. That was why the people who knew the king best were hesitant to approach him when they saw that he was in a condition that threatened his self-esteem. In the manoeuvres at Neisse in 1769 Seydlitz happened to see Frederick's horse give a shake and dump its royal master on the ground. The animal ran away but Seydlitz told his regimental surgeon to take no notice. 'So it was that the king stood on his own two feet for near a quarter of an hour, gazing impassively through his telescope at the movements of the troops. Seydlitz meanwhile looked to one side, as if he had observed nothing of what had happened to Frederick' (Nicolai, 1788–92, IV, 57; see also Zimmermann, 1788, 37).

Frederick came closest to the vision of the totalitarian master when he functioned as grand strategist, the maker of war and peace. Here he reaped the full reward of his stripped-down way of life. He repulsed, in the most brutal terms, every opinion that his ministers dared to venture on strategic affairs (*PC* 9, 26661). He was not distracted, like Maria Theresa, by child-rearing, court ceremonies, or baroque religious observances. He did not make the rounds of the Seven Holy Tombs on Good Friday. Nor was he entangled by any sense of obligation to deserving generals or statesmen. In the winter of 1760/1, when the courts of Vienna, St Petersburg and Paris were engaged in anxious debate on the coming campaign, Frederick's confidant d'Argens was amused to find the king sitting on the floor of his quarters in Leipzig, dividing his dogs' evening meal with his stick, with an air of apparently total unconcern (Nicolai, 1788–92, I, 46).

Once the campaigning seasons began, Frederick entered an environment which was less susceptible to direction. The fog of war descended densely over the theatre of operations, and on many occasions it deprived Frederick of all knowledge of events outside his immediate locality, as in Moravia in 1758 after the Domstadtl ambush, during the campaign of Bunzelwitz in 1761, and in the course of the invasion of Bohemia in 1778. The communication across the lower reaches of the Bohemian Elbe appears to have occasioned particular difficulties. It bedevilled the liaison between Frederick and Schwerin before the battle of Prague, and it isolated August Wilhelm from the royal army during the retreat from Bohemia after Kolin (PC 2937). Messages could pass with greater ease across the northern plains. The lofty spire of the Catholic church in Schweidnitz served as the watch tower of Lower Silesia, and in August 1761 and again in June 1778 Frederick arranged for the fortress commandant to signal Austrian movements to him through a simple code of rockets. Strangely enough he was never prompted to carry this notion one small step further, and establish a system of visual telegraphs.

In Napoleonic vein, Frederick once described the Duke of Bevern as an unlucky commander (Anon., 1788–9, III, 23), but he knew that misfortune could attend any general who ventured his reputation in the lottery of war. Mischance had attended his expedition in Bohemia in 1744, just as it dogged Prince Charles in the campaign of Hohenfriedeberg, and yet 'the kind of person who could not lead a patrol of nine men is happy to arrange armies in his imagination, criticise the conduct of a general, and say to his misguided self: "My God, I know I could do better if I was in his place!" ' (to Podewils, 14 July 1745, PC 1917).

We have already noticed how difficult it was for a commander to exercise control over a combat, once it was joined. The plan was usually concerted verbally with the generals on the eve of the battle; on the actual day Frederick might control the alignment and pace of the advancing troops, as at Leuthen, but thereafter he could seek to influence events beyond range of his voice only by scribbling orders on scraps of paper (using the back of the nearest staff officer as a rest), and dispatching von Oppen or some other aide-de-camp to carry the note to its destination.

Out of all of Frederick's actions, the affair at Burkersdorf was the most tightly controlled. Each corps or brigade commander had his precise task, and he was sent on his way by the king in person. Leuthen was the nearest counterpart among the big battles.

Some of the other battles were a chronicle of accidents and heroic expedients, such as those which turned out well at Hohenfriedeberg, Rossbach and Liegnitz, or less happily, as at Hochkirch. On occasion Frederick was separated from large elements of his army, whether

intentionally, as at Torgau, or under force of circumstances as at
Chotusitz. At Mollwitz, Lobositz and Torgau the king absented
himself from the field before the action was over. At Kolin the
character of the battle changed fundamentally once the Prussian
army got engaged in the frontal attack: 'Then the combat became
general, and what was most annoying of all was that I was reduced to
the role of spectator, not having a single uncommitted battalion at
my disposal' (*Oeuvres*, IV, 129). The day of Prague was notable for
the fact that the high command on both sides was rendered literally
hors de combat. Browne and Schwerin were struck down by gunfire in
the early stages; Prince Charles of Lorraine was in the grips of a
psychosomatic seizure, and King Frederick, who was afflicted with
gastric trouble, exerted little discernible influence on the train of
terrible events.

Inevitably, when we turn to Frederick's relations with his officers, we
touch not only on the life of the Frederician army but the collapse of
the post-Frederician state in 1806–7. This happening was associated
with a divorce between the ruling circles and the rest of society, and
with a failure of military leadership. It is not too much to say that the
battles of the Silesian Wars and the first campaigns of the Seven Years
War were won by generals who had been trained up in the reign of
Frederick William I, and that Jena-Auerstedt was lost by the generals
of Frederick the Great.

We come first to the charge of social exclusivity. Frederick
certainly maintained that the officer corps was the preserve of the
nobility, and he largely banned the middle classes (between 5 and 10
per cent of the population) from the holding of commissioned rank.
Prince Henry, who moved in intellectual circles, told his brother as
early as 1753 that dangerous social divisions were resulting from the
practice of holding all but the military aristocracy at a distance from
the spiritual life of the state (Herrmann, 1922, 261).

The injustice of the thing was not so evident to Frederick or his
admirers. In Austria, the standing of the army suffered from the fact
that many of the higher aristocracy disdained to commit themselves
to a military career. In Prussia, on the other hand, not a little of the
prestige of the service derived from the connection that Frederick so
sedulously maintained between military obligation and the social
privileges of the nobility.

It was the cult of honour which, in Frederick's view, made the
aristocracy so valuable an asset for the army: 'In general terms, the
noble has no career open to him but to distinguish himself by the
sword. If he forfeits his honour, he is denied refuge even in his
paternal house . . . A commoner, on the other hand, may indulge in

low deeds, and resume his father's trade unabashed' (*Oeuvres*, VI, 95; see also Pauli, 1758–64, I, 230).

Otto Büsch (1962) indicates that the cantonal system introduced stultifying military relationships into the countryside, by making recruitment depend on the landowning aristocracy. Contemporaries, however, were much more alert to the opposite process – the influence on the military ethos of rural life, which brought with it the habit of command, a familiarity with the dangers of the hunt, and a childhood influenced by the tales of past wars (Pauli, 1758–64, I, 228–9; Seidl, 1781, III, 386; Garve, 1798, 159–60; see also p. 11).

As some further justification of Frederick's military-social system, we may point out that it was never as exclusive or as rigid as the one which operated in France in the last years of the *ancien régime*. The documentary basis had been overset when the *Heroldsamt* had been abolished in 1713, and Frederick was seldom entirely certain as to who was, or was not, of noble blood. In Pomerania, for example, many families availed themselves of the old Polish legal principle which associated nobility with the simple ownership of land, and which, in the celebrated case of the village of Czarn-Damerow, made aristocrats out of all the community save the watchman and the swineherd. For some pretentious folk (the *Nominaladel*) nobility was something that was acquired by attention to mannerisms, and a judiciously timed insertion of the 'von' before the surname. Others, more deserving, were awarded patents of nobility for valiant service in the field. The former peasant Koordshagen, who became a captain of hussars and a noble, was sitting at the royal table when Frederick asked him from which aristocratic house he sprang. Koordshagen replied: 'I come from no such line, Your Majesty. My parents are simple country folk, and I wouldn't change them for any others in the world!' Frederick was genuinely moved, and he exclaimed: 'That was well said!' (Hildebrandt, 1829–35, IV, 124).

Altogether, the privileges of Frederick's nobility had their roots in function rather than caste. The king would have rejected any suggestion that the holder of a military commission had a right to carry his authority into areas of civilian life (which establishes an important distinction between the notions of Old Fritz and the militarism of Wilhelmine Germany). For some time after the Seven Years War, a number of the younger officers of the victorious army got into the habit of swaggering about the provincial towns. Frederick was determined not to allow this bumptious behaviour in Berlin, and on the advice of Zieten he appointed the strict and honourable Lieutenant-General Ramin as governor:

Ramin fulfilled the duties of his office with all the more rigour

because he proceeded from the supposition that, in any
confrontation, the civilian was careful to avoid offending the
soldier, and the blame nearly always rested on the military
man. We find a characteristic sentiment in his first address to
the officers: 'Gentlemen, you have no idea how horrible I can
be!' (Hildebrandt, 1829–35, III, 58)

Saldern held to the same principles at Magdeburg (Küster, 1793,
91–3).

It was, perhaps, in the professional conditioning of his officers,
rather than the maintenance of their social exclusivity, that
Frederick is more to blame in historical perspective. This comment
will appear still stranger when we consider that Frederick sincerely
believed that he was making excellent provision for the future leadership of the army:

I put my officers through their paces unremittingly, while
explaining the reasons for my actions. I never tire of preaching,
and whenever I detect young officers who seem to have some
talent I call them to me, and instruct them with all possible
care. Do you know of another prince who goes in for teaching
like me? (Catt, 1884; see also 'Principes Généraux', 1748,
Oeuvres, XXVIII, 41)

Thus Frederick compiled his Éléments de Castramétrie (1770) in
order to expand the vision of his generals beyond their immediate arm
of service, and instil the confidence that was requisite for independent command.

Frederick extended considerable freedom to the detached generals in the Seven Years War, and he insisted that they must take
decisions on their own head, without having recourse to councils of
war (PC 7796, 7805, 8609, 9189, 9414, 9839). When the generals in
question were theatre commanders, like Lehwaldt, Dohna, Hülsen,
Ferdinand of Brunswick or Prince Henry, who were likely to lose
contact with royal headquarters for considerable lengths of time,
Frederick was careful to furnish them with wide-ranging political
and strategic overviews, so as to inform their judgment (PC 9791,
9798, 9887). These admirable principles were complemented by
Frederick's refusal to allow himself to be bound by questions of
seniority, when it was a question of pushing a good man forward (PC
10882).

Why did these attentions ultimately bear so little fruit? For a clue
to the answer, we must return to Prince Henry's prophetic memorandum to the king of 1753. There he pointed out that the nobles were
paying so heavily for their privileges that they might be considered

the victims rather than the beneficiaries of the system:

> In every other country in the world the nobility represent the
> first class of the body of the state, and they are given freedom of
> choice as to what profession they wish to take up. But here the
> father is compelled to deliver up his as-yet uneducated son at
> the age of fifteen to the mercy of men of low extraction. These
> folk seek to humiliate the young man by bringing him down to
> their own level, and the result is that he finally adopts their
> own base habits. (Herrmann, 1922, 259)

This tyrannical treatment was prolonged by Frederick in his
everyday relations with his officers. The memoirs and records are
replete with examples of his contemptuous refusals of requests to go
on leave or retire, his obscenely phrased denials of permissions to
marry, his shattering rebukes to erring officers (which usually had
some foundation of justice), and his astonishing ingratitude to men
who had deserved well of him (which certainly did not).

Officers who over the years had schooled themselves to endure
such a life were incapable of transmuting themselves into prodigies of
independent enterprise when they were on campaign. Few commanders were confident enough to take Frederick at his word when he said
that he had given them their heads, and in any case they suspected
that, when they had to render account, only offensive action or a very
obstinate defence were likely to commend them to their master.
There was a despairing resignation in the way that Lehwaldt and
Wedel threw themselves at the Russians at Gross-Jägersdorf and
Paltzig, or that Fouqué took up station in the path of superior forces at
Landeshut. Only two commanders usually had the nerve to tell
Frederick when it was better to hang back. One was Prince Henry,
who was reinforced by his birth and his military reputation, and the
other was Seydlitz, who maintained a kind of moral superiority over
the king until the end. It was all too easy for the run-of-the-mill
officer to find safety and occupation in the fulfilment of narrowly
conceived duties (Guibert, 1778, 126; Moore, 1779, II, 150–3;
Riesebeck, 1784, II, 139; Warnery, 1788, 250; Retzow, 1802, II, 164;
Lossow, 1826, 98; Preuss, 1832–4, I, 52; Yorke, 1913, III, 217; Tharau,
1968, 126). Guibert saw the Silesian regiments at the manoeuvres at
Neisse in 1773, and he observed:

> Most of the officers, whether infantry or cavalry, turn out to be
> no more clever than ours, when they find themselves out of
> their regular order of battle, and forced to rely on their
> intelligence to cope with problems which arrive at unexpected
> times or places. In matters of detail I saw them commit the most

stupid blunders, the most incredible improbabilities. (Guibert, 1803, II, 170)

The Prussian officers, so prompt to sacrifice life, health and liberty at royal behest, nevertheless retained a sense of individual dignity and corporate worth that was not at the king's command. In the Seven Years War it strengthened them in their collective refusal to carry out what, by twentieth-century standards, was the very unatrocious atrocity of devastating royal palaces in Saxony. Every officer in the regular army whom Frederick directed to carry out the deed refused the commission outright and was willing to take the consequences. Saldern declared: 'Your Majesty may send me to attack the enemy batteries, and I will readily obey. But to act contrary to my honour, oath and duty is something which my will and conscience do not permit me to do' (Küster, 1793, 42). To men like these, loyalty to the king was part of their code of obligations, but not the totality. 'Honour' was a commodity they carried about with them, and not something they consigned to the keeping of another. Here was an essential difference in the ethos of a Frederician officer from that of the SS, to whom honour and loyalty were the same thing – 'Meine Ehre heisst Treue'.

Saldern was able to resume his successful career, after a long period of disfavour, but there was no such reprieve for the defenceless Lieutenant-Colonel Johann Friedrich von der Marwitz, who was forced to leave the army. Marwitz lived out the rest of his days in retirement, but he never regretted that he had withstood the king, and his tombstone bore an epitaph of his own composition which clarified the principle for posterity:

He chose Disgrace, when Obedience was incompatible with Honour. (Augstein, 1968, 93)

Almost every study of Frederick tells us about the artificial constitution of the Prussian army of his time, and the repressive treatment of the rank and file. Certainly there was an element of contrivance in a system which maintained a standing army of 160,000 troops from a base of 4,500,000 souls. This force was the equivalent in absolute terms of the British Army of the early 1980s, and it was twelve times greater in proportion to the size of the population.

Frederick's achievement was made possible by the expedient of recruiting one-third or more of the establishment from foreign mercenaries. Experience showed that half of these men would run off as soon as they could, and the consequence was an unremitting rigour of supervision, reinforced by the threat of the gauntlet and other terrible punishments.

The following words were penned by the dark, tyrannical Old Fritz of the period after the Seven Years War:

> As for the soldiers, all you can do is to imbue them with *esprit de corps*, in other words the conviction that their regiment is better than all the other regiments in the universe. It sometimes happens that the officers must lead them into considerable danger, and since ambition can exert no influence on the men, they must be made to fear their officers more than the perils to which they are exposed, otherwise nobody would be able to make them attack into a storm of missiles thundering from three hundred cannon. Good will can never motivate common men in dangers of this order – we must resort to force.
> ('Testament Politique', 1768, Frederick, 1920, 147)

The well-known brutalities were, however, just one element among many in Frederick's relations with his soldiers. Frederick knew that the life of his men was one of ill-rewarded danger and privation, and he was ready to take issue with Quintus Icilius, Voltaire, Guibert or anybody else who made light of their endurance and courage.

In his last illness, Frederick told Dr Zimmermann:

> In the course of my campaigns all my orders relating to the care of the sick and wounded soldiers have been very badly observed. Nothing in my life has occasioned me more chagrin than when I have seen that those brave men, who offered up their health and life so bravely for the fatherland, had their diseases and wounds so wretchedly attended to. They have often been treated barbarously, and many a poor soldier has died from lack of proper care. (Zimmermann, 1788, 124–5; see also *PC* 9839)

There is no reason why we should not take Frederick at his word. In 1788 Warnery occasioned great offence when he asserted that Frederick had deliberately allowed many wounded soldiers to die of infection when their lives might have been saved by amputations. The king was thereby supposed to have spared the state of maintaining cripples after the war (Warnery, 1788, 430). This suggestion was indignantly refuted by the first royal *Chirurgus* Theden, who pointed out that Frederick valued conservative treatments for their own sake. He described how after the battle of Chotusitz the king had seen a number of company *Feldscherer* clustered around an interesting amputation that was in progress. He was repelled by their ghoulishness, and exclaimed: 'Oh you utter shits!' (Nicolai, 1788–92, III, 337).

Unfortunately, this same squeamishness, together with Frederick's inability to work cordially with experts of any kind, held him at a distance from many things that ought to have received his closest attention. The soldiers received a poor return for the considerable sums which he devoted to his field hospitals (Nicolai, 1788–92, III, 336; Küster, 1793, 156; Dreyer, 1810, 36), and he remained unaware of the collapse of his medical services in the War of the Bavarian Succession, until Dr Zimmermann enlightened him on the subject in the summer of 1786. On Zimmermann's suggestion Frederick at once appointed Dr Fritze as *Oberaufseher* in Magdeburg, with special responsibility for supervising the *Feldscherer*.

The Frederick of the Seven Years War was a consummate master of the skills of leadership. He had a quasi-Napoleonic recall of the names and faces of old soldiers. On the march he spoke to his men in their Low German dialects, and he tolerated familiarities for which he would have cashiered an ensign. In this respect the British were much more on their dignity than was Frederick himself. In the War of American Independence an officer in the contingent of Hanau artillery was forced to intervene on behalf of one of his gunners, who had caused great offence by staring at an English officer. ' "Now", I asked the cannonier, "Why did you look at the officer?" He replied, that "he had served His Majesty, the King of Prussia, for eight years, and was allowed to look at him whenever he met him; and, moreover, he had never been reproved for so doing" ' (Pausch, 1886, 112).

Frederick had not yet shrunk into the Old Fritz of the 1768 Testament, and he could still maintain:

> My troops are good and well disciplined, and the most
> important thing of all is that I have thoroughly habituated
> them to perform everything that they are required to execute.
> You will do something more easily, to a higher standard, and
> more bravely when you know that you will do it well. I
> encourage my soldiers and excite their sense of honour. I give
> them rewards, and I hold out the prospect of still further
> recompenses, when it seems necessary. ('Principes Généraux',
> 1748, *Oeuvres*, XXVIII, 40)

The Frederician military discipline was certainly harsh, and it was judged to be so by the standards of the time. Was it also unreasonable? Probably not.

In the first place, Frederick had to impose effective control on men who were of aggressive temperament and unpredictable behaviour. He recalled the case of a wounded grenadier at Mollwitz who had commandeered a riderless horse, ridden into the cavalry battle, and returned with an Austrian senior officer as his prize. 'I was struck by the courage of this grenadier . . . and I ordered good care to be taken of him . . . When he had fully recovered from his wound I made him an officer, and on his first day of duty in this capacity he deserted. Now there's something for your philosophers to chew on!' (Catt, 1884, 242).

Industrious and intelligent soldiers escaped the punishments altogether, and if their careless comrades were punished severely it is worth emphasising that as recruits they had all undergone a training that was noted for its gentleness and patience (Riesebeck, 1784, II, 135; Mirabeau-Mauvillon, 1788, 116; Toulongeon (1786), 1881, 291). Individual monsters, like Lieutenant-Colonel Scheelen of the First Battalion of the Garde, were capable of driving their miserable soldiers to suicide. They had their counterpart in every army, but they did not necessarily represent what Frederick desired for his own. As governor of Berlin, Möllendorff declared in 1785: 'It is not rascals, scum, dogs and ruffians that His Majesty wishes to have in his service, but honest soldiers – the same people as ourselves, even if the chance of birth has favoured us with higher rank' (Schnackenburg, 1883b, 94).

Whereas drill is prized in modern times for its spiritual worth, in the eighteenth century it formed an inherent part of tactics. It was this utilitarian aspect that was stressed by Frederick: 'In Prussia, the soldier is trained to do precisely what he will execute on the day of battle, and nothing superfluous' (Toulongeon (1786), 1881, 392). Expert observers noted that the Prussian troops had an easy bearing under arms, and that on manoeuvres Frederick looked for a satisfactory performance of the essentials of each movement, and not an absolute precision of timing and alignment.

The bleakness of military life was alleviated by the very salutary distinctions which the Prussian army observed between the periods that were spent on and off duty. The parades in Berlin were held only on Sundays and feast days, which was less frequently than in Paris. With the exception of the Garde, the troops throughout the monarchy were accommodated in civilian billets, not barracks, and they were not disturbed overmuch by military demands. Outside the seasons for reviews and manoeuvres the native men went back to their villages. The foreigners, once they had been put through their paces on the square for a couple of hours each morning, were left to pursue whatever private occupation they wished. Likewise on campaign Frederick did not fatigue his troops by drills, when he was satisfied that they had acquired the basic tactical proficiency.

Such differences were respected by the men. The king enjoyed the informalities of the march, but

> as soon as the army reached the place of assembly Frederick turned into a different person, his adjutants sped in all

directions with his orders, and a solemn silence descended on
the scene. Everybody stood hushed and mute in rank and file,
their eyes on the single man at their head. An old grenadier
once said: 'It was if our Lord God had descended to earth in a
blue coat!' (Hildebrandt, 1829–35, VI, 30)

Discipline was in its turn an aspect of *Subordination*, an untrans-
latable term which in the Prussian service had connotations of
responsiveness and harmony, and the smooth articulation of a chain
of command which reached from the sovereign of the private soldier.
The personal leadership of Frederick and the generals had something
to do with it, and so did simplicity of life and a lack of ceremony. The
ultimate reward was reaped on the battlefield: 'When you open fire,
you cause a massacre. When you bring your cavalry into play, you
annihilate the enemy amid scenes of frightful butchery' ('Principes
Généraux', 1748, *Oeuvres*, XXVIII, 6–7; see also 'Testament Politique', 1752, Frederick, 1920, 86–7; 'Règles de ce qu'on exige d'un bon
commandeur de bataillon en temps de guerre', 1773, *Oeuvres*, XXIX,
57; Guibert, 1778, 390; Moore, 1779, II, 147; Riesebeck, 1784, II, 141;
Mirabeau-Mauvillon, 1788, 61; Lossow, 1826, 101; Toulongeon (1786),
1881, 166; Marshal Belle-Isle, quoted in Gr. Gstb., 1890–3, II, 40).

Among the native troops, the discipline and *Subordination* were
reinforced by what was called the 'military spirit' (see Warnsdorff, in
Volz, 1926–7, II, 290–1). This was a compound of many instincts and
impulses. The Prussian officer admired a certain austerity of temperament, as manifest, for example, in the ideal of *Contenance Halten*
(the stiff upper lip) under fire, or the rejection of decorations and
orders of chivalry as an inducement for an officer to do his duty. The
other ranks were moved by religious allegiance, the 'small unit
cohesion' of the military sociologists, and local and national loyalties
such as those that were evident in the Pomeranians of the regiment of
Manteuffel (17), 'upright and cheerful, strong and reliable, and loyal
to their prince – in other words honest men after the old German style'
(Haller, 1796, 327).

The king himself, frenchified to the fingertips, was not unresponsive to racial pride: 'Our Northern peoples are not as soft as the
Westerners. The men in our country are less effeminate, and consequently more virile, and more hard-working and patient, if also, I
must admit, somewhat less refined' (to Voltaire, 5 December 1742,
Oeuvres, XXII, 121–2).

Outward appearances were a matter of some importance, and
'only unreflective folk would consider this splendour as something
useless: on the contrary, it increases the courage and morale of the
soldiers, and enhances the dignity of the army' (Archenholtz, 1974,

16–18). Many of the items of uniform had a distinctively 'Prussian' appearance. In 1792, in the course of the long debate concerning the memorial statue to Frederick, the artist Daniel Chodowiecki explained that he and most of the general public rejected the notion of an Old Fritz in classical garb, and were 'for the clothing which Frederick wore from his youth until his dying day. This is what I call "the Prussian Costume". It was devised by his father, carried by the entire Prussian army, and is now imitated by all the other armies in the world' (Volz, 1926–7, III, 276–7).

The military spirit was produced by the working of time and tradition, and the efforts of a monarch who led his armies in war and devoted himself to the interests of his peoples in time of peace. By the end of the reign the affectation of weariness had long since given way to the reality. In 1785 a boy watched from a crowd when Frederick returned from a review to the palace of Princess Amalie in the Wilhelmstrasse in Berlin. He led his old crippled sister up the steps, and the couple disappeared inside. The spectators stood for a few minutes in silence, then went their way:

> And yet nothing had really happened! There was no splendour,
> no fireworks, no salutes of cannon, no drums or fifes, no music,
> nothing to keep the crowd amused beforehand. It was just a
> seventy-three-year-old man, badly dressed and covered in dust,
> who was returning from his laborious daily task.

(Friedrich August Ludwig von der Marwitz, in Volz, 1926–7, III, 202)

Maps

Key to Maps

 Prussian infantry battalion (v. approx. 700 field strength in Seven Years War; grenadier battalion 625-50)

 Prussian infantry regiment of two battalions

 Prussian cavalry regiment (v. approx. 800 field strength in Seven Years War)

 Austrian unit

 Unit of Austrian ally or auxiliary (French, Russian, Saxon or of the *Reichsarmee,* according to context)

 Heavy gun (12-pounder or more)

Infantry regiments are designated by a simple number; fractioned numbers indicate a grenadier battalion drawn from companies of the relevant regiments.

C = cuirassier
D = dragoon regiment
H = hussar regiment

Full identification and details of units are to be found in the author's *The Army of Frederick the Great* (1974) (Prussian), *The Army of Maria Theresa* (1977) (Austrian), and *Russia's Military Way to the West* (1981) (Russian).

Heights are given in metres

 The area of a town or village, as far as the outer limits of garden fences. The buildings were usually arranged along the edges of the streets

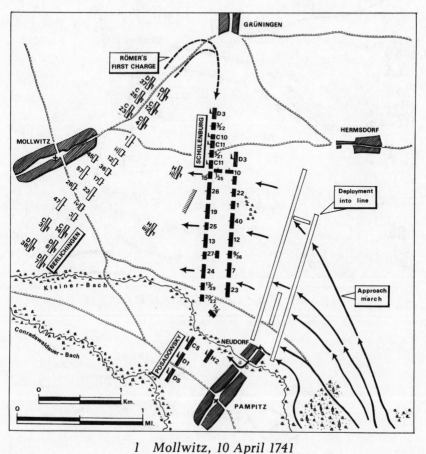

1   Mollwitz, 10 April 1741

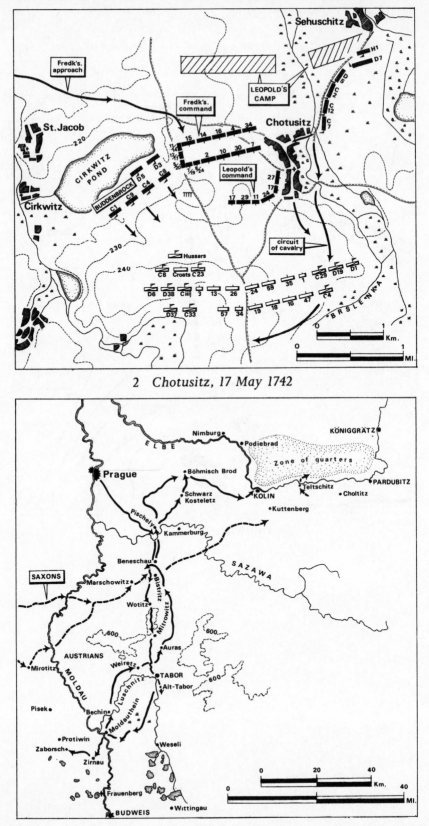

2 *Chotusitz, 17 May 1742*

3 *Bohemia, 1744*

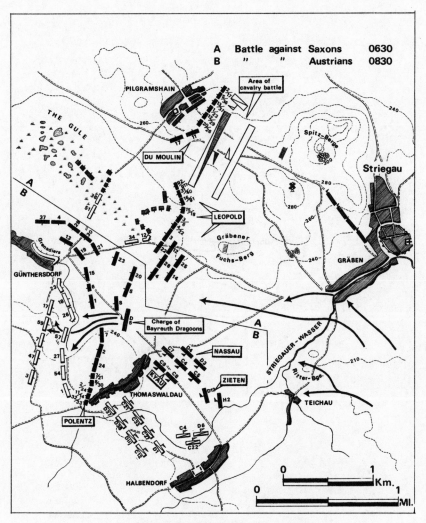

4   *Hohenfriedeberg, 4 June 1745*

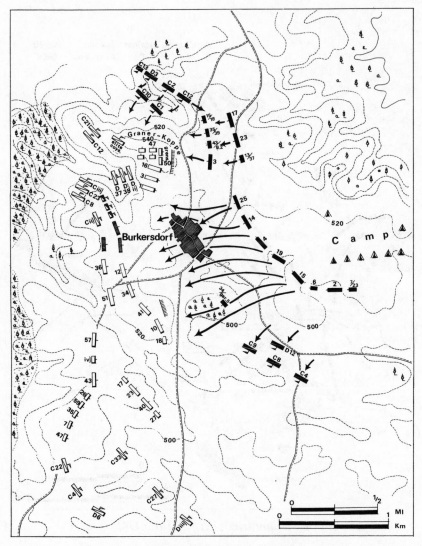

5 *Soor, 30 September 1745*

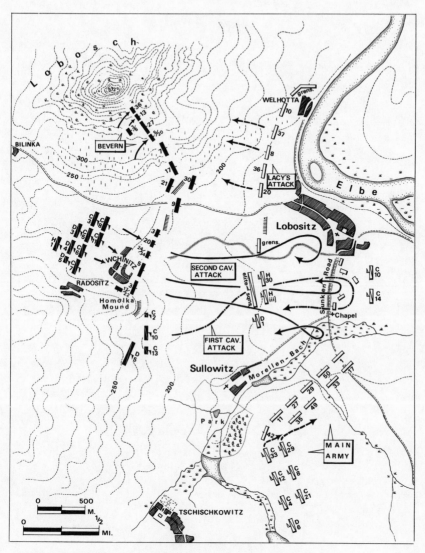

6   *Lobositz, 1 October 1756*

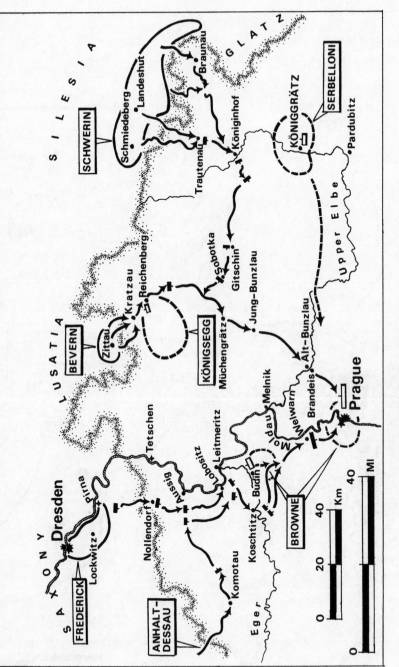

7 *Invasion of Bohemia, 1757*

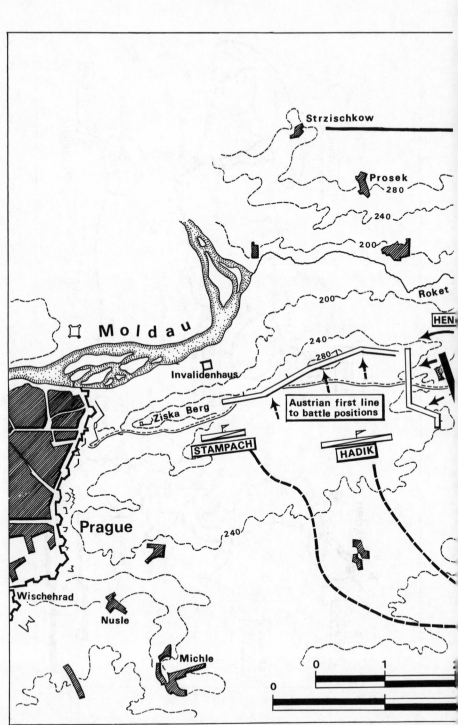

8   *Prague, 6 May 1757*

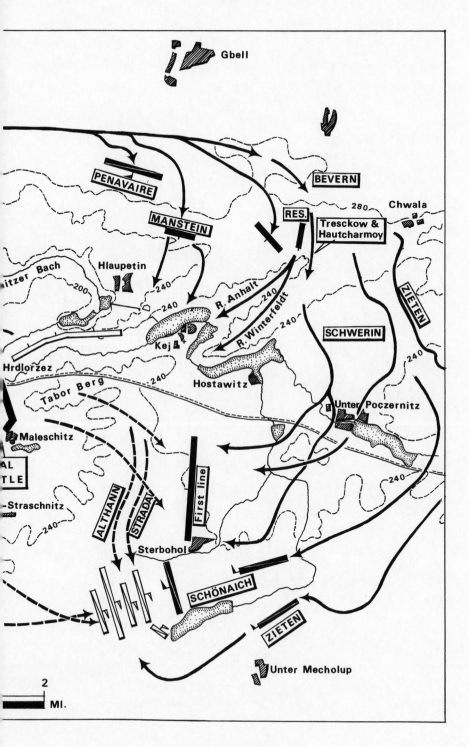

Gbell

PENAVAIRE

BEVERN

MANSTEIN

RES.

280   Chwala

Tresckow &
Hautcharmoy

itzer Bach   Hlaupetin

200

240

R. Anhalt

240

ZIETEN

240

240

Kej

R. Winterfeldt

SCHWERIN

240

Hrdlorzez

240

Hostawitz

Tabor Berg

240

Unter Poczernitz

Maleschitz

240

AL
TLE

First line

-Straschnitz

240

STRADA

ALTHANN

Sterbohol

SCHÖNAICH

ZIETEN

2

Unter Mecholup

MI.

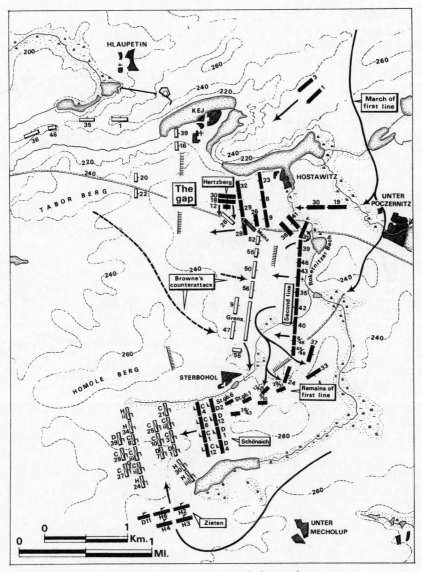

9 *Prague – the breakthrough*

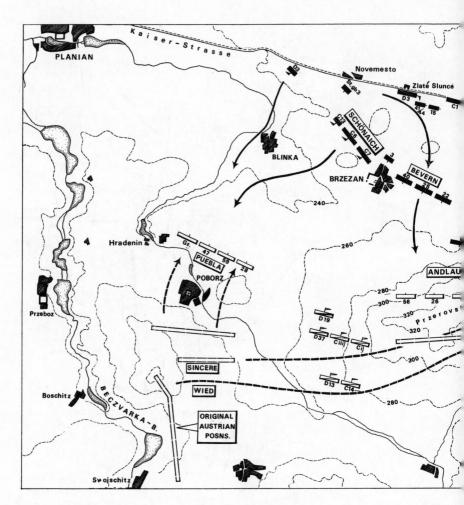

10   Kolin, 18 June 1757

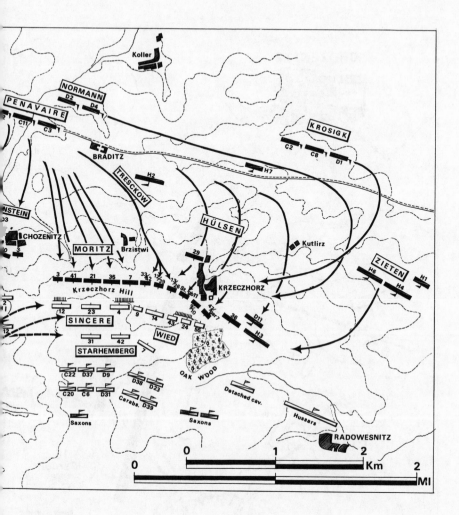

Koller

NORMANN
D2   D4

PENAVAIRE
C11   C3

KROSIGK
C2   C8   D1

BRADITZ

H7

TRESCKOW   H2

NSTEIN
D3

HÜLSEN

CHOZENITZ

MORITZ   Brzistwi   Kutlirz

29

ZIETEN
H6   H1
H4

3   41   21   35   7   33 2   12   13 26 St 5 17   KRZECZHORZ
Krzeczhorz Hill   39

12   23   4   9   14   43   24   58   D11   H3
SINCERE   9 10
                        47 Carr 7   38
WIED

31   42
STARHEMBERG

C22   D37   D9
                    OAK W'OOD
C20   C6   D31   D38   D23
        Carabs.   D39   Detached cav.

Saxons   Saxons   Hussars

RADOWESNITZ

0   1   2
                              Km
0   1   2
                              MI

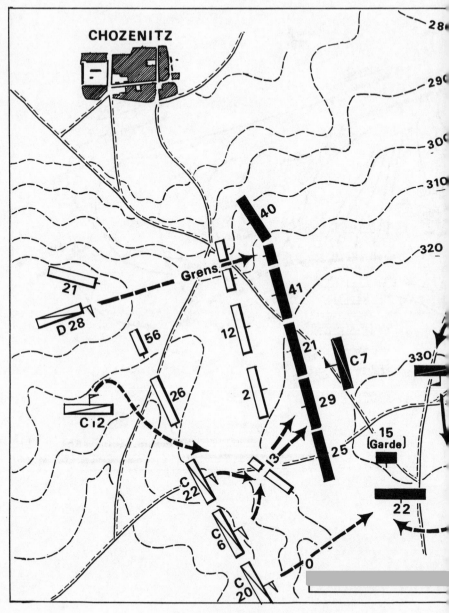

11   The end at Kolin

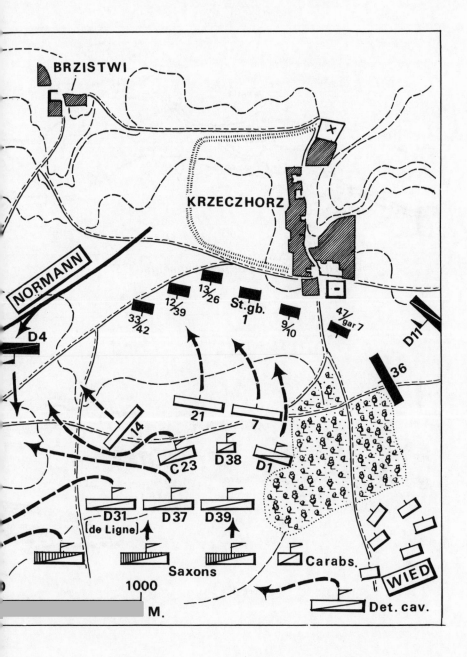

BRZISTWI

KRZECZHORZ

NORMANN

D4

33/42

12/39

13/26

St.gb.
1

9/10

47/gar 7

D11

36

21

7

14

C23

D38

D1

D31
(de Ligne)

D37

D39

Saxons

Carabs.

WIED

1000

M.

Det. cav.

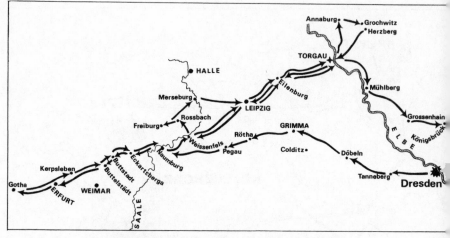

12   *The Rossbach-Leuthen campaign, 1757*

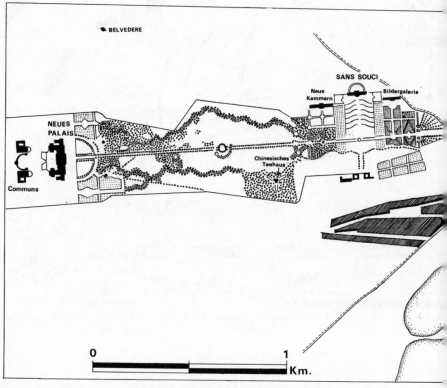

13   *Frederician Potsdam*

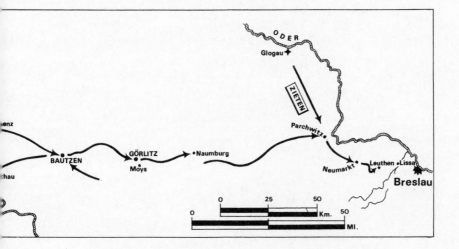

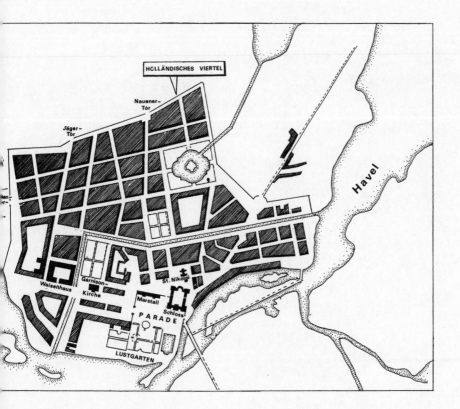

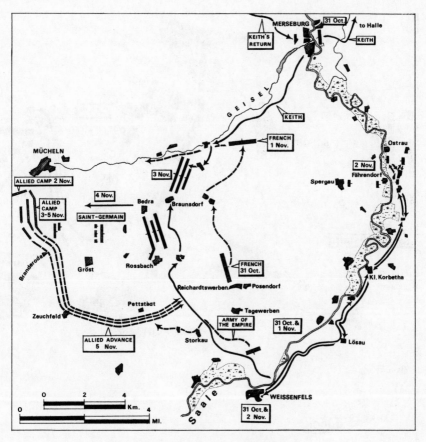

14   Before Rossbach

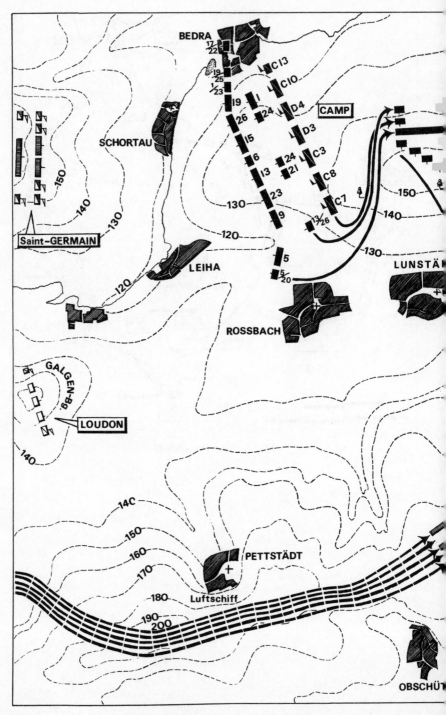

15   Rossbach, 5 November 1757

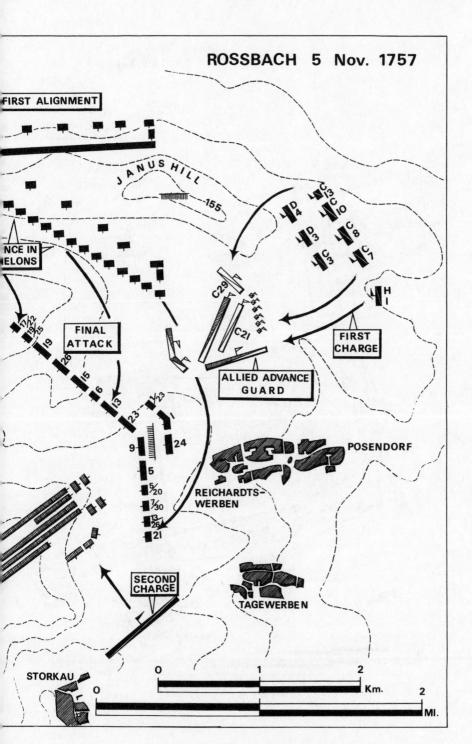

ROSSBACH   5 Nov. 1757

FIRST ALIGNMENT

JANUS HILL

155

C13
C10
D4
D3
C8
C3
C7

H1

C29

C21

FIRST
CHARGE

17/22
19/25
19
26
15
6
13
23
1/23
1
9
24
5
5/20
7/30
13/26
21

FINAL
ATTACK

ALLIED ADVANCE
GUARD

NCE IN
ELONS

POSENDORF

REICHARDTS-
WERBEN

SECOND
CHARGE

TAGEWERBEN

STORKAU

0   1   2
                              Km.

0   1   2
                              MI.

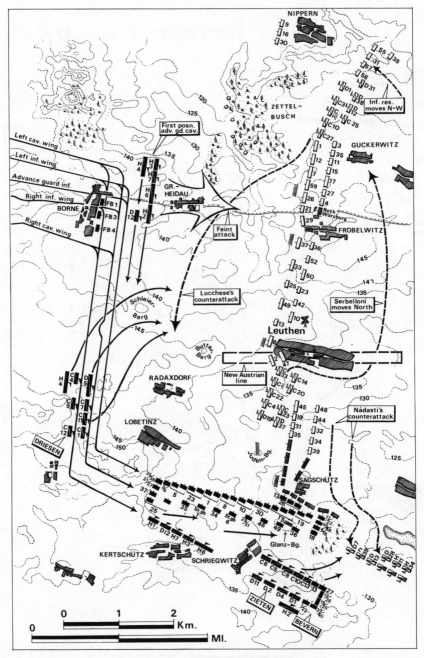

16   *Leuthen, 5 December 1757*

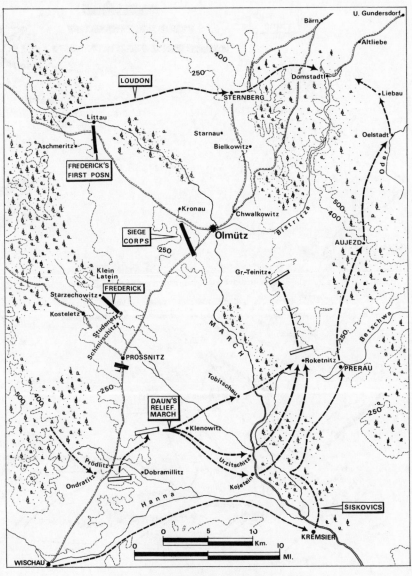

17   *Campaign of Olmütz, 1758*

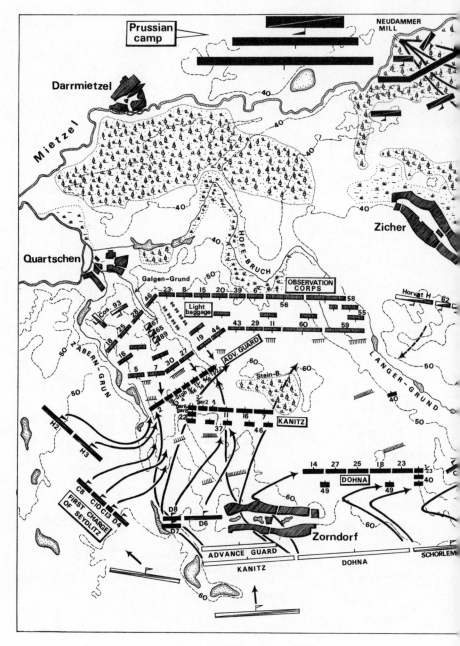

18 Zorndorf, 25 August 1758

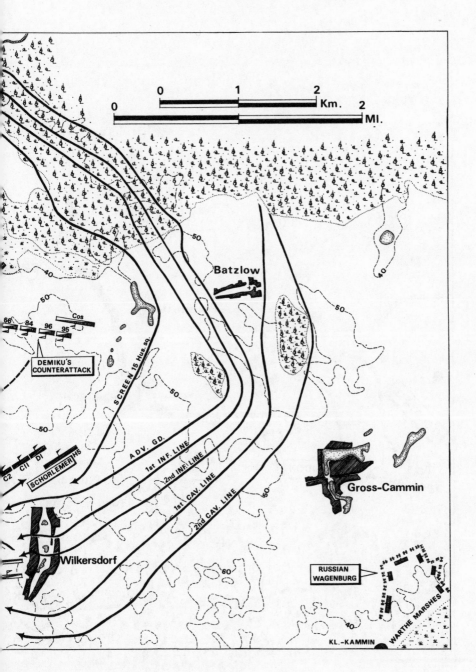

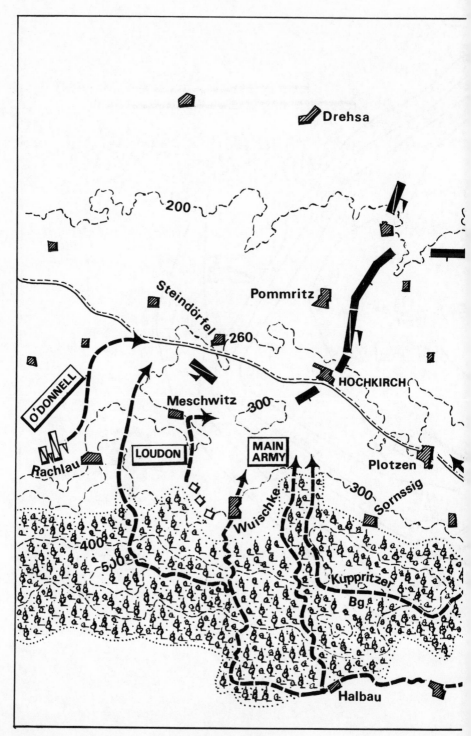

19   *Around Hochkirch*

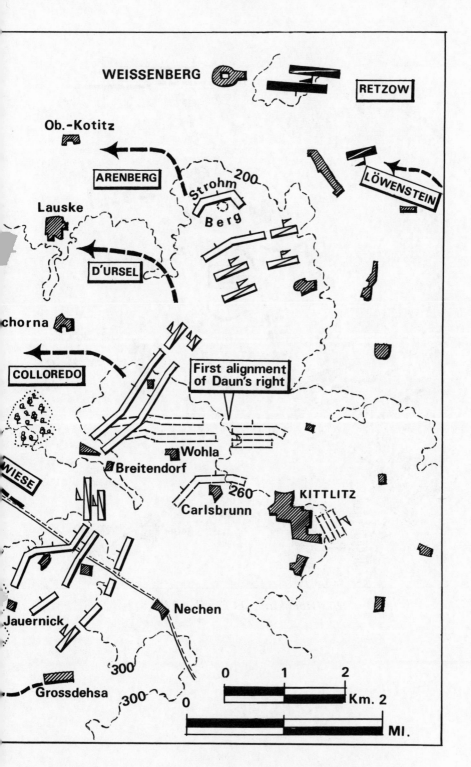

WEISSENBERG

RETZOW

Ob.-Kotitz

ARENBERG

Strohm
200
Berg

LÖWENSTEIN

Lauske

D'URSEL

chorna

COLLOREDO

First alignment
of Daun's right

WIESE

Wohla
Breitendorf

260
Carlsbrunn

KITTLITZ

Nechen

Jauernick

300

Grossdehsa
300

0

0   1   2
Km. 2

MI.

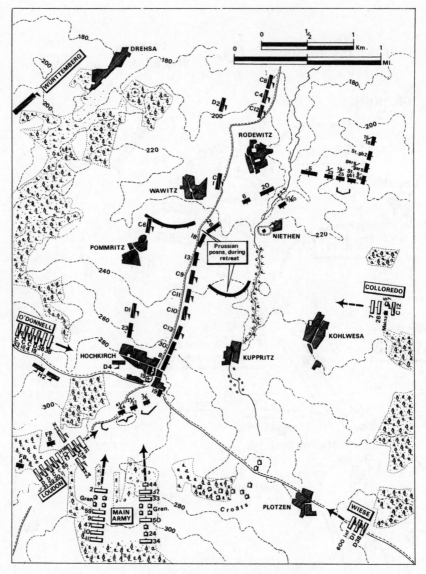

20   *Hochkirch, 14 October 1758*

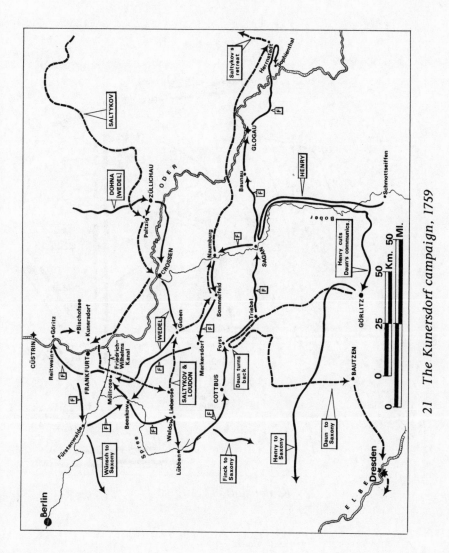

21 *The Kunersdorf campaign, 1759*

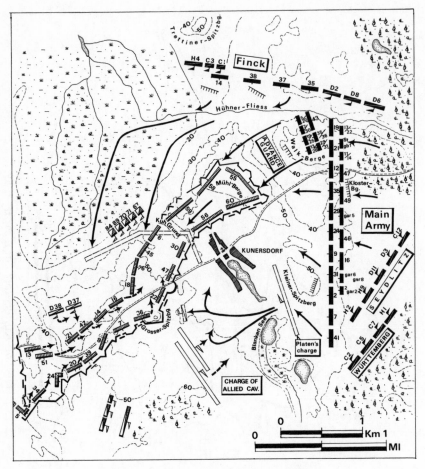

22   *Kunersdorf, 12 August 1759*

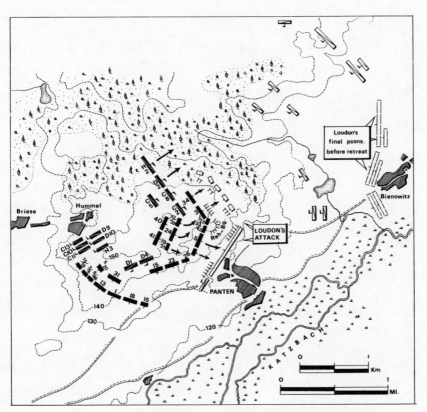

23   *Liegnitz, 15 August 1760*

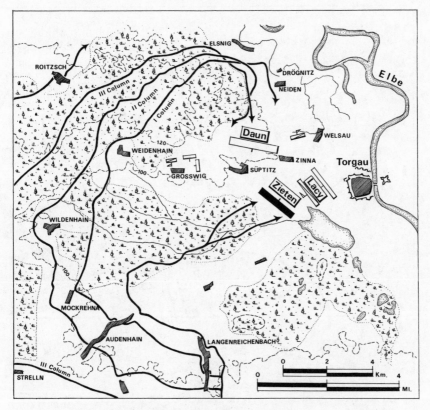

24   *Torgau – the turning movement*

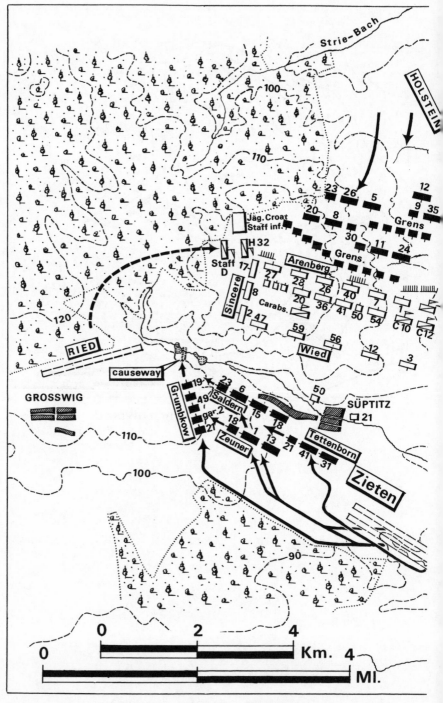

Strie-Bach

HOLSTEIN

100

110

23 26   5   12
20   9   35
8   Grens.
Jäg. Croat
Staff inf.   30   11   24
H 32   Grens.
Staff   17
D   27   28   40
Sincere   8   26   41 50   7
Carabs.   20 36   54
2 47   C 10   C 12
59
120   56
RIED   Wied   12
                                      3
causeway
GROSSWIG   50
                              SÜPTITZ
19   23 6   21
49 Saldern 15
gar. 2 18   1   18
21   13 21 Tettenborn
Zeuner   41   31
110
                              Zieten
100

Grumbkow

90

0   2   4
0 ──────────────────── Km. 4
──────────────────── MI.

25   Torgau, 3 November 1760

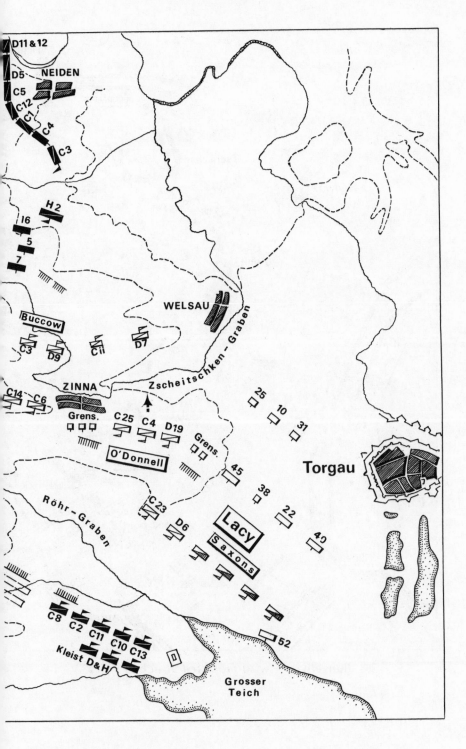

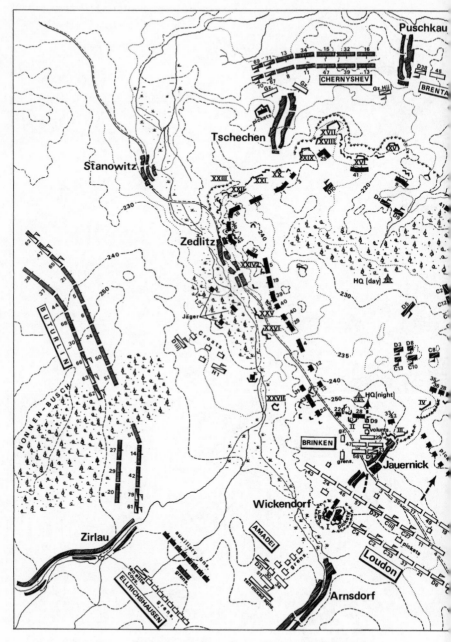

26　*Bunzelwitz – with projected attack of allies*

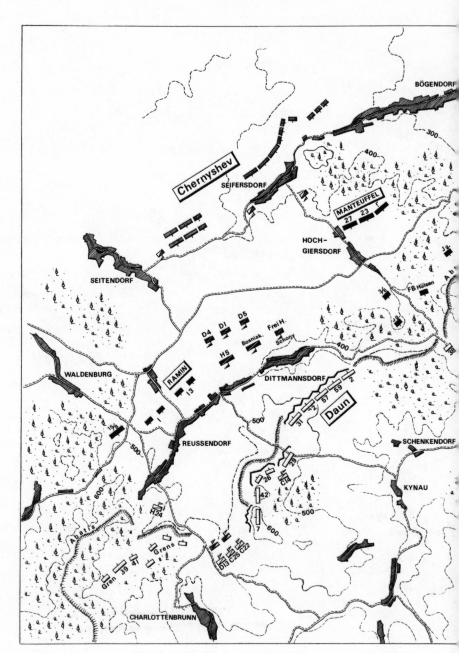

27   *Burkersdorf, 21 July 1762*

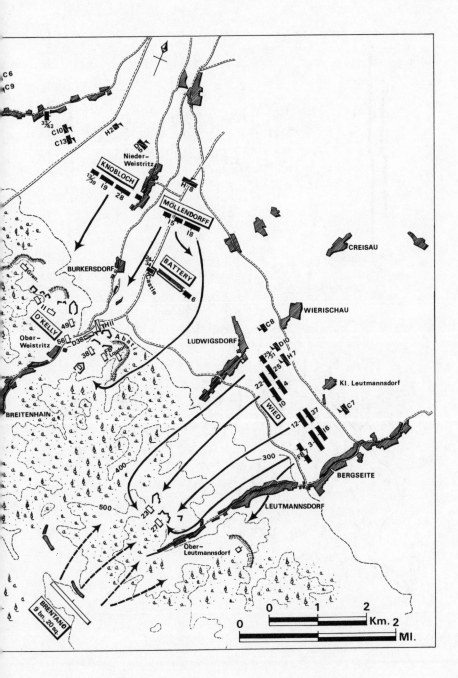

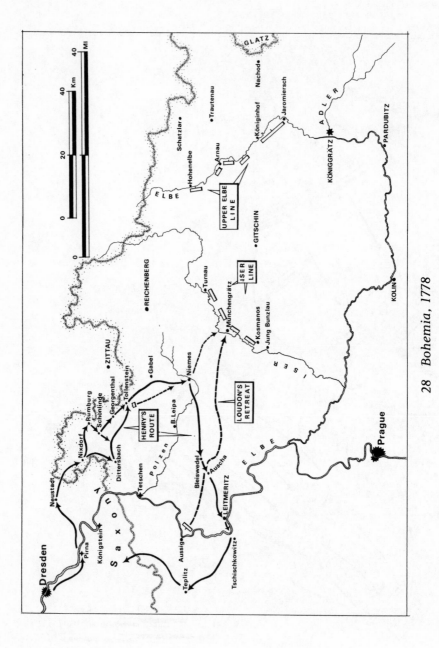

28 Bohemia, 1778

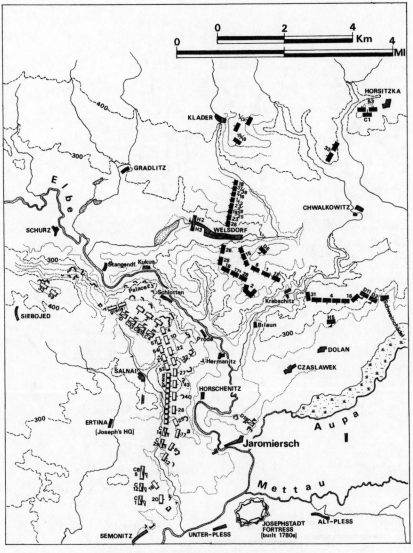

29   *The Jaromiersch position, 1778*

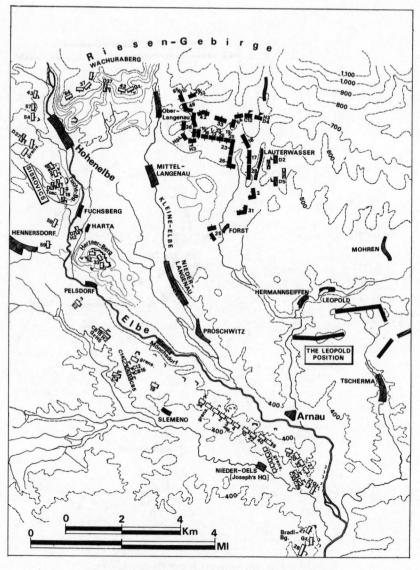

30   *The Hohenelbe-Arnau position, 1778*

Bibliography

Among many excellent works I particularly commend Koser (1921) for narrative detail, Schieder (1983) for the treatment of foreign policy, and Johnson (1975) for internal administration.

Abbt, T. (1761), *Vom Tode fürs Vaterland*, Berlin.

Adams, J.Q. (1804), *Letters on Silesia*, London.

Agramonte y Cortijo, F. (1928), *Los Ultimos Años de Federico il Grande según les Diplomáticos Españoles, Franceses y Prusianos de su Tiempo*, Berlin.

Allan, W. (1977), 'The Image of a King', *The Connoisseur*, London.

Ammann, F. (1887), *Die Schlacht bei Prag am 6. Mai 1757. Quellenkritische Untersuchungen*, Heidelberg.

Andreas, W. (1938), 'Friedrich der Grosse und der siebenjährige Krieg', *Historische Zeitschrift*, CLVIII, Munich and Berlin.

Anhalt-Dessau, L. (1860), *Selbstbiographie des Fürsten Leopold von Anhalt-Dessau von 1676 bis 1703*, Dessau.

Anon. (1756–75), *Allerneueste Acta Publica*, 37 vols, many places of publication. Bound sets of contemporary pamphlets.

Anon. (1758), *Abbildung derer Gemüthseigenschaften Friedrichs des Grossen*, Lippstadt.

Anon. (1772), *Recueil de Lettres de S.M. le Roi de Prusse, pour servir à l'histoire de la guerre dernière*, 2 vols, Leipzig.

Anon. (1784a), *Anekdoten vom König Friedrich II*, no place of publication.

Anon. (1784b), *Positiones der unter dem unmittelbaren Befehl Sr. Majestät des Königs von Preussen im Jahre 1778 sich befundenen Armee in Schlesien und Bohmen*, Altenburg. Very detailed and useful.

Anon. (1784c), *Zehn Briefe aus Oesterreich an den Verfasser der Briefe aus Berlin*, no place of publication.

Anon. (1786), 'Anekdoten vom König Friedrich II', *Militärische Monatsschrift*, IV, Berlin.

Anon. (Unger, ?) (1787–9), *Anecdoten und Karakterzüge aus dem Leben Friedrichs des Zweiten*, 12 vols, Berlin.

Anon. (Unger ?) (1788–9), *Beyträge zu den Anecdoten und Charakterzügen aus dem Leben Friedrichs des Zweiten*, 4 vols, Berlin.

Anon. (1844), *Ueber die grossen Kavallerie-Angriffe in die Schlachten Friedrich's und Napoleon's*, Berlin.

Anon. (1874), 'Ueber das Verpflegungswesen im siebenjährigen Krieges', *Jahrbücher für die deutsche Armee und Marine*, XII, Berlin.

Anon. (1881), 'Drei Jahre im Kadetten-Corps (1758–60)', *Jahrbücher für die deutsche Armee und Marine*, XXXIX, Berlin.

Anon. (1884), 'Erinnerungen an die letzte Campagne Friedrichs des Grossen', *Jahrbücher für die deutsche Armee und Marine*, LIII, Berlin. By a first lieutenant in a West Prussian regiment.

Anon. (1886), *Zur Schlacht von Torgau*, Berlin.

Archenholtz, J.W. (1840), *Geschichte des siebenjährigen Krieges in Deutschland*, 2 vols, Berlin. Served in the regiment of Forcade.

Archenholtz, J.W. (1974, reprint), *Gemälde der preussischen Armee vor und in dem siebenjährigen Kriege*, Osnabrück.

Arkhiv Knyazaya Vorontsova (1870–95), 40 vols, Moscow.

Arneth, A. (1863–79), *Geschichte Maria Theresias*, 10 vols, Vienna.

Ash, T.G. (1981), *'Und willst du nicht mein Bruder sein' . . . Die DDR heute*, Hamburg. On the 'rehistorisation' of Frederick and other figures in East Germany.

Aster, C.H. (1848), *Beleuchtung der Kriegswirren zwischen Preussen und Sachsen vom Ende August bis Ende October 1756*, 2 vols, Dresden.

Augstein, R. (1968), *Preussens Friedrich und die Deutschen*, Frankfurt-am-Main. Wide reading under a light-hearted guise.

Bach, A. (1885), *Die Graffschaft Glatz unter dem Gouvernement des Generals Heinrich August Freiherrn de la Motte Fouqué*, Habelschwerdt.

Baeumler, A. (1944), 'Die Idee les Reiches. Der Führergedanke in der deutschen Geschichte', *Offiziere des Führers*, I, Berlin.

Balke, Feldprediger (1885–6), 'Das Tagebuch des Feldpredigers Balke', *Internationale Revue über die gesammten Armeen und Flotten*, third year II-IV, fourth year II, Hanover. Disappointingly impersonal.

Bangert, D.E. (1971), *Die russisch-österreichische Militärische Zusammernarbeit im siebenjährigen Kriege in den Jahren 1758–1759*, Boppard.

Barsewisch, C.F. (1863), *Meine Kriegs-Erlebnisse während des siebenjährigen Krieges 1757–1763*, Berlin. He was a young officer in the regiment of Wedel.

Barthel, K. (1977), 'Friedrich der Grosse in Hitlers Geschichtsbild', *Frankfurter Historische Vorträge*, Wiesbaden.

Basler, O. (ed.) (1933), *Wehrwissenschaftliches Schrifttum im 18. Jahrhundert*, Berlin. Esp. for Prussian military cartography.

Baumgart, W. (1972), 'Der Ausbruch des siebenjährigen Krieges. Zum gegenwärtigen Forschungsstand', *Militärgeschichtliche Mitteilungen*, XI, Freiburg.

Becher, P. (1892), *Der Kronprinz Friedrich als Regiments-Chef in Neu-Ruppin von 1732–40*, Berlin.

Belach, A. (1758), *Der Christ im Kriege, und in der Belagerung*, Breslau and Leipzig.

Berenhorst, G.H. (1798–9), *Betrachtungen über die Kriegskunst*, 3 vols, Leipzig.

Berenhorst, G.H. (1845–7), *Aus dem Nachlasse von Georg Heinrich von Berenhorst*, 2 vols, Dessau.

Bernhardi, T. (1881), *Friedrich der Grosse als Feldherr*, 2 vols, Berlin.

Bertuch, J.G. (1781), *Über Erziehung des künftigen Soldaten*, Berlin.

Besterman, T. (1956), *Voltaire's Commentary on Frederick's 'Art de la Guerre'*, Geneva.

Bethcke, Captain (1905), 'Die Gaudi-Handschriften für das Jahr 1758', *Beihefte zum Militär-Wochenblatt*, Berlin.

Bethcke, Captain (1907), 'Die Gaudi-Handschriften für das Jahr 1759', *Beihefte zum Militär-Wochenblatt*, Berlin.

Bleckwenn, H. (ed.) (1971, etc.), *Das Altpreussische Heer. Erscheinungsbild und Wesen*, Osnabrück. An important series of monographs on many aspects of the old Prussian army. Still in progress. ISBN 3-7648-0187-5.

Bleckwenn, H. (ed.) (1971, etc.), *Altpreussischer Kommiss – Offiziell, Offiziös, und Privat*, Osnabrück. Reprints of old military literature, esp. eyewitness accounts. Still in progress. ISBN 3-7648-0864-0.

Bleckwenn, H. (1978), *Brandenburg-Preussens Heer 1640–1807*, Osnabrück.

Blumenthal, L.J. (1797), *Lebensbeschreibung Hans Joachims von Zieten*, Berlin. By a female relation of the old hussar.

Boehm-Tettelbach, A. (1934), 'Der Böhmische Feldzug Friedrichs des Grossen 1757 im Lichte Schlieffensche Kritik', in Elze, W. (ed.), *Schriften der Kriegsgeschichtlichen Abteilung im Historischen Seminar der Friedrich-Wilhelms-Universität Berlin*, IX, Berlin.

Böhm, W. (1870), 'Wie stellen sich die Thaten Friedrichs II. dar in der deutschen Literatur seiner Zeit?', *Zeitschrift für preussische Geschichte und Landeskunde*, VII, Berlin.

Bonin, U. (1877–8), *Geschichte des Ingenieurkorps und der Pioniere in Preussen*, 2 vols, Berlin.

Bosbach, E. (1960), *Die 'Rêveries Politiques' in Friedrichs des Grossen Politischem Testament von 1752. Historisch-politische Erläuterung*, Cologne and Graz.

Boswell, J. (1953), *Boswell on the Grand Tour. Germany and Switzerland 1764*, London.

Boysen, F.E. (1795), *Eigene Lebensbeschreibung*, Quedlinburg.

Brabant, A. (1904–31), *Das Heilige Römische Reich teutscher Nation im Kampf mit Friedrich dem Grossen*, 3 vols, Berlin. Uncompleted.

Bräker, U. (1852), *Der arme Mann im Tockenburg*, Leipzig. Bräker was forcibly recruited into the regiment of Itzenplitz.

Bratuschek, E.C. (1885), *Die Erziehung Friedrichs des Grossen*, Berlin.

Bremen, W. (1888), *Die Schlacht von Kesselsdorf am 15. Dez. 1745*, Berlin.

Bremen, W. (1905), 'Friedrich der Grosse', in Pelet-Narbonne, D. (ed.), *Erzieher des preussischen Heeres*, III, Berlin.

Broucek, P. (1982), *Der Geburtstag der Monarchie. Die Schlacht bei Kolin 1757*, Vienna.

Brown, M.L. (1959), *American Independence through Prussian Eyes*, Durham (North Carolina).

Brüggemann, F. (1935), *Der siebenjährige Krieg im Spiegel der zeitgenossischen Literatur*, Leipzig.

Brühl, Count (1854), *Correspondenz des . . . Grafen von Brühl mit dem . . . Freiherrn von Riedesel*, Leipzig.

Brunschwig, H. (1947), *La Crise de l'État Prussien à la Fin du XVIIIe Siècle et la Genèse de la Mentalité Romantique*, Paris.

Brunswick, Prince Ferdinand of (1902), 'Réflexions et Anecdotes vraies, mais hardies sur la Campagne de 1756', *Urkundliche Beiträge*, I, Heft 4.

Burchardi, H. (1897), 'Der kartographische Standpunkt beim Beginn des siebenjährigen Krieges 1756 in den betheiligten Ländern', *Beihefte zum Militär-Wochenblatt*, Berlin.

Burgoyne, J. (1876), 'Observations on the present military State of Prussia, Austria and France' (1767), in *Political and military Episodes . . . from the Life and Correspondence of the Right Hon. John Burgoyne*, ed., E.B. Fonblanque, London.

Büsch, O. (1962), 'Militärsystem und Sozialleben im alten Preussen 1713–1807', in Veröffentlichungen der Berliner Historischen Kommission, VII, Berlin.

Büsching, A.F. (1788), Abhandlung des Charakters Friedrich des Grossen, Halle. Important details from one of Frederick's attendants.

Bussmann, W. (1951), 'Friedrich der Grosse im Wandel des europäischen Urteils', in Deutschland und Europa (a Festschrift for H. Rothfels), Düsseldorf.

Butterfield, H. (1955), 'The Reconstruction of an historical Episode. The History of the Enquiry into the Origins of the Seven Years War', in Man on his Past, ed. H. Butterfield, Cambridge.

Buttlar, K.T. (1894), 'Zur Kapitulation von Maxen', Forschungen, VII.

Buxbaum, E. (1907), Friedrich Wilhelm Freiherr von Seydlitz, Leipzig. Useful, though some of the detail is suspect.

Caemmerer, R.C. (1883), Friedrich des Grossen Feldzugsplan für das Jahr 1757, Berlin.

Carlyle, T. (1858–65), History of Friedrich II of Prussia, called Frederick the Great, 6 vols, London.

Carlyle, T. (1940), Thomas Carlyle. Journey to Germany Autumn 1858, ed. R.A. Brooks, New Haven.

Catt, H. (1884), Unterhaltungen mit Friedrich dem Grossen. Memoiren und Tagebücher von Heinrich de Catt, ed. R. Koser, Leipzig. A most important source. However, Catt was not above rearranging his memories for dramatic effect.

Cauer, E. (1865), Über die Flugschriften Friedrichs des Grossen aus der Zeit des siebenjährigen Krieges, Potsdam.

Cauer, E. (1883), Zur Geschichte und Charakteristik Friedrichs des Grossen.

Cogniazzo, J. (1779–80), Freymüthige Beytrag zur Geschichte des östreichischen Militairdienstes, 2 vols, Frankfurt and Leipzig.

Cogniazzo, J. (1788–91), Geständnisse eines oestreichischen Veterans, 4 vols, Breslau 1788–91. Cogniazzo was certainly 'an Austrian veteran', but his writings are coloured by his dislike of Daun and his worship of Frederick.

Colin, J. (1907), L'Infanterie au XVIII Siècle. La Tactique, Paris. See chapter 3 for the Prussian influence.

Cornwallis, C. (1859), Correspondence of Charles, First Marquis Cornwallis, 3 vols, London.

Corvisart-Montmarin, Lieut-Col. (1880), 'Das Jahr 1757 und seine Bedeutung für die preussische Artillerie', Jahrbücher für die deutsche Armee und Marine, XXXV, Berlin.

Craig, G.A. (1955), The Politics of the Prussian Army 1640–1945, Oxford.

Craig, G.A. (1984), The End of Prussia, London.

Creuzinger, P. (1903), 'Friedrichs Strategie im siebenjährigen Kriege', part 2, vol 2, of his Die Probleme des Krieges, Berlin.

[Crillon] Mémoires Militaires de Louis de Berton des Balbes de Quiers: Duc de Crillon (1791), Paris.

Crousaz, A. (1874), 'Die Cavallerie Friedrichs des Grossen. Eine Militairhistorische und Charakterstudie', Jahrbücher für die deutsche Armee und Marine, XII, Berlin.

Daniels, E. (1886), Zur Schlacht von Torgau am 3. November 1760, Berlin. By a pupil of Delbrück.

Decker, C. (1837), Die Schlachten und Hauptgefechte des siebenjährigen Krieges . . . mit vorherrschender Bezugnahme auf den Gebrauch der Artillerie, Berlin.

Delbrück, H. (1890), *Die Strategie des Pericles erläutert durch die Strategie Friedrichs des Grossen*, Berlin.

Delbrück, H. (1892), *Friedrich, Napoleon, Moltke. Aeltere und Neuere Strategie*, Berlin.

Delbrück, H. (1900–20), *Geschichte der Kriegskunst im Rahmen der Politischen Geschichte*, 4 vols, Berlin.

Delbrück, H. (1904a), 'Ein Nachwort zu Kosers Aufsatz über Friedrichs des Grossen Kriegführung', *Historische Zeitschrift*, XCIII (new series LVII), Munich and Berlin.

Delbrück, H. (1904b), 'Zur Kriegführung Friedrichs des Grossen, ein zweites Nachwort', *Historische Zeitschrift*, XCIII (new series LVII), Munich and Berlin.

Demek, J. and Strída, M. (1971), *Geography of Czechoslovakia*, Prague.

Demeter, K. (1965), *The German Officer Corps in Society and State 1650– 1945*, London.

Denina, K. (1788), *Essai sur la Vie et le Règne de Frédéric II, Roi de Prusse*, Berlin.

Dette, E. (1914), *Friedrich der Grosse und sein Heer*, Göttingen. Most perceptive.

Ditfurth, F.W. (1871), *Die Historische Volkslieder des siebenjährigen Krieges*, Berlin.

Dohm, C.W. (1814–19), *Denkwürdigkeiten meiner Zeit*, 5 vols, Lemgo.

Dominicus, Musketeer (1891), *Aus dem siebenjährigen Krieg. Tagebuch des Preussischen Musketiers Dominicus*, Munich.

Dopsch, A. (1982), *Das Treffen bei Lobositz*, Graz. An Austrian challenge to the accepted Prussian version of events.

Doyle, J.B. (1913), *Frederick William von Steuben and the American Revolution*, Steubenville.

Dreyer, J.F. (1810), *Leben und Taten eines Preussischen Regiments-Tambours*, Breslau.

Droysen, H. (1906), 'Die Briefwechsel zwischen Kronprinz Friedrich von Preussen und Fürst Joseph Wenzel von Liechtenstein', *Forschungen*, XIX.

Droysen, H. (1916), 'Tageskalender Friedrichs des Grossen vom 1. Juni 1740 bis 31. Marz 1763', *Forschungen*, XXIX. An invaluable biographical aid.

Droysen, J.G. (1873), *Zur Schlacht von Chotusitz*, Berlin.

Droysen, J.G. (ed.) (1877), 'Die preussischen Kriegsberichte der beiden schlesischen Kriege', *Beihefte zum Militär-Wochenblatt*, Berlin.

Duffy, C. (1964), *The Wild Goose and the Eagle. A life of Marshal von Browne 1705–1757*, London.

Duffy, C. (1974), *The Army of Frederick the Great*, Newton Abbot.

Duffy, C. (1977), *The Army of Maria Theresa*, Newton Abbot.

Duffy, C. (1981), *Russia's Military Way to the West, Origins and Nature of Russian Military Power 1700—1800*, London.

Duffy, C. (1985), *The Fortress in the Age of Vauban and Frederick the Great*, London.

Duncker, M. (1876), *Aus der Zeit Friedrichs des Grossen und Friedrich Wilhelms III.*, Leipzig. Esp. for eyewitness accounts of Kolin.

Dundas, D. (1785), *Remarks on the Prussian Troops and their Movements*, British Library, King's MSS. 241.

Dutens, M.L. (1786), *Itineraire des Routes les plus Fréquentées*, London.

Duvernoy, Lieut-Col. (1901), 'Die Anschauungen Friedrichs des Grossen vom

Festungskriege vor Ausbruch des siebenjährigen Krieges', *Beihefte zum Militär-Wochenblatt*, Berlin.

Easum, C.V. (1942), *Prince Henry of Prussia, Brother of Frederick the Great*, Madison.

Eelking, M. (1856), *Leben und Wirken des Herzoglich Braunschweig'schen General-Lieutenants Friedrich Adolf Riedesel*, 3 vols, Leipzig.

Ergang, R. (1941), *The Potsdam Führer. Frederick William I, Father of Prussian Militarism*, New York.

Falch, O. (1860), *Was sich die Schlesier vom Alten Fritz erzählen*, Brieg.

Fann, W.F. (1977), 'On the Infantryman's Age in eighteenth century Prussia', *Military Affairs*, XLI, no. 4, Kansas.

Fitte, S. (1899), *Religion und Politik vor und während des siebenjährigen Krieges*, Berlin.

Fontane, T. (1906–7), *Wanderungen durch die Mark Brandenburg*, 4 vols, Stuttgart and Berlin.

Fouqué, H.A. de la Motte (1788) (ed. G.A. Büttner), *Denkwürdigkeiten aus dem Leben des Königl. preuss. Generals von der Infanterie Freiherrn de la Motte Fouqué*, 2 vols, Berlin. Esp. for the correspondence with Frederick in winter 1758.

Frauenholz, E., Elze, W., Schmitthenner, P. (1940), 'Das Heerwesen in der Zeit des Absolutismus', vol IV of *Entwicklungsgeschichte des Deutschen Heerwesens*, Munich.

Frederick the Great (1859) (ed. K.W. Schöning), *Militärische Correspondenz des Königs Friedrich des Grossen mit dem Prinzen Heinrich*, 4 vols, Berlin.

Frederick the Great (1920), 'Die Politischen Testamente Friedrichs des Grossen', published as supplement to *Politische Correspondenz Friedrichs des Grossen*, Berlin.

Frederick the Great (1926) (ed. J. Richter), *Die Briefe Friedrichs des Grossen an seinen vormaligen Kammerdiener Fredersdorf*, Berlin.

Frederick the Great (1927) (ed. E. Müller), 'Briefe des Kronprinzen Friedrich an Hans Christoph Friedrich von Hacke', *Forschungen*, XL. For young Frederick's progress in military affairs.

Freytag-Loringhofen, Freiherr (1897), 'Die Schlacht bei Torgau am 3. November 1760', in *Beihefte zum Militär-Wochenblatt*, Berlin.

Freytag-Loringhofen, Freiherr (1912), 'König Friedrich als Kriegsherr und Heerführer', *Beihefte zum Militär-Wochenblatt*, Berlin.

Friedel, J. (1782), *Briefe über die Galanterien von Berlin, auf einer Reise gesammelt von einem Österreichischen Offizier*, no place of publication.

Friederich, Lieut-Col. (1908), 'Die Schlacht bei Zorndorf am 25. August 1758', *Beihefte zum Militär-Wochenblatt*, Berlin.

G., D. de (1767), *Tactique et Manoeuvres des Prussiens. Pièce Posthume*, no place of publication. An eyewitness account of manoeuvres before the Seven Years War, with one of the earliest descriptions of the *Deployiren*.

Garve, C. (1798), *Fragmente zur Schilderung des Geistes, des Charakters, und der Regierung Friedrichs des Zweiten*, Breslau. Very perceptive.

Gerber, P. (1901), 'Die Schlacht bei Leuthen', *Historische Studien veröffentlicht von E. Ebering*, XXVIII, Berlin. Useful detail.

Geuder, F.C. (1902), *Briefe aus der Zeit des Ersten schlesischen Krieges*, Leipzig. Geuder was the envoy of the Prince of Orange, 1740–2.

Gieraths, G. (1964), *Die Kampfhandlungen der brandenburgisch-*

preussischen Armee 1626–1807, Berlin. Lists of garrisons and combats of Prussian regiments.

Giersberg, H.J., and Schendel, A. (1981), *Potsdamer Veduten*, Potsdam.

Gillies, J. (1789), *A View of the Reign of Frederick II of Prussia*, London.

Gisors, Comte de (1868) (ed. C. Rousset), *Le Comte de Gisors 1732–1758*, Paris. Gisors (son of Marshal Belle-Isle) had a long conversation with Frederick in 1754.

Goltz, C. von der (1906), *Von Rossbach bis Jena und Auerstedt*, Berlin. On the army in Frederick's later years.

Görlitz, W. (1953), *The German General Staff. Its History and Structure 1657–1945*, London.

Goslich, D. (1911), *Die Schlacht bei Kolin 18. June 1757*, Berlin.

Gotzkowsky, J.C. (1768–9), *Geschichte eines Patriotischen Kaufmanns*, 2 vols, Augsburg.

Granier, H. (1890), *Die Schlacht von Lobositz am 1. Oktober 1756*, Breslau.

Granier, H. (1891), 'Der Prinz von Preussen und die Schlacht bei Lobositz', *Forschungen*, IV.

Grosser Generalstab (German General Staff) (see Abbreviations) also: 'Briefe preussischer Soldaten', (1901) *Urkundliche Beiträge*, I. II.
    'Friedrich des Grossen Anschauungen vom Kriege in ihrer Entwicklung von 1745 bis 1756' (1899), *Kriegsgeschichtliche Einzelschriften*, XXVII, Berlin.
    'Die Taktische Schulung der Preussischen Armee durch König Friedrich den Grossen während der Friedenzeit 1745 bis 1756' (1900), *Kriegsgeschichtliche Einzelschriften*, XVIII–XXX, Berlin.

Guibert, J.A. (1778), *Observations sur la Constitution Militaire et Politique des Armées de S.M. Prussienne*, Amsterdam.

Guibert, J.A. (1803), *Journal d'un Voyage en Allemagne, fait en 1773*, 2 vols, Paris.

Haeckl, J. (1912), *Geschichte der Stadt Potsdam*, Potsdam.

Hahn, O. (1912), *Friedrich der Grosse und Schlesien*, Kattowitz.

Hahn, W. (1858), *Hans Joachim von Zieten*, Berlin.

Haller von Koenigsfelden, F.L. (1787), *Vie de Robert-Scipion de Lentulus*, Geneva and Paris.

Haller von Koenigsfelden, F.L. (1796), *Militärischer Charakter und Merkwürdige Kriegsthaten Friedrichs des Einzigen*, Berlin.

Hanke, M., and Degner, H. (1935), *Geschichte der Amtlichen Kartographie Brandenburg-Preussens*, Stuttgart.

Hartkopf, H. (1940), *Generalleutnant Wilhelm Sebastian von Belling*, Stettin.

Hartung, F. (1955), 'Der Aufgeklärte Absolutismus', *Historische Zeitschrift*, CLXXX.

Haworth, P.L. (1904), 'Frederick the Great and the American Revolution', *American Historical Review*, IX.

Heinrich, Prinzessin (1908) (ed. E. Berner, G. Volz). 'Aus der Zeit des siebenjährigen Krieges. Tagebuchblätter und Briefe der Prinzessin Heinrich und des Königlichen Hauses', *Quellen und Untersuchungen zur Geschichte des Hauses Hohenzollern*, IX, Berlin.

Heinzmann, J.G. (1788), *Beobachtungen und Anmerkungen auf Reisen durch Deutschland*, Leipzig.

Helfritz, H. (1938), *Geschichte der preussischen Heeresverwaltung*, Berlin.

Henckel von Donnersmarck, V.A. (1858), *Militärischer Nachlass des König-*

lich preussischen Generallieutenants . . . Henckel von Donnersmarck, 2 vols, Leipzig. Detailed and important. By an adherent of Prince Henry.

Henderson, W.O. (1958), *The State and the Industrial Revolution in Prussia 1740–1870*, Liverpool.

Henderson, W.O. (1963), *Studies in the Economic Policy of Frederick the Great*, London.

Herrmann, O. (1888a), 'Ueber Parolebücher und Notizkalender aus dem siebenjährigen Kriege', *Forschungen*, I.

Herrmann, O. (1888b), 'Gaudi über die Schlacht bei Torgau', *Forschungen*, II.

Herrmann, O. (1891), 'Zur Charakteristik des Gaudischen Journals über den siebenjährigen Krieg', *Forschungen*, IV.

Herrmann, O. (1892), 'Die Schiefe Schlachtordnung in der Schlacht bei Mollwitz', *Forschungen*, V.

Herrmann, O. (1894), 'Von Mollwitz bis Chotusitz. Ein Beitrag zur Taktik Friedrichs des Grossen', *Forschungen*, VII. Traces the origins of the Oblique Order to the First Silesian War.

Herrmann, O. (1895), 'M. Lehmann über Friedrich den Grossen und den Ursprung des siebenjährigen Krieges', *Forschungen*, VIII.

Herrmann, O. (1910), 'Olmütz', *Forschungen*, XXIII.

Herrmann, O. (1911), 'Zur Schlacht von Zorndorf', *Forschungen*, XXIV.

Herrmann, O. (1912), 'Der Feldzugsplan Friedrichs des Grossen 1758', *Historische Vierteljahrsschrift*, XV, Dresden.

Herrmann, O. (1913a), 'Der "Sieger" von Torgau', *Forschungen*, XXVI.

Herrmann, O. (1913b), 'Friedrich bei Kolin', *Forschungen*, XXVI.

Herrmann, O. (1914), 'Probleme Friderizianischer Kriegskunst', *Forschungen*, XXVII.

Herrmann, O. (1918), 'Prinz Ferdinand von Preussen über den Feldzug vom Jahre 1757', *Forschungen*, XXXI.

Herrmann, O. (1922), 'Eine Beurteilung Friedrichs des Grossen aus dem Jahre 1753' (by Prince Henry), *Forschungen*, XXXIV.

Hertzberg, Comte de (1787), *Huit Dissertations . . . lues dans les Années 1780–1787*, Berlin.

Hildebrandt, C. (1829–35), *Anekdoten und Charakterzüge aus dem Leben Friedrichs des Grossen*, 6 vols, Halberstandt and Leipzig.

Hinrichs, C. (1941), *Friedrich Wilhelm I*, Hamburg. Good, but completed only up to 1713.

Hinrichs, C. (1943), *Der Allgegenwärige König. Friedrich der Grosse im Kabinett und auf Inspektionsreisen*, Berlin.

Hintze, O. (1919), 'Friedrich der Grosse nach dem siebenjährigen Krieg und das Politische Testament von 1768', *Forschungen*, XXXII.

Hintze, O. (1920), 'Delbrück, Clausewitz und die Strategie Friedrichs des Grossen', *Forschungen*, XXXIII.

Hoen, M. (1909), 'Die Schlacht bei Prag am 6. Mai 1757', *Streffleurs Militärische Zeitschrift*, Vienna.

Hoen, M. (1911), 'Die Schlacht bei Kolin am 18. Juni 1757, *Streffleurs Militärische Zeitschrift*, Vienna. These two works are the most thorough and convincing of all Seven Years War battle studies.

Hoffmann, A. (1903), *Der Tag von Hohenfriedeberg und Striegau*, Oppeln.

Hoffmann, A. (1912), *Unter Friedrichs Fahnen. Tagebuch-Blätter, Briefe und sonstige neue Beiträge zur Geschichte der schlesischen Kriege*, Kattowitz.

Hoffmann, J. (1981), *Jakob Mauvillon. Ein Offizier und Schriftsteller im Zeitalter des bürgerlichen Emanzipationsbewegung*, Berlin. Esp. for the evaluation of Mirabeau and Mauvillon's *Monarchie Prussienne* of 1787.

Hoppe, Musketeer (trans. and ed. M. Lange) (1983), 'A Truthful Description of the Bloody Battle of Zorndorf', *Seven Years War Association Newsletter*, I, no. 5, Brown Deer (Wisconsin).

Hordt, Comte de (1805), *Mémoires Historiques, Politiques et Militaires de M. le Comte de Hordt*, 2 vols, Paris.

Hoven, J. (1936), *Der preussische Offizier des 18. Jahrhunderts. Eine Studie zur Soziologie des Staates*, Zeulenroda.

Hubatsch, W. (1973), *Frederick the Great of Prussia. Absolutism and Administration*, London.

Hülsen, C.W. (1890), *Unter Friedrich dem Grossen. Aus den Memoiren des Aeltervaters 1752–1773*, Berlin. One of the best of the eyewitness accounts. He was a subaltern in the regiment of Below.

Hürlimann, M. (1933), *Die Residenzststadt Potsdam. Berichte und Bilder*, Berlin.

Huschberg, J.F. (ed. H. Wuttke) (1856), *Die drei Kriegsjahre 1756, 1757. 1758 in Deutschland*, Leipzig.

Immich, M. (1893a), *Die Schlacht bei Zorndorf am 25. August 1758*, Berlin.

Immich, M. (1883b), 'Zur Schlacht bei Lobositz', *Forschungen*, IV.

Ingrao, C.W. (1982), 'Habsburg Strategy and Geopolitics during the Eighteenth Century', in Rothenberg, Kiraly and Sugar, 1982.

Jähns, M. (1885), *Heeresverfassung und Völkerleben. Eine Umschau*, Berlin.

Jähns, M. (1889–91), *Geschichte der Kriegswissenschaften vornehmlich in Deutschland*, 3 vols, Munich. A huge bibliography containing long extracts from many otherwise inaccessible sources.

Janson, A. (1913), *Hans Karl von Winterfeldt, des Grossen Königs Generalstabschef*, Berlin.

Jany, C. (1901), 'Das Gaudische Journal des siebenjährigen Krieges. Feldzüge 1756 und 1757', *Urkundliche Beiträge*, I, Heft, 3.

Jany, C. (1903), 'Die Gefechtsausbildung der preussischen Infanterie von 1806', *Urkundliche Beiträge*, I, Heft, 5.

Jany, C. (1904), 'Der preussische Kavalleriedienst vor 1806', *Urkundliche Beiträge*, VI.

Jany, C. (1907), 'Zum Friedenstage. Das Treffen von Burkersdorf am 21. Juli 1762', *Beihefte zum Militär-Wochenblatt*, Berlin.

Jany, C., and Menzel, A. (1908), *Die Armee Friedrichs des Grossen in ihrer Uniformierung*, Berlin. Superbly illustrated.

Jany, C. (1912), 'Aus den Erinnerungen eines Leibpagen des Grossen Königs' (i.e. Puttlitz), *Hohenzollern-Jahrbuch*, Berlin.

Jany, C. (1923), 'Der siebenjährige Krieg. Ein Schlusswort zum Generalstabswerk', *Forschungen*, XXXV.

Jany, C. (1928–9), *Geschichte der Königl. preussischen Armee bis zum Jahre 1807*, 3 vols, Berlin. Reprinted Osnabrück 1967. The 'bible' of every serious student.

Jany, C. (1941), 'Einige Bemerkungen zur Schlacht bei Torgau', *Forschungen*, LIII.

Johnson, H.C. (1975), *Frederick the Great and his Officials*, New Haven.

Johnson, H.C. (1982), 'Frederick the Great. The End of the Philosopher-King Concept', paper delivered to the International Commission of Military History, Washington, 1982.

Kaeber, E. (1907), *Die Idee des europäischen Gleichgewichts in der Publizist-ischen Literatur vom 16. bis zur Mitte des 18. Jahrhunderts*, Berlin.

Kalisch, C.G. (1828), *Erinnerungen an die Schlacht bei Zorndorf*, Berlin.

Kalkreuth, Field-Marshal (1839–40), 'Kalkreuth zu seinen Leben und zu seiner Zeit . . . Erinnerungen des General-Feldmarschalls Grafen von Kalkreuth', *Minerva*, 1839, IV; 1840, II–IV, Dresden. As dictated to his son. Very critical of Frederick.

Kaltenborn, R.W. (1790–1), *Briefe eines Alten preussischen officiers, verschiedene Charakterzüge Friedrichs des Einzigen betreffend*, 2 vols, Hohenzollern, 1790–1. Another unsympathetic portrayal of Frederick. Major Kaltenborn was forced to leave the army in 1780, and he was acquainted with Frederick only in the king's later years.

Kaltenborn, R.W. (1792), *Schreiben des Alten preussischen Officiers an seinen Freund*, Hohenzollern. (In answer to Ziesemer, 1791.)

Kann, R.A. (1982), 'Reflections on the Causes of Eighteenth-Century Warfare in Europe', in Rothenberg, Kiraly and Sugar, 1982.

Kapp, F. (1858), *Leben des amerikanischen Generals F.W. von Steuben*, Berlin.

Kaunitz, W. (1974), 'Votum über das Militare 1762', in 'Zeitgenossische Studien über die Altpreussische Armee', *Altpreussischer Kommiss* (ed. J. Bleckwenn), Osnabrück.

Keibel, R. (1899), *Die Schlacht von Hohenfriedberg*, Berlin.

Keibel, R. (1901), 'Die schräge Schlachtordnung in den beiden ersten Kriegen Friedrichs des Grossen', *Forschungen*, XIV.

Keith, J. (?) (1759), *A Succinct Account of the Person, the Way of Living, and of the Court of the King of Prussia. Translated from a Curious Manuscript in French, found in the Cabinet of the Late Field Marshal Keith*, London.

Kessel, E. (1933), 'Friedrich der Grosse am Abend der Schlacht bei Torgau', *Forschungen*, XLVI.

Kessel, E. (1937), 'Quellen und Untersuchungen zur Geschichte der Schlacht bei Torgau', *Schriften der Kriegsgeschichtlichen Abteilung im Historischen Seminar der Friedrich-Wilhelms Universität Berlin*, Allgemeine Reihe, XVII, Berlin.

Kilmansegg, E.F. (1906), 'Über Entstehung und Bedeutung der unter Friedrich dem Grossen abgehaltenen Manöver', *Beihefte zum Militär-Wochenblatt*, Berlin.

Kling, C. (1902–12), *Geschichte der Bekleidung, Bewaffnung und Ausrüstung des Königlich preussischen Heeres*, 3 vols, Weimar.

Knesebeck, E.J. (ed.) (1857), *Ferdinand Herzog zu Braunschweig und Lüneburg während des siebenjährigen Krieges*, 2 vols, Hanover.

Koschatzky, W., and Krasa, S. (1982), *Herzog Albert von Sachsen-Teschen 1738–1822*, Vienna.

Koser, R. (1890), 'Zur Schlacht bei Mollwitz', *Forschungen*, III.

Koser, R. (1891), 'Tagebuch des Kronprinzen Friedrich aus dem Rheinfeldzuge von 1724', *Forschungen*, IV.

Koser, R. (1894), 'Eine französische Schilderung des preussischen Heeres von 1748' (i.e. Valori's *Observations sur le Service Militaire du Roi de Prusse*), *Forschungen*, VII.

Koser, R. (1898), 'Bemerkungen zur Schlacht von Kolin', *Forschungen*, XI.

Koser, R. (1900), 'Die preussischen Finanzen im siebenjährigen Kriege', *Forschungen*, XIII.

Koser, R. (1901), 'Zur Geschichte der Schlacht von Torgau', *Forschungen*, XIV.

Koser, R. (1904a), 'Die preussische Kriegsführung im siebenjährigen Kriege', *Historische Zeitschrift*, LVI (new series), Munich and Berlin.

Koser, R. (1904b), 'Zur Geschichte des Preussischen Feldzugsplanes vom Frühjahr 1757', *Historische Zeitschrift*, LVII, Munich and Berlin.

Koser, R. (1910), 'Prinz Heinrich und Generalleutnant von Möllendorf im bayerischen Erbfolgekrieg', *Forschungen*, XXIII.

Koser, R. (1921), *Geschichte Friedrichs des Grossen*, 4 vols, Stuttgart (reprinted Darmstadt 1963).

Krause, G. (1965), *Altpreussische Uniformfertigung als Vorstufe der Bekleidungsindustrie*, Hamburg.

Krauske, O. (1894), 'Die Briefe des Kronprinzen Friedrich von Preussen an den Fürsten Leopold und an die Prinzen von Anhalt-Dessau', *Forschungen*, VII.

Krieger, B. (1914), *Friedrich der Grosse und seine Brüder*, Leipzig.

Krieger, L. (1975), *An Essay on the Theory of Enlightened Despotism*, Chicago.

Kröger, M.E. (ed. K.T. Gaedertz) (1893), *Friedrich der Grosse und General Chasot*, Bremen. Chasot's recollections, as conveyed through his friend Kröger. Important for Hohenfriedeberg.

Krogh, G.K. (ed. A. Aubert) (1913), 'Prag und Kolin. Ein glücklicher und ein unglücklicher Tag aus dem Kriegsleben des Grossen Königs. Nach dem Tagebuch eines norwegischen Offiziers', *Beihefte zum Militär-Wochenblatt*, Berlin.

Kunisch, J. (1978), *Das Mirakel del Hauses Brandenburg*, Munich.

Küster, C.D. (1791), *Bruchstück seines Campagnelebens im siebenjährigen Kriege*, Berlin. The recollections of a *Feldprediger*. Has a very vivid account of Hochkirch.

Küster, C.D. (1793), *Characterzüge des preussischen General-Lieutenants von Saldern*, Berlin.

Küttner, K.G. (1801), *Reise durch Deutschland*, Leipzig.

[Lafayette] *Memoirs and Correspondence of General Lafayette* (1837), 3 vols, London.

Laubert, M. (1900), 'Die Schlacht bei Kunersdorf am 12. August 1759', Berlin. Good, but written before the Russian sources became known.

Laubert, M. (1912), 'Die Schlacht bei Kunersdorf nach dem Generalstabswerk', *Forschungen*, XXV.

Laukhard, F.C. (1930), *Magister F. Ch. Laukhards Leben und Schicksale*, 2 vols, Stuttgart. For life in the regiment of Anhalt-Bernburg.

Lehmann, M. (1886–7), *Scharnhorst*, 2 vols, Leipzig. For Scharnhorst's visit to Prussia 1783.

Lehmann, M. (1891), 'Werbung, Wehrpflicht und Beurlaubung im Heere Friedrich Wilhelms I', *Historische Zeitschrift*, LXVII, Munich and Berlin.

Lehmann, M. (1894), *Friedrich der Grosse und der Ursprung des siebenjährigen Krieges*, Leipzig.

Lehndorff, E. (1907), *Dreissig Jahre am Hofe Friedrichs des Grossen*, Gotha. Lehndorff picked up much gossip as chamberlain to the queen.

Lehndorff, E. (1910–13), *Nachträge*, 2 vols, Gotha.

Lemcke, J.F. (ed. R. Walz) (1909), 'Kriegs- und Friedenbilder aus den Jahren 1754–1759. Nach dem Tagebuch des Leutnants Jakob Friedrich von

Lemcke 1738–1810'. *Preussische Jahrbücher*, CXXXVIII, Berlin.

Ligne, C.J. (1795–1811), *Mélanges Militaires, Littéraires et Sentimentaires*, 34 vols, Dresden.

Ligne, C.J. (1923), *Mémoires et Lettres du Prince de Ligne*, Paris.

Ligne, C.J. (1928), *Fragments de l'Histoire de ma Vie*, 2 vols, Paris.

Lippe-Weissenfeld, E. (1866), *Militaria aus König Friedrichs des Grossen Zeit*, Berlin.

Lippe-Weissenfeld, E. (1868), *Fridericus Rex und sein Heer. Ein Stück preussischer Armeegeschichte*, Berlin.

Lojewsky, J.G. (1843), *Selbstbiographie des Husaren-Obersten von . . . Ky (sic)*, 2 vols, Leipzig.

Lossow, L.M. (1826), *Denkwürdigkeiten zur Charakteristik der preussischen Armee unter dem Grossen König Friedrich dem Zweiten*, Glogau. Many acute observations.

Luvaas, J. (1966), *Frederick the Great and the Art of War*, New York. A selection and critique of the military writings. The only source of the kind in the English language.

Macaulay, T.B. (1864), *Critical and Historical Essays*, 2 vols, London.

McNeill, W.H. (1982), *The Pursuit of Power. Technology, Armed Force, and Society since A.D. 1000*, Oxford.

Malachowski, D. (1892), *Scharfe Taktik und Revuetaktik im 18. und 19. Jahrundert*, Berlin.

Mamlock, G.L. (1904), 'Krankheit und Tod des Prinzen August Wilhelm, des Bruders Friedrichs des Grossen', *Forschungen*, XVII.

Mamlock, G.L. (1907), *Friedrichs des Grossen Korrespondenz mit Ärzten*, Stuttgart.

Mansel, P. (1982), 'Monarchy, Uniform and the Rise of the *Frac* 1760–1830', *Past and Present*, XCVI, Oxford.

Marcus, H. (1927), *Friedrichs des Grossen Literarische Propaganda in England*, Brunswick, Berlin and Hamburg.

Marshall, J. (1772), *Travels . . . in the Years 1768, 1769, and 1770*, 3 vols, London.

Martiny, F. (1938), 'Die Adelsfrage in Preussen vor 1806', *Vierteljahrsschrift für Sozial und Wirtschaftgeschichte*, Beiheft XXXV, Stuttgart and Berlin.

Massenbach, A.L. (1808), *Rückerinnerungen an grosser Männer*, 2 vols, Amsterdam.

Mauvillon, J. (1756), *Histoire de la dernière Guerre de Bohême*, 3 vols, Amsterdam.

Mauvillon, J. (1794), *Geschichte Ferdinands Herzogs von Braunschweig-Lüneburg*, 2 vols, Leipzig.

Meyer, C. (1902), *Briefe aus der Zeit des Ersten Schlesischen Krieges*, Leipzig.

Meyer, P. (1955), *Zeitgenossische Beurteilung und Auswirkung des siebenjährigen Krieges (1756–1763) in der Evangelischen Schweiz*, Basel.

Mirabeau, H.G., and Mauvillon, J. (1788), *Système Militaire de la Prusse*, London. Separate printing of part of their *Monarchie Prussienne* of 1787. See the discussion in Hoffmann, J. (1981), pp. 245–76.

Mitchell, A. (1850), *Memoirs and Papers of Sir Andrew Mitchell K.B.*, 2 vols, London.

Mitford, N. (1970), *Frederick the Great*, London. Good on the king's friendships. Finely illustrated.

Mittenzwei, I. (1979), *Friedrich II. von Preussen. Eine Biographie*, East Berlin.

Mollwo, L. (1893), *Die Kapitulation von Maxen*, Marburg.

Mollwo, L. (1899), *Hans Carl von Winterfeldt*, Munich and Leipzig.

Mollwo, L. (1913), 'Friedrich der Grosse nach der Schlacht bei Kunersdorf', *Forschungen*, XXV.

Mönch, W. (1943), *Voltaire und Friedrich der Grosse*, Berlin.

Moore, J. (1779), *A View of Society and Manners in France, Switzerland and Germany*, 2 vols, London. By the father of Sir John Moore.

Müller, J.C. (1759), *Der wohl exercirte preussische Soldat*, Schaffhausen. Reprinted Osnabrück 1978.

Müller, L. (1788), *Tableau des Guerres de Frédéric le Grand*, Potsdam. By a lieutenant of engineers. Short but interesting.

Natzmer, G.E. (1870), *George Christoph von Natzmer, Chef der Weissen Husaren*, Hanover.

Naude, A. (1888), 'Aus ungedruckten Memoiren der Brüder Friedrichs des Grossen. Die Entstehung des siebenjährigen Krieges und der General von Winterfeldt', *Forschungen*, I.

Naude, A. (1892a), 'Zur Schlacht bei Prag', *Forschungen*, V.

Naude, A. (1892b), 'Berichte des Prinzen Moritz von Anhalt-Dessau über die Schlachten bei Prag, Kolin, Rossbach, Leuthen und Zorndorf', *Forschungen*, V.

Naude, A. (1893), 'Das Korps des Feldmarschalls Keith in der Schlacht bei Prag. Entgegnung gegen H. Delbrück', *Forschungen*, IV.

Naude, A. (1895–6), 'Beiträge zur Entstehungsgeschichte des siebenjährigen Krieges', *Forschungen*, VIII–IX.

Naumann, *Regiments-Quartiermeister* (1782–5), *Sammlung ungedruckter Nachrichten so die Geschichte der Feldzüge der Preussen von 1740 bis 1779 erläutern*, 5 vols, Dresden.

Nelson, W.H. (1972), *Germany Rearmed*, New York. For the survival of Prussian stock in the West German army.

Nettelbeck, J. (1821), *Ein Lebensbeschreibung von ihm selbst*, Leipzig.

Netzer, H.J. (ed.) (1968), *Preussen – Porträt einer politischen Kultur*, Munich.

Nicolai, F. (1788–92), *Anekdoten von König Friedrich II von Preussen*, 6 vols, Berlin.

Nisbet, H.B. (1982), ' "Was ist Aufklärung?" The Concept of Enlightenment in Eighteenth-Century Germany', *Journal of European Studies*, XII, Part 2, No. 46, Chalfont St Giles.

Noack, K.H. (1979), 'Friedrich II. und der Altpreussische Militärstaat im Urteil der Geschichtsschreibung der BRD', *Revue Internationale d'Histoire Militaire*, XLIII, Potsdam.

Ollech, General (1883), *Worin besteht der Unterschied und die Gleichheit der Armee Friedrichs des Grossen mit der heutigen Armee unseres Vaterlandes?*, Berlin.

Orlich, L. (1842), *Fürst Moritz von Anhalt-Dessau. Ein Beitrag zur Geschichte des siebenjährigen Krieges*, Berlin. A useful collection of letters.

Ortmann, A.D. (1759), *Patriotische Briefe*, Berlin and Potsdam.

Osten-Sacken, O. (1911), *Preussens Heer von seinen Anfängen bis zur Gegenwart*, I, Berlin. Good.

Paczynski-Tenczyn, Lieutenant (1896), *Lebensbeschreibung des General Feldmarschalls Keith*, Berlin.

Palmer, J.M. (1937), *General von Steuben*, New Haven.

Palmer, R.R. (1943), 'Frederick the Great, Guibert, Bülow. From Dynastic to

National War', *Makers of Modern Strategy* (ed. E.M. Earle), Princeton.

Paret, P. (1966), *Yorck and the Era of Prussian Reform 1807–1815*, Princeton.

Paret, P. (ed.) (1972), *Frederick the Great. A Profile*, London.

Pauli, C.F. (1758–64), *Leben grosser Helden des gegenwärtigen Krieges*, 9 vols, Halle.

Pauli, C.F. (1768), *Denkmale berühmter Feld-Herren*, Halle.

Pausch, G. (1886), *Journal of Captain Pausch*, Albany.

Peters, Captain (1902), 'Die Österreichischen Befestigungen an der Oberen Elbe', *Mittheilungen des K. u. K. Kriegs-Archivs*, V, Vienna.

Pfeiffer, E. (1904), *Die Revuereisen Friedrichs des Grossen, besonders die schlesischen nach 1763*, Berlin.

Pilati di Tassulo, C.A. (1777), *Voyages en différens Pays de l'Europe*, 2 vols, The Hague.

Pilati di Tassulo, C.A. (?) (1784), *Briefe aus Berlin über verschiedene Paradoxe dieses Zeitalters*, Berlin and Vienna 1784.

Piozzi, H.L. (1789), *Observations and Reflections made in the course of a Journey through France, Italy and Germany*, 2 vols, London.

Podewils, O.C. (1937), *Friedrich der Grosse und Maria Theresia. Diplomatische Berichte von Otto Christoph von Podewils*, Berlin.

Pounds, N.J. (1979), *An Historical Geography of Europe 1500–1840*, Cambridge.

Preitz, M. (1912), *Prinz Moritz von Dessau im siebenjährigen Kriege*, Munich and Berlin.

Preuss, J.D. (1832–4), *Urkundenbuch zu der Lebensgeschichte Friedrichs des Grossen*, 5 vols, Berlin.

Prittwitz und Gaffron, C.W. (1935), *Unter der Fahne des Herzogs von Bevern. Jugenderinnerungen*, Breslau. By a former subaltern in the regiment of Bevern.

Proebst, H. (1939), *Die Brüder. Friedrich der Grosse, August Wilhelm, Heinrich, Ferdinand*, Berlin.

Pross, H. (1968), 'Preussens klassische Epoche', in Netzer, 1968.

Prutz, H. (1895), 'Zur Kontroverse über den Ursprung des siebenjährigen Krieges', *Forschungen*, VIII.

Radda, K. (1879), *Der baierische Erbfolgekrieg und der Friede zu Teschen*, Teschen and Leipzig.

Rehfeld, P. (1944), 'Die preussische Rüstungsindustrie unter Friedrich dem Grossen', *Forschungen*, LV.

Retzow, F.A. (1802), *Charakteristik der wichtigsten Ereignisse des siebenjährigen Krieges*, 2 vols, Berlin. He was a subaltern in the Seven Years War, and son of the ill-used Lieutenant-General Wolf Friedrich von Retzow.

Riesebeck, K. (1784), *Briefe eines reisenden Franzosen über Deutschland*, 2 vols.

Ritter, G. (1954), *Staatskunst und Kriegshandwerk*, Part I, *Die Altpreussische Tradition 1740–1890*, Munich. English trans. *The Sword and the Scepter. The Problem of Militarism in Germany*, Part I, *The Prussian Tradition 1740–1890*, Coral Gables (Florida), 1969.

Rosenberg, R.R. (1958), 'Bureaucracy, Aristocracy and Autocracy, the Prussian Experience 1660–1815', *Harvard Historical Monographs*, XXXIV, Cambridge (Mass.).

Rosinski, H. (1966), *The German Army*, London.

Rothenberg, G., Kiraly, G.K., Sugar, P.E. (eds) (1982), *East Central European*

Society and War in Pre-Revolutionary Europe, New York.

Rothfels, H. (1926), 'Friedrich der Grosse in den Krisen des siebenjährigen Krieges', *Historische Zeitschrift*, Munich and Berlin, CXXXIV.

Sack, F.S. (1778), *Brief über den Krieg*, Berlin.

Sagarra, E. (1974), 'The Image of Frederick II of Prussia in Germany in the Century before Unification', *European Studies Review*, IV, No. 1, London.

Salmon, T. (1752–3), *The Universal Traveller*, 2 vols, London.

Sanders, H. (1783–4), *Beschreibung seiner Reisen*, 2 vols, Leipzig.

Scharfenort, L.A. (1895), *Die Pagen am brandenburg-preussischen Hofe 1415–1895*, Berlin.

Scharfenort, L.A. (1914), *Kulturbilder aus der Vergangenheit des Altpreussischen Heeres*, Berlin.

Scharnhorst, G. (1790), *Handbuch für Officiere*, Hanover.

Scharnhorst, G. (1794), *Unterricht des Königs von Preussen an die Generale seiner Armeen*, Hanover.

Scheffner, J.G. (1823), *Mein Leben*, Leipzig. For his recollections of service as a subaltern in the regiment of Ramin.

Schieder, T. (1979), 'Macht und Recht. Der Ursprung der Eroberung Schlesiens durch Konig Friedrich II. von Preussen', *Hamburger Jahrbuch für Wirthschafts- und Gesellschaftspolitik*, 1979, Hamburg.

Schieder, T. (1982), 'Friedrich der Grosse und Machiavelli – das Dilemma von Machtpolitik und Aufklärung', *Historische Zeitschrift*, CCXXXIV, Hamburg.

Schieder, T. (1983), *Friedrich der Grosse: ein Königtum der Widersprüche*, Frankfurt.

Schlenke, M. (1963), *England und das friderizianische Preussen 1740–1763*, Freiburg and Munich.

Schlözer, K. (1878), *General Graf Chasot*, Berlin.

Schmettau, F.W. (1789), *Über den Feldzug der preussischen Armee in Böhmen im Jahre 1778*, Berlin. Important.

Schmettau, G.F. (1806), *Lebensgeschichte des Grafen von Schmettau*, 2 vols, Berlin.

Schmidt, K. (1911), *Die Tätigkeit der preussischen Freibataillone in den beiden ersten Feldzügen des sienbenjährigen Krieges (1757–8)*, Leipzig. Takes an unusually favourable view of these units.

Schmitt, R. (1885–97), *Prinz Heinrich von Preussen als Feldherr im siebenjährigen Kriege*, 2 vols, Greifswald.

Schnackenburg, E. (1883a), 'Die Freicorps Friedrichs des Grossen', *Beihefte zum Militär-Wochenblatt*, Berlin.

Schnackenburg, E. (1883b), 'Heerwesen und Infanteriedienst vor 100 Jahren', *Jahrbücher fur die deutsche Armee und Marine*, XLVI–XLVII, Berlin.

Schnackenburg, E. (1895), 'Friedrichs der Gr. persönliche Fürsorge fur die Verwundeten und Kranken seines Heeres', *Jahrbücher für die deutsche Armee und Marine*, XCIV, Berlin.

Schnitter, H. (1979), 'Die Schlacht bei Torgau 1760', *Militärgeschichte*, 1979, No. 2, Potsdam.

Schoenaich, *Rittmeister* (1908), 'Die Exekution gegen Herstal im September und Oktober 1740', *Beihefte zum Militär-Wochenblatt*, Berlin. A useful study of a neglected episode.

Schöning, *Geheime-Rath* (1808), *Friedrich der Zweite, König von Preussen*, Berlin. By one of Frederick's attendants.

Schultz, W. (1887), *Die preussischen Werbungen unter Friedrich Wilhelm I. und Friedrich dem Grossen*, Schwerin.

Schwarze, K. (1936), *Der siebenjährige Krieg in der Zeitgenossischen deutschen Literatur*, Berlin.

Schwerin, D. (1928), *Feldmarschall Schwerin*, Berlin.

Scott, H.M. (1983), 'Whatever happened to Enlightened Despotism?', *History*, LXVIII, No. 223, London.

Seidl, C. (1781), *Versuch einer Militärischen Geschichte des bayerischen Erbfolge-Kriegs im Jahre 1778*, 3 vols, Königsberg.

Seidl, C. (1821), *Beleuchtung manches Tadels Friedrichs des Grossen Königs von Preussen*, Liegnitz.

Shanahan, W.O. (1982), 'Enlightenment and War. Austro-Prussian Military Practice, 1760–1790', in Rothenberg, Kiraly and Sugar (1982).

Sherlock, K. (1779), *Lettres d'un Voyageur Anglais*, London.

Silva, Marquis de (1778), *Pensées sur la Tactique, et la Stratégique*, Turin.

Skalweit, S. (1952), *Frankreich und Friedrich der Grosse. Der Aufsteig Preussens in der Öffentlichen Meinung der 'Ancien Regime'*, Bonn.

Södenstern, A. (1867), *Der Feldzug des Königlich preussischen Generals der Infanterie Heinr. Aug. Baron de la Motte Fouqué*, Kassel.

Spaethe, W.E. (1936), *Fridericus erobert Schlesien*, Breslau.

Steinberger, J. (ed. A. Kahlert) (1840), *Breslau vor hundert Jahren. Auszüge einer handschriftlichen Chronik*, Breslau.

Stille, C.L. (1764), *Les Campagnes du Roi de Prusse, avec des Réflexions sur les Causes des Evenemens*, Amsterdam. Excellent.

Stolz, G. (1970), 'Generalleutnant Daniel F. von Lossow (1721–83)' *Zeitschrift für Heereskunde*, CCXXXI, Berlin.

Stutzer, D. (1978), 'Das preussische Heer und seine Finanzierung in zeitgenossischer Darstellung 1740–1790', *Militärgeschichtliche Mitteilungen*, XXIV, Freiburg.

Szent-Ivany, G. (ed. Colonel Sommeregger) (1911), 'Die Schlacht bei Prag im Jahre 1757', *Mitteilungen des K. u. K. Kriegsarchivs*, 3rd Series, VII, Vienna.

Taysen, A. (1880), *Die Militärische Thätigkeit Friedrichs des Grossen im Jahre 1780*, Berlin.

Taysen, A. (1882), *Zur Beurtheilung des siebenjährigen Krieges*, Berlin.

Taysen, A. (1886), *Die Militarische Thätigkeit Friedrichs des Grossen während seines letzten Lebensjahres*, Berlin.

Taysen, A. (1891), *Die äussere Erscheinung Friedrichs des Grossen*, Berlin.

Tempelhoff, G.F. (1783–1801) *Geschichte des siebenjährigen Krieges in Deutschland*, 6 vols, Berlin. An inspired re-working of the uninteresting original by H.E.E. Lloyd.

Temperley, H. (1915), *Frederick the Great and Kaiser Joseph*, London.

Tettelbach, A.B. (1934), 'Der böhmische Feldzug Friedrichs des Grossen im Lichte schlieffenscher Kritik', *Schriften der Kriegsgeschictlichen Abteilung im Historischen Seminar der Friedrich-Wilhelms Universität*, IX, Berlin.

Thadden, F.L. (1967), *Feldmarschall Daun*, Vienna. Esp. for Giannini's report on the Spandau manoeuvres of 1753.

Tharau, F.K. (1968), *Die Geistige Kultur des preussischen Offiziers von 1640 bis 1806*, Mainz.

Thiébault, D. (1813), *Mes Souvenirs de vingt Ans de Séjour à Berlin*, 4 vols, Paris.

Thiébault de Liveaux, J.C. (1788–9), *Vie de Frédéric II Roi de Prusse*, 7 vols, Strasbourg.

Thürriegel, J.C. (1766), *Merkwürdige Lebensgeschichte des Generalmajors Herrn v. Gschray*, Frankfurt and Leipzig. Reprinted Osnabrück 1974.

Tielke, J.G. (1776–86), *Beiträge zur Geschichte des Krieges von 1756 bis 1763*, 6 parts, Freiberg. By a highly regarded Saxon staff officer. The maps are of astonishing accuracy.

Toulongeon and Hullin (ed. Finot, J., Galmiche-Bouvier, R.) (1881), *Une Mission Militaire en Prusse, en 1786*, ris. Important.

Trenck, F. (1789), *Mémoires de Frédéric Baron de Trenck*, 3 vols, Strasbourg and Paris. Entertaining but unreliable.

Troschke, T. (1865), *Die Beziehungen Friedrichs des Grossen zu seiner Artillerie*, Berlin.

Unger, W. (1906), *Wie ritt Seydlitz? Eine Studie über Pferde Reiter und Reitkunst in der Kavallerie Friedrichs des Grossen*, Berlin. Good.

Valori, G.L.H. (1820), *Mémoires des Négociations du Marquis de Valori*, 2 vols, Paris. There is a copy of this very rare book in the public library in Troyes, France.

Varnhagen von Ense, K.A. (1834), *Leben des Generals Freiherrn von Seydlitz*, Berlin.

Varnhagen von Ense, K.A. (1836), *Leben des Generals Hans Karl von Winterfeldt*, Berlin. Varnhagen wrote in a sensational style, but he was skilful at tracking down eyewitnesses and curious detail.

Ventré-Nouvel, J. (1981), 'L'Alliance Franco-Bavaroise-Prusso-Saxonne contre l'Autriche pendant la Campagne de Bohême de 1742', paper presented to the conference of the International Commission of Military History, Montpellier.

Vitzthum von Eckstaedt, C.F. (1866), *Die Geheimnisse des sächsischen Cabinets, Ende 1745 bis Ende 1756*, Stuttgart.

Volz, G.B., and Küntzel, O. (1889), 'Preussische und österreichische Acten zur Vorgeschichte des siebenjährigen Krieges', *Publicationen aus den K. Preussischen Staatsarchiven*, LXXIV, Leipzig.

Volz, G.B. (1907), 'Ein österreichischer Bericht über den Hof Friedrichs des Grossen', *Hohenzollern Jahrbuch*, Berlin.

Volz, G.B. (1926–7), *Friedrich der Grosse im Spiegel seiner Zeit*, 3 vols, Berlin. A rich storehouse of a wide range of contemporary accounts.

Volz, G.B. (1909), 'Friedrich der Grosse am Schreibtisch', *Hohenzollern Jahrbuch*, Berlin.

Volz, G.B. (1913), 'Friedrich der Grosse nach der Schlacht bei Kunersdorf, Eine Entgegnung', *Forschungen*, XXVIII. In answer to Mollwo's article of 1913.

Volz, G.B. (1923), 'Die parchwitzer Rede', *Forschungen*, XXXV. For the most authentic version of the famous speech.

Volz, G.B. (1926), *Friedrich der Grosse und Trenck*, Berlin.

Waddington, R. (1896), *Louis XV et le Renversement des Alliances*, Paris.

Waldeyer, W. (1900), *Die Bildnisse Friedrichs des Grossen und seine äussere Erscheinung*, Berlin.

Warnery, C.E. (1785–91), *Des herrn Generalmajor von Warnery sämtliche Schriften*, 9 vols, Hanover.

Warnery, C.E. (1788), *Campagnes de Frédéric II, Roi de Prusse, de 1756 à 1762*, Amsterdam.

Weber, H. (1890), 'Venezianische Stimmen zum siebenjährigen Krieg', *Forschungen*, III.

Wedell, M. (1876), *Ein Preussischer Diktator. Karl Heinrich von Wedell*, Berlin.

Wengen, F. (1890), *Karl Graf zu Wied, Königlich preussischer Generallieutenant*, Gotha. Esp. for the campaign of 1762.

Westphalen, C.H. (1859–72), *Geschichte der Feldzüge des Herzogs Ferdinand von Braunschweig-Lüneburg*, 5 vols, Berlin.

Wiarda, T.D. (1792–1817), *Ostfriesische Geschichte*, 10 vols, Aurich and Leer.

Willebrandt, J.P. (1758), *Historische Berichte und practische Anmerkungen auf Reisen*, Frankfurt and Leipzig.

Wiltsch, J.E. (1858), *Die Schlacht von nicht bei Rossbach oder die Schlacht auf den Feldern von und bei Reichardtswerben*, Reichardtswerben.

Winter, G. (1886), *Hans Joachim von Zieten*, 2 vols, Leipzig 1886.

Witzleben, A. (1851), *Aus alten Parolebüchern der Berliner Garnison zur Zeit Friedrichs des Grossen*, Berlin.

Woche, K. (1969), 'Christian Nikolaus von Linger. Offizier unter drei Königen', *Zeitschrift für Heereskunde*, XXXXIII–XXXIV, Berlin. On the veteran gunner.

Wolfslast, W. (1941), *Die Kriege Friedrichs des Grossen*, Stuttgart.

Wraxall, N.W. (1806), *Memoirs of the Courts of Berlin, Dresden, etc.*, 2 vols, London.

Wuttke, H. (1842–3), *König Friedrichs des Grossen Besitzergreifung von Schlesien*, 2 vols, Leipzig.

Yorke, P. (1913), *The Life and Correspondence of Philip Yorke, Earl of Hardwicke*, 3 vols, Cambridge. For Major-General Joseph Yorke's visit to the campaign in Moravia, 1758. His letter of 31 July is the best single description of Frederick's daily life on campaign.

Zedlitz, C.A. (1776), *Sur le Patriotisme considéré comme Objet d'Éducation dans les États monarchiques*, Berlin.

Ziesemer, Feldprediger (1791), *Briefe eines preussischen Feldpredigers verschiedene Charakterzüge Friedrichs des Einzigen betreffend*, Potsdam. In answer to Kaltenborn.

Zimmermann, J.G. (1788), *Ueber Friedrich den Grossen und meine Unterredungen mit Ihm kurz vor seinem Tode*, Leipzig.

Zimmermann, J.G. (1790), *Fragmente über Friedrich den Grossen*, 3 vols, Leipzig.

Zottmann, A. (1937), *Die Wirschaftspolitik Friedrichs des Grossen. Mit besonderer Berücksichtigung der Kriegswirtschaft*, Leipzig and Vienna.

Index

401

CENTRAL EUROPE

—————— PRUSSIAN BORDERS 1740

-------- LATER EXTENSIONS

North
Sea

Cpgn.

HOLSTEIN

STRALSUN
SWEDE
POMER

Demmin

HAMBURG MECKLENBURG

United

BREMEN
VERDEN

(1744)
Emden
O.
FRIESLAND

WESER

ELBE

Rheinsberg   Zehdenic
Neu-Ruppin

Salzwedel
ALTMARK
Stendal

SPA

Amst.

Provinces

EMS

Lingen

MINDEN

Hanover

HANOVER

BRUNSWICK

Rathenow
Brandenburg

PO

MAGDEBURG

MÜNSTER

RAVENSBERG

Minden

Bielefeld

Halberstadt

Wittenberg

CLEVE

Wesel

MARK

Soest

Westphalia

HOHENSTEIN

HALLE

Geldern

Crefeld

COLOGNE

Rossbach

LEIPZIG

AACHEN

RHINE

Dresde

a

S

FRANKFURT

Philippsburg

France

Württemberg

REGENSBURG

DANU

STRASBOURG

Bavaria

Munich